I0457846

THE SYNAGOGUE AND THE CHURCH

Filiation, Divorce and Reconciliation

XAVIER MAINGUY

Copyright © 2025 by Xavier Mainguy

Paperback: 978-1-967820-42-9
Hardcover: 978-1-968667-70-2
eBook: 978-1-967820-43-6
Library of Congress Control Number: 2025909353

All rights reserved. No part of this publication may be reproduced, distributed, or
transmitted in any form or by any electronic or mechanical means, without the prior
written permission of the publisher, except in the case of brief quotations embodied in
critical reviews and certain other noncommercial uses permitted by copyright law.

This is a work of nonfiction.

Ordering Information:

Prime Seven Media
518 Landmann St.
Tomah City, WI 54660

Printed in the United States of America

To my wife Monique and my daughter Mathilde

Prefaced by Sir Haïm Korsia

Chief Rabbi of France, Member of the French National
Academy (www.institut-de-france.fr)

I t is an honor and an immense responsibility to have been entrusted with writing the preface to this book, whose subject matter is both delicate and essential. Delicate, because it addresses centuries of often complex, sometimes painful, and now more fraternal relations between Judaism and Christianity. Essential, because it reminds us that, despite the trials and tribulations, our histories are deeply intertwined and that our common future depends on our ability to build bridges.

Xavier Mainguy's remarkable work explores an often-neglected area: that of our common heritage. Too often, our differences have been emphasized, but it is time to state clearly once again that Judaism is the source from which the Christian faith sprang. The Hebrew Bible, which we call the Tanakh, is the foundation of monotheistic faith throughout the world and throughout history. Our patriarchs, prophets, and sages are also recognized by Christians. This connection is an undeniable theological and historical truth. Far from being an obstacle, it is the most solid foundation on which we can build mutual, respectful, and sincere understanding.

Our sages teach us that the world was created by the divine word, and that from a single source, humanity diverged into multiple paths. The link between Judaism and Christianity is more than a mere historical coincidence; it is rooted in a deep theological foundation, that of faith in one God, creator of heaven and earth. The Torah, our foundation, is also the soil in which the Christian Scriptures took root. The story of Abraham, our common father, symbolizes this call to faith that transcends borders and generations, as it is written in Genesis: "I will make you into a great nation, and I will bless you; I will make your name great, and you will be a blessing." (Gen. XII, 2). This shared heritage calls us to recognize our spiritual kinship and to work together for a more just and fraternal world.

Over the centuries, the Jewish people have faced constant persecution. From the Babylonian exiles to the destruction of the two Temples in Jerusalem, from the medieval pogroms to the burning of our sacred books, and up to the unspeakable horror of the Shoah, we have been confronted with enduring hatred. Yet, in the midst of turmoil, we have never ceased to turn to the Eternal One. We have preserved the Torah, passed on our traditions, and kept our faith and identity alive. This resilience is not the result of chance, but of fidelity to the divine Word, unshakeable hope, and faith in our covenant with God. This is the lesson we offer to the world: even in the thickest darkness, the light of faith never goes out. It is this absolute conviction that I found in Apollinaire when he proclaimed, "The twilight will never defeat the dawn."

I have been able to experience moments of sharing and dialogue that offer hope and are the fruit of these years of building a new history of brotherhood. Each time we had these exchanges, I felt as if I were in that heavenly Jerusalem, which is but a reflection of the earthly Jerusalem where brothers know how to find each other. Yes, it is like a messianic time suspended between worlds but already present.

The work that made this possible would not have been possible without courageous men and women, peacemakers who chose dialogue over anathema, understanding over prejudice. I think of all those people, such as Pope John XXIII and Pastor Marc Boegner, who, within the Catholic Church and the Protestant Churches, were able to reach out to acknowledge the mistakes of the past and commit to a future of reconciliation. I think of the confident heroes of a story of brothers reunited, such as Jules Isaac, who was able to capture this moment in his prophetic words on the Church's transition from teaching contempt to teaching esteem, or Chief Rabbi Kaplan, or Edmond Fleg. Their courage and vision remind us that peace is not a pipe dream, but a work in progress. May this book shine a light on them and inspire new generations to follow their example and continue, in turn, to sow the seeds of peace, tolerance, and brotherhood between Jews and Christians.

Foreword

The subject of the relations between the Synagogue and the Church has been established in religious, historical, and sociological debates. It is animated by theologians, historians, and sociologists, whose list is very long. It was necessary, following the judgments of the court of Nuremberg in 1946, to examine in depth the first causes and their consequences in this monstrous conflict, which made so many victims. Among them, so many are Jewish. In the list of these specialists, there is Jules Isaac, with his fundamental book, "The Teaching of Contempt," followed by another work in the form of a question, "Does anti-Semitism have Christian roots?" and also "Jesus and Israel." He was one of the very first to fully explore the religious causes of the rift that occurred over the centuries between these two distinct entities. They are so close to each other; however, if only by the etymology of their name, one in

Greek derived from "Sunagôgê" and the other in Latin, "Ecclesia", both mean: "assembly". They are also close, in their finality, as places of worship to the same God: one, the Creator and Savior of Israel, and by the "New Covenant", of all humanity. With this basic idea, it seemed interesting to highlight the three major periods of their respective evolution: their genesis, the development of each other, and then the painful divorce that permanently separated their destiny. Finally, in the third part, I wanted to evoke the ways of reconciliation and mutual communion so highly desirable for peace and harmony between religions and beyond in society as a whole. These three periods justify the title of the book: "Filiation, Divorce and Reconciliation". To give a credible account of this long journey through time in these few pages, it was naturally necessary to be very synthetic, multiply the shortcuts, and span the centuries without ever losing the common thread; I hope I did. This book reflects the thought of someone who attaches great importance to the texts of the Bible, those of the Old Testament as well as those of the New. He considers them to be sacred, as ultimate depositories of the life and truth of dogma, as the Apostle John himself declares in the 1st Chapter of his Gospel, verses 1 to 14, when he says that, "this Word was God" and that it was incarnated; "... the Word was made flesh, and dwelt among us, full of grace and truth" (Jn 1:14). To attach oneself to the truth of the texts of the Bible, in a similar undertaking, was the first and foremost condition to be able to formalize a coherent theological and historical reflection in such a disparate set of facts. The truth of the Bible texts was also necessary to conclude with concrete ideas and proposals and thus permanently seal the reconciliation between the Synagogue and the Church. This book will appeal to a wide audience; it should be particularly suitable for Christians of all faiths, accustomed to frequent references to the sources of the Bible. It should also appeal to readers of the Jewish faith, in many ways reinforcing their views on this historical phenomenon. Although it is built on strong biblical convictions, it is open to academic circles, historians, sociologists, theologians, and intellectuals of any literary or scientific discipline. It can speak to all those who seek, even broadly, a real meaning to history, and singularly to that of Europe as a whole. The third part highlights the peacemakers who, in the past, saved Jews solely out of the impulse of their conscience. It should also speak to all those who today discover the Hebrew roots of their Christianity by participating in the life of many Judeo-Christian associations, messianic church unions, places of Judeo-Christian worship, etc.

What is the motivation of an evangelical Christian to write such a work? If he is not a pastor, a theologian, or even a historian, why undertake this adventure with the risk of getting bogged down in places that have become so common in a tragedy that will never be? He wants to express the feelings and reflections inspired by this particular destiny of Judeo-Christianism, which did not say his name, or rather, was ashamed of his Jewish roots. He wants to account for the complexity and the impossibility of understanding Christianity detached from these same roots. A necessary historical reminder is made as much on the origin of the Synagogue as on that of the Church, legitimate daughter of the first, to underline their essential characteristics. He also wants to show how badly sick the whole of Europe has been in the divorce between the Synagogue and the Church. A disease that we want to believe, however, that these nations are now cured, without being able to certify it for future times. While going through these centuries of greatness and decadence, he took the opportunity to propose some concepts that will be interesting to develop in another work, such as the "biblical causality in history" and also a brief introduction to the notion of "Biblical Law". A window was quickly opened on social history in Europe regarding the message of the Bible; Was this opening possible? The answer is in the following pages. Other surprises await the reader in the three parts of this book. We hope they contribute to his spiritual edification and knowledge of this significant chapter of Christianity. Ultimately, the goal that has been sought, from the very beginning of this enterprise, is to progress together, in the knowledge of the Bible as well as in the understanding of its influence on the individual and collective scale, nationally and internationally.

Table of Contents

---

[1] Deicide people - Jules Isaac, L'Enseignement du mépris, Fasquelle, Paris, 1962 ; Grasset, 2004

[2] Melito of Sardis - Accusation against the Jews. In "Peri-Pescha". The Harvard Theological Review Vol. 91, No. 4 (Oct. 1998), pp. 351-372 (22 pages)

Introduction

We are a collective of individuals gathered around the Bible and History. There is a doctor, two pastors, two engineers, a former chief of staff of the CEO of our national airline Air France, there is also a professor of a Faculty of Evangelical Theology and then we count among us all those who, close or distant, present or disappeared have contributed to the progress of reflection, documentation and ultimately, the solution to this tragedy in three acts. I am the pilot in this boat because it was enough for me to take the pen, or rather the computer, so that waves of words, thoughts, reasoning, and historical and theological reminders show me the course. This is my only justification because this theme has been present in my heart for years, and it had to come out one day. I am part of an Evangelical Church that has in its ranks a pastor, himself a member of the network, "Jews for Jesus". His motivation and assistance were instrumental in the development of the book. I am not a theologian, historian, or pastor, but rather an actor in a debate far from over. I want to do as the prophet Isaiah says in chapter 37 verse 15, "For Zion's sake, I will not shut up." Not being a specialist is a handicap because this literary project does not fall into any well-defined academic category with its codes, vocabulary, and conventions. However, it is also an advantage to be able to free oneself from its elements of style and professionalism. It also means gaining freedom of writing to place oneself resolutely on the side of readers sensitive to these three realities of a painful story, but which evolves in a rather positive sense. In this work, the logic of words and their sequences is called upon as well as that of lived experience. It is to make the texts speak for themselves, by the strength of each of their thoughts, by the power of words and deductions that must flow like water, when they are a call to life itself, as the Gospel of John so rightly reminds us in chapter 1:4; "Life was the light of men". It is to arrive at consensual and necessary conclusions because of the circumstances and facts that converge toward a recognition of the prophetic character of the Bible. It is adding pleasure to the reading of a subject that is sometimes terribly lacking. It is also to bring closer, by the power of words, the literary and historian, the theologian and churchman, the sociologist and philosopher, discourse and its consequences. This is the challenge this book faces to make its subject alive and positive.

Objective: the quest for truth, justice and reparation

For most Evangelical Churches, all denominations combined, the filiation of the Church in the Synagogue is self-evident as they are immersed in the culture of the biblical texts that they comment on every Sunday to their parishioners. However, do they really live the blessing promised by the Lord in the book of Genesis 12:3 to all who bless Israel? Do they participate in this effort to restore relations between them and the synagogues, as the apostle Paul prophesied in his epistle to Romans 11:15 when he said: "For if their rejection was the reconciliation of the world, what will be their reintegration, if not a life of the dead?". There is certainly much to be said and done in this area and our work is a contribution to the Gospel vision of, "the restoration of all things" according to the words of the Apostle Peter spoken in Acts 3:21. It is one of the evangelical publications on this major issue, alongside the remarkable collective work published by CNEF in[3] 2021 entitled "Anti-Semitism – It's Time to React", which is a clear stand for the people and nation of Israel. This work, like ours, will certainly help the Evangelical Churches and with them, their parishioners, to experience the promised blessings to those who bless Israel. Moreover, our work will allow the readers, we hope, to pass from the field of intuition or even prejudice to that of reality and finally to the truth of historical and theological facts, in one of the greatest misunderstandings in the history of humanity. In fact, at the beginning of Christianity, there was only one entity whose vocation was the teaching and celebration of worship of the Eternal God, the creator of everything existing in the universe, namely the Synagogue. Then, after the ministry of Jesus Christ spanned only a few decades, with the

---

[3]   CNEF: National Council of Evangelical Churches in France

contribution of converts from the pagan world, the Church was considered a particular branch of Judaism in the Roman Empire until approximately the middle of the second century. However, under the influence of various factors, whether geopolitical, academic, or theological, increasingly profound differences appeared between it and the synagogue until anti-Judaism and then anti-Semitism became an official doctrine of Christianity, especially after his consecration by Emperor Theodosius as the official religion of the Roman Empire in the year 392 AD. Indeed, while the synagogue remains relatively equal to itself during the post-exile centuries, it is considered, after the emperor Constantine as the enemy declared by the Church. A succession of affirmations, discourses, and various teachings characterized this evolution which soon took place in his theology, until the twentieth century. Then with time, starting from religion, the curse will spread to all the Jewish people and culminated after the First World War, in a will of total annihilation, during the domination of continental Europe by the German Third Reich. There was no better word to define it than genocide, which means the crime against a race or group of men, women, children, and the elderly, without consideration other than their membership to a particular ethnic group. Strongly involved in this human and moral disaster, the churches have not only failed in their mission, but they have also destroyed themselves, with the consequence, among other things, the collapse of the religious practice of Christianity throughout Europe in the aftermath of the war. It is a drama in 3 acts that we want to present in the following chapters, it is thus worded, The Synagogue and the Church: filiation, divorce and reconciliation. Fortunately, the end is much more beautiful than the beginning, for today the Lord is doing a great work of reparation for Israel, for theological truth, and historical justice. After the destruction of 1945 comes the resurrection of 1948 with the return of the exiles to Eretz-Israel. Beyond this great historical miracle, powerful religious revivals bring millions of men and women around the world, to find in the Bible itself, the Jewish roots of their Christian faith.

Method and sources

This theme is not new in literature as in the circles of study of the cross-memory of Judeo-Christianity, far from it. An abundant literature has been produced both, to expose and to explain the distortions of the meaning of Christianity towards Judaism, which appeared from the first centuries of their common history. On the other hand, the "Reconciliation" part remains strangely unexplored, as if the best wishes of the world were still up against a kind of invisible wall of incompatibility between the Synagogue and the Church. However, this is not the case, and this part contains the highest added value of the book because it offers a positive vision of their relationships, based on the solid foundations of the Bible. The first two, respectively, are the genesis of the Church in a Jewish context, then the disastrous record until very recently of their intertwined history. In its broad outline, the plan is chronological; it travels through space and time from the time of the scribe Ezra to the peace of Abraham, the aptly named in 2020. However, for the needs of certain developments, the story can borrow shortcuts, sometimes abrupt, or, on the contrary, ignore entire centuries. It is not possible to cover such a subject exhaustively. We wanted to retain only what is significant in a singular story and bring our analysis as rational, emotional, and spiritual. At first glance, reason seems to have little place to occupy in a subject as immersed in passions, metaphysics, and theology as this one. However, this book must satisfy all those who like the accuracy of facts, dates, places, and characters in their respective context. Therefore, particular attention has been paid to these objective criteria so that they can be satisfied and serve as a basis for adhering to our theses and convictions. We write more with the heart than with the computer, so there is a place left for feelings that cannot be reduced by simply stating historical facts. In working on this subject, we find the emotions of the disciples of Emmaus when they said about their encounter with Jesus Christ; "Did not our hearts burn within us when he spoke to us on the way and explained the Scriptures to us?" (Lk 24:32). An emotion that we want to make palpable runs through these lines because it is about the sum of sufferings, hopes and ultimately victories accumulated by generations of believers who have finally found in God love, justice and reparation. The third characteristic of our analysis is spiritual in the biblical sense of the term. It tends to respond positively to questions such as: "Does this history make sense today?", "What is the specific place of the Evangelical Churches in this religious complex?" and "Is it possible to elaborate a doctrine of good and evil?" And this one, "How am I personally concerned about Synagogue's relationship to the Church?" And again, "How can I participate in the work of reconciliation?". Other questions certainly come to mind for those interested in this hot topic. Without wanting to make the complete catalog, we will try to ask for some of them, among the most relevant.

This work is intended for all those for whom the relations between the Synagogue and the Church remain mysterious, as they are so complex and marked by this sinusoidal evolution, passing through the high point of natural and harmonious filiation, at the bottom of the heartbreaking divorce and then again at the top of the happy reconciliation. It is intended above all for people curious about human adventures, history, and practical theology, where one can put directly into relation: words, actions, and their consequences. They will find here most of the basics necessary to understand this singular historical phenomenon of Europe which, after its monstrous crimes, struggles until today to find its identity. We wish to create dialogue and consensus, around our theses and our objective of bringing knowledge, edification, personal enrichment, and wherever necessary, a systematic return to the texts of the Bible.

Although all the truth is not yet fully established on this subject, it has already aroused abundant literature. We are first indebted to the late Pastor Jean-Marc Thobois who, to bring it to light, has done an enormous amount of documentation and investigation, both historical and theological. From his writings and lectures, we have removed most of our framework and much of its development. Another great missing person who helped us powerfully is the historian and sociologist Jules Isaac who lost all his family in the Nazi concentration camps and sought to understand what the origin of this outburst of anti-Semitic hatred was. He has left us a considerable body of studies and salutary positions to break the human and social impasse of anti-Semitism. His two major works: "The Teaching of Contempt", followed by "Does Anti-Semitism have Christian roots?", unequivocally raise the question of the historical responsibility of Christian religions of many in spreading anti-Semitism to the heart of European societies. Another witness of this troubled 20th century, particularly helpful to us, it is the author Léon Poliakov, who has greatly participated in the demystification of relations between Christians and Jews, more specifically in his book: "History of anti-Semitism". We have sought in the remarkable "Précis d'histoire de l'Église", written by the pastor and historian Jean Marcel Nicole, important chronological landmarks of the life of the Church over the centuries. We have drawn on many other sources, which we want to thank here, even in a rather global way; they were all valuable for the construction of this work. They are in the footnotes every time we refer to them.

CHAPTER I

Filiation

1. The founding texts of Judaism

1.1 The Torah

B efore the Synagogue, there are in Judaism texts of which some words are sacred, and consequently, they became so in Christianity. However, what is before the "Word"? The second verse of the first chapter of Genesis answers this question: "the Spirit of God". It is the answer to one question by another because what is "spirit"? In its first Hebrew sense, the word "Rouakh" evokes the wind, invisible and yet impetuous. It represents movement and animates living beings. It precedes them and succeeds them according to his species. Charged with mysteries, the "Rouakh" sometimes refers to life itself, not an organic life but rather metaphysical and eternal. In the Gospel of John 3:5, Jesus Christ states that the condition for seeing and entering the Kingdom of God is "to be born of water and the Spirit". The Latin meaning "spiritus" and the Greek meaning "pneuma" each have a similar definition; it is a breath, then, later comes the meaning of the divine breath, an abstract inspiration, a mythological and metaphysical construction. From the Christian texts of the first centuries, this idea develops widely in the public sphere with the many different meanings known to it as: "to have good or bad spirit", "to make the spirit", "the presence of spirit", etc.

This preliminary reflection, however, makes it possible to establish the divine order, which is also for us humans, an order both chronological and also psychological; there is first, "the Spirit", then comes the "Letter", which is given to the people of the Hebrews. The genesis of these people is located between these two spaces of time by a complex detour of family relations from Abraham to the foot of Mount Sinai, when Moses delivers this famous "Letter" or "Word» or «Law" or "Law". Remarkably, the precedence of the Spirit over the Letter will be unceasingly recalled throughout the texts of the Bible in both the Old and New Testaments, until this definitive word of the Apostle Paul in his Second Epistle to the Corinthians; 2 Cor 3:6 "He has also enabled us to be ministers of a new covenant, not of the letter but of the spirit; for the letter kills, but the spirit quickens". Indeed, the letter can kill, and this is what we will see in the second chapter, but before that, the word is given to the Hebrew people by God himself. What a privilege and what a wonderful vocation for these people who, from antiquity, have the best constitution in the world. Nothing resembles this spiritual law as much as civil, in the mythologies of the surrounding peoples who have no other religious horizon than the forces of nature or as in the Greeks, the eternal questioning of their philosophy. Later, King David will sing the praises of this divine Law in Psalm 119 in particular. It is difficult for any sane person and even more difficult for a jurist to understand how a law can bring such great joy and fervor. David had no doubt understood that it was a gift of God, the expression of the power of his Word at the same time as his grace. It is noted that the 10 commandments (Ex 20. 1-2) address both the people and the individual, something that the legal texts of nations do not do, generally neutral and descriptive. It is because God addresses the heart of man as much as his intelligence. Personal as well as collective history, what has been called, "the Ten Commandments" or more precisely, "the Ten Words", constitutes the very heart of the Torah[4]. This is composed of the first five books of the Bible called in Christianity the "Pentateuch" (Penta in Greek means 5).

The Torah is, therefore, the founding text of the Synagogue; its teachings, and its history are recalled every Sabbath day among the people who gather there to listen to them. The Ten Commandments are followed by many others, a total of six hundred and thirteen, which concern life in society as well as private life, worship of the Eternal God as well as religious liturgy. Some parts develop the philosophical aspects of the Law of God, such as the question of free will in the

---

[4]   Torah: The Written Law - Torah, on www.jewishvirtuallibrary.org

human condition. Indeed, in the book of Deuteronomy, chapter 28:1-14, the Lord places man before a choice that is, either following His commandments with the related blessings or deviating from them with the corresponding curses (De 28:15-44). This choice itself is extremely innovative for the Israelites compared to other nations of that time. Long before the Protestant Reformation that brought it back into the spotlight, he raised the question of free will in the face of the Law of God, which can thus be summarized: "Is there genuine happiness outside of God's ways?" The answer is no; however, it must be argued solidly by a whole science that will be born in the Talmudic discussion and will continue in Christianity under the name of casuistry. It is a question of studying the Law of God concerning the various cases of practical life, for which its applications could lead to divergent interpretations. The number of these cases tends towards infinity, and the discussions they generate have never ceased. From these in-depth case studies were born in the 17th century, in Europe, a large part of the so-called "Enlightenment" Philosophy.

1.2 The Hebrew Bible, the Tanakh[5].

It was formed at the time of Ezra by a college of sages called "The Great Assembly". Together, they fixed the canon of the Hebrew Bible, thus passing the teaching of Judaism from an oral tradition to that of writing. Its name is in Hebrew "the Tanakh", which refers to the three parts that compose it, namely: The Torah, the Nevi'im, and the Ketuvim. Its formation and integration as a canon of the Jewish faith followed a long and complex path. These three parts are as follows:

1. T ת: the Torah ה ר ו ת The Law or Pentateuch

These are the texts of Genesis, Exodus, the Law of God, Leviticus, Numbers, and Deuteronomy, as they were received by Moses on Mount Sinai. The Jewish and Christian traditions attributed to him the writing of these five books. However, the investigations of scholars and theologians have questioned this hypothesis. In the 16th century, the philosopher Baruch Spinoza, in his treatise "Politico-religious,"

---

[5]   Tanakh - The word is the Hebrew acronym of "כתובים-נביאים-תורה" Meaning "Torah-Nevi'im-Ketuvim"

attributes the texts of the Torah to the Scribe Ezra. Later, the idea of a gradual compilation between the 8th and the 5th centuries BC by several authors, obeying the same inspiration, was born.

2. N נ: the Nevi'im נביאים The Prophets

These books contain historical accounts of the formation of the kingdom of Israel, its division after the reign of Solomon and the destruction of both by the king of Assyria for the first in 722 BC and by the king of Babylon for the second in 587 BC. They form the chronological sequence of the Pentateuch not without underlining the interventions of God in it. From this point of view, they have value of jurisprudence because they highlight the applications of the divine Law to all kinds of concrete situations of life during these chaotic phases of national construction. They also have a theological value by considering the oracles and interventions of God during this period as well as a moral scope, since these texts constantly appeal to the individual conscience. Thus, they pave the way for universalism of the Bible message, which is why rabbis use it to argue and illustrate their preaching and commentaries in the Synagogue.

The Nevi'im also contains the books of the prophets who accompanied the political and social evolution of the nation up to the scribe Ezra. They present each other's personal views according to the context in which each person finds themselves. The prophets respond to God's call, injunctions, and revelations to warn, counsel, or judge according to their knowledge of the Law of the Lord. They play a major role in shaping the minds of generations of Israelites and their memory is honored and taught well beyond the time of their ministry until today. There are fifteen in order:

Isaiah, Jeremiah, Ezekiel, Hosea, Joel, Amos, Obadiah, Jonah, Micah, Nahum, Habakuk, Zephaniah, Haggai, Malachi, Zechariah.

3. K ך: the Ketuvim כתובים (the Other Writings or Hagiographies).

They are considered as poetic and hagiographical texts and their insertion into the canon of the Bible was not without difficulty. This is particularly the case for the Book of Esther and the Song of Songs. This third part of the Tanakh, is finalized only at the beginning of the 2nd century BC. Each book has its own style, sometimes quite far from the other books of the canon of the Bible. Nevertheless, their inspiration and finality fully justified their place among the canonical texts.

The Ketuvim (כתובים, "Writings") are as follows:

1. The Psalms
2. Proverbs
3. Job
4. Song of songs
5. Ruth
6. Lamentations
7. The Ecclesiastes
8. Esther
9. Daniel
10. Ezra and Nehemiah
11. Chronicles - I and II

Faced with the circumstances of life, these books are rich in moral content, case study and expression of feeling. They facilitate the identification of the reader with the one who speaks and testifies to his or her experiences of blessing as of misfortune. It can be said that as a whole the Ketuvim are the founders of a Jewish humanism, which will be found over the centuries in its literature and philosophy among its known or unknown authors. From this point of view, it is not surprising that the collective and superficial popular culture in Christianity has retained them over the centuries, rather than the dogmatic and legal works of the other books of the Bible. However, for all those who wanted to deepen these texts beyond superficial knowledge, they proved to be of extraordinary richness for the construction of faith and personality. Examples abound on this subject, and it is not our purpose to want to demonstrate it in extenso; let us nevertheless quote the value of the Psalms in the field of messianic prophecy and that of the Proverbs on the personal cultivation of good feelings and the search for wisdom according to God. Let us also quote in the book Esther the faith in him, who overturns the mountains and adverse circumstances and makes them favorable. Let us note in the book of Daniel, the submission to the divine Word rather than to that of a man was he king, and finally, in Ezra and Nehemiah, the courage, the determination to want to rebuild by faith what the adversary destroyed. The Ketuvim demonstrate to each of their pages perhaps more than elsewhere in the Bible, that there is certainly the Law but also and above all the Spirit, that there is the rule but at the same time the mercy of the Lord and his love for his people and all humanity. This spiritual reality is forcefully recalled when Jesus Christ addresses the Samaritan woman in the Gospel of John (4:22-26); "You love what you don't know; we worship what we know, for salvation comes from the Jews. But the hour is coming, and it has already come, when the true worshippers will worship the Father in spirit and in truth; for these are the worshipers whom the Father asks. God is Spirit, and those who worship Him in spirit and in truth must. The woman said to him, I know that the Messiah must come (the one called Christ); When he comes, he will tell us all things. And Jesus said to him, I am, I who speak to you."

1.3 The Bible called "Septuagint"[6]

After the founding of the city of Alexandria in 331 BC, in honor of the Greek conqueror Alexander the Great, an important Jewish minority settled there and prospered in all kinds of activities. At that time, Hebrew as a common language had already almost disappeared; it is Aramaic that is most used in the whole country of Canaan and up to the borders of present-day Iraq. However, Greek culture is crowned with the prestige of the winners and comes with it a considerable amount of literary and philosophical works of high quality. Since worship in the synagogue is open to non-Jews, the Greeks come in large numbers, which is found in the New Testament, where they are called the "Hellenists" and also the "God-fearing" in the Acts of the Apostles (Acts 17:17). It is probably for this reason that around 270 BC, king Ptolemy II of the Lagid dynasty founded by one of the generals of Alexander the Great, wished to know better the thought of the Jews who populate his kingdom. Thus, he asked that all the books of the Bible known at that time be translated from Hebrew into Greek by a collective of seventy-two scholars divided into twelve groups of six scholars, each belonging to one of the

---

[6] Septuagint: The Greek Old Testament made by seventy-two Jewish translators at the request of Ptolemy II Philadelphus (285 – 247 BC)

twelve tribes of Israel. It is from this number that this version of the Bible takes its name because seventy is said and written, as "Septuagint" in some regions of eastern France, Switzerland, and Belgium. Three original texts of the Bible of the Septuagint, called Codex, have reached us; they contain, in addition to the Old Testament, the New Testament, thus marking the continuity of the revelation of God by his Word. This is the Codex Sinaiticus, dating from the 4th century AD and discovered in 1844 by Constantine Von Tischendorf, a researcher working for the universities of Leipzig in Saxony on the one hand and Saint Petersburg in Russia on the other. It is also the Codex Vaticanus, the oldest, and the Codex Alexandrinus. The first was divided for a long time between the museums of Saint Petersburg, that of London, and the monastery of Saint Catherine of Sinai in present-day Egypt. An online version makes it possible to find its unity[7]. The second, the oldest, is in the Vatican Museum. Jerome of Stridon, better known as Saint Jerome, made a translation into Latin called "the Vulgate" towards the end of the 4th century AD, which serves as the basis for the Catholic and Orthodox versions of the Bible. The third Codex, owned by the Crown of England, was placed at the British Library in London. Research on it indicates that it was written in Alexandria, from where it takes its name. The three versions are remarkably close to each other as well as to the Old Testament text of the Masoretic Bible in Hebrew[8]. However, the Bible of the Septuagint in its part of the Old Testament has not been recognized as canonical by the experts of Judaism. It contains indeed added books called apocryphal[9] books, which are not part of the canon of the sacred texts of Judaism. Protestant theologians at the time of the Reformation recognized the Hebrew Bible rather than the Septuagint as the canon of the doctrine for Christianity.

1.4 The Talmud[10 & 11]; define the Talmud

From the law to its application and explanation, the Talmud presents itself as a monumental sum of knowledge, experience, and exegesis, built from the

---

[7] Online version: Codex Sinaïticus
[8] Masoretic Bible: History of the Hebrew Masoretic text. pdf (levigilant.com)
[9] List of apocryphal books: https://www.kingjamesbibleonline.org/Apocrypha-Books/
[10] Talmud – https://sacred-texts.com/jud/talmud.htm
[11] Talmud - Chabad.org

Pentateuch and the Law of God. Since its elaboration, until today, it is inseparable from the history of Judaism and still constitutes a large part of its inspiration. We see the first traces of it with the problematic of the transmission of the divine Law when the Lord said to Moses; "These are the commandments, laws and ordinances which the Lord your God has commanded to teach you, so that you may put them into practice in the land which you are about to take possession of; so that you may fear the Lord your God, and observe, every day of your life, you, your son, and the son of your son, all his laws and commandments that I prescribe to you, and that your days may be prolonged. You will therefore listen to them, Israel, and you will take care to put them into practice, so that you may be happy and multiply much, as the Lord, the God of your fathers, has told you, promising you a land where milk and honey flow. Listen, Israel! The Lord, our God, is the only Lord. You will love the Lord your God with all your heart, with all your soul, and with all your strength. And these commandments, which I give you today, will be in your heart. You will teach them to your children, and you will talk about them when you are in your house, when you go on a trip, when you lie down, and when you get up. You will bind them as a sign on your hands, and they will be like borders between your eyes." (Dt 6.1-8). This passage, like many others, implies the duty to pass the Law of God on to successive generations who will come during the duration of time. It will first be transmitted orally.

1.5 The writing of the Talmud

Most historians believe that it is under the ministry of the priest and scribe Ezra that the transition is made from the oral to the written sum of the religious commentaries on the Torah. In chapter 8:6-8 of the book of Nehemiah, the Levites clearly take over the teachings of Ezra from the people; "Ezra blessed the Lord, the great God, and all the people answered, raising their hands: Amen! amen! And they bowed and bowed before the Lord, their face against the earth. Joshua, Bani, Scheerebia, Jamin, Akkub, Schabbethai, Hodija, Maaseia, Kelitha, Azaria, Jozabad, Hanan, Pelaja, and the Levites, explained the law to the people, and each remained in his place. They read distinctly in the Book of the Law of God, and they gave meaning to it so that they might understand what they had read". This chapter emphasizes the written form of the divine instructions and their systematic study by the Levites. It is as if the oral testimony to the Law and to the prophets had become insufficient and that Scripture brought him the seal of eternity. The development of a scriptural culture in Judaism is concomitant with that of the synagogue, the decentralized gathering place of the people during and after the period of exile. The rules of worship and liturgy are established from this time, and they will know little evolution until today. The authority of the Law in its present form is recognized from the 5th century BC. However, in the intertestamental period, the canon of the sacred books of the Old Testament is still debated in the religious circles of Judaism. It is crucial to distinguish between what is sacred and what is not through an impenetrable boundary to profane thoughts. This radical separation made interpretation and exegesis necessary in order to meet the innumerable needs of both individual and collective life. This work is undertaken by sages, from the period of the Second Temple, around the year 520 BC until the 2nd century AD. It is carried out mainly by Levites since they had responsibility for religious matters. They were called the repeaters or "Tannaïm" in Hebrew. The idea of repetition is interesting because it emphasizes the will to be faithful in time to the successive opinions, opinions and exegesis of the Pentateuch, formulated by the "masters". However, are the masters themselves reliable? This question and many others of the same nature will be the subject of extensive debate within Judaism and will involve many successive comments adding to the precedents. This uninterrupted literary sequence, dealing with everything concerning the application of the divine Law, is recorded in writing in what has become, "The Mishnah", a word meaning "repetition" in Hebrew. Although written, the Mishnah is a faithful transcription of the oral rabbinic tradition, which has the Pentateuch at its source. During its evolution, it will give birth from the end of the 2nd century AD to the Talmud. We are still far from its final texts, which will come only after the 5th century AD. Two Talmuds will be successively elaborated, the first chronologically is that of Jerusalem, while the second came about 2 centuries later is the Talmud of Babylon. In the time of Jesus, the abundant oral and written rabbinical traditions are closely intertwined to the point that confusion reigns over their respective value concerning the sacred texts. In the Gospel of Matthew, Jesus Christ bears witness to this when he declares; "Why do you transgress God's commandment for the sake of your tradition?" (Ma 15:3).

1.6 The Talmud of Jerusalem[12]

The destruction of the temple in the year 70 AD, rested as a necessity, the problem of a decentralized Judaism without its place of sacrifice. The country was devastated, and a large part of its population was forced back into exile to the diaspora centers. However, under Emperor Hadrian, the worst remained to come after the revolt of Bar-Kokhba in 135 AD because Jerusalem was razed and its very name was changed for nearly 350 years to that of, "Aelia-Capitolina". The city became a military garrison, now under the supervision of a special administration of the occupiers. The Jews were expelled from Judea, and everything was done to erase their memory of this region, which was now forbidden to them. It is from this period that the name of Palestine is attributed to it by the Romans, a name derived from the Hebrew "Philistine". Faced with these destructions, the rabbis undertook further north in Galilee, as well as in some academies of the diaspora, an important work of reconstruction of a more literary Judaism. These are the comments and discussions on the Mishna formalized by the "Rav" that is to say, the "Masters", from the 2nd to the 5th century, approximately. Together, they gradually formed the so-called Talmud of Jerusalem, more out of nostalgia than realism since the Jews no longer had access to that place. Thus, it takes over the Mishnah from which he covers all the treaties. However, it brings more than ancestral repetition, a new orientation towards discussion and teaching. The context of his conception was not favorable to it because the Roman occupier, following the revolt of Bar-Kokhba multiplied the prohibitions of all kinds against the Jewish minority and their culture. The reading and dissemination of rabbinical texts was prohibited and towards the end of the Talmud a Christianity hostile to Judaism became the religion of the empire.

1.7 The Talmud of Babylon[13]

It was composed after that of Jerusalem, in the sixth century AD. This is the result of the work of the sages of the large Jewish diaspora in the Middle East,

---

[12] Jerusalem Talmud - https://www.jewishvirtuallibrary.org/talmud-jerusalem
[13] Babylonian Talmud - https://religionsfacts.com/the-babylonian-talmud-a-collection-of-ancient-rabbinical-teachings/

the one that had remained in the Persian empire and had not followed the call for the return of the exiles in Judea at the time of Ezra and Nehemiah. However, they did not all come from these eastern regions, some representatives of the Jewish academies such as that of Alexandria also participated in this work. This voluminous series of documents has benefited from a better historical and social context for its elaboration than the Jerusalem Talmud. The result is therefore deeper and better structured than this one, which is why most Jewish communities and especially those of the Orthodox, study it first. It was written in Aramaic and Hebrew, it borrows from La Mishna its structure in six distinct parts, but it brings them additional developments called "Gemara" after each of them. The word means "completion" or "perfection", these are the comments of the Mishnah intended to link with the "Tanakh", the Hebrew Bible also called in Judaism, First Testament rather than, Old Testament. The Babylonian Talmud later had remarkable additional contributions such as those of Rabbi Shlomo ben Itzhak HaTzarfati (1040-1105 AD) better known as, "Rashi" and those of the Rabbis Moses Nahmanide and Shlomo Ben Aderet in the 13th century. Still, others have continued to renew a genre that has become a classic of Jewish literature. In this area, we can mention the works of Rabbi Yom Tov Asevilli (1250-1330 AD) of Zaragoza and Rabbi Bethal Ashkenazi of Jerusalem in the sixteenth century who contributed to a major theological and literary work, that will never be entirely completed. The Babylonian Talmud was first printed in its entirety in Venice in 1520.

1.8 Reflection on the founding texts of Judaism – Parallelism and the difference between the Talmud and scholasticism[14].

Deprived of its Jewish roots, Christianity is impoverished at the same time as the Western Roman Empire is decomposing. It was a time when pagan myths, some theological wanderings, and distortions of the meaning of New Testament texts appeared in its doctrine as in its ecclesiology. The Talmud, whose diffusion begins from the 6th century, is a form of systematic investigation of the texts of the Mishnah that has no equivalent in Christianity. In order to stand out from it

---

[14] Scholastics – https://www.britanica.com/topic/Scholasticism

while seeking its method and its prestige, the theologians of the High Middle Ages will attempt the difficult or the impossible union, between Christianity and the philosophy of the Greco-Latin world, starting with Aristotle's, the most famous among them. With it appear different attempts to find the basis of a Christian rationalism. From this point of view, we remember the premonitory reflection of the apostle Paul in his first letter to the Corinthians; "The Jews ask for miracles and the Greeks seek wisdom" (1 Cor 1:22), this was already there in his time, an indication of the great fame of Greek philosophy. Thus, would Christianity impose itself as an immediate fact of consciousness in the same way as instincts, reason, metaphysical or scientific speculation or the search for causes in physics? Detached from its Jewish history, it would then impose itself as evidence of the observance of the laws of morality ethics and nature. Between the eleventh and fifteenth centuries, scholasticism produced a considerable amount of knowledge, thus giving pride of place to the learning of dead languages such as Greek and Latin, still taught today in many religious and non-religious academic institutions. It will allow the foundation of a vast network of universities throughout Europe, including the famous Sorbonne in Paris. However, this philosophical as well as theological science is confiscated by the clergy and does not reach the people of believers whom it is nevertheless intended to form. Rather than explaining the world and its relationship to Christianity, it butts on its multiple contradictions and becomes a source of confusion for all those who want to believe and know at the same time. It is generally a philosophy of reason, a sensitive world, subordinated to essences or ideas, intelligible forms, which interpret phenomena and give them meaning. Today theological studies in Protestant and Catholic academies are based on the Greco-Latin intellectual contribution more than on the Bible and the Talmud. From the 16th century onwards, scholasticism was doubly challenged by the humanism of the Renaissance and especially by the Protestant Reformation, one of which brought a real blossoming of the arts and the scientific spirit, while the other allowed Christianity to rediscover its biblical roots. In his, "Controversy Against Scholastic Theology" written in 1517 Martin Luther[15] would say; «the philosophers of the Middle Ages delivered the keys of theology to pagan morality". The reformers accuse the scholastic of having "Hellenized" Christianity

---

[15]   Martin Luther: Controversy Against Scholastic Theology

to the point of having dissolved the revelation of the living Eternal God and savior of humanity in the hazardous and relative speculations of the thinkers of Greco-Latin antiquity. In addition, its pagan mythologies and polytheism were finally considered incompatible with Christianity.

1.9 Reflection on the founding texts of Judaism – Is the Talmud missing in the Christian culture?

History can only be remade in the form of a novel or euchronia, which makes it possible to rearrange the order you want the causes and their consequences. One thing is certain, however, is that Christianity would have gained much more by cultivating this memorial link with the Talmud so as not to depart as much as it did from its Jewish origins. One can especially regret a posteriori this excessive culture of difference and systematic opposition to everything that referred directly or indirectly to them. It has degenerated, even among those who have been called "The Fathers of the Church", in manifestations of pride, contempt and superiority, contrary to the spirit and the letter of the good news of the Gospel. The apostle Paul had anticipated the possibility of this temptation among the non-Jewish converts when he told them; "... and you stand by faith. Do not abandon yourselves to pride, but fear" (Rom 11:20). There was certainly much to be gained in the systematic study of the Talmud in the Christian academies. As an example, we can cite "the Midrash", this method of exegesis and hermeneutics allows us to elaborate new prescriptions concerning the divine Law while distinguishing the sacred from the profane. It brings to the study the openness that the repetition of sacred texts does not have in that it promotes questioning about them. This method and the experience it has brought to Judaism is reminiscent of the value of the dialectic founded or rediscovered by Protestant philosophers such as Johann Gottlieb Fichte[16] and Friedrich Hegel, to name but a few. There are in the Hebrew root of the word "Midrash" the notions of: seek, question, and examine, which have unquestionably favored the openness of mind including the scientific mind, in those who have applied this method. The six orders of the Talmud of

---

[16]   Johann Gottlieb Fichte: Doctrine of Science (1794)

Babylon are particularly interesting for the knowledge of the application of the Law of God in the various areas of personal and collective life.

The contributions of Jewish thought compared to those of Greco-Latin thought could be endlessly detailed, without finally bringing more clarity to the message of the Bible itself. Nor can one live in the eternal regret of what has not been, as if it could constitute a becoming. Rather, it is a new chapter in Judeo-Christian relations that must be opened, based on the universal heritage of the Bible and the imprint of love, respect, and hope that must be cultivated. But ultimately, this is what matters most for the salvation of the soul, the sacred foundation of both Christianity and Judaism.

1.10 Reflection on the founding texts of Judaism – Emergence of a hierarchy of norms between the Law of God and the oral tradition

With time, alterations of meaning appeared between the Law of God and oral traditions, and, in order not to harm its higher authority, it was long been forbidden to put them in writing. This period comes after the tables of the Law were engraved in stone, that is, approximately, from Joshua and the period of the judges to that of the kings of Israel. This separation is full of teaching because it emphasizes the distinction that the Levites wanted to express, charged with religious questions between, the sacred and the profane, between the divine Law and the tradition of men. From the point of view of constitutional law, almost 3,500 years ahead of schedule, it establishes a hierarchy of norms widely used in our domestic law texts and today's international treaties, namely, first; to put in writing the philosophical, moral, and immutable founding principles of the nation. Second, to develop the body of legislation in broad areas: civil, criminal, and commercial... and third, at the basis of this hierarchy, the regulatory area, which specifies the details of the application of the laws. This pyramidal arrangement is still the model for the functioning of political democracy because it harmoniously combines the timeless and the temporal. Thus, we see permanently going into oblivion, a mass of legislative and regulatory texts, because they no longer have any value or application in each social context, while remaining at the top of the pyramid, the laws, the founding and unifying texts of the nation.

1.11 Reflection on the Founding Texts of Judaism – The Organization of Power in the People: The Distinction Between Religion and Politics. (Nb 1.47)

The cohesion of the Hebrew people during their turbulent history is remarkable; it has been consolidated thanks to these three unique characteristics of Judaism: the Torah, the Synagogue, and the Levites.

The Torah, the revealed, eternal, and living Word, is constantly being investigated by successive generations of Jews since it was given by God and written by Moses or by another author who came later. Thus, the Jewish people are a people who seek the Lord and find Him in this Word. However, they do not obtain all the answers to their questions, for the Torah acts as a mirror (2 Cor. 3:18, James 1:22-25) in which man can see both the image of the perfect God, since that is how he was created, but also his own imperfection, since he is mortal, subject to temptation, sin, and ultimately failure. The image is perfect, but virtual; man is real but imperfect. From this double vision arises the need for a savior, for the people as for the individual. Thus, the messianic hope was born at the same time as the Torah, and it is found abundantly in the historical, poetic, and prophetic books of the Bible. The Torah through the ages and its vicissitudes is the crucible of the Jewish people, its rallying point, its confession of faith to which everyone adheres to form an innumerable multitude on the scale of time.

2. Synagogue - Place of worship and memory

2.1 Origins of the Synagogue

During the migration in the desert of Sinai, the book of Exodus tells us that the place of worship to the Lord was the Tabernacle, it was move constantly, it was a removable and transportable tent. All the details of its construction were indicated by God to Moses at the same time as the Law on Mount Sinai. This is where God wanted to reside among His people, a place of prayer, revelation, and sacrifice to the Lord. This was also where the Ark of the Covenant resided, a particularly sacred object for the Jewish people. All activities concerning the exercise of worship were reserved exclusively for the Levites. After the conquest of the land of promise, this itinerant place lost its meaning since the people settled. Much later, during the reign of King David, the need arose to build a "house" for the Lord, even though he does not dwell in a house made by human hands. This truth is emphasized by the words of the prophet Isaiah when he says, "Thus says the Lord, Heaven is my throne, and the earth my footstool. What house could you build for me, and what place would you give me? All these things my hand made, and all have received existence, saith the Lord. Behold, I will look to him who suffers and has a depressed mind, to him who fears my word" (Isa 66:1-2). It was Solomon, son of David, who built a temple for the Lord. This magnificent space, dedicated to the ultimate worship, will also serve as a place of pilgrimage for the entire people during the major religious events that will be celebrated there. It was destroyed in 587 BC, during the invasion of the country by the king of Babylon, Nebuchadnezzar II. Before this major event, all the religious activity revolved around the temple, the ceremonies, and the sacrifices practiced by the Levites in its enclosure. With the fall of Jerusalem began a painful period of deportation and exile away from the promised land and its spiritual center, Jerusalem. From then on, the need arose among the exiles for a cult that was at the same time collective, devoid of sacrifice, and decentralized in the small and large Jewish communities, which were born successively in the two empires of Babylon and Persia. Thus, was born the synagogue (תסנכ תיב Beit Knesset). For most experts, they place its birth in the captivity of Babylon, where its existence would be attested (Ez, 11.16) by the expression miqdaš me'at, designating a sanctuary. Some experts even think that it was born before the exile in the time of King Josiah, following the move to honor again the books of the Law of God. The prophet Jeremiah speaks of those houses of the people (Jer 39:8) burned by the Chaldeans, who might have prefigured the synagogue. In any case, the birth of the synagogue is confirmed in the postexilic era; it is the logical continuation of the work of the Prophet Ezra. Worship as we know it today took shape gradually from that time, with its order, its rules, and its liturgy. The religious services were led and supervised by priests, who from the Hasmonean period (168 – 37 BC) were divided into two major groups: the Pharisees and the Sadducees. The former leads the synagogues in cities, villages, and in all the distant communities of the diaspora.

Their influence was strengthened before and during this interval of time during which they fought against the growing influence of Greek philosophy on the people of Israel. The Sadducees constituted the aristocracy of priests, directing the religious and civil activities of the temple. Their origin goes back to the time of the high priest, "Sadok" of the lineage of Jesus Christ, referred to in the Gospel of Matthew (Mt 1:14). Their elitist behavior and collusion with the successive occupiers of the country of Israel have distanced and often discredited them in the eyes of the people.

2.2 Inside the Synagogue

It is the place where the Jewish believers of a city gather to pray, meditate, and receive a teaching on the Bible and its traditions. Its general layout resembles more or less in miniature that of the great temple of Jerusalem. It, therefore, has a square where the assembly meets, a candelabra, sometimes very big. It has the form of the "Menorah", this seven-pointed candlestick whose detailed realization is mentioned in the book of Exodus 25:31-40. One of its branches is permanently lit to recall the continual presence of God alongside his people. The head of the synagogue presides over the worship from an elevated platform. This place recalls the place of the sacrifice of the Tabernacle at the time of the pilgrimage in the desert. In an enclosure generally even higher is "The Ark of the Covenant", it is the equivalent of the "Holy of Holies", that is, of the great temple of Jerusalem. This is where the scrolls of the Torah are kept. It also has annex rooms for the various events of the community's life. Some of them are reserved for the in-depth study of the Torah, Hebrew, and texts of the Jewish tradition. They enable the emergence of a vast culture that has nourished generations of Jewish children and adults around the world. The synagogue also promoted the development of the "Yeshiva", a Talmud and Torah teaching center run by a rabbi. These "Yeshivot" amplify the teaching role of the synagogue. They bring it, its future leaders and contribute greatly to the spread of Jewish faith and culture among Jews and non-Jews alike. Christianity, especially in its Catholic version, has taken the same paths to build its places of worship; it does indeed include the square, which is the vast gathering place of the parishioners, the light that shines constantly testifying to the presence of God, and the choir where are the consecrated hosts, which only the clergy has the right to manipulate. Protestantism did not take up this parallelism with the arrangement of the synagogue; it was enough in many cases to keep the forecourt and put in the center of the choir a large open Bible, usually quite old, to bear witness to what is now accessible to the reading and instruction of all. This Bible is in the middle of a bare decor where usually stands also an empty cross. This is intended to enhance both by contrast. The parallelism with the synagogue in Christianity extends well beyond the buildings designed for worship, because one will see religious teaching seminars on their side for the improvement of the faith of those called to the ministry. In considering this brief retrospective on the history and definition of the synagogue, it can be seen that the Church in its genesis and its functioning did not invent anything fundamentally different from the synagogue; the word "Church" has, for its Latin root, "ecclesia" which equally means, "assembly" as the "Synagogue". This common semantic origin shows that there is well in time; first the synagogue and then the church, one being the mother of the other, one showing the way to the other.

2.3 Worship in the Synagogue

It is a group of elders who run and discipline the synagogue (Lu 6:22; Jn 9:22, 12:42, 16:2). At the head of it, there is a head of the synagogue, the various services such as: building supervision, accounting, household tasks, are provided by members of the community according to their respective abilities. This simple and pragmatic organization will be found in the churches of the first century and throughout their history until today.

2.4 The order of worship

The worship functions themselves were not reserved for a predetermined person. Any member of the synagogue present could read the prayer, while the interpretation was reserved for ministers. This characteristic is attested in the Gospels and the apostolic texts (cf. Jesus and Paul). Worship consists of the following four main parts:

a) The prayer, including the Schemna, corresponding to the confession of faith from the books of Deuteronomy 6:4,9 11-13,21, and that of the Numbers (Nb 15:37-41), and the prayer itself.

b) The Bible reading was given by one of the assistants and consists of two parts:

    1) Reading of the law is introduced and concluded with a prayer.

    2) The reading of the part of the First Testament called "the Prophets". It serves as the basis for a message preached to the people.

c) Preaching is a practical exegesis of the text read (Ma 1:21-39 and parallel narratives, Ma 6.2; Lu 4.20, 6.6, 13.10; Jn 6.59, 18.20; Ac 13.5).

2.5 The Levites

Unlike the other eleven tribes of Israel, that of the Levites did not receive a well-defined territory in inheritance when the land of promise was shared. Otherwise, they have received a mission: to direct worship to the Lord among the people, to manage objects dedicated to its celebration, and to teach the Torah. As guarantors of the preservation of the texts of the Law, they were also vested with the judicial power to judge civil and religious matters under the Law of God. In order to provide for their needs, the principle of the dime was instituted. The statement of the Eternal God in the book of Numbers (Num 18:20-24) is unambiguous in this regard: "The Lord said to Aaron, Thou shalt have nothing in their land, and there shall be no part for thee among them; I am your share and your possession among the children of Israel. I give as possession to the sons of Levi all tithes in Israel, for the service they do, the service of the tent of meeting. The children of Israel will no longer approach the tent of meeting, lest they commit sin and die. The Levites will serve in the tent of meeting, and they will remain charged with their iniquities. They will have no possession among the children of Israel: it will be a perpetual law among your descendants. I give as possession to the Levites the tithes which the children of Israel will present to the Lord by elevation. Therefore, I say unto them, they shall have no possession among the children of Israel". These decrees of divine power upon the tribe of Levi deserve a time of reflection and study. Indeed, they laid down several fundamental principles, the first of which is that of the separation of powers. If the 11 tribes of Israel have the administrative, economic, and military charges of the country, each in its territory, only one exercises the religious power, which is also judicial. It is transversal because it is recognized by all the tribes that obey it. It is also normative because it is the ultimate reference for all the children of Israel who can appeal to it in cases of dispute or difficulties of interpretation. The second principle is that of the written Law: as soon as it is pronounced, the Law of the Lord is engraved on tablets of stone to last and pass through the trials of time and resist the whims of the reign of men on earth. Unlike all religions that emerge from the human imagination, what must be worshipped in Judaism is the God who creates everything, unique, invisible, and accessible to man only by His Word. It therefore has a sacred value, superior to all other words spoken by men, even the greatest. The third principle of the Law of God consists of a doctrine of good and evil. To apply the law is to do good, not to apply it is to do evil. This extreme shortcut of the relation to the Law of God, in fact to God himself, did not remain in this state because from verse 18, Moses fulfilled the function of a Levite by becoming the intermediary between God and the people. The Law of God is laid out in a series of extremely difficult details to follow for an average intelligence. It treats of human matters but also, civil law, commercial law, marriage, inheritance laws, strangers of respect due to them, and many questions on worship to the Eternal God and on life itself, nature, animals... Amidst all these seemingly disordered prescriptions, a constant reminder: God is merciful (Ex 20:5, 22:27, 33:19, 34:6). His grace appears in his Laws at the same time as his rigor, it is even inseparable from it, and this is where the role of the Levites is paramount. They mediate, interpret, and contextualize the Law of God for the people so that it applies to both personal and social life. They therefore exercise a juridical function for all that concerns the relation to the laws, but even more, it is normative for questions of morals, for uses and it is pastoral for the individual and collective relation to God. This landless tribe was thus given a considerable role in sharing Canaan, the promised land. Over the centuries it has left an impressive line of great servants of both the Lord and the people. Among these illustrious names can be mentioned chronologically: Moses, his brother Aaron and his sons, Samuel, Elijah, Ezekiel, Ezra, Haggai, Jeremiah,

Zechariah. These three great principles will be found in full, in what was not yet Great Britain at the end of the 17th century under the pen of various puritan or agnostic thinkers such as: John Locke[17] (1632 – 1704), John Milton[18](1608 – 1674) and Thomas Hobbes[19](1588 – 1679) as in the great debates of the pre-revolutionary period in France in the 18th century. Indeed, the separation of powers is the central feature of political democracy as we have known it for our greatest benefit, in most European countries and North America for generations. It reminds men of the difficulties of exercising the power, whether political or religious. It also reminds us that the one who exercises power is only a transient of time, an ephemeral depositary of an authority that is soon withdrawn from him because he is mortal. As soon as he arrives at power, he must think of his succession because it is not, he who remains but rather the institution he serves. After the exile and as a result of the many vicissitudes of Israel's political life, the genealogical bonds of the tribes were completely lost, however, the religious and social services provided by the Levites remained. At the time of Jesus, this power in Jewish society was shared between the following three entities: the most numerous the Pharisees, the Sadducees, who were close to the political power and administrators of the temple and the very rigorous Essenes group, who used to live far from the world and its temptations. According to some authors, John the Baptist himself descended from a Levite would have been one of them. They had a definite influence at that time, since the text of Matthew 3:5-6 tells us that "the inhabitants of Jerusalem and all of Judea and the surrounding Jordan came to him".

3. The Preaching of Jesus and the Apostles in the Synagogues

There are many examples in the New Testament where the Lord Jesus and the apostles entered synagogues to teach, to meet the people, and their leaders. The following references in the New Testament give specific examples of Jesus and his apostles entering and teaching in the synagogues:

---

[17]   John Locke https://www.britannica.com/biography/John-Locke
[18]   John Milton https://www.britannica.com/search?query=John+Milton
[19]   Thomas Hobbes https://www.britannica.com/search?query=Thomas+Hobbes

3.1 Matthew 12.8: "For the Son of man is master of the Sabbath. From there, Jesus entered the synagogue."

Here we are witnessing the disputes between Jesus Christ and the Pharisees about the Sabbath. Indeed, this chapter begins with the disciples' picking sheaves of wheat on a Sabbath day. The representatives of the religious world are scandalized by this rather banal act. Indeed, everything seems forbidden on a Sabbath except contemplation, prayer, and piety. Therefore, the question arises as to where the will of God is truly, concerning the Sabbath rules. The religious world willingly makes canonical laws of religion imperative orders that do not support any exception or derogation. With such an application of these rules, we understand that they become instruments of domination and judgment to accuse, condemn, and exclude. However, unlike the religious world, Jesus Christ introduces new laws and rules. Not that he abolishes the old ones, but rather that he interprets them in a spirit of love of compassion, and wisdom, with this question to which the Pharisees have difficulties answering: "Was the Sabbath made for man or man for the Sabbath?". He concludes by saying: "the son of man is master of the Sabbath" (Mt 12:8). In other words, the Spirit of the Lord is superior to religious rules, even if they have their importance and place in the life of the believers. He recalls this truth that religious have often forgotten to acknowledge: "I take pleasure in mercy and not in sacrifice" (Mat 9:13), and concludes with this well-known formula, "For I have not come to call righteous, but sinners" (Lk 5:32). It is interesting to note in this passage that the synagogue is a place of dialogue and intense social life for the Jewish community. The mischievous question posed by the religious to Jesus Christ, namely: "Is it permissible to make a healing on the Sabbath days?" Nevertheless, allows him to clarify a major theological question concerning the observance of its rules. Indeed, the answer to the question is this: "It is therefore permissible to do good on the Sabbath." This statement complements what we have seen above; it highlights the superiority of life itself over the rules of religion. It subordinates these to it, as if religion were not an end, rather a set of formal means and benchmarks by which the faithful can come closer to God and his holiness. This statement, that is, the superiority of the Spirit over the rule and the letter, will be found throughout the teachings of the New Testament, as the apostle Paul recalls when he states in 2 Corinthians 3:6: "He has also enabled us to be ministers of a new covenant, not of the letter but of the Spirit; for the letter kills, but the spirit quickens". Unfortunately, over the centuries of its history, we know that Christianity has relied more on the rule than on the Spirit to subjugate peoples and individuals. It put on the boots of the Roman emperors rather than the sandals of the apostles of Jesus Christ to spread throughout Europe a formal Christianity, and no longer an individual conversion to Jesus Christ's teachings. However, despite all his faults and theological wanderings, for the authentic born-again Christians, the hope of the reign of the Holy Spirit and the Word of Jesus Christ remained alive.

3.2 Mark 1.21: "And on the Sabbath Jesus first entered the synagogue and taught."

This passage is an example of what could be done in the synagogue, namely, teaching. What teaching did Jesus bring? Several passages in the Gospels show that Jesus constantly referred to the teachings of the Torah and the historical accounts of the people of God recorded in the Bible. Even then, the Bible was formatted into its main components. The synagogue was organized around the meditation of certain passages of the Bible, and a corresponding liturgy recalled the key points of the Jewish faith. It was in this context that Jesus as a Rabbi recognized by his peers, could teach. We know that he was not a Pharisee and claimed no religious title in the hierarchy of Judaism of his time. However, because of his perfect knowledge of the Scriptures, the Jewish tradition, and the liturgy of worship in the synagogue, Jesus was recognized as a teacher, as a Rabbi. In this capacity, he could teach as was practiced, which demonstrates, in passing, the great spiritual and intellectual freedom enjoyed by the community of the faithful in the synagogue at that time. This freedom to interpret and to teach from the texts of the Bible has alas been lost in the churches of the multitude from the height of the Middle Ages until today, when knowledge of the Sacred Scriptures has been confiscated by an ecclesiastical hierarchy that has also arrogated for centuries, regalian rights over the whole of society. It is only with the appearance and multiplication of the Evangelical Churches of professing believers that one will find again in the 16th century and until today, this possibility for the laity to comment and teach the texts of the Bible. This passage also shows the universal character of the knowledge of God. If Jesus, who was not a religious person, could receive a complete revelation of the Word of God without going through high theological studies and without having made a particular initiatory journey, it meant that all of us, can access a measure of the knowledge of the Holy Scriptures and the revelation of God's will for our lives. Teaching and being taught are the major needs of Christians converted to Jesus Christ. It is through teaching that the principles, references, and achievements of the conversion to the Lord are transmitted. The elders and Jesus Christ with them had understood it well, and it is through the teaching that the values of Judeo-Christianity have been transmitted ever since.

3.3 Mark 1.23: "There was in their synagogues a man who had an unclean spirit, and cried…"

First of all, we read in the previous verse: "… that they were struck by his doctrine, for he taught as having authority and not as the scribes". This preliminary remark nevertheless highlights a crucial question that has kept all its value nowadays, namely: is the religious world capable of directing the entire society and being normative for its uses and morals? Even today, the debate is far from closed, and ambiguity remains great in many societies where the weight of religion on social life is still considerable. This is particularly the case in France, where secularism has tried to replace what religious norms have left as a legacy in this area. At the time of Jesus, several testimonies show the importance, even the preponderance of the synagogue at the local level, while the Sanhedrin led the nation jointly with the Roman occupier from Jerusalem. This remark also shows how tired people were of hearing the religious discourses devoid of any practical significance from their scribes. This is like the contemporary situation where we see deserted religious buildings because the public is tired of an empty belief. On the contrary, the words of Jesus spoken in the synagogue are powerful and full of authority; they restore life to the body and hope to the soul of the faithful. However, this verse is a window into the life inside the synagogue. This man is seen in the Gospel of Mark (1:23), with an unclean spirit and he shouts. Did he have the right to behave like this, and was it common at that time, that the unfortunate of the country may implore by shouting their distress in the very enclosure of the place of prayer and the consecration of the people? The Bible does not answer these questions directly, however, several passages in the New Testament suggest that the synagogue could also be a place of therapy for individual suffering as evidenced by this verse: "On another Sabbath day Jesus came into the synagogue and taught. There was a man with a dry right hand "(Lk 6:6). The continuation of this passage shows that the liberating and saving word of Jesus Christ, most often clashes with the religious formalism that prevails within the synagogue. Is this the beginning of the divorce between the Synagogue and the Church? There are here the seeds of a radical separation between the two entities. We see that, to gain in freedom as in audience, Jesus will seek outdoor spaces such as the hills, the edge of the sea, sometimes even arid places, and it is said that each time, he attracted large crowds, despite the discomfort and remoteness of the country's towns and villages. One example of this is found in this verse: "He went down with them, and stopped on a plateau, where there were a crowd of his disciples and a multitude of people from all over Judea, Jerusalem, and the sea country of Tyre and Sidon" (Lk 6:17). Labeled as scandalous, the preaching of Jesus Christ nevertheless founds its way among the people of those who sought life and spirit in vast natural spaces, under the sky and in the deserts, away from religious formalism, to which they often understood very little. This historical and sociological reality is reminiscent of the evolution of Christianity through the ages, from the freedom of converts professing their faith in the Lord Almighty, savior and liberator, to a Christianity of multitude, hyper structured by a rigid and dominating hierarchical power. It underlines the permanent imbalance that has been observed since the Old Testament in the religious life of the People of God, between charism and structure, which always tends to stifle it. This imbalance was found in full in Christianity as soon as it deviated from the letter and the Spirit of Jesus Christ. This tendency existed in historical Judaism long before Jesus Christ came; the structure systematically persecuted the charism. This context prevailed over the emperor Constantine until very recently, at the end of the 20th century. In the end, these religious forms offered the population little connection with the revelation of the Holy Scriptures. They did not give access to pastoral ministry, which was often notoriously insufficient for the local population. Under these conditions, the Protestant Reformation took the first steps in the right direction by opening the Bible again and letting it speak directly to the Christian people. It brought him a pedagogy and an explanation of the message of the

Bible far superior to all the mysteries of Greco-Latin scholastic theology, which became confused and obscure to his ears and heart.

3.4 Mark 1.39: "And he went to preach in the synagogues throughout Galilee and cast out the demons."

Therefore, Jesus Christ exercises his ministry in synagogues and drives out demons. The text does not explicitly tell us whether he drives them inside or outside the synagogue. In fact, it does not matter that he did it both inside and out. The text is a brief description of his ministry, where preaching is intimately linked to healing. This connection is remarkable between word and action, it perfectly translates the notion of incarnation, which was an aspiration of the whole people since the time of Moses. Indeed, it was given at the same time as a promise that the Lord had made to him, as it is indicated in this verse found in the second book of the Chronicles chapter 7 and verse 14, "if my people, upon whom my name is invoked, humble themselves, pray, and seek my face, and if they turn away from their evil ways, I will answer him from heaven, forgive his sin, and heal his land". Moreover, the Word of God is followed by concrete effects, and finally, it speaks to the mind, heart, and body. This passage from word to deed is entirely new for the people who soon see in Jesus the Messiah of whom the prophets had spoken from ancient times. The verses of Mark 1:33 & 34 show the extent of Jesus' work as well as his great popularity: "And the whole city was gathered before his door. He healed many people who had various diseases; he also cast out many demons". Healing is and remains today, the obvious sign of God's favor. It is a confirmation of its intrinsic truth as "Word of life", as this statement of Jesus Christ in John 6:63 reminds us: "the Words I have spoken to you are spirit and life".

3.5 Mark 5.36 : "But Jesus, without taking these words into account, said to the chief of the synagogue, Fear not, but believe only."

The relations of Jesus Christ with the religious authorities are not always hostile or full of duplicity; This verse and the scene in question amply demonstrate this.

Indeed, being cornered by the almost certain death of his daughter, the head of the synagogue does what everyone in the crowd would have done. With humility, he rushes to the feet of the Lord, imploring him, seeking healing for his child. By the way, the text reports this unexpected encounter with a woman suffering from chronic hemorrhage for more than twelve years. This is by no means a superfluous digression because in these two very different situations, Jesus Christ expresses in a few words, a fundamental principle of the Christianity, namely: the faith saves. He says, in one verse the 34th: "your faith has saved you" and in the other verse 36th: "Fear not, only believe". In the urgency, he does not tell the woman or the head of the synagogue in whom and in what way to have faith. However, in his words, it is clear that it is faith itself is the right attitude of both heart and mind. In the woman's case, it is through faith that she moves to touch the garment of the Lord, that is, anticipating that Jesus Christ has the power to heal her. The head of the synagogue also expresses these same qualities differently: he shows remarkable humility, although he is head of the synagogue, he does not appeal to any of his titles, culture, or traditions. Thus, stripped of all that could have raised him above his fellowmen, he goes to meet the Lord, imploring him, not for himself, but for his young daughter. These two very distinct characters, moreover, have in common the exercise of faith to find salvation. The text speaking of their faith also shows us their humility, their expectation, and the sincerity of their request. It shows us that, in this disposition of heart only, God grants prayer and saves the unfortunate, according to what is written in the letter of James 4.6: "God resists the proud, but he gives thanks to the humble". We find in the whole Bible these inseparable formulas: "... he saves the unfortunate" and again, "... he saves the sinners" or similar. These expressions, repeated in the biblical texts, show to everyone at the same time the way of salvation and its indispensable prerequisite, namely: humility, stripping oneself of pride and selfishness, and coming to him with repentance. In this reference to the text of Mark 5:36, where is the synagogue? Although it is absent from the staging in this passage, it appears well in the background of this double healing by the character of its leader. One can see that it has the following meaning in the shadow: God heals whom he wants when he wants, the religious person, as the one who is not. He is in the synagogue as well as outside it. He is sovereign in Israel as he also rules over the nations. All those who call upon him with humility and self-emptying can find salvation and healing in him. With this statement, what is the synagogue for? It remains indispensable in this setting as a reminder of the necessary teaching that it brings to each faithful believer. Faith, so precious before God, must be nourished, framed, educated, and strengthened throughout the believer's life, individually and collectively. This is where it takes its full place and meaning. It has proved its value and its greatness by its ability to preserve, despite countless persecutions, the heritage and the radiance of Judaism from the time of Ezra until today. While a great number of nations and religions were born and perished in space and time, Judaism and with it, the nation of Israel, passed through countless storms and survived to this day. The churches, in turn, received this spiritual heritage and took on their own along with the missions that the Lord had given to the synagogue, without in any way replacing it. In this sense, they were well into a matrilineal filiation with the synagogue.

3.6 Luke 4.15 & 16: "He taught in synagogues and was glorified by all. He went to Nazareth, where he had been raised, and, according to his custom, he entered the synagogue on the Sabbath. He got up to read"

One can easily imagine the stunning astonishment and the disbelief of the people gathered in the Synagogue who hear the strange and prophetic words spoken by Jesus. First, we notice the rootedness of Jesus Christ in local Judaism and his regular practice of worship within the synagogue, since we are told here: "... according to his custom". This is one more confirmation among all those that can be noted. Here again, we notice the great freedom of reading and interpretation existing in the celebration of the Sabbath in the synagogue. The reminder of Isaiah 61:1-3 and the words of grace that he utters, first of all, arouse in the audience astonishment and benevolence. Is he not in the synagogue of Nazareth who saw him grow up, is he not the son of the carpenter, well known and honored in the city? But soon after, he makes an interpretation that will cause his listeners to be angry. He prophetically announces from verse 24 that the messiah who is to come will not do it for them, except for a few: "But, he added, I tell you in truth, no prophet is well received in his homeland". The next two quotations, verses 25 to 27, show that God's favor has been granted to strangers rather than to the people from the land of Israel, finishing by angering his audience. How dare he say such words of curse in the place of blessing? One can easily put oneself in the place of this public who awaits the messiah of Israel, to whom one of them comes to say that the one they hope will not come for them, but rather, for those who did not wait for him! What outrage, can we imagine a worse attack on the collective messianic hope of these people? As Christians, we know the continuation and the real significance of the words of Jesus Christ, which evoke here the tragedy of his destiny. Indeed, he was at the same time the Savior of Israel and also his scapegoat, rejected far away from his society by the religious world. This violence, going as far as the will to kill the supposed dissident, is reminiscent of the bewilderment and violence that accompanied the preaching of the message of the Protestant Reformation at the beginning of the 16th century, in the ecclesiastical hierarchy and even in the peoples of Europe. The excommunications, exclusions, attempted murders of Luther, and the numerous murders of Reformers are ample evidence of this. The defense of the structure against the charism of Jesus Christ was merciless, until the condemnation to the torture of the cross. So too, was the defense of the ecclesiastical structure against those who preached in the 16th century, the Reformation, the salvation by grace alone, and the superiority of the Bible's teachings over scholasticism. They suffered fire, iron, and blood price for daring to announce this good news.

3.7 Luke 4.28: "They were all filled with anger in the synagogue when they heard these things."

It is a fact; the teaching of Jesus Christ scandalized many of his contemporaries on several occasions. However, it was not radically scandalous, as if Jesus Christ was fighting Judaism as a resolute adversary. This passage in verse 15: "and he was glorified by all" and many others, shows that the crowd of listeners loves the discourse of Jesus, they love the practical philosophy that emerges from it, they love the lessons of common sense that he proposes in support of his doctrine. Moreover, his customary presence in the synagogue indicates that he places himself as the Messiah, in the most emblematic setting of Judaism, where the faithful of cities and villages gather. It is there, in fact, that the Torah and the Mishnah are taught, a significant part of which already had great intellectual and moral value.

He teaches these Eternal Truths founded from the antiquity of the people of Israel, and he pronounces these capital words in the Gospel of Matthew 5:17-19, which no Christian can ignore to know: "Do not believe that I came to abolish the law or the prophets; I came not to abolish, but to accomplish. For, I say to you in truth, until heaven and earth pass away, there shall not be a single iota, or a single stroke of letter, removed from the law, until all has happened. Whoever, therefore, removes one of these lesser commandments, and teaches men to do the same, will be called the least in the kingdom of heaven; but whoever observes them and teaches to observe them, he will be called great in the kingdom of heaven". In the Gospel of John 4:22, he also affirms this fundamental truth: "for salvation comes from the Jews." These words constitute the foundation of the eternal relationship between Judaism and the Church that will be born after his ascension to the Father. It is a relationship of filiation, in which all the richness of canonical, moral, and historical teaching, brought by the envoys and prophets of God over the centuries, and who bore witness to the truth of the Words of God, must be seen. From this wealth, no Church can dispense itself; however, with the divorce between the Synagogue and the Church, much of the drama that will be played out is the relegation and systematic oblivion of this wonderful science, similar to the sap of the tree. It should never have stopped feeding both, for the greater happiness of Israel and the nations.

Yet the teaching of Jesus Christ disturbs, amazes, stuns, and even scandalizes. What are the points on which his doctrine provokes such strong rejections that they push the elders of the people and later the Sanhedrin to want to kill him? We cited and developed this example in Luke 4:28, where listeners go from admiration to anger when Jesus tells them that the coming of the Messiah is not for them but for people and nations that are not waiting for him. In Matthew 15:12, Jesus Christ scandalizes the Pharisees on a very important theological point concerning tradition: what is the value to be attributed to it in the relationship of the believer to his God? In this area, it is already necessary to distinguish the sacred from the profane. This is what Jesus does when he declares in verse 6: "You destroy the word of God for the benefit of your tradition", he explicitly separates the relative and circumstantial content of the tradition of men from the teachings of the Mishna, from the sacred character of the Word of God, that is, the Bible as it already existed in his time. On the contrary, the Holy Book is sacred, and all its precepts are covered with the seal of Eternity. This point is firmly established by the verses in Matthew 5. 17-19 quoted above. If there were equivalence with tradition, the word of the Lord would then be in contradiction with itself and would also become relative and circumstantial. It could not finally serve as an eternal foundation for our faith. Certainly, one cannot understand his teachings without prayer, faith, questioning, research, personal experiences and especially perseverance. However, unlike human traditions, the Words of God have this clarity and vitality that formulas fixed in the space and time of the religious liturgy do not have. Christianity has not been exempted from this confusion, and the preachers relying on the texts of the Bible often cite this passage to question globally, a Judaism stifled by tradition. Based on this idea, they insist on the theological superiority of the New Testament. They could just as well cite the many examples in Christian history, where these confusions were multiple, blatant, and in full contradiction with the Word of God. In order not to overload the text, we will simply mention the doctrine of baptism as an emblematic example on this subject. In fact, the Evangelical Churches of professing peoples practice only the baptism of converts, according to the texts of the Bible (Mt 15:16 and 1P 3:21), while the Churches of multitudes continue to practice the traditional baptism of children, which radically changes its meaning.

3.8 Luke 7.5: "For he loves our nation, and he built our synagogue."

When he arrived at Capernaum, Jesus met a Roman centurion whose servant was ill and about to die. The fame of the Lord has come to him, and he hopes for a miraculous intervention. We are talking here about the attraction exerted by Judaism on the peoples integrated into the empire of the Mediterranean basin and singularly on the Roman occupier in Israel. Historians have shown that this was great and that Judaism enjoyed a certain consideration in all circles of society. What are the reasons for this undeniable appeal? The late Pastor Jean Marc Thobois has made abundant studies on this question, and he gives us his reflections in his writings and conferences[20] we can quote at leisure, not without paying him a tribute, supported posthumously to express our gratitude.

---

[20]   Jean-Marc Thobois - Jesus, the Jewish Messiah (Lecture, part 1)

Jews were present throughout the perimeter of the Roman Empire from its foundation and during the period of its expansion. Coming from different centers of the Jewish diaspora of antiquity, from Babylon, Persia, Alexandria, and many other urban centers, they settled in the great cities of the empire, until they formed, according to certain sources, ten percent of the population in some cities[21]. They enjoyed the recognition of the Roman administrative authorities and extensive privileges. Because of their exclusive worship of the Eternal God of the universe, they were not bound to worship the successive emperors to whom the title of "Pontifex Maximus"[22] had been given from the imperial period onwards. This high-ranking name is the one who makes a bridge between the gods and men. After the Bar-Kokhba[23] revolt in the year 135 AD and the great dispersion of the Jews that followed, many settled in Rome on the right bank of the Tiber, where they founded the Jewish quarter.

It is certain that Judaism exerted a strong attraction on the local populations and that it aroused many conversions among them. The reasons that can be advanced are singularly the same as those that prevail today, namely, intrinsic coherence. In contrast to the pagan mythologies of Greco-Roman antiquity, which offered a sometimes-fanciful description of the universal order, Judaism provides a satisfactory explanation of this one thing. The world was created by a good God who was also the father of nations and of individuals. He reigns over the elements; he is superior in power to the kings of the earth. Master of the infinitely great, he also probes the infinitely small and the depths of the human soul; nothing escapes his gaze. God is the creator of the universe; unlike pagan gods, whose origins are difficult to trace and who leave very little collective memory in the people. The God of the Hebrews is present from all times, which gives to his oracles and laws the seal of eternity, whose memory and teachings are recorded and transmitted faithfully from generation to generation. Moreover, Judaism proposes a solid doctrine of good, and evil based on a divine Law, that of the 10 Commandments. This excellent mark for the governance of the great affairs of a nation, as for the

---

[21]   History of The Jews in The Roman Empire.
[22]   Pontifex Maximus - https://study.com/academy/lesson/pontifex-maximus-overview-history.html
[23]   BAR KOKBA AND BAR KOKBA WAR - JewishEncyclopedia.com

behavior of the simple citizen, is the mark of its divine and Eternal character. To this set of intellectual and moral qualities must be added the jurisprudential contribution of the historical period of the kings of Israel. This greatly allowed the emergence in the Talmud of a large mass of ethical standards for the people that we have found up until today. All these laws and texts, together with those of the New Testament, are still the main source of inspiration for the Churches of the Reformation for the edification and instruction of their believers. It is certain that compared to the inadequacies and confusion of pagan mythologies of that time, Judaism was infinitely superior to them and never ceased, like it is today, to attract people who were fond of the culture of knowledge and morality.

3.9 Luke 13.10: "Jesus taught in a school on the Sabbath."

The repetition of the passage quoted above in Luke 4:15 shows again, Jesus teaching in the Synagogue. We cannot go wrong. he is a regular at these gathering places of the Jewish people. One can even argue that he loves them because it is there that he can both affirm what must remain unchanged in the religious foundations of Judaism and also what must be reformed in order to bring to the people an authentic, strong and living faith. This short verse serves as an introduction to the following fundamental truths: the superiority of life overrule. In fact, God is above all, the God of life, creator of everything, including our body. As a result, in this passage (Luke 13:16), Jesus Christ, who is this incarnate God, has not refused grace to this tormented woman for 18 years. He did so, despite the strong opposition of the head of the synagogue, guardian of religious orthodoxy. By the way, we note the enthusiasm of the crowd, who praised this thought rather than that of their religious leaders. Another truth put forward in these verses is that the kingdom of heaven is characterized by distinctiveness from those governed by the kings of the earth. It is like a mustard seed, which is infinitely small and insignificant at first glance; however, it grows and extends its branches until it can shelter a whole population of birds from the sky. The latter are here the representation of lost, hopeless, and aimless men and women who find refuge in this large, majestic, and strong tree. This comparison, although very accurate, requires some reflection before being understood and accepted by the believer of the time, as of today. It is not certain that it was indeed in the synagogue at the time, except for a small number in the audience. The second comparison is no less enigmatic for most of the audience. Here, the image is that of a woman who kneads the dough and inserts yeast in very small quantities. However, it is this leaven that makes all the dough rise. This image of a daily domestic task performed moreover, by a woman, does not evoke in any way what a kingdom can be in the mind of the public. The latter thinks more of the struggles of political influence, of the means of conquest of power by arms to overthrow that of Rome, on the one hand, and on the other hand, to govern according to the justice of the Word of God. What does this woman, her dough, and her leaven come to do in the reconquest of the national independence that everyone has been dreaming of for so many years? Nothing, except that she participates without her knowledge, in the teaching given by Jesus Christ on the kingdom of heaven that he will establish, which will be built not on human forces, but as the apostle Paul tells us in his letter to the Romans, namely on: peace, righteousness and joy (Rom 14:17) coming into hearts as the fruit of the holy spirit. This kingdom of a new kind would spread gradually by the influence of one believer to another, then in Jerusalem, in Judea and Galilee, and later in the whole Roman Empire and even later to the ends of the earth.

3.10 John 6:59: "Jesus said these things in the synagogue, teaching at Capernaum."

The most difficult part of the teaching of Jesus Christ for the Jews of his time is the covenant by his body and blood, that is, the incarnation. The first words of the Gospel of John clearly evoke it when one reads in chapter 1.4, "In him was life; and the life was the light of men.". By making the connection with the above, one can only realize this evidence: "the Word of God is life". It is therefore embodied. From verse 50 onwards, what he says goes beyond the comprehension of all that a sensible man of his time can understand, whether he is a Jew or not: "This is the bread that comes down from heaven, that he who eats of it may not die. I am the living bread that came down from heaven. If anyone eats this bread, he will live forever; and the bread I will give is my flesh, which I will give for the life of the world". It is easy to understand that, as a result of this statement, the discussions are going well as the verse 52 says: "On this, the Jews argued among themselves, saying: How can he give us his flesh to eat?" However, in the following verse, Jesus becomes even more precise when he says to them: "Verily, verily, I tell you, if you do not eat the flesh of the Son of man, and drink his blood, you have no life in yourselves". What follows is an even clearer explanation of the need for the believer to live by the very life of the Lord Jesus Christ, hence this expression; "he who eats my flesh and drinks my blood" in verse 56. Verse 59 concludes this difficult explanation for both the apostles and the audience, and it gives this clarification: "Jesus says these things in the synagogue, teaching at Capernaum." The mystery of the Incarnation has therefore been exposed as a fundamental doctrine of Christianity in synagogues since its inception. It is not only his work that bears the seal of God, but his person does also. He is indeed the Eternal Son of God, recognized as such from the beginning of his ministry by John the Baptist in particular. He appears to many people in the crowd as an extraordinary phenomenon by the miracles he works, but his genealogy certainly links him to a royal origin. Isn't he often called "Son of David"? Other texts, some of which we have referred to, also show the opposite: the conflagration of his ideas with the religious practices of his time. Although he relied on the authentic words of the Bible, he was not understood by those to whom he addressed, including the apostles, who said in verse 60, "This word is harsh; who can listen to him? ". The passage in verse 66 marks the point of separation between some of the disciples who had followed him since the beginning of his ministry, but who did not understand the spiritual meaning of the incarnation, which exceeded their capability. On the other hand, he also emphasizes the strengthening of the adherence of certain apostles to the Eternal Words of Jesus Christ, when Peter declares in verse 68: "Lord, to whom would we go? You have the words of eternal life". The intellectual, spiritual, and moral path by which a man can find in Jesus Christ the salvation of his soul will be very difficult to go into for the religious people, for the rich, for those who rely on their merits and knowledge to comply with the requirements of the Law of God.

3.11 Acts 9:20: "And straightway he preached Christ in the synagogues, that he is the Son of God."

The first steps of Saul of Tarsus after his encounter with Jesus Christ are made in the Synagogue. His lightning conversion on the road to Damascus is not only a violent shock for himself, but also for all those who know him and see in him the persecutor of the nascent Church. This is what verse 21 says: "All those who heard it were astonished, and said, Was it not he who persecuted in Jerusalem those who invoked this name, and did he not come here to take them bound before the chief priests?" He became a fervent proselyte of the Christian faith and had lively discussions with the Hellenists. It is recalled here that despite the relegation of Greece as a political and military power to the benefit of Rome, it is still the Greek language and culture that dominate especially in the eastern part of the Roman Empire at that time. This influence remained particularly strong on Diaspora Jews. We also remember the ideological competition between the two opposing cultures, Greek and Jewish. It dates from the invasion of the region by the troops of Alexander the Great and the domination of the dynasties that succeeded him, namely, the Ptolemies and the Seleucids. The prestige of the philosophy of Greek authors such as Plato and Aristotle, had largely penetrated the circles of the Jewish intelligentsia. It was to the point that the Pharisees of Judea and Galilee often had to fight it in their preaching and their teachings. However, with the hindsight of the centuries that separate us from this time, one can easily see the fulfillment of God's sovereign will. Indeed, this influence that the Pharisees fought against was not without real benefits for both Judaism and Christianity. For the first, the Greek culture provided a set of methods and rhetorical processes that helped Hebrew, develop more rigor and formal logic in its theology as well as in its culture in general. For Christianity, it provided two essential vehicles for its expansion throughout the Roman Empire as Greek and Later Roman were the most widespread languages of that time. Particularly Latin, the language of the winners with its prestigious authors, completed later, this already rich cultural baggage for Christianity. It must be recognized, however, that from a relative benefit, one moved later, to an objective mischief. Indeed, with these considerable successive additions of Greek and Latin authors to the Gospel doctrine, Christianity took on a heavy heritage which, subsequently, masked from various European peoples, the original Bible texts and the Jewish foundations of the Christian doctrine, and singularly that of the salvation in Jesus Christ. It is precisely to this effort of clarification and return to the original texts that the reformers tackled in the 16th century. Their enterprise was continued and deepened by the various evangelical currents born in the wake of the

Reformation. Together, they allowed the sacred texts of the Bible to be honored again and placed at the top of the hierarchy in Christianity. By going through the centuries of the intertwined history of the Synagogue and the Church, one comes to this capital and definitive conclusion that the second could not have existed without the first.

3.12 Acts 13:14: "And they went into the synagogue on the Sabbath, and sat down."

Paul gives a didactic presentation on the coming of Jesus Christ and his ministry from the history of Israel. It appeals to the collective memory of the Israelites and, in so doing, lays down the fundamental principles of causality in history. Verse 5 indicates that Paul and Barnabas taught in the Jewish synagogues. This is a mark of what Jesus practiced in his time. In Antioch of Pisidia, the leaders of the Synagogue, with courtesy, gave Paul an invitation to comment on the reading of the Law and the prophets. Having risen, Paul makes a didactic presentation, that is, he does more than teach; he explains and demonstrates in detail at the same time, the origins of the Christian faith, starting with the formation of the Hebrew people in Egypt. The continuation of his discourse is only the succession of causes and their consequences; this is a very specific method of exposure to Judeo-Christian thought, which can be called: causality in history. It is the explanation of any phenomenon's occurrence by its cause. Widely used in the physical sciences, it can also be applied to the social sciences, with the specific difficulty that human behavior is not always reducible to its causes. It takes, in a way, a talented exegete to bring to light the hidden truths behind the chain of causes and consequences in men, and this is what the apostle Paul does on this occasion. This method is not only prevalent in the Old and New Testaments but will also be generalized in the following centuries to explain, justify, and perpetuate factual situations in Christianity. However, with time, this or that truth is distorted by usage and tradition. What made the force of it is relativized and reduced to a legend, and in the long run, no one can find the exact origin or the authority it had at the beginning. We do this or that because we have always done it, we believe this or that because we have always believed it. In this passage, the apostle Paul returns to the causes that brought the Lord, the God of Israel, to send his Son Jesus Christ into the nation to grant him salvation, for both the individual and the collective. In another even more explicit passage (Acts 7:1-60), Stephen, filled with the Holy Spirit, makes an even more detailed demonstration of causality in the history of the Jewish people. Going back even further in time, he invokes Abraham, the patriarchs, Moses, David, and the prophets to explain before the Sanhedrin that Jesus Christ, whose crucifixion they had asked for, rose from the dead and is truly the Son of God. Jesus himself used this explanation method widely when he taught in synagogues and in public places, where he gathered a large crowd.

3.13 Acts 17:17: "So he talked in the synagogue with Jews and God-fearing men, and in the public square every day with those he met."

The synagogue, a place of metaphysical exchange and speculation between experts and scholars, but also between people less advanced in the knowledge of the Scriptures, appears here in broad daylight. It is an extraordinary place of meeting and social exchange for Jewish culture, which at the same time reveals its universal character. In this chapter, we note the extraordinary popularity of the apostle Paul. Without the means of modern communication tools other than the power of words, he draws with him "a great multitude of Greeks fearing God". We also find here the attraction of Judaism on the local population mentioned above, since a large part of its audience was composed of Greeks. This passage also indicates, with a remarkable economy of words, the point of contact between Greek culture and Jewish culture. In verse 18, the text speaks of those Epicurean and Stoic philosophers who argue with Paul. Their astonishment is great, and they asked him to tell them more about what they take for "... foreign deities". Having reached the amphitheater, they offer the Apostle Paul an excellent platform to express himself before many people, on this new doctrine of a single God, creator and savior of all mankind. From verse 22 to verse 32, the apostle makes a remarkable synthesis intended for an audience that knows nothing about the Jewish conception of man, history, and human destiny. His conclusion, however, from verse 29 and following to verse 32, radically distances them from his discourse. This point of entry into the doctrine of Judeo-Christianity through the renunciation of idolatry, the necessity of repentance, the judgment on a fallen humanity, and the resurrection of the dead, seems to them insurmountable, inconceivable, and, except for a few, they mock. Before these events in Athens, verses 10 and following, it is said that Paul and Silas escaped at night from Thessalonica and arrived in Berea. In this city, the teachings of Paul are received with great interest and even haste, the text tells us. It is possible to think that the apostles often received a positive reception like this one, since they all began their ministry in the synagogues. The manifestations of hostility cited in the Bible texts were rather the exception than the rule when considering the number of times Paul and his companions entered synagogues. This is the thesis that the Pastor and theologian Jean-Marc Thobois[24] develops abundantly in his many writings and conferences. The radiance of the intelligence of the apostle Paul is strong among the notables of the city because men and women of "distinction", the text tells us (v 12) came to listen to him. In the Synagogue of Berea, religious leaders do what any religious leader should have done from the beginning of the Christian adventure: examine the Scriptures daily to see and understand whether what they were told was correct (v11). This short passage applies forcefully to the doctrine of Christianity and its ecclesiology. This attitude of humility before the sacred texts is certainly essential to seek and highlight the fundamental truths on which they take root. It is a question, in fact, for the leaders of the Synagogue as for the men of the Church, of teaching with truth, under the inspiration of the Holy Spirit as the Lord wants when he says to the Samaritan woman; "But the hour cometh, and now is, when the true worshippers shall worship the Father in spirit and in truth: for the Father seeketh such to worship him. (Jn 4:23)". The history of both Judaism and Christianity is parallel from this point of view; both easily forgot the cornerstone, that is to say, these fundamental truths in question to the benefit of human tradition, the frivolity that pleases the crowd and sometimes even the blatant doctrinal counter-meaning. It is to this work of reflection and investigation, accompanied by prayers and personal consecration, that the Reformers, first Protestants, then Evangelicals, have been working thoroughly until today. Amid great opposition, they have done so, so that

---

[24] Jean-Marc Thobois: Israel in the present time and the Church's attitude towards Israel - YouTube

the Word of God may again be exposed and explained in all its dimensions to believers of different peoples throughout the world. Returning to this passage, we see in verse 5 that unfortunately, this beautiful harmony does not last long because troublemakers soon arrive from Thessaloniki, forcing Paul and Silas to leave the city of Berea.

3.14 Acts 18:4: "He spoke in the synagogue every Sabbath, and persuaded Jews and Greeks."

Paul works in tent making with Aquila and Priscilla. This information could go unnoticed if it were not indicative of Paul's condition. Although he is dedicated to the ministry of evangelization and the teaching of Christianity in the synagogues and wherever he could, Paul is here for a time making tents to provide for his material needs. It is a window open to his concrete situation, showing that he did not always benefit from the support of the communities he had formed or the synagogues that had welcomed him. It is also a teaching for the nascent Evangelical Churches whose resources are sometimes very limited. They cannot always assume both the salary of the pastor, the rental of a room, and the various financial commitments necessary for the worship services. As a result, their pastor works in the secular world and ensures his salary. This is not always a comfortable situation, and it is not that of the Apostle Paul who will exercise this profession only for a short period, since it is said in verse 5: "But when Silas and Timothy came from Macedonia, he gave himself entirely to the Word, attesting to the Jews that Jesus was the Christ". The word "... entirely" is a clear indication that henceforth he had ceased to make tents. However, this dual status also has the advantage of being able to start a Church, without this financial constraint, sometimes being too heavy to bear. A pastor who works with his hands and talents is also a witness to the biblical value of work as a service to God and the community. These situations are in fact extremely varied; no theological basis opposes it; these are questions of personal choices and opportunities. Some communities have made this activity both temporal and spiritual, a general rule of their functioning, and they pay no pastor. This is particularly the case of the Evangelical Mennonite communities, very present in eastern France, Switzerland, the Netherlands, and Germany. They are mainly found in the USA in the state of

Pennsylvania and Canada in the Province of Alberta. After this time spent with Aquila and Priscilla, Paul has great activity in various synagogues where he teaches and debates abundantly with the religious leaders, to demonstrate the truth of Jesus Christ in the universal plan of divine salvation. In verse 8, a major event shakes the Synagogue of Corinth because its leader, Crispus, believes in Jesus Christ the Messiah of Israel with his whole family. For this reason, the apostle might have feared social unrest in the city accompanied by great persecution. However, in verses 9 and 10, the Lord speaks to him in a vision, assures him that no harm will be done to him, and encourages him to continue speaking without fear. Corinthians also believed in Paul's preaching, and they were "baptized". The question that can be asked is what represented at the time, baptism in the rites and ceremonies of the Synagogue? Nothing before John the Baptist is indicated in the Old Testament on Baptism. However, it can be assumed that it existed before him by elements of context. Indeed, nowhere does the Bible indicate that this is a new rite in Judaism that would have been established by him. On the contrary, it is said in Mark 1:5 that many people went to the desert to be baptized: "And there went out unto him all the land of Judaea, and they of Jerusalem, and were all baptized of him in the river of Jordan, confessing their sins". Other passages go in the same direction, so baptism was not unknown in the Judaism of the time of Jesus Christ. Its origin probably lies in the ritual of ablutions, very present in it. This ritual toilet was ordered in the Law of the Lord not only for hygienic reasons, but also for its moral value, the water carrying away with it, the impurities of the body, including moral faults, and finally, sin in general. Chapter 14 from verse 8 of the book of Leviticus makes the connection between the physical wound and the moral fault, since according to the text, the leper must make for the day of his purification both a sacrifice of atonement and a sacrifice of guilt. The connection of the health of the body with that of the spirit is made here and is found even in the New Testament where the preaching of Jesus Christ and that of the apostles, is accompanied by the healing of the bodies. A complex and long protocol is described in this passage of Leviticus, where one notices that the patient is placed outside the camp, he is in quarantine somehow. Is this where the practice of baptism, like John the Baptist in the desert or the Jordan, comes from? We have no answer from the Bible on this point, nevertheless, it can be suggested. Baptism is therefore outside the Synagogue; however, it is not outside the Judaism of the time, and it will be the mark of entry into the Church for all generations of Christians who will come after the apostles. This use preserved much more in its sense of moral purification than physical hygiene, was sacralized by Jesus Christ himself on several occasions when he declares in Luke 7:29-30 "And all the people that heard him, and the publicans, justified God, being baptized with the baptism of John. But the Pharisees and lawyers rejected the counsel of God against themselves, being not baptized of him.". And also, in Mark 16:16 when he utters his last words before his ascension to the Father: "He that believeth and is baptized shall be saved; but he that believeth not shall be damned."

3.15 Acts 18.19-20: "And he came to Ephesus, and left them there: but he himself entered into the synagogue, and reasoned with the Jews. When they desired him to tarry longer time with them, he consented not.»

This passage, like the precedents concerning the activity of Paul, shows well the preponderant role of the Synagogue in his ministry. Whether he is well received or not, the filiation of the Synagogue to the Church is better understood by reading these verses. The last part of the sentence, verse 20, shows the favorable reception of the Jews towards Paul. This characteristic of his activity is again found in the Synagogue, teaching, edification, and exhortation to conversion. We can assume, with Pastor Jean-Marc Thobois, who demonstrated it in one of his conferences[25], that this benevolence towards the apostle was rather the norm than the exception, as he often went to preach. This is an opportunity for us to revisit the entire relationship of the Synagogue with Christianity at its origin. For many Christians, including those familiar with the biblical texts, the Jews rejected the teachings of Christ at the same time as his person. A great guilt weighs on these people and the many persecutions they suffered are basically only a logical consequence of this rejection. This is often the simplistic reasoning of many, even among the most learned people. This is the famous causality mentioned above

---

[25]   Jean-Marc Thobois: Israel in the present time and the Church's attitude towards Israel
        - YouTube

in history: "They rejected, they are cursed". However, these simplistic assumptions are false and are opposed abundantly by biblical references and examples in the third part of the book on the "Reconciliation". A careful reading of the Gospels shows, as we did above, the rootedness of Jesus in his Jewish people, spirituality and culture. We can also read how often the apostles were welcomed and at ease in the synagogues to preach the Gospel. Except for the cases cited in the New Testament, it was not considered a "New Doctrine". It was often interpreted as an interesting development of Judaism. The opposition and sometimes the violence that accompanied the preaching of the Cross, and of the Gospel, is the fact of a small number of influential and, not of the Jewish people as a whole. It remained, indeed, very distant from this politico-religious trial in which its opinion was never asked. One finds here a phenomenon that will reproduce "in extenso" in Christianity from its formation as the official religion of the Roman Empire with, "the Edict of Thessaloniki"[26], that is, the establishment of a religious monopoly and the culture of orthodoxy to the detriment of the search for truth according to the texts of the Bible. The exercise of this monopoly can be summarized in this formula: "The struggle of the structure against charisma". In the Gospels, this struggle is led by an intellectual and political elite in the service of the Roman occupier called the Sadducees. This party, formed by a politico-religious aristocracy, had religious only the name. Essentially turned to the preservation of their many privileges since they were also administrators of the temple; they did not care about the preaching of Jesus Christ, of which they perceived, nevertheless, the revolutionary dangers for the established order. In the New Testament, they represented this structure that fought vigorously and with the help of the means of politics, the enthusiasm aroused in the people, by the preaching of the Gospel. The Sadducees were far from popular in the nation of Israel, their compromises with the Roman occupier, their notorious corruption in the management of the temple affairs and their superficial religiosity made them the constant target of criticism from the population, many passages in the Gospels bear witness to this (Mat 16:6; Lk 20:27). The Pharisees, on the other hand, were much closer to the people and exert great social influence because of their activities in the service of the local population. Born practically at the

---

[26]   Thessaloniki Edict - The Edict of Thessalonica in 380 - World History Edu

same time as the Synagogue in the postexilic period of the time of Ezra, they allowed the expansion of a decentralized Judaism, far from the Jerusalem Temple, wherever Jewish communities were, including in the distant Persian Empire and up to the borders of India. In the west of it, a large diaspora was formed in ancient Greece and then throughout the Roman Empire. Here again, a careful reading of the Gospels shows at once the rootedness of Jesus in the Synagogue and Jewish culture. It also shows his occasional opposition to the excesses and abuses of power of which this religious system was at fault concerning the texts of the Law of God and their spirit. The age-old struggle of the structure against the charisma embodied by Jesus Christ found its ultimate expression because it was only a tiny minority of the Pharisees who spoke jointly with the Sadducean[27] party and the Sanhedrin, for the crucifixion of Jesus Christ. The people, for their part, remained largely alien to this unequal struggle between the two powers: one secular and the other spiritual. The tragic outcome that we know shows the triumph of the first over the second. However, over time, the work of the apostles, that of future disciples, and the early Church, reversed all that, and we saw the second triumphing over the first to demonstrate that the influence of the spirit was far superior to that of the politico-religious parties, whatever they were. Thus, neither the Roman Empire with all its power nor the party of the Sadducees with its politico-religious monopoly would prevent the emergence of a Christianity of conversion, increasingly vigorous throughout the Mediterranean basin. Another fundamental lesson of the crucifixion of Jesus Christ we must not miss; in this botched trial of Jesus Christ, in this performance to show the strength of the structure against the charisma, these are two well-identified human powers that have been judged and condemned by history and by the texts of the New Testament. It is a part of the religious world with its dogmatic rigidity, its sordid politico-financial interests, and its insensitivity to the needs of the people. On the other hand, it is also the pagan world, represented by the Roman occupier, totally ignorant of the religious realities of the Hebrew people. It is indeed this one which will finally condemn Jesus Christ to death based on this iniquitous trial, where it is a question of Jewish legends that they understand nothing. Finally, it is rather in consideration of his immediate interests, to defend the established

---

[27] Sadducee: https://Judaism_enc.en-academic.com/16976/SADDUCEES

order, that the Romans in the person of Pontius Pilate, prefect of Judea, condemned to death Jesus Christ. It was this Roman occupier who finally gave the fatal order to kill Jesus Christ. Thus, are gathered in the New Testament, symbolically but also concretely and for eternity, the condemnation of two powers: the religious world and the pagan world. It recalls the verses of the apostle Paul on the condemnation of the human race as a whole, when he says in his epistle to Romans 3:9-12, "9 What then? Are we better than them? No, in no wise: for we have before proved both Jews and Gentiles, that they are all under sin; As it is written, There is none righteous, no, not one: There is none that understandeth, there is none that seeketh after God. They are all gone out of the way, they are together become unprofitable; there is none that doeth good, no, not one". In writing these lines, he quotes a verse from the Ecclesiastes who, in the Old Testament, reached the same conclusion (Ec 7:20), he also quotes a short passage from Psalm 5:9. The iniquity of the human race is thus demonstrated, the religious world and the pagan world are both enclosed in the same condemnation being both equally guilty of the death of Jesus Christ. This demonstration invites everyone, therefore, to question their condition before God because it also means personal guilt, the need for repentance, and individual conversion to live in newness of life with the help of the Holy Spirit. It is a long demonstration to exonerate the Jewish people from the death of Jesus Christ. It is still necessary today, so much the reductive and simplifying work of prejudices and time has been powerful and harmful to extend to all the Jewish people, the condemnation that should be carried out only on the actors guilty of this drama.

3.16 Acts 19.8: "He entered the synagogue and for three months spoke out boldly, and argued persuasively about the kingdom of God."

Paul is now in Ephesus, where he is well received in the synagogue since we are told in verse 8: "let him speak freely", for a rather long period of 3 months, until different points of the doctrine of Christianity do not offend some, to the point that; "When some stubbornly refused to believe and spoke evil of the Way before the congregation, he left them, taking the disciples with him, and argued daily in the lecture hall of Tyrannus." (v9). Very interesting is Paul's strategy, whose objective remains intact despite adverse circumstances: prevented from speaking in the synagogue, he does so in a school. For two years, he preached and taught to such an extent that "all those who lived in Asia, Jews and Greeks, heard the word of the Lord", says verse 10. It doesn't matter where, if the doctrine of salvation in Jesus Christ is preached. This strategy is reminiscent of that of the desert pastors, implemented much later during the 16th century until the 18th century in France, at the time of severe persecution against the Protestants. The "Pastors of the desert" preached then, in barns, in the open, in forests, in caves, including at night to hide from their pursuers. Despite all the strength of King Louis XIV against them, the Word of God never ceased to be preached and spread across the country. It shows that it is not the place of preaching that is important, but rather the message itself and the hearts that receive it. Extraordinary miracles follow Paul's preaching, verse 12 tells us, "So that from his body were brought into the sick handkerchiefs or aprons, and the diseases departed from them, and the evil spirits went out of them.". This unusual practice recalls the woman's blood loss gesture in the Gospel of Matthew 9:20 and other similar passages in the Synoptic Gospels. This woman wanted to be content with touching the hem of Jesus Christ's garment. Still, when he turned to her, he gave her a miraculous healing and accompanied her with an Eternal Word, "... he said, Daughter, be of good comfort; thy faith hath made thee whole. And the woman was made whole from that hour." (v22). Thus, the objects recall the effective and miraculous presence of the divine for these sick. They are healed not by these, but by reminding them of the Word of God preached by Paul, in which they put their faith. However, the following verses reveal the rapid distortion of this punctual practice by unscrupulous individuals who have little regard for the means of acquiring money (Acts 19:13-19). In their evil spirit, it is the object and not the Word of God that works the miracle, so it is enough to possess it to bring about the miracle. This shortcut is unfortunately common in the history of both Judaism and Christianity. It is recalled that Aaron, under pressure from the people, tired of waiting for the return of Moses from Mount Sinai, had made a golden calf and had declared it the god of the Hebrews, thus surrendering the people to shameful idolatry (Ex 32:4). It is also remembered that during the whole period of the kings of Israel and Judah, the idols of Baal, the Astartes, the high places of idolatry and all the deities foreign to the Eternal the God of Israel remained in the land. We remember that some kings fought them vigorously while others were rather complicit in their presence. Idolatry is a characteristic feature of all humanity; to be attached to the object and not to its creator is found everywhere in this world. Man raises to heaven the objects he has created, he makes them his idols, he gives them an immoderate cult, and through them he celebrates himself. Christianity was not spared this sin, which violates the first commandment of the Decalogue as defined in Exodus 20:1-6: "Then God spoke all these words: I am the LORD your God, who brought you out of the land of Egypt, out of the house of slavery; you shall have no other gods before me. You shall not make for yourself an idol, whether in the form of anything that is in heaven above, or that is on the earth beneath, or that is in the water under the earth. You shall not bow down to them or worship them; for I, the LORD your God am a jealous God, punishing children for the iniquity of parents, to the third and the fourth generation of those who reject me, but showing steadfast love to the thousandth generation of those who love me and keep my commandments". These are the first words of the Basic Law of both Jewish and Christian peoples. However, over time, they have been forgotten even by those who were responsible for teaching and putting them into practice. Thus, from the early Middle Ages, especially in churches, but also in many public places, images of biblical scenes flourished. Over the centuries, artists, some of whom have left a great name in the history of art, have endeavored to create sculptures, paintings, and countless objects of piety, to communicate the faith and love of God. Over time, these creations of all kinds were the subject of a true cult, encouraged by religious dignitaries from the top down the ecclesiastical hierarchy. The form took precedence over the substance, the tradition over the Bible, and the images over the teaching. The entire period of the Middle Ages, followed by the Renaissance and Baroque periods, will portray God in an image, despite the first commandment of the Torah. From the 16th century onwards Protestantism would go against this trend; its places of worship would be much more stripped, especially among Calvinists, to honor the incarnate verb rather than the work of talented artists. The most visible consequence of this drift from the sacred text to profane images is naturally the idolatry of the visual opposed to the spiritual life according to God, namely, by "spirit and truth" (Jn 4:24). This attachment took the turn of a relentless fanaticism in Europe during the rise of Protestantism and especially in France. All kinds of heinous crimes were committed during this period to defend plaster statues, images, and inert objects. For many of them, these artistic creations of all kinds still exist today in places of worship. However, no one thinks of destroying them; it is through the crowd's indifference that they have lost their metaphysical power. Testimonies of a bygone era belong more to the culture of people than to religion.

3.17 Theological context: the common messianic hope between Jews and Christians

From an anthropological point of view, one can only note the obvious parallelism between the messianic hope in Judaism on the one hand and that which exists in Christianity on the other, regarding the return of the Lord Jesus Christ in glory. These two hopes, which in many ways are but one, could have been cultivated both in synagogues and in churches, to find together points of theological and practical convergence, allowing for a mutual harmony. In this regard, there are endless regrets about what has not happened in history. However, what has not been in the past may well come in the future, and it is from this perspective that this work is being built. Before opening this blessed part called: "Reconciliation", we must go through the very unfortunate, which has for title: "Divorce"

3.18 An undeniable filiation and analogies between the Synagogue and the Church

It is therefore certain that the Synagogue existed since about the 6th century BC, long before the coming of Jesus, and that the message it brought to the people was rooted in the teachings of the Torah and the rabbinical Bible of his time. That of the Synagogue directly inspires the liturgical order of worship in Christian communities. The writer and journalist Bernard Lazare[28] describes, in the introduction of chapter three of his book, "Antisemitism: its history and causes", this filiation in terms that could not be more precise: "The Church is a daughter of the Synagogue; she was born of her; thanks to her, she developed,

---

[28]   Bernard Lazare: Antisemitism: its history and causes, ch III Léon Chaillet Éditeur 1894

she grew up in the shadow of the temple and, barely vaguely, she opposed her mother.... The early Christian assemblies had, like the Synagogue for theological source, the Torah and the Bible, inspired by the available translations, one being the Hebrew Masoretic Bible and the other the Greek Septuagint Bible. They both wanted to gather "The People of the Book" faithful to the Sacred Scriptures and thus prolong Jewish theology by giving it the universal perspective of the New Testament.

CHAPTER II

Divorce

Anti-Judaism in Stone - Allegory of the Synagogue (Ecclesia and Synagoga) Blindfolded, the spear broken and the tables of the Law collapsed, one of the representations of medieval European anti-Judaism (Saint-Etienne Cathedral of Metz, France)

1. The Jewish theocracy against the Church in the New Testament

It would be contradictory to state now that the Synagogue was opposed to the Church from its origin, when we demonstrated in the first part that there was in general harmony and theological filiation from one to the other. However, as the New Testament amply indicates, misunderstandings and conflicting situations have not been lacking between them from the beginning of their relations. So, there are two states of their relations: on the one hand, the theological and practical filiation, which was self-evident in most cases, as we have seen previously and on the other hand, the doctrinal conflicts, they dispute and more or less definitive separations of which the Gospels and the pastoral letters of the New Testament speak. We can examine the causes of the opposition between the Synagogue and the Church, and group them into four parts, each time reflecting on what we know about the history, the letter, and the spirit of the Bible texts.

1.1 The force and violence of words; blasphemy and the resurrection of the dead.

Violence and murder are attached to certain words and to the one who pronounces them, since they contain stakes of spiritual and temporal power. It is clear in this passage from the Gospel of Matthew 26:57-66, shortly before the crucifixion: "Those who had arrested Jesus took him to Caiaphas the high priest, in whose house the scribes and the elders had gathered. But Peter was following him at a distance, as far as the courtyard of the high priest; and going inside, he sat with the guards in order to see how this would end. Now the chief priests and the whole council were looking for false testimony against Jesus so that they might put him to death, but they found none, though many false witnesses came forward. At last, two came forward and said, "This fellow said, 'I am able to destroy the temple of God and to build it in three days.'" The high priest stood up and said, "Have you no answer? What is it that they testify against you?" But Jesus was silent. Then the high priest said to him, "I put you under oath before the living God, tell us if you are the Messiah, the Son of God." Jesus said to him, "You have said so. But I tell you, From now on you will see the Son of Man seated at the right hand of Power and coming on the clouds of heaven." Then the high priest tore his clothes and said, "He has blasphemed! Why do we still need witnesses? You have now heard his blasphemy. What is your verdict?" They answered, "He deserves death". The New Testament presents this situation in which it is not only the Lord, the God of Israel, who is blasphemed or at risk of being blasphemed, but also Diana, the pagan goddess of the city of Ephesus (Acts 19:37). In the Bible, blasphemy is the contempt done to God himself or a deity placed above the reign of men. On the other hand, what is clear in the Old and New Testaments is not clear in the pagan world, where the gods, principalities, and various dominations are often clever abstract constructions that nevertheless justify the exercise of power and unjust constraint on the population. This is indicated in several passages of the Word of God, taken in Ephesians 1:21, when the apostle Paul exhorts the Ephesians to consider the absolute superiority of Christian hope over any other form of power:

"...Far above all principality, and power, and might, and dominion, and every name that is named, not only in this world, but also in that which is to come:". It can therefore be concluded that blasphemy, although it is generally considered the supreme insult to what is elevated, is ultimately a very convenient term for judging and condemning a person. It is enough for those who judge to decree that the other has blasphemed this or that sacred symbol, sometimes quite abstract or esoteric to the community, to condemn him. We will find this abuse of power throughout the history of Christianity, where it is images, statues, titles, words, dignitaries, or any other artifice, which have been in turn blasphemed by some and condemned by others, despite or because of their sometimes very relative sacredness. It can also be concluded that this concept has a universal value far beyond Judaism, Christianity, and Greco-Latin culture. It is an anthropological reality that is encountered in all human societies. The idea of blasphemy is found for the first time in this Bible passage where a stranger by his father and Israelite by his mother blasphemed and cursed the name of God (Lev 24:15-16). After consulting the Lord, the elders and the wise pronounce the verdict: "And thou shalt speak unto the children of Israel, saying, Whosoever curseth his God shall bear his sin. And he that blasphemeth the name of the LORD, he shall surely be put to death, and all the congregation shall certainly stone him: as well the stranger, as he that is born in the land, when he blasphemeth the name of the LORD, shall be put to death".

Thus, much later, the Romans will carry out the condemnation pronounced against Jesus by the high priest for allegedly blaspheming, outside the walls of Jerusalem, on Mount Golgotha. Blasphemy is, therefore, a word that kills its author. In the case of the trial done to Jesus Christ, it can be observed that it is not the Synagogue that instructs him, but rather a very small number namely: the high priest Caiaphas, the scribes and the elders of the people (Ma 26.57), that is, the narrow circle of representatives of the Jewish theocracy of the time. The people as a whole remained largely alien to this case, having been neither consulted nor represented in the final decision. Many passages in the New Testament indicate, on the contrary, that the popularity of Jesus Christ was high, especially when it is written: "... and a great crowd followed him" (Ma 8:1, 13:2, 19:2, 20:29...). This real dichotomy between the narrow circle of accusers of Jesus and the benevolence he enjoyed in general in the country will make even more unjust the anathema that Christianity will later cast on the Jewish people.

Another often-pronounced term is provocative to some Jews, and when Jesus Christ explained it will arouse their determined opposition. It's about: resurrection. We know from the New Testament texts that there is a theological boundary between the Sadducees and the Pharisees. The former, in fact, are firmly opposed to the idea of the resurrection of the dead. Several passages clearly show this, including this one: "... Being grieved that they taught the people, and preached through Jesus the resurrection from the dead. " (Acts 4:2). The second many more, are divided on this question whose stake is much more important than it seems because, the resurrection of the dead becomes an integral part of the messianic hope mentioned in several texts of the Bible. There are two opposing religious conceptions, and the Sadducees, guardians of both the temple and the dogmatic orthodoxy, want to put an end to the spread of this message, which seems subversive in many respects. Their determination is such that they are plotting to assassinate the apostle, Paul. He owes his salvation only to the swiftness of the tribune Lysias, who withdrew him from their criminal intentions.

As a defense and explanation, the Apostle tells Governor Felix, "²⁹Except it be for this one voice, that I cried standing among them, Touching the resurrection of the dead I am called in question by you this day" (Acts 24:21). These are the same words he used for his justification before the Sanhedrin when the high priest Ananias had just ordered him to be struck (Acts 23:2-6). The resurrection, a fundamental point of discord in the Judaism of that time, leads to violence and murder. However, it is not in the synagogue that this violent opposition is born; it is rather in the religious politico hierarchy that it is noticed because it fears the fervor of an exuberant messianism that would question its power. Naturally, the fear aroused by the resurrection message will not be found in Christianity since it is part of its doctrinal foundations. On the other hand, the messianic hope always present in a fraction of the people will sometimes take violent forms, as it will be the case at the time of the Reformation between 1524 and 1526 in Germany, during the revolt of the peasants. It was a brief but violent manifestation of one of these millennial currents, which were frequent during Christianity. They announced the advent of the reign of God on earth, the end of the Law, the end of history, and of the order established by men. These mystical-religious currents have unfortunately produced excesses and exaltations that have rather condemned their cause most of the time. Jesus Christ in his day foretold this when he declared his disciples in the Gospel of Matthew 24:5 and 24:11, that many will come and try to usurp his titles and prerogatives by pretending to be the true Messiah of Israel. He says in verse 5; "For many shall come in my name, saying, I am Christ; and shall deceive many". In verse 11, this warning returns with this prophecy: "And many false prophets shall rise and shall deceive many".

1.2 Exclusion from the Synagogue because of Jesus Christ

The Gospel as a testimony of the Jewish society of his time, offers very instructive sequences on the permanence of human behavior. Reading some passages it can be seen that those of today are hardly different from those of yesterday when it is written in the Gospel of John 9:20-22, about this blind young man healed on

---

²⁹ Doctrinal opposition: Rejection of the gospel by the leaders of the Jewish diaspora - Jean-Marc Thobois – YouTube à 28›05.

a Sabbath day: "His parents answered them and said, We know that this is our son, and that he was born blind: But by what means he now seeth, we know not; or who hath opened his eyes, we know not: he is of age; ask him: he shall speak for himself. These words spake his parents, because they feared the Jews: for the Jews had agreed already, that if any man did confess that he was Christ, he should be put out of the synagogue". Parents, like many others, are sensitive to the threat of exclusion. Conformism and gregarious instinct prevail over the nevertheless brilliant manifestation of the truth by this miraculous healing. The social pressure is such that the parents fear being driven out of the synagogue and soon, one can assume, from the whole society. Under these conditions, it is not easy to express a personal judgment based on the truth of experience. Indeed, two discourses are opposed: that of the witness against that of the theologian. Where is the manifestation of the truth, and which of these two opinions should be believed? In Judaism, the ambiguity is great because the social conditioning around the Mosaic religion remains very strong since God renewed the Law given to Moses, the Sacred Covenant with his people. In it, however, the exercise of individual free will also existed as it is clearly expressed in the following passages of the Torah; "Behold, I set before you this day a blessing and a curse..." (De 11:26; 30.1; 30.15...) as well as in other texts recalling this fundamental expression (Jer 21:8; Is 28:16). The "I set before you" and similar expressions show that it is up to the individual to make the choice, to take the right path, and not to God to impose it on him. We see, therefore, that individual responsibility remains intact in both the Old and New Testaments. Rather than give thanks to God for this extraordinary miracle, the parents of this blind young man from birth are seized with fear and react with conformity so as not to upset the leaders of their synagogue. On the contrary, with baptism according to the teaching of Jesus Christ, taking a personal position is valued and even contributes to the manifestation of God's justice according to this passage, Luke 7:29-30; "And all the people that heard *him*, and the publicans, justified God, being baptized with the baptism of John. But the Pharisees and lawyers rejected the counsel of God against themselves, being not baptized of him". This baptism is required of an adult by the teaching of Jesus Christ himself. It begins with an individual awareness, which leads to repentance and the desire to live in newness of life with Jesus Christ as Master and Lord. It is done in public, so that it may serve as a personal witness to the people gathered for the occasion. Finally, it is the expression of a personal will outside any religious or social pressure, which has the consequence of being able to be practiced from adolescence and throughout the entire life. Indeed, it is not a compulsory religious rite but rather a personal commitment, as this passage from the Apostle Peter's First Epistle attests: "The like figure whereunto even baptism doth also now save us, not the putting away of the filth of the flesh, but the answer of a good conscience toward God, by the resurrection of Jesus Christ:" (1Pe 3:21). Unfortunately, historical Christianity, despite the teaching of Jesus Christ emphasized in Matthew 28. 18 & 19, where he insists on the personal commitment, departed from the practice of the baptism of repentance and conversion. The historian of the Church Jules-Marcel Nicole[30] traces around the third century the increasingly frequent practice of infant baptism, contrary to the doctrine of the Gospel, but undoubtedly considered more convenient by some, to the "making" of small Christians in large numbers. It is encouraged by theologians of this period, such as Origen and Cyprian, while it is fought by others, including Tertullian, the theologian of Carthage, in the name of doctrinal coherence. In doing so, a mass Christianity was introduced, and with it, this fear of displeasing the ecclesiastical hierarchy. This thick conformism around religious practices and questionable initiatory rites, very far from doctrinal truth, will continue for centuries until today. The Reformation, however necessary on this point as on many others, has become blasphemy, anathema, and sacrilege, with sometimes real risks of condemnation for their authors. In the 13th century, Christianity went so far as to establish a "dogma police" with the creation of the Inquisition Court. Its extensive powers allowed the sentence to be more or less severe depending on the judgments it pronounced against the defendants. These ecclesiastical courts were not definitively abolished until the early 19th century, when they only remained in Spain. In the 16th century, a new Catholic order was established to counter the Protestant Reformation and defend the pope, their doctrine, and Catholic institutions. This order has taken the name of "The Society of Jesus", later called "Jesuit". Its members, organized as a real army corps with a general at their head, took charge as soldiers, the defense and expansion of Catholicism. Very intrusive into the European royal courts, they were successively driven out

---

[30]   Jean marcel Nicole: Précis d'Histoire de l'Église p 30 et 38

of Portugal in 1759, France in 1763, and Spain in 1767. Finally, the company was dissolved in 1773 before being restored in 1814 by Pope Pius VII. Since then, its activities have been mainly academic, legal, and missionary. This detour by the behavioral analysis about this blind man healed on a sabbath day in the Gospel of John (9.20-22), and by the history of Christianity, shows how in these two examples and Judaism also, one has gone from a grace and a personal choice to a constraint, to mass conformism and an unjustified social obligation[31].

1.3 The Synagogue against the Church: competition between the two assemblies

The Judaism of the time of Jesus Christ was far from uniform; it varied not only theologically but also geographically due to a large diaspora spread throughout the empire and beyond to Mesopotamia. Pilgrims came from far and wide, as indicated, especially in the book of Acts (Acts 2:5). Additionally, it is known that in Judea, Samaria, and Galilee, Aramaic was spoken, while Greek was commonly practiced in much of the empire. The legacy of Alexander the Great, along with the prestige of Greek culture and philosophy, strongly influenced diaspora Judaism, resulting in a de facto separation between the Hebrew synagogues near the historic heart of Jerusalem and those of the diaspora, who spoke Greek and were more distant. This part of Judaism, known in the New Testament as "Hellenistic" (Acts 9:29), consisted of Jews descended from families who had emigrated over the centuries from the scribe Ezra and from the reconstitution of the nation of Israel after exile. These synagogues were present everywhere and had a great capacity to welcome non-Jews who sought spiritual truth and hope. They offered much more than the mystery religions with their countless mythologies. They were an opening to the true knowledge of the Eternal God and a solid conception of man and nature. In addition, they practiced dynamic proselytism, encouraged the conversion of pagans, and taught them the basics of Jewish culture (Matt 23:15; Acts 2:10,6:5). Thus, it is not the birth of Christianity that radically changes the synagogue; it is rather the demographic weight of non-Jews increasingly important in its midst, which is the cause. This major

---

[31] Society of Jesus – https://www.jesuites.com/qui-sommes/jesuites/

sociological fact leads, during the 1st century AD, to a progressive separation between two entities that no longer recognized each other and are soon in competition against each other, for the pagans they seek to convert. The apostles on many occasions will pay the price when they are driven out, beaten or vilified by the representatives of the Hellenistic synagogues in which they will soon no longer be able to preach salvation in Jesus Christ (Acts 5:40). The apostle Paul recounts in his epistles, including 2 Corinthians 11:24-25, the beatings he endured for preaching the Gospel: "Of the Jews five times received I forty stripes save one. Thrice was I beaten with rods, once was I stoned, thrice I suffered shipwreck, a night and a day I have been in the deep". Reading verses 4 to 12 of chapter 18 of the Book of Acts, one gets the impression that they represent different scenes of what the first disciples of Jesus Christ experienced in their work of evangelization. Spontaneously like Paul did, wherever they were, they went to the synagogue (v 4): "And he reasoned in the synagogue every sabbath and persuaded the Jews and the Greeks". Then verse 6 describes this violent protest they had to endure like Paul: "The Jews then made opposition and engaged in insults". In the face of this, Paul's reaction, as no doubt that of many disciples of Jesus Christ placed in the same situation, was as follows: "... And when they opposed themselves, and blasphemed, he shook his raiment, and said unto them, Your blood be upon your own heads; I am clean: from henceforth I will go unto the Gentiles". This conclusion opens the door to the evangelization of the pagans and the progressive constitution of churches independent of the synagogue. One can legitimately assume that the situation of Paul described in these 8 verses was repeated several times. These examples, which Jesus Christ prophesied when he said, "They shall put you out of the synagogues: yea, the time cometh, that whosoever killeth you will think that he doeth God service." (Jn 16:2), show that in this period it happens that the synagogue expels the Gospel and its representatives from its places of worships. The competition between the two types of community is emphasized by the Apostle Paul in the following verses, 1 Thessalonians 2:13–16 "Therefore we thank God continually that in receiving the word of God, which we have made heard, you have received it, not as the word of men, but as it truly is, as the word of God, which acts in you who believe. For you, brethren, have become imitators of the Churches of God which are in Jesus Christ in Judea, because you too have suffered from your own compatriots the same evils they have suffered from the Jews. It is these Jews who made the Lord Jesus and the prophets die, who persecuted us, who do not please God, and who are enemies of all men, preventing us from speaking to the pagans so that they may be saved, so that they never cease to fill up their sins. But anger finally reached them". However, it is necessary to recall here what was said in the first part, namely, the unbreakable filial bond between the Synagogue and the Church. That there were exceptions is certain, however; the history of the Synagogue and the Church recalls that of these prophets of the Old Testament rejected by an oligarchy of priests and so-called prophets more interested in their position of power than in the search for truth as these two examples indicate, one found in the book of Jeremiah: 23.25: "I have heard what the prophets say, who prophesy in my name the lie, saying: I have had a dream! I had a dream!" and the other in Isaiah 1:14; "Your new moons and your appointed festivals my soul hates; they have become a burden to me; I am weary of bearing them". We must not forget that all these radical exclusions remain, in fact, internal to Judaism. By taking the image of a circle, they reflect the opposition that there is between, the absolute and intangible Law of God on a point of this circle and at its diametrically opposite end, the life of men and their contradictions, while there are in the center, the love and mercy of God as the eternal and ordaining axis of the balance of all things. Positions are extreme and clear throughout the history of the Hebrew people, denunciation of abuses of dominant position, mutual anathemas between different parties are numerous, repeated, and sometimes even violent. However, despite all these differences and oppositions, there remains within the People of God a fundamental mutual communion with the Law, with the history, and with the destiny of Israel. As the apostle Paul demonstrates in his entire epistle to the Romans, Christianity fits perfectly into this story, both dramatic and glorious.

1.4 The Synagogue against the Church; Jewish nationalism versus Christian universalism

Since the return of the exiles and the great reforms undertaken in many areas by Ezra and Nehemiah, the nation of Israel has revived. It has regained the worship service of the Lord; its spiritual values are taught by an increasingly dense network of synagogues. Its temple is that of Zorobabel, but it is quite modest compared to the splendor of the first, built in the time of King Solomon (Es 3:7-13). However, it is yet again the spiritual center of its religious life, and Jerusalem is again its political capital. The nation lives again, but it is only one of the many provinces of the Persian empire, and independence under the guidance of a righteous and pious king, perfectly fulfilling the Law of God, is slow to materialize indeed. In the year 334 AD, Alexander the Great arrived as a victor in Judea, which he submitted, like the other parts of his immense empire, to an intense policy of Hellenization. His successors, the Seleucid and Ptolemy kings, disputed Judea, which passed under the control of the first in 200 BC. It is a period of political domination exercised by one dynasty and another, and yet it is also a time of flourishing Jewish culture throughout the Mediterranean basin, where a large diaspora is developing. At that time, the emigration of the Israelites was no longer forced, but voluntary, and they multiplied throughout the empire, establishing centers of their spirituality and culture. We owe to King Ptolemy II the translation of the Bible into Greek around 270 BC. It is named "Septuagint" after the group of 72 Scribes (Septante in old French) who worked tirelessly on this achievement. While it was not considered entirely authentic by Jewish orthodoxy in relation to the original Hebrew texts, it enabled many non-Jews of Greek culture to understand Jewish religion and philosophy. Much later, independence will come in the form of a revolt against King Seleucid Antiochus IV Epiphanes. Indeed, he had decided, a forced march of Hellenization of all Judea, and also to consecrate the temple of Jerusalem to "Zeus", the king of the gods among the Greeks. Under the leadership of Judas Maccabeus[32], the whole country rose and gained independence in 150 BC, after long and perilous fights. The country remained for a long time in a struggle against its former masters, and this dearly acquired political freedom did not bring the concretization of the promises it had aroused. Indeed, the internal struggles, the confusion of powers, the corruption of the elites plunged into troubles with repetitions, the Hasmonean dynasty, which came after the Maccabees brothers. It was far from a reign of peace and justice, and of the Messianic hope when the Romans seized the country in 37 BC. But what was left of it at that time? It should be noted that under this dynasty, Judea

---

[32]   Nick Page: New Bible Atlas, P 69 – Edition Footprint Present Time

experienced a remarkable territorial expansion, reaching the shores of the Mediterranean between 142 and 135 BC[33]. At the time of the Hasmonean king Alexander Jannaeus, between the year 103 and 76 BC, the country was approximately within its current limits. In the north it is on the border of Lebanon, it had not yet reached the desert of the Negev in the south, but it already included in the west, all the maritime frontage that we know today, including the city of Gaza and even beyond, in the center Samaria and Judea, while to the east, the Golan Heights was integrated into the country as well as an eastern part of the Jordan bank in present-day Jordan. It is also a period of great fruitfulness on the religious, spiritual, and intellectual levels. The synagogue was established as a center of local piety and a center of community life with its schools, artistic and literary life. At this time, the Mishna experienced great developments and allowed many rabbis, who animated a prosperous and dynamic diaspora, to strengthen the biblical faith. However, in the time of Jesus Christ and long after, Judaism would want to be exclusive and nationalist; it would often confuse in one celebration the worship of the Lord and that to the glory of Israel, its people. In many cases, it would want to exclude from his community those who professed this dual belonging to Christianity and Judaism as Jesus Christ spoke about in this passage: "They shall put you out of the synagogues: yea, the time cometh, that whosoever killeth you will think that he doeth God service." (Jn 16:2). Thus, we see the difficult synthesis between Judaism and Christianity on the theological and national level, yet the root is the same. With the years and the centuries, this exclusion, which is at the beginning only exceptional, will become the rule on one side as on the other, and the gap between the two currents of the faith of Abraham will not cease to widen until the murders of the Shoah[34]. At the time of Jesus Christ, Israel was small with its population relative to that of the Roman Empire, their master, yet it had all the assets of a great nation. What is truly lacking in this moment of his destiny for the fulfillment of the promises of blessings made by the Eternal God to Abraham and his seed? He lacks the Messiah as well as all of us, he lacks the one who has the power to change hearts and minds so that the promise of the forgiveness of sins and the return to grace as

---

[33] Nick Page: New Bible Atlas, P 72 & 73 – Edition Footprint Present Time
[34] Nick Page: New Bible Atlas, P 74 – Edition Footprint Present Time

before the fall of Adam and Eve is fulfilled. By saying this, one abruptly passes without transition from history and politics to the field of personality and psycho-sociology because the long-awaited Messiah will come, and with him, the Eternal God changes the paradigm of his revelation for men. His message places the question of the exercise of power and freedom at the level of the person, his heart, and his feelings, and no longer at the level of national institutions or even at the level of religion. From ancient times, this reading of the founding texts of Judaism was obvious, since the divine Law is addressed as much to the individual as to the community of Israel, with its constant reminders to ethics, to individual integrity and responsibility before the Almighty Eternal God. Jesus Christ comes as the Reformer of hearts and thought, he is not the founder of a new religion, but he creates a relationship with God by his sacrifice on the cross of Calvary. Nor did he found a nation, and in this sense he disappointed many of his disciples who had hoped that he would put an end to Roman rule and restore the kingdom of Israel, as this passage from the Book of Acts testifies: "[6] When they therefore were come together, they asked of him, saying, Lord, wilt thou at this time restore again the kingdom to Israel? And he said to them, It is not for you to know the times or the seasons, which the Father hath put in his own power. But ye shall receive power, after that the Holy Ghost is come upon you: and ye shall be witnesses unto me both in Jerusalem, and in all Judaea, and in Samaria, and unto the uttermost part of the earth" (Acts 1:6-8). Another statement of Jesus Christ emphasizes this lack of political project in his message, and yet it is pronounced during his trial, in a compound and for eminently political characters. It is this one: "[35]Jesus answered, My kingdom is not of this world: if my kingdom were of this world, then would my servants fight, that I should not be delivered to the Jews: but now is my kingdom not from hence" (Jn 18:36). These and other passages with the same meaning, have been interpreted by many, and especially by the thinkers of an anti-Semitic theology, as the act of dissolution of Israel as a nation. The Jew who converts to Jesus Christ would cease to be part of Israel because he would pass from the national messianic hope of Israel to that of the universal redemption of humanity in Jesus Christ. For many Christian theologians even today, the call to conversion of the Jewish people implies the disappearance

---

[35]   The Holocaust - Holocaust Memorial Holocaust Memorial - memorialdelashoah.org

of Israel as a nation. Over the centuries, this reasoning would have had disastrous consequences for Christian ethics and theology because it contains a striking syllogism that has often been overlooked by its authors. If the message of Jesus Christ leads to the disappearance of Israel as a nation, does it not lead to the disappearance of all other nations as well? But the history of Christianity shows exactly the opposite; with its expansion into the nations, their role and power have only strengthened over the centuries, until they rose with pride and violence against Israel. Thus, the dramatic prophetic declaration of Ezekiel came true; "For the day is approaching, the day of the Lord is approaching, a dark day: it will be the time of the nations" (Ez 30:3). The Bible in many passages speaks of this: "Time of nations", whose precise definition remains rather enigmatic. We know, however, from the text of the Gospel of Luke that this time must come to an end after Jerusalem has been trampled by the nations: "Jerusalem will be trampled at the feet by the nations until the times of the nations are fulfilled" (Lk 21:24). We can even risk seeing the destruction of the exacerbated nationalism that prevailed in Europe before and during the Second World War, as the end of this time of nations. It is indeed the end of a time of domination of European nations over immense areas of influence, by colonialism. This is the end of a time of confusion between nationalism and Christianity, with the retreat of the official churches and religious practice in general. They now face multiple ideological, scientific, and sociological challenges that they do not provide an answer to. The end of the time of the nations as the main vector and support for the truth of the Gospels means the reduction of these to a socio-historical role of their own, while the message of the whole Bible gains in autonomy, in force, and truth with the tireless preaching of the Evangelical Churches. Although it was not until 1948 that God's authority for the restoration of Israel was realized, according to the quote, "... the times and moments that the Father has set with his own authority" (Acts 1:6). The Year 1948 was indeed a very long time to wait on a human scale. However, the new context of the "end of the time of the nations" is much better from the point of view of evangelical truth. Indeed, God blesses Israel today as he blesses all nations according to the prophecy of the righteous Simeon quoted at the beginning of the Gospel of Luke: "[29] Lord, now lettest thou thy servant depart in peace, according to thy word: For mine eyes have seen thy salvation, Which thou hast prepared before the face of all people; A light to lighten the

Gentiles, and the glory of thy people Israel" (Lk 2:29-32). In conclusion, Christianity does not imply the abolition of Israel as a nation or the disappearance of Israel as a recognized universal anthropological reality. The late 20th and early 21st centuries have demonstrated that nationalism can align with the universalism of the Old and New Testaments, as long as it avoids excessive pride of the nations, leading to the negation of others and ultimately to war.

2. The Church Against the Synagogue

2.1 The struggle of structure against charisma in Christianity

From the second century after Jesus Christ, it is the opposite that occurs: the pagans take as their own what appears as anti-Judaism in the apostle Paul, of which they make hasty and dangerous generalizations. This is particularly the case with this passage from his first epistle to the Thessalonians; "For ye, brethren, became followers of the churches of God which in Judaea are in Christ Jesus: for ye also have suffered like things of your own countrymen, even as they have of the Jews: Who both killed the Lord Jesus, and their own prophets, and have persecuted us; and they please not God, and are contrary to all men: Forbidding us to speak to the Gentiles that they might be saved, to fill up their sins alway: for the wrath is come upon them to the uttermost" (1Thes 2. 14 – 16). They clumsily assimilate and convey his arguments, in full, without bringing to them the slightest nuance. They castigate the infidelity of Israel towards their God, as if they were without reproach themselves before him. They are at the origin of the separation between the Synagogue and the Church and of Christian and pagan anti-Semitism, combined in the same devastating rejection of Judaism. They paved the way for a kind of right to hatred, which will not cease to manifest itself over the centuries until the monstrous epilogue of the Shoah during the Second World War in the 20th century.

According to the Bible, we understand that the religious world and the pagan world are whole, locked in the same condemnation, and both need Jesus Christ, the savior of humanity. This is one of the lessons to be learned from his condemnation, pronounced and carried out jointly by the religious and pagan worlds. But what about the Christianity that came after this iniquitous trial and the glorious resurrection of the Messiah? Is it exempt from this heavy legacy that weighed on the Jewish world? Has the structure fought against the charism or given it free rein for the expression of the truths, oracles, and divine inspiration that the people of God need? It is striking to note this strictly parallel evolution of the Christian world compared to the Jewish world. Passing in a few decades, from the situation of a persecuted minority to the official religion of the state, Christianity becomes the persecutor in its turn of all the religious minorities, which could overshadow the exercise of its power. It soon confiscates the knowledge which is now reserved only to a minority, which passes through a long and tedious initiatory journey, far from the simplicity of the Gospel, before reaching, for some only, in the "high" spheres of ecclesiastical power around the person of the pope. Although a human being like any other, he is excessively sacralized by an array of ecclesiastical dignitaries. He bears a strange resemblance to the powerful Roman emperor whose titles he borrowed, such as "Pontifex-Maximus" along with some of its attributes, such as the dual temporal and spiritual power, to name but two. When the Protestant Reformation occurred, the whole structure rose against the charisma of Martin Luther. The latter, who initially had no intention of leaving the Catholic Church, was soon forced to do so because of the violent hostility of the structure and the incompatibility of the new doctrine he brought with the old. Strange story indeed, because Protestantism, once settled, rather in the countries of the north of Europe, will behave in the same way, in a rigid structure and hostile to the movements of several Evangelical reforms that will be born within it. Fortunately for them, as for Protestantism in general, the power of the Word of God will confuse all attempts to stifle the charisma of the great reformers who will come after its founders. In other words, and to simplify, the Bible once opened can no longer be closed by kings and their armies, nor by the ecclesiastical structure and its dogmas, nor by any power as powerful as it may be. Consequently, the hostility of the structure against the charisma will gradually lose intensity with the growing awareness among the people that the Christian faith is first and foremost a personal commitment rather than a collective one. A trivial comparison can help to understand this phenomenon of appropriation by the people of the Word of God: can one put back into the barrel the wine spilled when it was broken? Another factor in reducing the hostility of the structure towards charisma is the erosion of religious matters in social life, the growing secularization of popular activities, as well as that of their elites. These factors have sometimes radically cut, as in France, the close link they once had with religious power. From this point of view, in most countries, it can be said from a sociologist's perspective that in the 21st century, the structure lost its eternal fight against charisma. The latter has spread despite it, and today, numerous living communities such as the Evangelical Churches of Pentecost are eagerly seeking charisma and their beneficial effects on individual and collective life. However, it should not be inferred that the structure is destined to disappear in favor of charisma. The dynamic that can be observed is rather that of a harmonious and beneficial complementarity for the expansion and blossoming of a Christianity of conversion. This positive development is seen with the naked eye in the spectacular progression of the Churches of born-again Christians in all latitudes and in the social transformation that they operate, such as in South Korea, Brazil, and many other countries of Africa and Latin America. With them, poverty is vanishing everywhere, popular education, hygiene, and economic development are on the rise.

2.2 The Destruction of Jerusalem in 70 AD and the destruction of Judaism after the revolt of Bar Kokhba (132-135 AD).

The destruction of the temple is the destruction of the place of the presence of God. It is followed by a great dispersion of the Jews in the four corners of the Roman Empire and even well beyond. This major event has been and is often interpreted by some Christians as the sign of the fall of the Jewish people before God and their condemnation by one of His final judgments. At first sight this interpretation finds its legitimacy in the words of Jesus Christ himself when he declares to his disciples admiring the splendor of the temple: "Jesus says, As for these things which ye behold, the days will come, in the which there shall not be left one stone upon another, that shall not be thrown down" (Lk 21:6). His prophecy was fulfilled in the year 70 when the Roman general Titus took over the city of Jerusalem after a long siege of five months and he destroyed the temple. That was a bloody victory and a culmination of a revolt begun in the year 65 AD, by riots in Caesarea against the Roman procurator Gessius Florus. He was a brutal and corrupt individual who would go as far as to use the wealth of the temple for himself, causing a new outbreak of violence in Jerusalem. Growingly, all the cities of Judea and Syria would rise in a general war against the Roman occupier. The first Judeo-Roman war that followed began in 66 BC according to the account of the Jewish historian Flavius Josephus and it ended when the Roman legions of Titus besieged, looted then destroyed Jerusalem and the temple of Herod in 70, as well as the strongholds of the Jews, Gamla in 67and[36] Masada in 73. After a relative calm, the revolt or war of[37] Quietus took place again between 115 and 117 AD. The Jews and the Romans fought against each other during the Trajan War against[38] the Parthian Empire in the East. According to historians, it was characterized by a strong involvement of the Jewish and Judeo-Christian diaspora, particularly in Cyrenaica, Alexandria, Cyprus, and even in Babylonia, where Jews were numerous and very anti-Roman. In the end, however, nothing could prevent the final victory of Roman General Lusius Quietus. More serious and devastating was the revolt of Bar Kokhba[39] in 132[40] to 135 AD. This was also the last of the Judeo-Roman wars. Consequently, a large population displacement occurred, and many Jews were enslaved and deported to Rome. Judea changed its status, becoming a province of a Roman garrison, with increased numbers. All Jews in the empire were subject to a special tax, called the "Fiscus Judaicus". Jerusalem was now called "Aelia Capitolina". Thus, renamed and emptied almost entirely of its Jewish population, its occupants are veterans of the 5th legion "Macedonia", but also more widely by Greeks[14] and Syrians. The city would regain its original identity only under Emperor Constantine I[st], almost 200 years later. From this unhappy period will be born the legend of the, "Wandering Jew", which will be transformed over the centuries into Jews "stateless", with the most degrading innuendo such as: "traitor" and "conspirator", because stateless and stateless because wandering and finally, plotter because without any local roots. However, after the defeats and humiliation of Jerusalem, communities

---

[36] Nick Page: New Bible Atlas, P 119 – Edition Footprint Present Time
[37] Flavius Joseph: War of the Jews Volume IV, 1,9. Gamla, la "Massada du Nord", by Liorah Chekroun, Jewish Tribune, no. 42, November 2008
[38] Yigaël Yadin, Masada, the last citadel of Israel, Hachette 1966
[39] Heinrich Graetz, History of the Jews - Uprising of the Judeans under Trajan and Hadrian (98-135), § III [archive]
[40] Trajan - https://romanempirehistory.com/roman-emperors/trajan/

will persist for a long-time further north in Galilee and south in Alexandria, but soon the people of Israel will be in diaspora in all the great cities of the empire and even beyond.

2.3 Passage from Hebrew to Hellenism 1st to 4th Century AD

"John 7:35 - What did the Jews say to each other, Where will he go, that we may not find him? Will he go among those scattered among the Greeks, and teach the Greeks?" This transition is a turning point in the history of the Church, it is the transition from Hebrew to Hellenism with its major consequence, that is, its divorce from the Synagogue. Following the destruction of the temple, a logic of Hellenization is gradually taking shape. The apostles are now gone, and the Church of Greek and Latin, non-Jews, is numerically the largest. It then changed its general direction, on the strategic, practical, and theological level, and gradually moved away from Judaism. Thus, Christianity creates an increasingly marked cleavage with the Synagogue and allows an anti-Semitism, sometimes even violent, to develop within it. The apostle Paul (Rom 11:1-18) foresaw it and warned Christians from the Greco-Roman world against a complex of superiority against the Jews. Unfortunately, as early as the 2nd century AD, some theologians, to mark their difference with the Synagogue and Judaism in general, went so far as to condemn and reject entirely the Jewish origin of Christianity. This deliberate rejection has lasted with more or less intensity until today. Over centuries, it will cause calamitous consequences for the Jews first, but also and by extension for the whole so-called Christianized Europe. Thus, the drama of the people of Israel is also that of Christianity because one has never been able to recognize in Jesus Christ his messiah, because of the caricature made by the other as a whole.[41]

2.4 Progressive separation and curse

We saw in the New Testament that from the beginning of Christianity, theological and practical continuity between the Synagogue and the Church was not self-evident. Two situations are characteristic of this development: the first is that of

---

[41]   Jesus, the Jewish Messiah (part 1) - Jean-Marc Thobois — 8'40 - YouTube

Hebrew Christianity near its capital, Jerusalem, as long as it remained accessible to Jews. The second is that of a Hellenistic Christianity, which was very numerous in the diaspora. With the ministry of the apostles and the contribution of the new converts, it is developing rapidly, as several passages of the New Testament show us: (1 Cor 10:32) "Be not in scandal to the Greeks, nor to the Jews, nor to the Church of God," and also this one: "There is no more Jew or Greek, there is no more slave or free, there is no more man or woman; for all of you are one in Jesus Christ" (Gal 3:28). This last passage expresses by a shortcut that, in the Christian conception, the national belonging of the individual takes second place. It shows that there is, first and foremost, man before God. Now this God is indeed that of the Bible, creator, savior, and redeemer. In addition, the term "Greek" is applied here as a generalization to non-Jews by different authors of the New Testament. This is because at that time, Greek was spoken by all the peoples of the eastern Mediterranean region of the Roman Empire.

2.5 Rivalry: Rome triumphs against Jerusalem destroyed - Influence, power, and prestige of Rome[42]

Rome triumphed in the year 70 and even more in 132, after the last Judeo-Roman war, and posed as a spiritual rival of Jerusalem, which was destroyed, humiliated, and placed under its domination. As the capital of the empire, Rome bears witness to its power, wealth, and authority over a myriad of peoples. By a strange mimicry, the imperial city exerts a strong attraction on the bishop of Rome and its nascent church. The latter soon claimed for himself a power similar to that of the emperor, over all the churches of the western empire. Growingly, it tends to become the center of all important decisions of the church. A struggle of influence developed between the great bishoprics, Rome against Alexandria, Antioch against Ephesus, Constantinople against Damascus, etc. When the last emperor, Romulus Augustulus, was deposed in 476, the already very divided Roman Empire collapsed. The only power that remained within it was the Catholic Church, which had no other major bishopric as a competitor in the entire Western

---

[42] JM Nicole. The History of the Church – Ed: IBN L'Institut Biblique de Nogent-sur-Marne, France. p 34 to 37 and p 63

part of the former empire. In a few key stages, the bishopric of Rome becomes the seat of Roman Catholicism, whose claim to be universal is inscribed in the use of the word "catholic", which means in Greek, "universal". The juxtaposition of these two adjectives: "Catholic" on one hand and "Roman" on the other is a major contradiction in these terms because how is it possible that what is universal would also be concentrated in a single geographical place of power? Isn't this monopoly of dogma and major decision-making the negation of the ministry of the Holy Spirit in every Christian individual and community? This contradiction did not prevent it from imposing itself throughout Western Europe, from the time of Emperor Constantine to the Protestant Reformation of the 16th century, as the only authorized expression of Christianity in the West.

2.6 Emancipation of Christianity through texts – Is Christianity extension of Judaism or new religion?

In the 1st century, Christianity remained well integrated with Judaism; it did not become truly autonomous until it had its canonical texts, towards the end of the 4th century BC. Indeed, it was only in 363 at the Council of Laodicea and in 397, at the Council of Carthage, that the list of books retained by the Church to form the New Testament was fixed, although the Apocalypse of John did not yet appear in it. The arrival of many pagans in the churches has gradually distanced Christianity from its Jewish roots. At that time, the weekly service passed definitively from Saturday to Sunday, the day of the resurrection of the Savior. The first 4 Gospels are the exposition and illustration of the doctrine of Jesus. The links with the Old Testament or First Testament are everywhere present because their authors are all Jews with the exception of the apostle Luke, who is believed to be, nevertheless, part of these Greek proselytes, very close to the Synagogue, perfectly integrated with Jewish culture and theology. Turned inwards in Judaism for the salvation of Israel and outwards in the salvation of the whole human race, the New Testament takes no other doctrinal and theological support than the biblical conception of the universe and mankind than the Old Testament. From this point of view, it remains its continuity, of which it constitutes the extension and the universal version of the revelation of God. It does not expect much from the kings of the earth and the powerful of this world, just peace and quietness, not to prevent the preaching of the message of the Bible, as this passage from the first epistle of the apostle Paul to Timothy emphasizes; "I therefore exhort, first of all, to make prayers, supplications, petitions, thanksgiving, for all men, for kings and for all those who are raised in dignity, so that we may lead a peaceful and quiet life, in all piety and honesty. This is good and pleasant before God our Savior, who wants all men to be saved and come to the knowledge of the truth. For there is one God, and also one mediator between God and men, Jesus Christ man, who gave himself as a ransom for all. This is the testimony given in his own time, and for which I have been established as a preacher and apostle, I speak the truth, I do not lie, instructed the heathen in faith and truth" (1Ti 2:1-7). What is good and pleasing to God, therefore, is not adherence to a doctrine of the state or nation, but rather an attitude of the heart to lead a peaceful and quiet life. With the hindsight given by history, we can make this passage a double reading; the first is a skeptical confirmation of what the apostle Paul says, given the failure of the kings of the earth to establish justice and peace permanently in this world. The second is optimistic because it interprets the wisdom expressed here by the apostle Paul as an act of faith in the future. It is the hope of a time when the prayers and supplications of believers will be answered, and therefore all men will be able to learn in peace, to know God the Savior. Indeed, it must be remembered that the conversion of hearts takes place in peace and especially in the peace of God, according to this passage from apostle James: "The fruit of justice is sown in peace by those who seek peace" (Ja 3:18) and this of the apostle Paul; "And the peace of God, which surpasses all understanding, will keep your hearts and thoughts in Jesus Christ" (Phi 4:7). The New Testament is therefore a doctrine of peace, love, the grace of God for all men and of salvation in Jesus Christ through repentance and new birth. He places at the center of his developments the individual, as he is, in his complexity and in front of the wonderful destiny that God promises him, from the moment he repents and accepts the sacrifice of Jesus Christ for the salvation of his soul. Long before the theories of individual and collective behavior appeared in Europe and the USA, at the beginning of the twentieth century, it constituted from the origin of Christianity, a remarkable treatise on psychology and social ethics for individual and also collective formation by the ministry of local Churches. One, finds in the same way in this, the function devolved to the Synagogue since its origin that is to say; form, teach, build, train, pray, transmit and defend a spiritual and cultural heritage based on the message of the Bible. Did the Synagogue and the Church share a common destiny, one waiting for its messiah and the other for his return? One can imagine that Christianity followed paths approximately parallel to those of the Synagogue, with its academies, the more or less in-depth study of the Mishnah and then of the Talmud, and that in its turn reported on its experiences and the value of its rules and principles. Early Christianity was not far from this pattern; it was extremely decentralized, far from uniform, and allowed many voices to be heard. Just like the Synagogue from its origin, it had to fight the false doctrines, deviations, and heresies that appeared within it. Together with the apostles and their successors, it cultivated the extraordinary riches of the New Testament for the construction of personality, for the education of children, for work ethics, the expression of individual talents, life in society, and many other areas of life. The innumerable works written by evangelical Christian authors on the same subjects, intended for an audience of believers, bear witness to this today. However, after several centuries of expansion in the Roman Empire, the attraction of Christianity continues to deprive of their public, the pagan mythologies, many of which are falling into disuse. Some historians[43] believe that by the middle of the 4th century BC, Christianity already represented 5% of the population, sometimes with higher concentrations in regions of the empire, such as North Africa in particular.

2.7 Christianity is the stake of the power in ancient Rome.

With its progression throughout the empire despite the last persecution under Emperor Diocletian (244 – 312 AD), Christianity became, despite itself, a major power issue. In this evolution, the bishop of Rome claimed for himself more prerogatives than his colleagues, on the pretext of his proximity to the central power of the empire. Historian and theologian Jules-Marcel Nicole[44] talks about the growing temptation of power among the bishops of Rome and their

---

[43] Arnold Hugh Martin Jones - Constantine and the conversion of Europe INTERNET ARCHIVE p 73 -201

[44] Jean-Marcel Nicole: Éditions de l'Institut Biblique de Nogent-sur-Marne - Précis de l'histoire de l'Église p 92

increasingly imperialist manifestations in the church's life. From the 4th Century[45] AD, its union with the empire made it an essential link in the exercise of civil power. Thus, in just a few years, we have gone from a Christianity of personal conviction to a Christianity of social conformity. The anti-Christian persecutions cease, and the Church increasingly takes on the garments of the spiritual and royal authority over the whole empire. Emperor Constantine (305 – 337) converted to Christianity, and yet, more importantly, he intervened in its doctrinal matters. He inaugurated a type of relationship between the state and the Church that has been called the "Caesaro-papism", which is characterized by putting under the guardianship of one and its domination to serve the political and social objectives of that one. It is he who decided on the convocation of the Council of Nicaea (325 AD), a very important one, for the precision it brings to the doctrine of the Churches. This founding text of Christianity is then, supplemented in 381 by the declaration of the Council of Constantinople, convened by the emperor Theodosius I, to which were added details on the Holy Spirit and subtracted its conclusion made of anathemas against Arianism. With these two councils, both qualified as ecumenical, Christianity as a whole now has a real confession of faith, also called: "Symbol of Nicaea-Constantinople". This period is nevertheless quite short because the Western empire gradually collapsed before disappearing in 476, when its last emperor, Romulus Augustus, was deposed. There is but only one power left in Rome, that of the Church, which will become all-powerful during the Middle Ages, including over the kings of medieval Europe. The "Césaro-papism" is then gradually reversed, and it is the Church that tends to dictate its laws and ordinances to the sovereigns of a continent increasingly fragmented and divided into regional, tribal, and rival factions. In the image of the empire itself, the Church, which for a long time was only a mosaic of more or less extensive obedience's throughout the empire, was gradually gathering around two major entities, one in the west with Rome and the other in the east with Constantinople as their capital, respectively. However, from the 9th century, going from conflicts to ruptures, liturgical and theological differences appeared between them, and two centuries later, in 1053, a real schism happened, so much the gap between

---

[45]   Jean-Marcel Nicole: Editions of the Bible Institute of Nogent-sur-Marne - Précis of the history of the Church p 35

these two main branches of Christianity was deep. Henceforth, for the Church of the West, it is the authoritarian way chosen to evangelize, to discipline and to guide; it is no longer a question of convincing with gentleness and with truth[46], according to the counsel which the apostle Paul gives to his pupil Timothy: "... preaches the word, insists on every occasion, favorable or not, repeats, censors, exhorts, gently and instructing" (2Ti 4:2). Rather, it wants to impose itself as the sole holder of spiritual power, often confused with temporal power. It takes the name of the Catholic Church, the last term meaning universal. It serves as both a spiritual and a temporal project to bring under its magisterial authority all the tendencies of Christianity and all the peoples of Western Europe into its fold. To this end, the Catholic Church adopts a structure and an organization that recall those of the disappeared Roman Empire. It develops in a spirit of conquest and absolutism, resolutely rejecting the method of investigation of the Judaism of the Mishnah and the Talmud.

2.8 New doctrinal foundations for the Western Church: imitations of the rules and institutions of the Roman Empire

One of the first signs of this authoritarian trend appeared with the appointment of the popes to Rome. This name, derived from the Greek "papas", evokes the affection of the child towards his father. During the persecution under Emperor Diocletian, from the year 306, the use of this title was attributed to Metropolitan Peter of Alexandria by the Christians of this city[47]. Originally, there were several popes; they were present from the IIIrd and the IVth centuries. The title was then reserved for ecclesiastical dignitaries and mostly for some eminent bishops. Originally the pope was the bishop of Rome, but gradually he was detached from the mass of believers and even from the ecclesial hierarchy, he became the sole and unique representative of the authority over the church. From the eleventh century[48] on, he affirmed his temporal prerogatives as well as his spiritual powers, on the nations on the one hand and on the Church on the other. Leo 1st

---

[46] Charles River Editors - The Great Schism: The History and Legacy of the Split Between the Catholic and Eastern Orthodox Churches in 1054

[47] Saints & Sinners: The History of the Popes. primevideo.com

[48] Alain Rey - Historical dictionary of the French language. Lerobert.com P 2552

known as "The Great"[49] (from [440] to [461]) is considered by the historian Jules-Marcel Nicole as the first pope to assert himself as sovereign over all Christendom. In fact, at the Council of Chalcedon in the year 451, he refused to recognize equality of status with the Bishop of Constantinople and monopolized for his benefit the meaning of the Gospel passage in which Jesus Christ declared to the Apostle Peter: "And I say unto thee that thou art Peter, and that upon this stone I will build my church, and that the gates of the underworld shall not prevail against it. I will give you the keys to the kingdom of heaven: what you bind on earth will be bound in heaven, and what you loose on earth will be loose in heaven." (Ma 16:18-19). He thus created for his benefit the idea of an uninterrupted apostolic succession sitting in Rome since the apostle Peter, and he added to the symbol of Nicaea-Constantinople this eminently conflictual formula: "Rome has always had primacy"[50.] No doubt to further increase his prestige and power over the spirits as well as the kings, the pope puts on the clothes of the Roman emperors of the time of their glory and calls himself: "The supreme pontiff"[51] that is to say the "Pontifex-Maximus". Thus, succeeding the pagan high priests of the Roman religion, the bishop of Rome takes this singular title of sovereign, "Pontiff". This term comes from the Latin, "pontifex", etymologically, he is the one who makes the sacred bridge" between gods and men. It was used in ancient Rome to designate the members of one of the four priestly colleges of the Roman religion, the pontifical college, which in turn designates the dignity of the great pontiff the, "Pontifex Maximus". He is the one who cannot be compared or surpassed in dignity or power. Directly derived from the pagan mythologies of ancient Rome, this title expresses its continuity in Christian Rome. It testifies to the will of power of its leader; one foot in paganism, another in Christianity, this sovereign will not cease to cultivate the ambiguity of his status during the papacy's long history. He is both, bishop of Rome, but also head of the heads of a multitude of parishes to the ends of the earth and head of the states and domains that he would appropriate during the course of history, often by intrigue and war.

---

49 Pape Leo 1st - Saint Leo I | Biography, Papacy, Legacy, & Facts | Britannica
50 Jean Marcel Nicole. Church History Précis Ed IBN p 64.
51 Pontiff - Etymology, Origin & Meaning

2.9 The organization in prefecture

From Latin praefectus, from praeferre with, prae meaning before, and facere meaning to do. The word has first the general meaning of master; the one who is placed before or above others, who is responsible for... Then by imitation, it migrated into the religious field with these particular expressions like prefect apostolic, prefect of congregation, prefect of doctrine, in the image of what was done in ancient Rome.

2.10 The Diocese[52]

According to the, "Dictionnaire historique de la langue française", this name is borrowed from medieval Latin, "diocese Issa". It is an administrative organization of the Roman Empire. It is used in Christian Latin about an ecclesiastical circumscription entrusted to a bishop. This geographical area, with its specific perimeter and demographics, is subject to its authority for religious affairs. Hierarchical organization: another borrowing from ancient Rome is the highly hierarchical organization of the Church into distinct regional administrative units, just like the territorial structure of the empire. In addition to the distinctions of nation or region, the diocese was originally an administrative unit of the territories of the Roman Empire. The Greek root of the word "dioikêsis", evokes the management of a house by caring parents. This term and its meaning were taken up in Latin Christianity. The dioceses were placed under the jurisdiction of a bishop who exercises legislative and executive power in his diocese on behalf of the pope. He must submit to the pope, but he is almost sovereign in his constituency, and very often he will behave as such. He is assisted by vicars who represent him according to his needs throughout his diocese. At the bottom of this hierarchy, the parish priests have the real responsibility of the parishes and are in constant contact with the faithful people in each town and village. With the evolution of ecclesiastical terminology, the vicar has sometimes become the assistant of the parish priest for certain pastoral tasks. This organization is pyramidal, and authority always comes from above. With

---

[52] Diocese - Etymology, Origin & Meaning

the gradual nationalization of religion, episcopal authority will extend over time to civil and political affairs. From the Middle Ages until the modern era, the keeping of the register of baptisms, marriages, and deaths in parishes allowed a rigorous control of the identity of their citizens and later of their political opinions. None of the dimensions of social life will escape their gaze: baptism, religious practice, marriage, family life, descent, profession, titles, fortune, trials, affairs, inheritance... The individual remains from the cradle to the tomb, placed under the watchful eye of this ecclesiastical power far superior to that of princes and even that of kings.

2.11 Cardinal, Cardinals[53]

According to the, "Dictionnaire historique de la langue française", this word is borrowed from the Latin "Cardinalis", which means hinge, gong, pivot, which also gave it the meaning of, south, north, east, and west poles. In the Catholic organization, the cardinals are dignitaries, superior to the bishops, specially assigned permanently to a particular regional or national church. He is a prelate chosen by the pope; their assembly constitutes the electoral college of the papacy. They are the ones who elect the new pope on the death of the previous one or when the latter is replaced. Here we find again the idea of ancient Rome of the "College of High Priests" electing the "Pontifex-Maximus".

2.12 Distinction between religious and secular[54]

This trend, which began in the third century, only strengthened in the following years. The clergy conceives itself as a set of ministries having followed a more or less long initiatory path that radically distinguishes them from the rest of men. They attribute to themselves numerous titles and powers not found in the New Testament. The word "Ministry," which gave the title of "Minister," is soon diverted from its original meaning of "Service" or "Servant" to become equivalent to a title of nobility (see appendices p 304) with the privileges and

---

53   Cardinal - Etymology, Origin & Meaning
54   Jean Marcel Nicole: Précis d'Histoire de l'Eglise P 62 Ed IBN

distinctions attached to it (see appendices). For their superior attributes to be well seen and recognized, ecclesiastics would wear more and more special clothes. This is the cassock, whose color, distinctive signs, and various additions follow a complex nomenclature to signify to the wearer its particular rank in the ecclesiastical hierarchy. The obligation of wearing long clothing covering the whole body for ministers of Christian worship is constantly reaffirmed by the various councils and especially by that of Trier in 1238 and that of Trent in 1542. The cassock for priests and parish priests reminds us that they do not work with their hands like the rest of men. This black artifice, mostly non-functional, closed at the neck by a white bar, permanently separates the clergy from the rest of society. It symbolizes the man without a body; he is freed from the vicissitudes of the flesh, from which only the head emerges as if it alone directed this body, which is now enslaved to the power of the mind. He is entirely dedicated to his priesthood and has renounced the world and its temptations. In the West this distinction is further reinforced by the extension of the obligation of celibacy for the high dignitaries of the Church and then, step by step for all his servants from the so-called "Gregorian" reform under the impetus of the Popes and especially of Gregory VII[55] (1073-1085), following the councils of the 11th century.

2.13 Rise of the monastic orders

We have seen that Christianity for the multitude had to face a major and intrinsic contradiction since it claimed to impose itself on the whole people, whether they are believers or not. From then on, the need quickly appeared to attempt, within it, an effective separation between those who wanted to conform or even more, to devote themselves sincerely to following the teachings of Christianity, and on the other hand, the mass of believers in name only, without any real attachment to it. Thus, monasticism was born from the will of some to live their faith in total purity, far from the world and its temptations. It appears from the 4th century with the "Anachoretes," also called, the hermits who lived in great solitude and destitution. This tendency to isolation and asceticism within Christianity is reminiscent of that of the Essenes in Judaism, which was revealed among others

---

[55] Gregorian Reform | Papal Power & Church Reforms | Britannica

by the Jewish writer Flavius[56] Josephus in his chronicles, "The Jewish wars"[57] as well as in "Antiquities Judaica". However, differences and multiple interests would appear over time. Indeed, the monastic orders, although guarantors of the solitude and piety of the monks, would open to the economic and social life of the countries where they were located, with their immense abbeys. Thus, some of them would become immensely rich as centers of agricultural production for the greater benefit of the bishoprics and their bishops.

2.14 Reflections on the Catholic Church's Imitation of the Temporal Power of the Roman Empire

The Roman Empire had shown remarkable qualities in its organization, its administration, its ways of communication, and the model of command of its highly hierarchical army. These qualities, added to those of some of its emperors, allowed it the exceptional expansion that we know. The proximity of the bishopric of Rome to this all-powerful central power certainly played an important role in the constitution of a church that gradually became imperial in its organization, theology, and government. The multiplication of its levels of command allowed it, as it allowed the Roman army, to direct vast areas with numerous and very diverse populations. It is not so much individual Christianity of conversion that it seeks rather, the submission of the multitude to the decrees of the Bishop of Rome. This pyramidal organization of power facilitates the transmission of messages and orders that go in priority from the top to the bottom of the pyramid. On the other hand, it does not allow the resolution of complex local problems and leaves no room for dialogue regarding the legitimacy of its power, with consideration of the Holy Scriptures. The pyramid works essentially from top to bottom, and so any problem from the base is first dealt with by the level above it, and so on to the top of the hierarchy if necessary. It is always the higher level that gives the answer or the solution by descending the entire hierarchical chain of ecclesial authority. This system of government is necessarily authoritarian; it produces decisions and decrees applicable by the interested

---

[56]   Jules-Marcel Nicole: Church History Précis p 64 Ed IBN
[57]   Jewish War, II, 8:2 - 13; Jewish Antiquities, XIII, 5:9; XV, 10:4.5; XVIII, 1:2 - 6

parties without real possibility of discussion on the fund as on the form. Often, the individual is left unanswered to their questions or solutions to their problems, which can become time traps for their entire lives. Another major disadvantage of this system of government is the absence of initiative because what is valued above all, is obedience and docility toward the hierarchy. On the other hand, initiative and experimentation are not favored because they could overshadow it. To show the faithful people that there are more teachings to draw from the personal exercise of faith and obedience to the Word of God is to deconstruct this pyramid of blind obedience to human traditions and teachings. This model of effective organization, when it comes to maneuvering large uniform units such as a territorial administration or an army, is no longer effective when it comes to governing the Lord's Church. Without being able to be exhaustive on the subject, one can still cite a major drawback to this form of organization; it is the sacralization of beings and their function in the hierarchy. We spoke quickly of the person of the pope who becomes ipso facto: "The Most Holy Father", that is to say, much more "holy" than the mass of the faithful people. It results from this verticality of the power of the ecclesiastical hierarchy that each one receives a greater or lesser share of this sacredness, of this spiritual aura which distinguishes him from other Christians. Characters with some merits are given more or less brilliant titles such as Monsignor, his Excellence, his Eminence, Father or Mother superior etc... The use of these superlatives from the top down of the ecclesiastical hierarchy acts as a separator in the community of the faithful. One finds in it, in fact, always someone superior to oneself, and he must therefore always seek the one of whom he is superior. In this evolution, the New Testament model and the advice of the Apostle Paul such as this one have been completely removed; "Do not aspire to what is high but let yourselves be drawn to what is humble. Be not wise in your own eyes" (Rom 12:16) and also; "Do not do anything out of partisanship or vain glory, but may humility make you look upon others as being above yourselves" (Phi 2:3) and finally this very clear statement of Jesus Christ himself on the question: "And call no one on earth your father; for only one is your Father, the one in heaven", all these exhortations to humility and service to others have unfortunately been forgotten. The verticality of the ecclesial organization was found in extenso as if by mimicry of the Roman Empire, in all civil society, especially in its Latin part. Extremely hierarchical and rigid, this model will have difficulty adapting to the successive turns of modernity that came much later from northern Europe and across the Atlantic with Protestantism, political democracy, and the expansion of individual law. This type of operation will see endless rivalries between men, questions of precedence between ecclesiastical dignitaries, and between princes and rulers. The confusion of powers will lead to that of the spirits and, far from favoring the unification of the nations and the return to the greatness of the Roman Empire, it will rather favor their division and their incessant rivalry. The limit to the expansion of this ecclesial as well as social model was finally the Synagogue, which had retained its type of internal relations unchanged since the time of the Hasmonean kings. This one, much more cellular and decentralized, was closer to the biblical and New Testament perspective. In 395, shortly before his death, Emperor Theodosius divided the empire into two parts, one in the East, the other in the West, with Constantinople and Rome respectively as capitals. He gave them to his two sons, but under repeated blows from invasions from northern Europe, as well as intrigues and corruption, the Roman Empire broke up and disappeared in the year 476. It remains in the East with Constantinople as its capital. However, this political division was the prelude to another that would later separate Christianity between the Eastern Churches and those of the West. In the former, questions of theology and discipline are no less intense than in the Western part. However, the exercise of supreme power would always remain shared between the great bishoprics: Constantinople, Alexandria, Antioch, Jerusalem.... These churches are called "autocephalous", and their respective bishops enjoy great autonomy. They are based on a theology of the councils of Nicaea[58] (325 AD), Constantinople[59] (381 AD), and Carthage[60] (390 AD) and are reinforced with those that would come after them. As in the West, they include the multitude of people who are therefore reputed Christians. They are no longer professing churches, and as in the West, their functioning becomes authoritarian with a less pronounced hierarchy but also closed to theological discussion based on the texts of the Bible. They will develop in the southern part of the empire

---

[58] First-Council-of-Nicaea.pdf
[59] First Council of Constantinople | Description, Christianity, History, Doctrine, & Significance | Britannica
[60] Carthage Council (390) - Charles Munier - Conciles de Carthage - La tradition du IIe Concile de Carthage (390) - Persée.fr

of Greek culture and later in eastern Europe to the north and east, in Ukraine, Belarus and even in the Russian far east. More than 1600 years after the division of the empire and after the progressive separation until the schism of 1054, between the Churches of the East and those of the West, their line of separation still passes through the same places namely: the border between Serbia in the east and the west, Croatia with Bosnia and Herzegovina further south-west. This disputed region has remained conflicted over its long history and is still a major failure of Christian brotherhood for Christianity today.

3. Imitations of the Rules and Institutions of Judaism in the Churches of the West and the East

3.1 Imitation and Diversion from the Sacred Law

This Christianity of multitude widely inspired as seen above by the pagan Greco-Latin philosophy, nevertheless kept some important and inseparable characteristics of Judaism. First of all, it is necessary to quote the fundamental texts namely: The Law of God or Decalogue (in Latin deca = 10); Christianity in the East and the West will not rule out the fundamental biblical explanation of the universe and its conception of man. In these major features, the two great communities remained close to each other, but also and above all, they remained inseparable from Judaism of which they recognized the God creator of man and of the universe, the Law given to Moses, and the God Savior of humanity by his Son Jesus Christ. However, neither Roman Catholicism nor Eastern Orthodoxy favored the reflection of believers on the Bible and on its founding texts for the Christian faith. In some cases,[61] they even opposed it, reserving for themselves the exclusivity of their interpretation. Over the centuries, Roman Catholicism made for its catechism a reduction of the ten commandments to their simplest expression, to which it added five laws or commandments as shown below. These have long had the force of law, both civil and spiritual. The Decalogue[62]: Exodus (20, 12 et s.), then Deuteronomy (Dt 5, 16 et s.)

---

[61] Index librorum prohibitorum - D_Dusto_Index_2008.pdf
[62] The Commandments of God - Exodus 20 NET - The Decalogue - God spoke all these - Bible Gateway

- One God you will worship and love perfectly.
- His holy name you will respect, fleeing blasphemy and false oath.
- The day of the Lord you will guard, serving God devoutly.
- Your father and mother will honor, your superiors alike.
- You will not kill.
- You will not commit adultery.
- You will not fly.
- You will not bear false testimony against your neighbor.
- You will not covet the house or the wife of your neighbor.
- You will not covet anything that belongs to your neighbor.

The five new orders[63] are:

- First commandment: On Sundays, the faithful are bound by the obligation to participate in Holy Mass and to abstain from servile works. The faithful will sanctify the feasts of precepts, in France: The Ascension is 40 days after Easter, the Assumption on August 15, All Saints on November 1st and Christmas on December 25th.
- Second commandment: Every believer is bound to confess his sins at least once a year.
- Third commandment: Every believer is bound by the obligation to receive Holy Communion at least every year at Easter.
- Fourth commandment: On the days of penance fixed by the Church, the faithful are bound by the obligation to abstain from meat and to observe fasting and prayer.
- Fifth Commandment: The faithful are bound by the obligation to provide for the Church.

The short-cut imitation of the Laws of the Lord in the Catholic catechism nevertheless remains very close to the true sacred text in Hebrew. The five[64] additional commands dating from the Council of Trent in 1551 do not bring anything new about the knowledge of God; on the other hand, they are all

---

[63] Church Precepts - 5 Precepts of the Church Explained
[64] https://catholicity.com/baltimore/catechism/lesson21.html - The Commandments of the Church; The First and Second Commandments

oriented towards submission to the orders and injunctions of the Catholic institution. Again, in other times, fortunately remote, these articles were pretexts for many abuses of power, including compulsory taxes for any citizen or subject, inspired by the 5th new command, despite his or her convictions. These discretionary measures remain today in many countries and do not contribute at all to the promotion of the Christianity of the multitude, which everywhere retreats in religious buildings, practice as in hearts of people. Rather, it reflects the survival of an era of systematic collusion between the two powers: religious and political. It can also be added that the obligatory character of these five commandments was intended, the control of the spirits, and that of the purses. Collusion with the political power of the ecclesial institution has often made it possible to make texts of civil law.

3.2 Jewish holidays and their transposition into Christian holidays: Passover/ Easter

It is undoubtedly the celebration that best characterizes Christianity. However, to understand it even superficially, the mass of the faithful Christians is necessarily referred to Jewish history in their condition of slaves in Egypt, loaded with heavy work and entirely submitted to the pharaohs. The understanding of the role of "the Easter lamb" and its transposition into the person of Jesus Christ can only be done by a preliminary teaching on chapter 12 of the book of Exodus in which, this is God himself who orders Moses and Aaron to establish what he defines as the "Passover of the Lord". In Hebrew, "Passover", or Passover in modern English, has the meaning "the passage above". That is, in Judaism, the blood of the lamb applied to the lintels of the doors of the Hebrews houses, served as a sign to the exterminating angel, to pass over their houses and spare them, as verse 13 states; "The blood will serve you as a sign on the houses where you will be; I will see the blood, and I will pass over you, and there will be no plague that destroys you, when I strike the land of Egypt". In Christianity, the perfect Lamb is Jesus Christ himself. For Judaism, this transposition is scandalous, and it became in Christianity the proof for many theologians to condemn Judaism without appeal. Yet, this is the cardinal point of its doctrine that must be remembered when it is said in the Gospel of John that Jesus Christ is the one who "takes away the sin of the world" (Jn 1:29). The universal vocation of the ministry of Jesus Christ found in this short passage as in many others, all its justification. This divine order has become a feast celebrated in both Judaism and Christianity. It is a real gateway into Jewish theology, which is also essential for understanding the rootedness of the Christian message in it.

3.3 Shavuot/ Pentecost

Originally Shavuot had the meaning found in the book of Exodus; "You shall celebrate the feast of weeks, the first fruits of the harvest of wheat, and the feast of the harvest at the end of the year" (Ex 34:22). Later in the Book of Numbers, this feast is characterized by the gift to the Lord of an offering of the first fruits of the harvest (Num 28:26). This is one of the three pilgrimages that gathered the people from as far away as they were into Jerusalem. There is also Pesach, celebrated seven weeks before, as well as Sukkot, which comes in September to celebrate the harvest. For a very long time, it remained a joy associated with the harvest period and the hope of the fruits that it would bring. It was originally called, "the Feast of Weeks" in reference to the seven weeks that separated it from Easter (Passover). The transposition of meaning came by comparison of the corruptible seed for the nourishment of the body with the incorruptible seed of the Law of God for the nourishment of the soul and spirit. The rabbinical teachings gradually reinforced this meaning by considering that the gift of the Law was for all the people of Israel a wonderful blessing from the Lord. It was for them, as permanent tutors, to promote their establishment and especially their development. The evocation among the Hebrews of the Law of God is always accompanied by great joy. It is compared to "the honey under the tongue[65]" and to the water that quenches, purifies, and fertilizes the seed. In Psalm 119, King David recalls all the blessings he received in his life when meditating on the Law of the Lord and putting it into practice as he expresses it in these few verses: "Your statutes are the subject of my songs, in the house where I am a stranger. At night, I remember your name, O Lord! And I keep your Law. This is my own, for I observe your ordinances. My share, O Lord! I say it is to keep your words."

---

[65] Cf. Jewish Encyclopedia 1906 & Kitov 2008 p 505.

(Ps 119:54-57). Concerning this feast, the evangelical theologian Yves Pétrakian makes this comment, "In the liturgies of the synagogue, Pentecost is called the feast of the promulgation of the Law", and this meaning inspires the whole ritual of the feast[66] ". Christians have made a new transposition of the meaning of Shavuot, which they called "Pentecost", in reference to the 50 days (Penta = 50 in Greek) that come after Easter. Jesus Christ was therefore considered the first fruits of a new and abundant harvest of hearts transformed by God's love. Through his voluntary sacrifice and glorious resurrection, he truly became the sacrificial Easter Lamb for the salvation of the whole world. He became the firstborn of a new harvest of souls regenerated by his blood and by the Holy Spirit. The somewhat enigmatic words of Jesus Christ about the coming of a "Comforter" (Jn 14:16 & 26; Jn 15:26; Jn 16:7 & 13), take all their meaning for the disciples in the upper chamber when they were baptized with "Spirit and fire". They then experienced the power of the Holy Spirit upon them, empowering them to witness wherever He would send them. The parallelism with Shavuot, is not direct however, it is real because in the Christian conception we also have this idea of the beginnings, of a new dawn for believers, thus clothed in the fullness of the revelation of God's plan and the power from on high to witness effectively to the truth of the Word of God.

3.4 Hanukkah/ Christmas

Hanukkah was instituted after the victory of the Maccabees over the king of the Greek dynasty of the Seleucids, Antiochus IV, in 165 AD. This victory is threefold because it is not only military but also spiritual with the purification of the temple and the return to the Jewish cult that followed it, and finally political, since it marks the regained independence for Israel after about 160 years under the domination of the Greek dynasties, first the Ptolemy and then the Seleucids. The rabbis did not fail to see the intervention of the God of Israel in this happy outcome. This was also confirmed to them by the "Miracle of the Vial" because during the feast of the consecration of the temple, there was barely enough oil for a day contained in a vial; however, it miraculously burned for eight

---

[66]   TopBible: Yves Pétrakian, Pentecost § 1

days. Hanukkah, which means in Hebrew, "Feast of Edification" for the reasons mentioned above, is also called the "Feast of Lights" to recall the miraculous light of the vial. The date of the festivities was set at the 25th of the month of Kislev, which corresponds more or less to the end of December of the Gregorian calendar. They last eight days, they are characterized by joy, celebration, and the idea of rebirth after darkness. In these days, fasting and penance are suppressed, the joy of salvation is indulged, and children are especially spoiled with treats and toys. Menorahs or candlesticks are constantly lit in the houses to recall the miracle of the vial. In recent years, giant menorahs have been lit in public spaces, in some cities in Israel, the USA, Europe, and Canada. The parallelism with the Christian holiday of Christmas is not obvious a priori; however, it exists even if very few Christians know "Hanukkah," while they know the relationship of Easter and Pentecost to the Jewish history to which these two festivals are attached. First, there is the date in winter, at the end of the year, as the birth of Jesus. There are lights, which express in Christianity the same idea as in Judaism, namely, the end of the period of darkness and the return to the light with the lengthening of the days. Both physical and spiritual darkness are confused in the same obstacle to the development of spirituality and life. The righteous Simeon would express it in his way when he said, seeing the child Jesus during his presentation in the temple, "Now, Lord, let your servant go in peace, according to your word. For my eyes have seen your salvation, salvation that you have prepared before all peoples, light to enlighten the nations and, glory of Israel, your people". The light to illuminate the nations is miraculous as that of the vial in Judaism. The New Testament makes no mention of the feast of Hanukkah, except under another name for which it also does not give an explanation, namely: "The feast of the Dedication". The Gospel of John places it in winter in this short verse: "The feast of the Dedication was celebrated in Jerusalem. It was winter (Jn 10:22)". It can be assumed that it was sufficiently well known and popular in the Judaism of that time to dispense with a definition intended for future generations of Christianity. Indeed, if it is quoted only once in the New Testament, it is found abundantly in the Old Testament, where, from the beginning of the history of Israel, the Eternal God had prescribed the dedication of the altar in these two verses of the Book of Numbers: "The princes presented their offering for the dedication of the altar on the day it was anointed; the princes presented their offering before the altar. The Lord said to Moses, The princes will come one by one, and on different days, to present their offering for the dedication of the altar" (Num 7:10-11). In the Bible, the meaning of the verb' dedication' consists in assigning an object, such as the altar (2Chr 7:5, No. 7.10-11), or a place of worship, such as the temple (Ps 30:1; Esd 6:16-17), to a sacred task or function. It does not concern a person, so when Jesus Christ, who is the incarnate verb, appears, there is a kind of mutation of meaning since he alone is "the first fruit" but also as a living body and the incarnate temple he is, "the dedication" (Jn 2:18, 20). Most sources, including the historical dictionary of the French language, referring to the definition of "Christmas" do not mention the obvious relationship with "Hanukkah". Some cite its appearance from the beginning of the 4th century, making this name a derivative of words from Latin, such as Navitas, which gave "Navidad" in Spanish, "Nata"l in Italian, and French, in religious vocabulary, "Nativité". Christmas has therefore also, from the beginning, the meaning of birth and rebirth. This festival is characterized by the relegation of the Jewish origins of Christianity into a religion that becomes the majority at the end of the Roman Empire. However, despite this distance, there are at least four common features between Hanukkah and Christmas: the date at the end of the year, the idea of renewal, and that of the light triumphing over darkness. The fourth feature they share is the demonstration of joy because in the Middle Ages, during happy events, such as the birth of the heir son, the coronation of the king, the visit of a prince or any other popular celebration, the crowd shouted with all their heart to manifest their joy: Noël! Noël! (Christmas! Christmas!). It can be assumed without being possible to establish with precision that the original Christianity, which was rather a Judeo-Christianity, celebrated Hanukkah by adding unambiguously its new meaning, which it had acquired henceforth. Throughout Europe, the feast of Christmas took second place after Easter in the liturgical calendar of Christianity, however the name is different according to the country; In the United Kingdom they speak of "Christmas", in Germany they say, "Weihnachten", the meaning of which is borrowed from ancient pagan customs celebrating the winter solstice and the return of daylight. In fact, while celebrating the birth of Christ, Christmas brought together some customary origins wherever Christianity spread. Today, with the progressive de-Christianization of Europe, it is rather this sense that predominates in modern society. It is a great family and social celebration, with from the end of the nineteenth century, the Christmas tree, which testifies to the persistence of life even in the heart of winter. For the children, there is the "Santa Claus" which appeared at the beginning of the XXth century, it is inseparable from this time of rejoicing. The cities are decorated and illuminated, and Christmas markets, more and more, animate the heart of cities. Holidays are granted in companies and administrations, so that all young and old enjoy the period of wonder of "Christmas".

3.5 Bar Mitzvah and Confirmation

For the 13-year-old boy, the Bar Mitzvah marks his change of status in the Jewish community. He is now regarded as an adult and leaves parental guardianship for the application of the commandments of God prescribed in the Law of the Lord. The prefix "Bar" means "son" while "Mitzvah" means; command or good deed, so the one who does his, "Bar Mitzvah" can enforce the commandments of the Law and do good for his family and community. He emancipates himself and becomes a man; he can be included in one, "Miniane", that is to say, a group of 10 men, allowing the holding of an office. He can also wear the prayer shawl called "Tallit", as well as the phylacteries or "Tephillin". Depending on his abilities, he can now replace the person in charge of the sung part and even the "Hazzan" who presides at the usual services of the Synagogue. This religious ceremony[67] is also an opportunity for parents to have a great family celebration. It appeared during the Middle Ages and spread rapidly throughout the diaspora. For young girls, a similar ceremony, the Bat-Mitzvah (Bat = Girl) was instituted in the 20th century, with some notable differences, namely, age, which is lowered to 12 because of their earlier sexuality. According to Jewish circles, more or less conservative or liberal, they receive powers and responsibilities comparable to those of young boys. Entrance into the world of adults, often celebrated with pomp in this way, has not only a religious meaning but also a social and confessional one. It confirms the young pre-adolescent's adherence to the confession of faith of Judaism, his and her entry into the people, and their commitment to serve it in one way or another with all of their heart and all their strength. This aspect of

---

[67] Bar Mitzvah - https://www.jewishvirtuallibrary.org/bar-bat-mitzvah-and-confirmation

the Bar-Mitzvah has promoted in Judaism the development of a kind of militancy based on the positive values of the Bible. Applied internally but also externally, it is found in many areas today, where the work of Jewish institutions is positive and can be found everywhere in present-day Western societies.

3.6 Solemn communion and Confirmation

In Christianity, the parallelism between confirmation and Bar Mitzvah is very pronounced. It is also a question of consecrating on a solemn day, the entrance of young boys and girls from 13 to 15 years, into the People of God and the community of the faithful. It was made necessary because baptism, which is, according to the texts of the Bible, a personal act and the expression of an adult's conviction, was diverted from its original meaning. We remember the teaching on baptism, according to the very words of Jesus Christ and his apostles; "He who believes and is baptized will be saved, but he who does not believe will be condemned" (Ma 16:16) and also; "This water was a figure of baptism, which is not the purification of the defilement of the body, but the commitment of a good conscience to God, and which now saves you, too, by the resurrection of Jesus Christ" (1P 3:21). Thus, the clear and precise teachings of the Word of God were substituted, with the support of the religious authorities from the 3rd to the 4th century BC, by the baptism of children for reasons of convenience at the same time as to control families and beyond, the entire social fabric. We have already seen above that from the 4th century; there was no longer any question of this baptism for the converts. It was then administered to children, so this to extend as far as possible the grip of a religion that transformed itself from day to day, more conquering and less convincing. From then on, the problem arose of the real and sincere adherence of the individual to Christian doctrine. Confirmation[68] was, therefore, as its name suggests, the solemn act by which the child, passing into adulthood between 13 and 15 years, personally confirms the commitments to follow the teachings of the religion taken by his parents and guardians, during his or her baptism. On the day of his confirmation, the Holy Spirit is administered to him by the bishop to help him understand and apply the

---

[68] Introduction to Catholicism/Confirmation — Confirmation.pdf

teachings he has received. The trap is closed on him and, even before the happy and unhappy experiences of life, the one who is still only a child in many respects is "certified" Christian by men and by religion. Consequently, these two acts: pedo-baptism and confirmation, which tend to replace the one and authentic Baptism instituted according to the Scriptures, being neither a personal decision, do not have the sacred value which had been given to them by Jesus-Christ in the plan of salvation.

3.7 Reflection on Bar Mitzvah and Solemn Communion

The first common trait is, by default, namely that neither in the Torah nor in the New Testament does one find a trace of this obligatory passage in the adult world with the consequences that this implies. The problem of personal adherence in Bar Mitzvah and Solemn Communion is similar in many respects: how, one who is still only a pre-teen make a serious commitment for his whole life based on this special day, where everything was decided in his place? However, there are differences between these two types of engagement. In Judaism, it is easy to understand that the Bar-Mitzvah serves as an introduction to the people of Israel, knowing that in the First Testament, God wanted to create for himself a people from the filiation of the patriarchs of Israel (Gen 12). We know that it is therefore fleshly at the same time as it is spiritual with the confession of faith in the Law of the Lord, and we can also add intellectual in the sense that the Law must be explained and meditated on by all the people from generation to generation. The major difficulty in this plan of life, which starts from circumcision to Bar Mitzvah and goes far beyond with many rules and obligations, is the truth and sincerity of the adherence of the young and later adult to the laws and decrees of the Torah. One of the thinkers who contributed the most to the questioning of this automatic adherence to the sacred texts is the philosopher Baruch Spinoza besides, he conflicted with his synagogue on these questions and was excluded from it. His thinking is indeed, with those of some other writers such as René Descartes and Thomas Hobbes and many others from the time of the Renaissance to the so-called "age of enlightenment", the pivot of an alternative to the power of religion by philosophy and reason. Wanting to be rationalists, the philosophers of this current implicitly question the normative power of religions over the

Judeo-Christian societies of their time. They methodically build a whole system of thought that radically distanced men from unconditional adherence to the dogmas of religion. First of all, this trend uses the power of deduction, that is to say; even before being created, facts, beings, and things existed, so they present themselves to human understanding as necessary and their nature as their causes and consequences must be analyzed in a methodical, objective, and deductive way. With this materialist conception of the universe, Spinoza elaborates a method close to mathematical reasoning. It starts from the intrinsic definition of the object, then from the axioms and postulates that can be formulated about it, it then makes proposals and demonstrations in perfect coherence with these findings. Finally, it manages in many cases to express the truth of the experience, allowing the searcher to express a theorem or a quasi-scientific truth about this object. It is an almost geometric demonstration that he would apply extensively to philosophy, history, sociology, and even religion. By submitting it to rationality, Spinoza attracted the wrath of the religious authorities of his time, whether Jewish, Protestant, or Catholic. Far from uses, prejudices, and social customs, he reconstructs on a quasi-mathematical model the power stakes of his time, showing particularly how religions have gone far beyond their initial prerogatives to dominate the mass of the people for political ends and lead them into fanaticism and absurdity. He demonstrated that finally, the latter being deprived of their "free will", they are no longer able to judge the good and the evil that they are meant to do. In this unfortunate drift, one takes the full measure of the abuse of power represented by both the Bar-Mitzvah and the solemn Communion, since in the name of a religion of peace, love, and social harmony, men were pitted against each other in war. He is with other philosophers' precursors of a democratic model of government and categorical rejection of any form of dictatorship. Through his work, he contributed greatly to the emergence of the very new concept for the time of "Separation of powers"[69], which was, however, very old since it was exposed in the Bible in many passages[70]. Certainly, these two sacraments and innocent feasts do not alone bear the full responsibility of the religious conflicts of[71] the 16th and 17th centuries, and others occurred after,

---

[69]   Baruch Spinoza - https://israeled.org/baruch-spinoza/
[70]   Theological-Political Treatise Edition Chapter 3 & Page. 53-70
[71]   Theological-Political Treatise Edition Chapter 5 & Page. 87-103

far from it. However, it is a perfect opportunity to point out that whenever man departs from biblical thought, as expressed in the texts, he takes the risk of making it loses the sacred meaning that the Eternal God wanted to give to it. In Christianity, the ambiguity is even greater because by introducing the individual to the Christian life by the new birth followed in general by the water baptism of an adult and finally by that of the Spirit, The Lord Jesus did not want to create a nation in the sense of the generational and traditional ties known to him. Christianity does not create one, "Christian nation" as Judaism creates a Jewish nation. It puts at the center of the construction of the Church, the individual and the question of his eternal salvation. The passage through commitment is therefore essential, it is that of an adult who has understood his condition of being lost without the help of his savior. This understanding, which appears at any age of life, is soon accompanied by the desire to follow the teachings of the Lord Jesus Christ, regardless of any traditional, family, or social pressure. It is a free act "par excellence" considered along with marriage as a major event in the existence of an adult. In this way, the bonds existing between Christians are, above all, spiritual and fraternal. Certainly, with time they often take this other dimension of affection and use, but there is nothing obligatory or binding in this personal allegiance to the principles and truths of Christianity. There is even the risk of abandonment, of rejection of the values of Christianity, and finally of the Word of God. This risk is clearly underlined when Jesus Christ states: "He who believes and is baptized will be saved, but he who does not believe will be condemned" (Mk 16:16). The implication here is very strong because whoever does not believe in His words, bears full personal responsibility. The Christian life with its blessings and the promises it possesses is thus everywhere compatible with the national culture, its manifestations, feasts and specificities except naturally when there is irreconcilable opposition of those with the biblical teachings, and also in case of persecution, as unfortunately it is still observed today. For this reason the Apostle Paul would emphasize in his two epistles, one to the Galatians and the other to the Colossians: "There is no longer any Jew or Greek, there is no longer any slave or free, there is no man or woman: for all of you are one in Jesus Christ" (Gal 3:28) and also; "There are neither Greeks nor Jews, neither circumcised nor uncircumcised, nor barbarians nor Scythians, nor slaves nor freemen; but Christ is all in all" (Col 3:11). Almost the same words show that belonging to different nations is not an obstacle to the conversion or brotherhood that the Christian has found in Christ. The balance and wisdom of God cannot be better expressed in these words explaining how adherence to Christianity passes through a free, authentic, and adult act. It is on this solid New Testament's foundation that the Evangelical Churches also called "Professing Churches", are built. They were born in 1523 in Zurich, Switzerland, with the Anabaptists only a few years after the Lutheran Reformation, and they had for a very long time to face the resolute hostility of the official churches, also called "multitude" both Protestant and Catholic. Spinoza is not only interesting because he opens philosophy and experimental sciences to a wide audience, but also because he applies his method of investigation to religion and more precisely to the knowledge of the God of the Bible. He did not return to religion; he returned to the biblical texts. Starting from these sources, he recognized that they established a doctrine of good and evil, also that God only precisely defines the nature of these two opposite poles. Thus, he says that it is normal to love this sovereign God and that there is bliss in the expression of this love. Far from being the theorist of atheism that some writers wanted to see in him, Spinoza also proposes a method of studying the Bible that was put into practice by all the Evangelical movements during his lifetime and those that came after him. It consists of systematically studying the Bible as a doctrinal and normative word for the faith of the believer. When a passage is obscure or seems contradictory to other theological statements and principles, on the one hand; be careful, if possible, to question this passage in its historical-social context and, on the other hand, to seek other passages throughout the Bible that provide another definition or expression of this difficult first passage in question. The reader can then discover, and this is what Spinoza did, that the Bible can be explained by itself, and to each major question that is asked, it answers with one or more solutions. For example; Many Christians who are not anti-Semitic think that the Jews who rejected the message of the Gospel have fallen from their place as a people who bear witness to God and his message, when the apostle Paul explicitly says: "I speak the truth in Christ, I do not lie, my conscience bears witness to it by the Holy Spirit: I feel great sadness, and I have in my heart a continual sorrow. For I myself would like to be anathema and separate from Christ for my brethren, my flesh parents, who are Israelites, to whom the adoption, and glory, and covenants, and law, and worship, and promises, and patriarchs belong, and from whom, according to the flesh, Christ, who is above all things, God eternally blessed. Amen!" (Rom 9:1-5). The reader could easily believe that the apostle declares here, the people of Israel irremediably lost because they did not recognize in Jesus Christ their savior. But this is not so in the mind of the apostle since a few verses later in chapter 11, he brings to this thought, alas, so widespread, a vigorous denial when he declares: "I therefore say: Has God rejected his people? Far from it! For I, too, am an Israelite, of the seed of Abraham, of the tribe of Benjamin. God did not reject his people, whom he knew in advance. Do you not know what the Scripture tells of Elijah, how he addresses God this complaint against Israel: Lord, they have killed your prophets, they have overthrown your altars; I was left alone, and they're trying to take my life? But what answer does God give him? I have reserved for myself seven thousand men who have not bowed their knees before Baal" (Rom 11:1-4). He concludes his thought with a definitive phrase: "For God does not repent of His gifts and calling" (Rom 11:29). Thus, Israel remains in the heart of God in the place He has chosen in all sovereignty. As a people, Israel is in no way guilty of the crucifixion of Jesus Christ, which has remained, as we have seen above, a politico-religious affair carried out by a small circle of Jewish and pagan leaders interested in its loss. However, in the spiritual sense, like all nations and individuals in all ages, it is also true because Jesus Christ, the Savior of the world, bore upon him the universal nature of man's sin, as the Apostle Paul states in this passage; "For we have already proved that all, Jews and Greeks, are under the dominion of sin, as it is written: There is no righteous, not even one; No one is intelligent, no one seeks God; All are lost, all are perverted; No one does good, not even one" (Rom 3:9-12). Innocent of the crime of ordering the crucifixion of Jesus Christ, he must be acquitted in this shameful trial that a cheap Christianity has made him for centuries. However, as the whole of humanity, it is nevertheless guilty in the spiritual sense of the term before God because there is not even a single righteous one on all the earth. The apostle demonstrates the need for all men to seek salvation in Jesus Christ, the Savior of mankind. What is remarkable in his demonstration is the analogy between the analytical method proposed by Spinoza and that used by the apostle, who also takes the texts of the Bible as the basis of his explanation. The methodological unity between Paul and Spinoza showed the way for a more rigorous exegesis than that of the scholastic tradition marked by hazardous recourse to the interpretation of some sages, to the tradition, and to the very relative wisdom of the Greek thought, Latin, and sometimes even pagan superstition[72]. The Dutch theologian Spinoza would have this memorable sentence on this subject: "What relationship can there be between Christ and Aristotle?[73]"

4. The theology of substitution[74]

4.1 The "Verus Israel" replaces the "Vetus Israel" or the new replaces the old

This operation of replacing one by the other took place in the history of Christianity with the idea that it had henceforth substituted itself for Israel in the favor of God and in his election to bring to the world the knowledge and witness given to his name, to his works, and glory. In his remarks on this crucial question, the French Protestant theologian Fadiey Lovsky summed up the painful evolution by saying that the first Christians of Greek or Roman origin had first said: "Israel is us too", then, "Israel is us", then finally, "Israel is only us". Although the idea of being found better in the heart of God does not make much sense when one considers what the Holy Scriptures say about human nature; «There is no right, not even one" (Rom 3:10). However, the Churches have zealously pursued it since the first centuries of their history and until very recently on the scale of time, towards the end of the 20th century[75]. The theology of substitution deserves, if it were possible, the sketch of a psychoanalysis to show how it is from Christianity, an exercise of complacent narcissism. To be found better in the heart of God is extremely difficult for men; we know

---

[72] Definition "PRIESTS AND LEVITES" - TopBible Dictionary — TopChrétien (topchretien.com)

[73] Scholastics - Jean-Barthélemy Hauréau, De la philosophie scolastique, Pagnerre éditeur, Paris, 1850, 2 vol. in-8°

[74] Theology of Substitution: Jesus, the Jewish Messiah (part 6) - Jean-Marc Thobois - YouTube at 17'59.

[75] Fadie Lovsky: Fadiey Lovsky auteur de L'église et les malades – Babelio - Tribute to Fadiey LOVSKY delivered on May 30, 2015, at the Temple of Grenoble by Pastor Alain MASSINI

from the message of the Bible that it is even downright impossible. First, there is the question of comparison: better than whom, what? The theologians of substitution have found how they have made easier what was difficult; it was indeed possible to be better before God than the Jews. Then it took scriptural references to engrave definitively this superiority in stone and eternity. These were found in the texts of the New Testament, even at the cost of blatant misinterpretations and multiple theological approximations. Thus, the sacred texts could themselves speak against Judaism and its theological heritage. The Old Testament was relegated, devalued and annihilated as a source of divine inspiration for Christian life. The Ten Commandments, the Magisterium of the Law of God with its many ordinances for ethics and social life, all the jurisprudence acquired since the conquest of Canaan by Joshua to the prophet Malachi, were no longer to have any influence on its existence. In Catholicism, this doctrine is constantly reaffirmed over the centuries, particularly at the Council of Florence (15th century), until the encyclical Mistici Corporis Christi by Pius XII, published in 1943 in the middle of World War II, while the physical destruction of the Jewish people in Europe reached its climax. It is around the year 150, that the nascent Christianity claims to be the "True Israel» (Verus Israel), which replaces "Ancient Israel" (Vetus Israel). This interpretation ignores the words of Jesus himself and those of the apostle Paul about the God who, "repent neither of his calling nor of his gifts" (Rom 11:29). The late Pastor Jean Marc Thobois makes a remarkable distinction between the group of Sadducees, this wealthy religious oligarchy, very close to Roman power, strongly opposed to the ministry of Jesus and the people of the Israelites who were not at all opposed and who, on the contrary, saw in him a liberator from their abuses of power. The theology of substitution goes even further in its enterprise of degradation of Judaism, since it dispossesses it of its sacred and cultural texts, such as the Old Testament and the Talmud. Indeed, Christianity became imperial and represented in its hierarchy by eminent theologians, some of whom were recognized by posterity as being "Fathers of the Church". Now they claim to be the only people able to understand and interpret the founding texts of Judaism. They reserved to themselves the right to rewrite certain passages; so, it is in the controversies called "disputation" between Catholic experts and theologians on one side and Jews on the other. In public, or in front of a large circle of representatives from both sides, they discuss the respective merits of their profession of faith and their sacred texts. These exchanges that could have been beneficial to both are far from being courteous and respectful. They are more like violent oratorical games and public trials, instructed against Judaism, in which everything is played in advance. In France, during the first "disputation", known and documented in 1242, between rabbis, including "Yehiel de Paris" and Catholic clergymen, the Talmud was condemned, and copies were burned publicly in place of Grève in Paris. Going back to the beginning of Christianity, a controversy of the same nature had opposed the second century, Justin of Nablus to Rabbi Tryphon. Although the form was very different, since it was more of an intellectual joust through writing, the conclusion was the same. It tended to promote Christianity and to demonstrate its superiority over Judaism. Other "disputations" remained famous, especially that of Barcelona in July 1263[76]. During 4[77] days of intense exchanges, the advantage seemed to go to the Jewish party, which had won the support of King James of Aragon. However, the Dominicans eventually obtained, with the support of Pope Urban IV, the exile of Rashi Ben Nahman, the leader of the Israeli delegation, and the prohibition of certain passages of the Talmud[78]. There was also the "disputation" of Tortosa (1413-1414)[79] in present-day Catalonia. It was the longest in the history of these attempts to convince Jews to convert to Catholicism, through dialogue most often accompanied by threats. It lasted more than a year, it was actually a trap for the leaders of Judaism, many of whom converted and led with them many of their coreligionists[80]. A few decades later, the infamous decree of the Alhambra[81] (February 1492) by which the Jews would be obliged to convert to Catholicism or leave the kingdom was published throughout the kingdom. Meanwhile, these

[76] Role of the Sadducees: Jesus, the Jewish Messiah (part 6) - Jean-Marc Thobois - YouTube at 26'25
[77] Yehiel de Paris: «La vie interne des communautés juives du Nord de la France au temps de Rabbi Yéhiel et de ses collègues», dans Le Brûlement du Talmud à Paris 1242-1244, Éditions du Cerf, 1999
[78] Judeo-Christian Disputation - Daniel J. Lasker, Jewish philosophical polemics against Christianity in the Middle Ages, New York 1977
[79] Léon Poliakov: History of Antisemitism – The Age of Faith 1. Edition Points P 152, 153
[80] Tortosa Disputation - Antonio Pacios Lopez, La disputa de Tortosa, Instituto Arias Montano, Madrid, 1957, 2 vol., 392p. et 621p
[81] Barcelona Disputation — Robert Chazan, The Barcelona "Disputation" of 1263: Christian Missionizing and Jewish Response [archive], Speculum, Vol. 52, No. 4 (Oct., 1977)

false mass conversions bring only misdeeds and give rise in the "conversos" the double complex of having left Judaism without having become frankly Christian. The decree of the Alhambra will only worsen this complex, as will be seen later.

4.2 The Persecuted Talmud in Christianity[82]

At the end of the 4th century, everything from Judaism was now considered cursed, harmful, and poisonous in the so-called Christian empire. Although they were reduced to second-class citizens in the Middle Ages, the Jews and their Talmud nevertheless exerted an undeniable influence on the public. Indeed, this voluminous intellectual production in relation to the spiritual values of the Bible, itself recognized in Christianity, is unparalleled. In 1553, during the Council of Trent (1545 – 1563), the Talmud was burned in Rome in a gigantic autodafé that would call many others, and in 1559, as part of the same council, intended to fight against the expansion of Protestantism, it was put on the index of forbidden books (Index Expurgatorius). In this unique attempt to dispossess Judaism of what belongs to it, Pope Pius IV ordered in 1565 that the very name of the Talmud disappear. This censorship will, of course, be circumvented, like the others, by semantic artifices and various codifications. Still, we measure the weight of the intellectual and spiritual constraint of the time. From the 16th century to the present day, the Talmud has remained largely within Jewish circles, and, like the entirety of Judaism, it has been set apart from Christianity. However, this period from 18th to 19th centuries was also that of the emancipation of Judaism and, for scholars and specialists, that of the multiplication of study centers of the Talmud throughout Europe.

4.3 The first theories and theorists of anti-Judaism

Today, we find everywhere in the press, on social networks as well as in debates on the issue, the term "Anti-Semitism" rather than "Anti-Judaism", which would

---

[82] Relations between Judaism and Christianity — Simon Claude Mimouni et Pierre Maraval, Le Christianisme des origines à Constantin, PUF, coll. « Nouvelle Clio », 2006, p.272, chap. Séparation entre Judéens pharisiens et Judéens chrétiens.

be more appropriate. In fact, as in the letter, anti-Semitism has become nowadays, anti-Judaism; its first meaning derives from its construction: anti, is to be against or opposed to; "Semite", refers to the people from the branch of "Shem", son of Noah in the Bible (Gen 6:10). After the flood, they left on the side of the East, the Jews and the Arabs are part of the Semitic peoples like many other ethnic groups in the Near and Middle East. Finally, "ism" is the suffix used to translate into a behavior or a philosophy the noun to which it is attached. The evolution of its meaning is rapid since this word appears for the first time in Germany under the pen of the Austrian Jewish essayist, Moritz Steinschneider in 1860 in the expression "anti-Semitic prejudices", in German, "antisemitische Vorurteile"[83]. From its formulation, this expression designates prejudice against Jews, and it is the meaning that remains until today. It is indeed extremely rare that the formula, "anti-Semitic prejudice" is applied to the Arab world or to another ethnic and social group other than the Jews. Does its very frequent use today, make it possible to hide that it is really about "anti-Judaism", like this other expression, "anti-Zionism", allows to disguise anti-Judaism? It is possible, however, that this widely used formula is indeed the cover-sex of anti-Judaism, which is why we will use this one rather than the other in the rest of this book. This is also the position adopted in his time, by historian Jules Isaac[84], in his systematic studies on this subject. Absolute and definitive word, the Bible is also all in nuance, in softness, in appeal to reason and conciliation between men. It expresses the God who judges the earth, men, and their transgressions of his Law, as well as the God of grace, of love and peace for all who seek his face, who seek the good both for themselves and for their fellow men. He does not deprive them of any happiness or good in the course of their lives, and if they are not spared from trials, they triumph by faith as so brilliantly explained in chapters 11 and 12 of the Epistle to the Hebrews. The revelation of the message of the Bible is therefore like a philosophy of happiness proposed to the Hebrews first, then by extension to all humanity by the spread of the New Testament, intervened with the Christian era. It has been seen, however, that many distortions of meaning have appeared since ancient Jewish times, as well as during the formation of the Church, both

---

[83] Anti-Semitism - Hannah Arendt, Sur l'antisémitisme, Les Origines du totalitarisme, t.1, Paris, Le Seuil, coll. « Points »

[84] Léon Poliakov: History of anti-Semitism: Edition Point. P 19, 20, 21, 25

Eastern and Western. Among these, one of the most notorious, absurd, strange, and dangerous is the inexorable rise of anti-Judaism in a Europe that is still only very partially Christianized after the fall of the empire of Rome in the West in the year 476 AD. Why was speaking out against Judaism a way to assert oneself more Christian at that time? And today, what remains of this propensity of the individual to grow by the lowering of the other and singularly of the Jew? Christianity in the course of its history is characterized by light and glory as well as by darkness and shame; on the question of anti-Judaism, unfortunately, it is rather these last two qualifiers that suit it. Opening the door to this dark story is not the easiest part of this work; it is like entering a nauseating cellar where swarms of vermin and evil beings thrive inside. The Bible teaches us not to judge men in order not to be judged ourselves (Mat 7:1), yet it also teaches us to judge and condemn doctrines (Eph 5:11; 1Th 4:1-6), strangers that enter into the theology of the Church at the expense of the purity of its message of salvation, life, peace, hope, and love. Two reference authors among many others, namely Jules Isaac and Léon Poliakov[85], have made extensive studies on anti-Judaism. They both indicate that before Christianity, there was no organic or institutional anti-Judaism. Of course, authors of antiquity, including Tacitus and Seneca, for example, have spoken against Judaism and some of its customs[86], but their position cannot be systematized and made a social generality as it will unfortunately be possible to do so much later in the so-called "Christian" Europe. We have seen that the criticism of Judaism found in the New Testament does not in any way establish a right to anti-Judaism for the generations of Christians who came after the time of Jesus Christ and the apostles. But very quickly, from the end of the first century and during the 20 others that followed, authors, theologians, dignitaries, sometimes even passed to posterity under the name of "Fathers of the Church", conducted a long course trial against Judaism, its founding texts, and its synagogues. Since we cannot be exhaustive, we present below and in chronological order some of these more or less famous figures, emphasizing each time that their anti-Jewish words have passed into posterity and have been woven into official or unofficial texts in Christian doctrine and teaching.

---

[85]   Léon Poliakov: History of anti-Semitism: Edition Calmann-Lévy. P 11.to 25
[86]   Jules Isaac: Teaching contempt. Bernard Grasset Edition - Paris

4.4 The difficult emergence of Christian identity from the biblical message and the pagan context

It is easy to understand that the Christian identity of the early days had great difficulty in emerging from Judaism on the one hand and paganism on the other. The historian of the Church Jules-Marcel Nicole speaks of these various deviations in his remarkable book, "Précis d'histoire de l'Église", he emphasizes one particularly, that of, "Gnostics", which theorized some knowledge with the ambition of knowing and explaining the mysteries of existence. The basis of their doctrine was to radically separate the universe between the spirit associated with good and matter associated with evil. In these basic principles, there were many similarities with Greek mythologies, in which the question of creation remained undetermined. God being perfect, he could not have created a world that was not. Intermediate minds had done all sorts of mediation work with humans that had led to their real situation here below. The problem of evil was not dealt in relation to the individual but rather by an observation of its presence and its nuisance for man, for society, and the material world in general. The same was true of the incarnation, it was incompatible with the complex mythologies that had taken place in the corpus of Christianity. Jesus Christ was therefore a spirit more than a man; from his sacrifice, one only wanted to retain the knowledge which he brought about, on man himself, and by it, salvation was accessible to him. This complex metaphysical architecture favored the emergence of a hierarchy between men that was equally so. There were the spirituals able to understand the mysteries, the psychics of lower rank could only hope for a very partial knowledge and finally the material spirits who were irremediably lost because they were unable to know and understand metaphysics. The distinction spirit/matter was very strong in the Gnostics and rarely corresponded to that which Jesus Christ made when he said, "What is born of the flesh is flesh, and what is born of the Spirit is Spirit" (Jn 3:6). Indeed, many of them advocated extreme asceticism, rejecting everything that seemed to be a concession to the pleasures of the flesh or simply of life; so, they condemned marriage and indulged in mortification of the body and prolonged[87] fasting. Others, on the other hand,

---

[87] Jules Marcel Nicole: Précis of Church History, Ed of the Bible Institute of Nogent-sur-Marne. P 27, 28

considered that matter, and therefore the flesh, was no longer important, and indulged in excesses in the other direction, without regard for the teachings of the Bible.[88]

5. Early Christianity: Leading Anti-Jewish Writers

5.1 Marcion of Sinope or the destruction of the biblical message[89]

Among the known Gnostics, the one who deviates most radically from the biblical teaching is Marcion de Sinope. He was born in 85, in the region of the Bridge on the shores of the Black Sea and died around 160 probably in Rome. He is the son of a wealthy shipowner of Sinope in present-day Turkey; he made the family business prosper. He is in Rome from the year 140 and is distinguished by every kind of generosity towards the Christian community. He appears as one of the very first destroyers of biblical thought as a whole. Indeed, he systematically opposes the Old and the New Testament, sees in the first only the God of anger and judgment, and totally rejects the Jewish teaching and tradition. In the New Testament, he sees the God of grace and mercy appearing in the fifteenth year of the reign of Emperor Tiberius, as a supreme being in Jesus Christ who did not go through the ordinary birth of men by a woman[90]. Unlike Jesus Christ, who declares, "Do not believe that I have come to abolish the law or the prophets" (Ma 5:17), Marcion develops a very personal doctrine in which he resolutely opposes the Jewish Law to the Gospel. He therefore discards the Torah and all that in the New Testament literature bears the mark of Judaism, proposing a summary text of the Gospel according to Luke and the ten epistles of the apostle Paul of his choice. He thus created another religion derived from Christianity, based solely on the writings of the apostles Paul and Luke, and for this reason, he was excommunicated by the representatives of the official Church in the year 144. However, he continued to preach his doctrine. He created his own "church", which would become a great success throughout the empire and even beyond, as far as Mesopotamia and the Persian Empire. His influence remained

---

[88] Gnostic - Gnosticism | Definition, Texts, Movements, & Influence | Britannica
[89] Marcion - Marcionite | History, Beliefs, Heresy, & Facts | Britannica
[90] Marcionite | History, Beliefs, Heresy, & Facts | Britannica

great in the so-called official Churches, both in the East and in the West. His doctrine has indeed enough to seduce; this God of love, who forgives and makes men happy, has no history; he is not incarnate since his origin is heavenly. This point of view remains close to the Greco-Latin mythologies, still a majority at that time in the empire. The rejection of the Law of the God of Israel in his crypto-Christianity makes it possible to escape from the normative power over existence it implies and therefore, from the guilt that it inexorably engenders in the individual, since this Law cannot be flawlessly fulfilled in the life of a man. Marcion's method is also very pleasant in more ways than one, since it allows him, at the same time, as a multitude of his imitators, to take in the Holy Scriptures only what suits him to the exclusion of any other part. Moreover, it opens the way to a very speculative hermeneutics, in which what is lacking in the rigor of exegesis can easily be compensated by interpretation of metaphysics, and also by tradition. Another quality that is found in Marcion is his ability to organize, structure, and develop a church parallel to those officially recognized. This is what brought him great success throughout the empire, where many communities, "crypto-Christian Marcionites," were born during his lifetime and long after his death. Is he the first theorist of anti-Judaism who will open a boulevard to racism against Jews that will come and grow with the centuries? Probably not if we want to be exhaustive about what was said and written in this field before him. However, it can be considered that it creates a new theological genre, based on the radical separation between the Old and New Testaments and the expurgation of any evocation of its Jewish origins. Lacking history and historiographical references, Marcion's crypto-Christianity de facto replaces the Bible to make history in its place. The thought, as the practice of Marcionism, will, despite the excommunication of the beginnings, find its place in official Christianity from the IVth and Vth centuries. This habit of not giving due value to the Old Testament and of not considering it as the eternal Word of God will be found throughout the history of Christianity. It will give rise to a convenient form of duality between the beneficial values of the New Testament, opposed to the decay of the Old one. For these reasons and given its importance in the evolution of Christianity, it is truly one of the leading theorists of anti-Judaism and will be followed in this by many others. Recovered unconsciously or consciously by many authors, we find in particular the praise of Marcion made by the Nazi ideologue, Alfred Rosenberg[91] in his book, "The myth of the Twentieth Century". As follows, he evokes his contribution to the formalization of racial Christianity: "In 150, the Greek Marcion defended the Nordic idea of a world order based on organic tension and hierarchies, in opposition to the Semitic representation of an arbitrary divine power and its limitless despotism". For this reason, he also rejects the "book of the law" of such "divinity", that is, the Hebrew Old Testament He inserted in his development the idea of a positive "Nordic" Christianity[92], which he believed was far superior to a negative Christianity of Semitic origin; "Negative and positive" Christianism's have always been in struggle and are fighting each other even harder today than in the past. The negative side is based on the Syro-Etruscan tradition, abstract dogmas and consecrated rites, the positive awakens again the forces of the Nordic blood, consciously and naively, as once the first Germans, when they invaded Italy and offered their lives to fertilize the uncultivated land". [93]

5.2 Justin of Nablus

He was a Theologian and philosopher of the early Church; he was born in the early years of the 2nd Century. He is also called "Justin martyr" because that is how he died, around 165 AD, condemned by the Roman justice of his time. He is known for helping to separate Christianity from Judaism radically. Indeed, in his book, "Dialogue with Tryphon", the latter being a rabbi, he develops the idea of the, "Verus Israel", the true Israel, opposed to "Vetus Israel", the ancient Israel. It is Christianity that would have become the "True Israel" as opposed to "the ancient Israel" that would have lost its place as the people of God and its witness to the world, because it did not recognize the ministry of Jesus Christ. This idea was enough to seduce the leaders of a Church that sorely lacked historical and doctrinal foundations after only a few decades of existence. Indeed, in their time, a large number of Christian communities were still, in fact, Judeo-Christian communities for which the risk of a return and a pure and simple reintegration into historical Judaism was great. Nevertheless, one can see how pretentious

---

[91] Alfred Rosenberg: Le Mythe du vingtième siècle, Éd Sorlot p. 71
[92] Alfred Rosenberg: Le Mythe du vingtième siècle, Éd Sorlot p. 34
[93] Alfred Rosenberg: Le Mythe du vingtième siècle, Éd Sorlot p. 34

and even more sacrilegious this idea is of having supplanted Israel in the heart of God was. Who can claim a similar title for himself? By what right, by what authority? This story of precedence over one another in the heart of God is reminiscent of the conversation between the apostles, which is found in the Gospel of the apostle Luke: "There was also a dispute among the apostles: which of them should be considered the greatest? Jesus said to them: The kings of the nations master them, and those who dominate them are called benefactors. May it not be the same for you. But let the greatest among you be as the least, and the ruler as the one who serves. For who is the greatest, who is at the table, or who serves? Isn't that the one at the table? And I, however, am among you as the one who serves." (Lk 22:24-27). Jesus clearly shows by his answer the type of government he wants to establish in his Church, that is, a government of service and mutual assistance; he who could have been, "at the table", is in fact, "the one who serves". This neglected Gospel word, like many others, has been replaced by condemnations, accusations like that of Justin of Nablus who does not hesitate to write in his Dialogue with Tryphon[94]: "After killing Christ, you do not even repent". Anger, threats, anathemas, relegation are all seeds of a deadly hatred against both Judaism, reduced to a role of permanent scapegoat and, by a boomerang effect, against the official Christianity, which will thus lose much of its soul and its message[95].

5.3 The "decide" people, Meliton of Sardis[96] (End of the[97] 2nd century)

Concerning this strange term, the Historical dictionary of the French language indicates that it is borrowed from Christian Latin, "deicida". It is found in this form in 1585, The Latin root of this word is formed of, "deus" which means God and, "caedere" become by contraction "cide" and which is found in homicide,

---

[94] Marcel Simon: Verus Israel, relations between Jews and Christians in the Roman Empire (135-425)

[95] Anti-Semitism: Yves Chevalier, L'Antisémitisme : Le Juif comme bouc émissaire, Cerf, 1998, publié avec le concours du CNRS et de la Fondation du judaïsme français

[96] Deicide people: papal bulls Concerning the Jews [archive]. Encyclopedia Judaica, Jewish Virtual Library

[97] Meliton of Sardis: On-Pascha-and-Fragments.pdf P 66 to 105

for a murder, parricide the murder of parents, infanticide the murder of a child, etc. However, the charge of crime "deicide" expressed in other words, goes back at least to the 2nd century, with Justin of Nablus. In his Dialogue with Tryphon, when he addresses the Jews in these terms, "Now again, in truth, your hand is raised for evil; because, after killing Christ, you do not even repent; you hate us, we who through him believe in the God and Father of the universe, you put us to death every time you obtain its power; always blaspheme you against him and his disciples, and yet we all pray for you and all men without exception". The term itself was written by theologian Peter Chrysologus[98], bishop of Ravenna from the year 433. Meliton of Sardis is a contemporary of Marcion; he exercised his ministry in the city of Sardes in Asia Minor, in present-day Turkey. He was one of the first authors to share his ideas on substitution theology. He thought that the Passover had no more reason to be, for what the apostle Paul writes in his epistle to the Corinthians on the comparison between the two leavens "the old and the new", tends to demonstrate, according to him, that Jesus Christ, being the new Passover, replaces the old, fallen into disuse. "Make the old leaven disappear, so that you may be a new dough, since you are unleavened, for Christ our Passover has been slain" (1 Cor 5:7). What is true in Christianity because it gives to this celebration the meaning of a new and universal Passover for the forgiveness of sins, is not true in the Jewish world because the first Passover retained all its value, whatever the Christian theologians may think. The idea of a forfeiture of the heritage of Judaism is everywhere present in Meliton of Sardis[99] because much of his apologetic work of Christianity is in fact based on the denunciation of Judaism, as this apostrophe to Israel sums up; "What have you done, Israel? You killed your Lord during the great feast. Listen, O ye descendants of the nations, and see. The Sovereign is outraged. God is slain by the hand of Israel". So, the first would be built on the ruins of the second. As for the example of Tertullian quoted later, the political and historical context can partly explain this tendency to look at Judaism as the party of the defeated. The defenders of Christianity are all the more inclined to go beyond the limits of gentleness and charity, which must

---

[98]   People of Deicide — Jules Isaac, Genèse de l'antisémitisme, Calmann Lévy, 1956. Philippe Bobichon, *JUSTIN MARTYR, Dialogue with Tryphon (Dialogue with Trypho), critical edition. VOLUME I: Introduction, Greek Text, Translation*, Fribourg, Editions Universitaires de Fribourg, 2003, 1120, p. 2-133, 6

[99]   Homily at Easter, 73-93. Meliton Easter, § 96

characterize them in principle since Judaism as religion, doctrine and philosophy is far from being defeated. This rivalry, these religious and ideological struggles, this anti-Jewish hatred, take root at this time in the Christianity of the masses, and they will remain there forever, pushing inexorably up to[100] the 20th century in its trunk and its ramifications the poison of anti-Judaism. In his "Easter Homily", Meliton of Sardis violently attacks the Jewish people, denouncing those who killed God with the accents of a court prosecutor; "God is put to death, the King of the Jews is condemned by the right hand of Israel". In this accusation, "God is put to death" brought against the Jews is in germ; this new concept stated above namely: the "deicide people". It is the perfect synthesis, the use of which will never be reserved in all of universal history, only to the Jewish people. Meliton of Sardis does not use this strange term, which will take place only later in doctrine, as in the homilies of some theologians of official Christianity. It is noted in Pope Gregory13th[101] in the 16th century, in his apostolic letter entitled "The ancient wickedness of the Jews", also in Jacques Bossuet[102], the famous bishop of the city of Meaux, in France in the 17th century when he wrote; "It was the greatest of all crimes: a crime hitherto unheard of, that is, the deicide, which also gave rise to a vengeance of which the world had not yet seen any example... The ruins of Jerusalem were still smoldering with the fire of divine wrath. It was not only the inhabitants of Jerusalem, but all the Jews, that you wanted to punish. At the time when the emperor Titus put the siege in front of the city, the Jews were there in a crowd to celebrate the Passover. [... Yet the hardening of the Jews, willed by God, made them so obstinate that after so many disasters, their city had to be taken by force.... Divine justice needed an infinite number of victims; it wanted to see eleven hundred thousand men lying in the square [...] and after that again, pursuing the remains of this disloyal nation, he dispersed them all over the earth". The French theologian, Félicité de Lamennais[103], is not left behind when he declares; "Since the deicide of the Jews, no greater crime had ever been committed". This concept, which wants to express what is the greatest crime of all time, is however empty if we refer to the definition that Jesus Christ gives of

---

[100] Anti-Judaism: Jules Isaac, L'Enseignement du mépris - suivi de L'Antisémitisme a-t-il des racines chrétiennes ? édition en 1962 et 2004
[101] Motu propio Gregory XIII 1581: Antiqua Judaeorum improbitas,
[102] Jacques-Bénigne Bossuet - LAROUSSE
[103] Lamennais, Essai sur l'indifférence en matière de religion, t. 1, 1817-1823, p. 313.

God himself in his dialogue with the Samaritan woman when he says; "God is Spirit, and those who worship him must worship him in spirit and in truth" (Jn 4:24). Upon reading this verse, the question that immediately arises in connection with the idea of deicide is: can one kill a spirit? Can we kill what is immaterial, what is metaphysical? Can we kill a mythology, a religion, an ideology, a particular conception of man and the universe? The answer is no, nothing, and no one can destroy what exists only in a man's heart and mind. So it is with ideas, traditions, and the whole metaphysical universe to which he refers to philosophize, to live, and to try to understand the meaning of his earthly pilgrimage. However, this accusing term of a crime that cannot exist will nevertheless flourish in the theology of Christianity. Although devoid of any real meaning, it will provoke in Europe from Christian antiquity until the middle of the 20th Century, all kinds of fantasies, outrages, conflicts, and monstrous persecutions against scattered Jewish minorities. This term remained in use in various forms until the 1970s, and in 1950, it was still present in the catechism for children. Thus appears the recurring theme of capital crime; of Israel-Cain, of Israel-Judas, of the murderous people, of the "deicide" people, who designate the Jews by this epithet, both withering and absurd. They are then left to the hatred of the Christian world. The work of the historian and sociologist Jules Isaac, on Jewish memory and interreligious dialogue with Catholicism, allowed this term in any form to be gradually excluded from rhetoric and Catholic theology.

5.4 Quintus Septimius Florens Tertullianus, known as Tertullian[104]

Tertullian is from Carthage, capital of ancient Tunisia. He was born between 150 and 160 and died around 220 AD. He left an indelible mark on Christianity because of the breadth of his knowledge and his zeal to defend it against its detractors and dividers. Very prolific, he left to posterity a considerable number of theological treatises on the most diverse subjects. One owes it, the first formalization of the dogma of the "Trinity", which is not defined in the New Testament. The Council of Constantinople in 381 will validate and clarify this concept, which has become one of the most important pillars of Christian

---

[104] tertullian.pdf

theology and has not been challenged by its three main branches: Protestantism, Catholicism, and Orthodoxy. He converted to Christianity around the age of 40. The spirit of holiness attracted him; he found there what corresponded to his deepest aspirations. In addition, Tertullian inaugurated a theology written in Latin which, for the time, was very innovative. In fact, originating in the eastern part of the empire, Christianity was written before him, only in Greek, mainly by the Hellenistic Judeo-Christian diaspora, of which some New Testament texts speak[105]. He fought vigorously against the heresy of Gnostics and particularly that of Marcion. However, in his treatise; "Against the Jews[106]", he joined him de facto in his condemnation of the people of Israel when he wrote: "Therefore, since it is recognized that the Jewish people are the first nation to come in the order of time, and that they were the first by the grace of their vocation to the Law, while our people are the youngest, whereas he only obtained the knowledge of divine mercy towards the end of time, there can be no doubt, following the sacred oracle, that the first people who are our eldest, that is, the Jewish people, are necessarily, enslaved to the youngest, and that the youngest, that is still the Christian people, does not triumph over the elder. For, if I ask the divine Scriptures, I see that the first of these two peoples, in time, abandoned God to serve idols, and, defecting from divinity, knelt before vile simulacrums, witnessing what the people said to Aaron: As soon as the gold that came from the bracelets of the women and the rings of the men, had been melted by the flame, and the head of a stupid animal had come out of the furnace, Israel, repudiating his God, paid homage to the idol in these words: 'These are the gods who have taken us from the land of Egypt'". The reference of this, "sacred oracle," by which the first is submitted to the second, in God's favor, is found in the book of Genesis (Gen 25:21-34). It builds on the difficult birth of Esau and Jacob, who were already fighting each other in the womb of their mother Rebekah. This initial conflict is followed by two others, which end at the detriment of Esau, since he loses successively his birthright and then the blessing of his father Isaac, who granted it instead to Jacob, under a fraudulent scheme (Gen 27:1-47). The eldest is therefore subject to the younger and his seed, which became the people of

---

[105] Acts 6.1 and Acts 9.29
[106] Tertullien-Oeuvres 3: Contre les Juifs (Adversus Judaeos)

Edom, often in struggle later against the people of Israel, will also be. The transposition of this biblical episode into Israel's relation to the Church is a risky extrapolation, far from being as obvious as Tertullian suggests; Indeed, why would one find in his text this idea of "enslavement" of Israel to the Church of nations and in this other about, "triumph", of it over Israël? Why these terms, which speak more of a campaign of annihilation than of the peaceful and unlimited progression of the biblical message among the nations? Where are the Words of Jesus; "I give you a new commandment: Love one another; as I loved you, too, love one another" (Jn 13:34) and also those of the apostle John in his first epistle; "Beloved, let us love one another; for love is of God, and whoever loves is born of God and knows God. He who does not love has not known God, for God is love" (1 Jo 4:7-8). On the contrary, these vengeful terms used foreshadow others that will come after Tertullian, where all kinds of bad feelings, complexes of superiority, rejection, condemnation, and finally hatred will be manifested. The politico-religious context could explain this semantic choice because Tertullian wrote in the years 190 to 220, at a time when everywhere triumphed the power of Rome. Jerusalem, for its part, was defeated and humiliated. The capital of Judaism, after losing its temple in 70 AD, had lost its name, since after the defeat of the revolt of Bar-Kokhba in 136, it is now called "Aelia-Capitolina". It is "trampled over by the nations" exactly as Jesus Christ announced in his time in this passage of the Gospel of Luke; "They will fall under the edge of the sword, they will be taken captive among all the nations, and Jerusalem will be trampled at the feet of the nations, until the times of the nations are fulfilled" (Lk 21:24). The Jews are no more than a people of migrants, a nation without land reduced for a long time, at the mercy of its sovereigns. Like many observers of his time, Tertullian notes the maturity of the Hebrew people with this sentence of great lucidity: "These events were announced to us because they had to be fulfilled and as they were fulfilled before our eyes, we recognize them". It is precisely in these conditions that the Gospel of peace finds all its meaning and its power to rebuild what has been destroyed. It is under these conditions that the words of blessings spoken by the God Almighty to Abram take on their full meaning when he declares; "I will bless those who bless you and I will curse those who curse you" (Gen 12:3). The words of Tertullian quoted above are not benevolent words to Israel, therefore they will be deprived of the blessing of the Lord and will bring instead to those who will take them back, the curse that was prophesized. They will, however, provide generations of students, teachers, and theologians, for centuries after him, with the doctrinal references necessary for the construction of militant anti-Judaism in the churches of the multitude. The other passage from Tertullian's writings from his title IV which calls for a similar commentary is this one; "Therefore, as we have established above that the prophets had foretold a new law, different from that which had been given to their fathers, when the Lord pulled them out of the land of Egypt, we are in the necessity of showing and proving, on the one hand, that the old law has ceased; on the other hand, that the new law, which had been promised, is now in force". A large part of Tertullian's demonstration is based on the fact that the Jews are now deprived of their spiritual center in Jerusalem; they can no longer make sacrifices in the temple, and therefore, they can no longer apply the Law of God. These words of Jesus Christ must be opposed to this affirmation on the Law of God; "For I say to you in truth, as long as heaven and earth do not pass away, there will not disappear from the law one iota or one stroke of a letter, until all has happened" (Mt 5:18). Unlike Tertullian, Jesus Christ thus seals for eternity the value of the Law of God. Whether it is applicable or unenforceable is not the issue, the important thing is to consider what is really applicable, namely its fundamental elements such as; the 10 commandments that each one strives in one's daily life to apply (Ex 20 1-26) and which have largely entered into the texts of our civil law. For academies around the world, Tertullian remains a master of Catholic Christian theology, especially, and he is cited as a reference for its doctrinal foundations[107]. He will be reproached, having joined for some time at the end of his life, the "Montanism[108]", a heretical current particularly rigorous in its doctrine and practicing a picky asceticism. Very few, however, will reproach him, the germs of anti-Judaism, much more dangerous in our opinion, which he sowed for future generations, in the heart of the Christian message. [109]

---

[107] Tertullian On the Trinity: Perichoresis | PDF | Logos (Christianity) | Trinity

[108] Tertullian — General Audience of Pope Benedict XVI, 30 May 2007

[109] Jules-Marcel Nicole: Précis d'Histoire de l'Église, Éditions de l'Institut Biblique de Nogent P 28.

5.5 Eusebius of Caesarea

He was born around 265 and died on May 30 , 339, bishop of Caesarea. He was very close to the emperor Constantine I[st], whom he was a great admirer. Eusebius of Caesarea was one of the first theorists of the Christian empire; for him political unification allowed religious unification with the state religion. The greatness of the Roman Empire and the triumph of Christianity are thus linked. The emperor is, in this context, the servant of God and as the image of the Son of God, the master of the universe. Eusebius of Caesarea thinks that the reign of Constantine is part of God's plan and that it was planned from all eternity. The emperor also receives the mission of guiding towards salvation and the Christian faith. It is actually the adaptation to Roman Christianity of the old Hellenistic idea of sacred royalty[110]. We have seen above that Jesus Christ did not form a nation in the political and institutional sense that we know of. This idea is therefore the personal extrapolation of a visionary who gives his fantasies the backing of a religion. It is very popular, not only in the generation of Eusebius of Caesarea, but much later, it will be at the heart of the political-social construction of the many kingdoms in Europe, including the most ephemeral of them. It has been a generator of endless wars and crusades between peoples, where pan-European ambitions, religion, law, dynasties, and peoples have mingled in an indescribable cacophony, ending in mutual annihilation. However, we cannot help but think of the wisdom of the Apostle John when he exhorts Christians not to go "further" in the doctrine of the Gospel when he says: "Whoever goes further and does not abide in the doctrine of Christ has no God; he who dwells in this doctrine has the Father and the Son" (2Jn 1:9). Returning to this idea formulated by Eusebius of Caesarea, we know that it is concomitant with the conversion of the emperor Constantine[111] that historians place in the course of the years 312 to 324 AD. Despite his heavy past as a man of war, intrigue, and murder to access power, far away from the Christian virtues, Eusebius of Caesarea is a fervent admirer. It seems that the conjunction of political and religious forces led to this time, a sort of apotheosis prefiguring the reign of God on earth, the end of history, and

---

[110] Caesaropapism History, Characteristics & Significance | Study.com

[111] The Life of the Blessed Emperor Constantine by Eusebius Pamphilus. Modernized and introduced by Stephen Tomkins. Edited and prepared for the web by Dan Graves.

the eternal golden age of the reign of men on earth. This victorious emperor converted to Christianity, intervened in religious life; he convoked the councils, set certain rules, appointed and dismissed the bishops, he inaugurated the era of "Caesar-Papism" by submitting "the church institution" to the will of political power. However, the message of the Gospel does not allow this confusion of powers; the empire becoming «Christian" is only a view of the human spirit. It is as if each of its citizens, from the greatest to the humblest, were converted to Jesus Christ by the sole will of the emperor. Christianity of personal conversion and submission to the texts of the Bible disappears; it is replaced by the socio-religious message, enameled with multiple theological wanderings, and intended to bring the multitude of pagans of the empire into the fold of the church institution. From then on, another Christianity appears; it is a hybrid version of it, of which the New Testament is no more than the empty shell and the moral guarantee for all kinds of enterprises of domination and conquest. It has become authoritarian, belligerent, imperialist, idolatrous of its works, and Caesar-Papism is gradually being reversed; it is now the church institution that directs kings and princes in Europe, from the early Middle Ages. This concept will unfortunately spread like wildfire in all its parts, from north to south and from east to west. It will bring with it a multitude of abuses of power on the human conscience, and it will distort the meaning of the Christian message by making it auxiliary to the royal power. Much later in the 17th century, it would still be in force, and its struggle against the Protestants of its own country, King Louis XIV[112] of France would declare, to assert national unity around his person, "A king, a faith, a law." Concerning Judaism, this conception will have serious consequences because if the populations of the empire and the kingdoms which succeeded it are reputed "Christian", why and how would a Jewish minority distinguish itself by witnessing to its spiritual and cultural difference? Would this not be a challenge to the dual authority of the prince and the church? The persistence of Judaism throughout ancient, medieval, and modern Europe, the rejection of a forced conversion to a Christianity far removed from its biblical foundations, will lead to the longest persecution that history has ever known, against a minority, against its religion,

---

[112] Louis XIV vs French Protestants - La révocation de l'édit de Nantes et ses conséquences (1685-1700) - Musée protestant

its culture, and even its physical integrity. It is unique in universal history because it is inscribed in the founding texts of the so-called Christian civilization, and it will be interspersed with periods of appeasement, more or less long depending on the places and circumstances. However, even after the emancipation of the Jews that appeared in the 18th century, they will remain suspended in a Europe durably marked by "The Teaching of Contempt", according to the expression of the historian Jules Isaac and the title of his work on this historical as well as theological theme. Eusebius of Caesarea was one of the first theorists of the Christian empire, and he was to be as much a historian of the Church as an uncompromising prosecutor against Judaism. Indeed, in his book, "Ecclesiastical history" he makes this comment about the destruction of Jerusalem and the dispersion of the Jews in all nations: "Such was the punishment of the Jews for the crime and ungodliness they had committed against the Christ of God". In his other hagiographic work, "Life of Constantine[113]", he lends to the emperor these words expressed at the Council of Nicaea; "It is regrettable to hear the Jews boast that without them, Christians cannot observe their Easter: moreover, since their deicide, they are blinded, cannot serve as a guide to anyone". In describing quickly, the emergence of this so-called Christian empire which took place after that of Rome and Constantinople, one cannot help but think of the warnings which the apostle Paul addresses to the Corinthians when he declares to them; "Already you are satisfied, already you are rich, without us you have begun to reign. And may you indeed reign, that we may also reign with you" (1 Cor 4:8). Without the authentic message of the Bible, without going through the Cross of Jesus Christ, without going through repentance or the New Birth, theorists believed they could build an easy Christianity for everyone, at the service of their hierarchy and the kings of the earth. Here again we think of these words of the Lord spoken at the time of his mock trial: "My kingdom is not of this world," Jesus also replied; "If my kingdom were of this world, my servants would have fought for me so that I would not be delivered to the Jews; but now my kingdom is not from here" (Jn 18). If we can no longer judge these different authors of, "the Christian empire" or those of anti-Judaism, some of whom are even among those who were called by abuse of language, "The fathers of the church", it is

---

[113]   The life of Constantine by Eusebius.pdf Ch 18, P1306

clear that they left, but that their writings remained and that they germinated over time until they became a deadly poison for generations of believers up to us.

5.6 Augustine of Hippo

Better known as Saint Augustine, he was born in 354 in Thagaste, a town about a hundred km south of the city of Annaba in present-day Algeria and died in 430 in Hippone, a city of which he was bishop for a long time. In the Catholic tradition, he is considered as one of the "Fathers of the Church" so much his influence was great on his doctrinal and theological formation. Concerning relations with Judaism, he supports the theology of substitution and judges the Jews as the "assassins of Jesus Christ". He calls the specialists of the Talmud, falsifiers, and his vehemence against the Jews is reminiscent of that of Justin of Nablus, Tertullian, John Chrysostom, and of many other dignitaries of the church institution. Like most of them, he thinks that the lowering of the Jewish people is the expression of God's judgment against his people. Now abandoned and abandoned by God, Jews are deprived of the right to interpret and comment on their own religious and cultural texts. They have only one role to play, that of bearing witness before the nations of the truth of the judgments of the Lord, and their mission is to be curators of the texts of the Law of God and of the Mishnah. They must especially guard those who evoke the coming of the Messiah and thus confirm that Jesus Christ is indeed the one they expected and rejected. The historian Jules Isaac quotes this passage from the teaching given by Augustine to his students on the passion of Jesus Christ, where the dramaturgy and repetition of the word "Jew" exaggerate the feeling of reprobation and horror aroused against the deicide people; "The end of the Lord has come, the Jews hold him, the Jews insult him, the Jews bind him, they crown him with thorns, they stain him with their spits, they scourge him, they condemn him with insults, they hang him from the wood, they search his flesh with their spears[114]". The passion of Augustine carries him far from the historical truth, since we know that it was the Romans who put Jesus Christ on the cross and who finished him with the spear that pierced his side.

---

[114]   Jules Isaac: Jesus and Israel P 162 E ditions Fasquelle. Quote: Sermon to Catechumens, 10, Latin Patrology XL,634.

This[115] capital judgment of Augustine of Hippo can be added: "The Jews were sons of God, but now they are sons of Satan. The true image of the Hebrews is Judas Iscariot, who sold the Lord for money. The Jew will never understand the scriptures and will forever bear the guilt of Jesus". The influence of Augustine of Hippo would be great in the propagation of the absurd and monstrous idea of the "deicide people". Indeed, he is one of those who introduced into the Catholic and Orthodox liturgy of Good Friday, what was called in Latin, "the improper", that is, the reproaches that Jesus Christ makes to his people for the trial and crucifixion he suffered. These litanies, sometimes chanted and recited piously in religious buildings, have done much to transmit reproach and curse into the European peoples against the Jewish people. They were suppressed in Catholicism after the Second Vatican Council only in 1965 however, they are still present in Orthodox churches. The transmission of such venom lasted about 1600 years, and still, its flow has not completely dried up today. It should be noted, however, that Augustine of Hippo did not want physical persecution of the Jews; because of their memory function, they must be preserved, but in a permanent status of inferiority. This is confirmed when he declares that they were not exterminated but dispersed; so that not having the faith that could save them, they were at least useful to us by their memories. "Our enemies by heart, they are by their books, our supporters and our witnesses".

5.7 John Chrysostom

John Chrysostom was born in Antioch about 344 or a few years later, he died in 407, after having been archbishop of Constantinople. He is one of those whom the Catholic tradition has called "The Fathers of the Church". This classification of authors, which has been in progress since the 16th century, has the effect of giving additional credit and authority to their spiritual and intellectual heritage. Although it has retained all its interest from the point of view of the historiography of Christianity of the East as well as of the West, the same cannot be said from the theological point of view, since we know how far it has strayed from its fundamental truths, and particularly regarding the relations

---

[115] Escaping the great deception" de Derek Frank

with Judaism. John Chrysostom is one of the "fathers of the church", the most venerated in the mythology of this imperialist Christianity which reaches in its time a form of apogee and preeminence over all other forms of worship. One speaks of John Chrysostom only by adding the epithet of "Holy" despite the violence and insults contained in his words towards Judaism. He is the author of the anti-Jewish doctrinal texts, "Adversus Judaeos " taken up from generation to generation, by both Eastern and Western Christianity. In addition to his filthy language, he exposes in his pages the doctrine of substitution in quasi-military terms: Christianity emerged victorious from its struggle against Judaism. For him, the destruction of Jerusalem and its temple deprived the Jewish religion of its spiritual center. Any sacrifice to the Lord has become impossible, and nothing that has been restored after this capital defeat can replace it. With regard to the Synagogue, he declared that it is something like, "lupanars" and about the Jews, he uses the language of the taverns when he qualifies them as, "treacherous bandits, destroyers, debauchees, like pigs, surpassing wild beasts in ferocity, who sacrifice their children to the devil, a criminal assembly of assassins of Christ". There are several sermons in particular where his hatred to Judaism and Jews is expressed; in the first, he claims that the Jews are ignorant, unable to understand their sacred texts: "They are ungodly, miserable, dogs, stubborn brains. Their people are like a herd of brutes and ferocious beasts. They have rejected Christ, so they are fit only for evil". The competition with the Synagogue must have been fierce at that time because in this letter he puts Christians before a radical alternative when he told them; "If the Jewish doctrines excite your admiration, you must find the Christian doctrines false". He exhorts them to flee the teaching of Judaism in this way; "Do not attend their synagogues, do not follow the Sabbath, fasting and other Jewish rites. If you meet Judaizers, warn them of the danger because you are the army of Christ, do not let yourself be diverted it would be extreme madness". John Chrysostom also said: "As God hates Jews, it is the duty of Christians to hate them" and also: "Many, I know, respect Jews and think that their current way of life is respectable. That is why I hasten to uproot and demolish this terrible opinion... the synagogue is not only a brothel and a theater, it is also a den of thieves and a shelter for wild beasts... when God abandons a people, what hope of salvation remains for them? When God abandons a place, that place becomes a home of demons". In another sermon he wants to show the vanity of the Passover sacrifice with this statement: "Do you not know that the Jews sacrifice in every part of the earth, except in the only place where the sacrifice is valid, that is, in Jerusalem; Do you not know that only there can they celebrate the Passover, as the Law says[116]; so do not conform to their illusory Passover." Other sermons preached in Antioch treat the Jews as "thieves, unclean, debauched, rapacious, miserly, craftsman of tricks, oppressors of the poor..." They made their crimes worse by immolating Christ". There is no longer any reflection or modesty in the vehement speeches of John Chrysostom against the Jews, he even goes so far as to proclaim against them total war and the call to murder. He declares: "in accordance with the sentiments of the saints, I hate the Jews and their synagogues, this is where the abode of demons is, they are just good to be slaughtered". These words[117], paraphrased from the quotations of "L'Adversus Judaeos[118]" by Walter Ze'ev Laqueur, a naturalized American German historian and political scientist, will have a great fortune in the following centuries. If a "saint" can thus appeal to the murder of the Jews, how much more reason, the simplest of the king's subjects will have the legitimate right to do so. Barely out of paganism, the popular masses left without instruction on Christianity and on its Bible roots, will soon retain from it only one easily applicable truth, namely: the right to hatred against the Jews. Following John Chrysostom, there will be theorists and theologians who will follow in his footsteps in a long-running anti-Jewish crusade, as for example, those quoted by the historian of anti-Semitism Bernard Lazarus[119] [120] Epiphanes, Diodorus of Tarsus, Theodore of Mopsuestes, Theodoret of Cyr, Cosmas Indicapleuste, Athanasius the Sinaite, Synesius, among the Greeks; Hilaire de Poitiers, Prudentius, Paul Orose, Sulpice Sévère, Gennadius, Venantius Fortunatus, Isidore of Seville among the Latins. The fatal legacy of John Chrysostom will be found even in the homilies of the clergy before and during the period of the Second German Revolution in the 20th century. This anti-Jewish

---

[116] Jean Chrysostome, Adversus Judæos, I, éditeur Migne, 1, p 847 & 848 - 8, I p 848 - 8, p 855

[117] Anti-Semitism (Lazarus)/IV - Antisemitism from Constantine to the eighth century – Bernard Lazare

[118] Walter Laqueur, The Changing Face of Antisemitism: From Ancient Times To The Present Day, Oxford University Press, 2006, p. 47 - 48.

[119] John Chrysostom, Adversus Judaeos, 1, 6.

[120] Bernard Lazare: Antisemitism Ed Léon Chailley 1894 – P 63 – 96

conformity will thus be part of the DNA of the Christianity of the multitude until very recently.

5.8 Jerome de Stridon and others....

He is also better known by the title "saint", which was attributed to him in Catholicism from the 16th century. He was born in 347 or 348 in Stridon, a locality disappeared today on the border between Slovenia and Croatia. He is the author of an extensive bibliography on the first historians and theologians of Christianity, including Origen and Eusebius of Caesarea. He is also the author of the Latin translation of the entire Bible, that is, for Christians, of the New and Old Testaments, gathered in what is called the "Vulgate". Jerome of Stridon began this work with the translation of the four Gospels, then he tackled the letters and epistles of the apostles. For the Latin version of the Old Testament texts, he relied on the one written in Greek, called the "Septuagint". Its influence is considerable in Catholicism because it gave it its indispensable doctrinal base, especially after the Protestant Reformation, which from the beginning of its history in 1517, had put in honor the whole Bible. He is recognized as one of the four Latin "Fathers of the Church" with Ambrose of Milan, Augustine of Hippo, and Gregory 1st. The Orthodox consider him a saint, he is a prolific writer, he has attached himself in all his work to the accuracy of the terms used in his translations of Hebrew and Greek, as in the comments he made. From this point of view, he greatly advanced hermeneutics in early Christianity. Highly dependent on Jewish culture and thought for his work, he frequents sages, rabbis and scholars in Bethlehem who bring him closer to their centuries-old teachings. Despite this deep rootedness in Judaism, Jerome of Stridon is a purveyor of texts violently anti-Jewish, he insults them by these words "Judaic serpents", he made of the traitor Judah, the emblem of the Jewish people, mocks their prayers which would be according to him, "than a donkey roar". He assured[121] , "... that a foul spirit had taken hold of the Jews" and he, who had learned Hebrew at the school of the rabbis said, no doubt thinking of the curse of[122] the Mines, whose meaning he distorted: "We

---

[121] Bernard Lazare : L'Antisémitisme Ed Léon Chailley 1894 P 63 - 96
[122] Jules Isaac: Israel and Jesus Ed Fasquelle P 361

must hate the Jews who, every day, insult Jesus Christ in their synagogues". As an interpreter of God's thoughts of Israel, he declared, no doubt more out of unconsciousness than daring; "there could never be an atonement for the Jews: God has always hated them". In his exegesis of the book of Zephaniah, he supports the thesis of the deicide people, which will find its place in the "patristic corpus", that is, the founding texts of the doctrine of the Western church left by the "Fathers of the Church". According to the French historian and writer Valéry Larbaud, the Vulgate accompanied by the comments of Jérôme de Stridon is: "one of the cornerstones of our civilization". The author of this conclusion probably did not measure to what extent this "cornerstone" in question could be heavy to bear and contained in it the curse that is in anti-Judaism. Soon, it would sporadically reverberate in all European nations until the volcano of hatred against the Jewish people, which was unleashed with the Nazi enterprise. The following quote from one of Jerome de Stridon's commentaries on the downfall of the Jewish people has the grandiloquent accents of an ancient drama: "This day is a day of fury, a day of distress and anguish, a day of devastation and destruction, a day of darkness and darkness, a day of clouds and fog...[123]". It is not without a certain sense of sadness that this last expression: "of clouds and fog", transformed into: "night and fog" became the code name of the deportation order of the Jews and opponents of the third[124] German Empire (NN, Nacht und Nebel), signed by Marshal Keitel[125] on December 7, 1941[126] . This evocative expression of darkness and mystery was taken up by the French filmmaker Alain Resnais in 1956 for his moving film on the deportation of Jews and concentration camps in occupied Europe during the Second World War. Speaking of the prayer of the Jews facing the wall of lamentations in Jerusalem, Jerome de Stridon says: "To this day, these hypocritical tenants are forbidden to come to Jerusalem, for they are the murderers of the prophets and especially of the last of them, the Son of God; unless they come to cry because they have been permitted to lament over the ruins of the city, for payment[127]". In fact, at the time when he wrote, Jerusalem no longer existed, it was renamed, it was called: "Aélia Capitolina" and

---

[123] Léon Poliakov: History of anti-Semitism, p 33 Antiquity Edition Calmann-Lévy
[124] Bernard Lazare: Antisemitism Ed Léon Chailley 1894 p 63 - 96
[125] Wilhelm Keitel: Biography | Holocaust Encyclopedia
[126] Night and Fog Decree | Holocaust Encyclopedia
[127] Jerome of Stridon: Pilgrimage to the Holy Land.

the Jews were forbidden to settle there, it was a city of Roman garrison where meet: soldiers, officials, merchants and craftsmen from all parts of the empire in the east. Curiously, no nation will settle permanently in this country, soon being almost entirely abandoned. From the Byzantine Empire to that of the Ottomans expelled in 1917, the country will never again regain political independence. The very name of Palestine will be lost, the conquest of the whole Middle East in the 7th century by Islam will not change anything to this relegation. Largely returned to the desert, Judea, Samaria and Galilee are only roads, places of passage, crisscrossed by caravans, between the great metropolises of the north in Syria, Anatolia and those of the south in Egypt. It is as if; without the presence of the Jewish people, this country had ceased to exist... What about the other theorists of anti-Judaism? It is impossible to list them all because they are so numerous and make the repetition of hateful words and feelings the foundation of their allegiance to a Christianity ever more distant from its biblical roots. Some of these figures are still highly regarded in Catholicism, as in Eastern Orthodoxy. It is about, Gregory of Nyssa (circa 331-394) who denounces, "the killers of the Lord", he reproaches the Jews for being," ... unbelievers who refuse to accept the testimony of Moses and the prophets on the Trinity and the Incarnation". We can also mention Origen (v. 185-253) also recognized and revered as, "Father of the Church" in Catholicism. He is the author of an impressive body of Old and New Testament studies. He was one of the first, if not the first theologian, to make the Jewish people collectively responsible for the crucifixion of Jesus, where the texts of the Gospels speak only of the chief priests and the Sanhedrin. Following this deliberate and sustained confusion, it was possible to theorize the theology of the replacement of Israel by the Church in the heart of God. This list must be concluded, for it teaches us nothing more than the hatred, contempt, and pride of those who have claimed the title of judge and prosecutor against the people of God. This is what one of the very first adversaries of Israel, namely Balaam, did not want to do (Num 31:8-16), who, despite the injunctions of his king Balak to curse Israel, blessed him three times instead. Let us also remember, Hilaire de Poitiers (300-367), he left behind definitive judgments on the Jewish people such as this one; "... a perverse people whom God has cursed forever".[128] We know of

---

[128] Night and Fog, The film | Holocaust Encyclopedia

him that he refused to eat with Jews and said of them: "The Jews are a people who glorify iniquity".[129] Ignatius of Antioch, born around 35 BC and died in martyrdom around 116 or 118, was bishop of this city between 110 and 115. He distinguished himself by practicing a severe separation between the Judeo-Christians, the different groups interpreting the person of Jesus, rather mythologically and in his eyes, the true Christians recognizing the earthly experience of Jesus-Christ, submitted to the bishops and gathered around the Eucharist. He did not grant Christian identity to these movements, and with regard to the former, he goes so far as to affirm that Judaism is the antithesis of Christianity. Much later,[130] with the Protestant Reformation of the 16th century, a new era opened for Christianity; this return to the simple and eternal teachings of the Word of God was a great hope for the peoples of Western Europe, enslaved to the only Catholic version of the message. However, Luther also sank into virulent anti-Semitism at the end of his life. He would speak foul words against the Jews, especially these; «Burn their synagogues and their schools; That which has not burned, bury it so that no stone or waste remains. In the same way they enter their houses and destroy them. Take their prayer books and their Talmuds. For in them there is nothing but ungodliness, lies, curses and curses. Forbid their rabbis to teach, on pain of death or mutilation". John Calvin, another great reformer of the sixteenth century who came a few years after Luther said of the Jews; "I have had many discussions with many Jews: I have never seen a drop of piety or a grain of truth or innocence; no, I have never found common sense in any Jew". He also wrote: "The stiff and rotten neck of the Jews deserves that they are constantly oppressed and without measure or end and that they die in their misery and without the mercy of anyone". One can be surprised at what the reformers have agreed to, the most extremist positions of the most anti-Jewish Catholics. In fact, they opened up the texts of the Bible to everyone's interpretation, but they excluded from grace those who spoke best of them, both in the apostolic letters of the New Testament and in the meditations of the entire Old Testament. Understand who can; of this major contradiction, will be reborn in a great part of Protestantism, all the ancient prejudices, the various judgments

---

[129] Night and Fog Decree | Holocaust Encyclopedia
[130] Jerome de Stridon - Pilgrimage to the Holy Land.

and condemnations against Judaism. From this point of view, the Reforms of the 16th century resemble the most sectarian and anti-Jewish Catholicism by the positions of their respective founders. Later, Luther's memory would be enlisted in the anti-Semitic crusade boasted by the theorists of Nazism. [131] [132]

6. The Endless List of Anti-Jewish Words Impossible to update

We have cited some of the most emblematic authors of anti-Judaism in the tumultuous beginnings of Christianity. If the list had to be drawn up to this day, it would be endless, no more than it would be relevant to make a scholarly exegesis of what they left to posterity since together they all converge towards the same idea developed above, that is, the downfall of Israel and its replacement by Christianity. What we will do in the following paragraphs is to highlight the common features of anti-Judaism and contrast them with the texts of the Bible. Thus, we will be able to see what the good personal attitude is and what is the good teaching of the Church towards Judaism. Everyone will then be able to realize that by approaching the letter as well as the spirit of the Bible, one reaches the harmony of Judeo-Christian relations without sacrificing the truth of the message. This is what the CNEF (National Council of Evangelicals in France) did in 2020, in its remarkable collective work, "Antisemitism[133]; it is time to act"

6.1 Forgetting the language of love and respect.

"May your gentleness be known to all men. The Lord is near" Philippians 4:5. The New Testament gave no other means to the Apostles and subsequently to their successors to spread the Good News, than the gentleness and love of others, as a witness to the transformation of their hearts. What a personal challenge, nothing else to assert and support one's convictions with others than love and respect for those who are like him, who also represent the image of God, and

---

[131] Derek Frank (former pastor in Geneva) "Escaping the great deception."
[132] Escaping the great deception" de Derek Frank
[133] Anti-Semitism – Led by E tienne Lhermenault. Édition: Excelsis

who also need the grace of God. Thus, the witness is stripped of any form of artifice, he has nothing to offer except the personal experience he has made of his own conversion to Jesus Christ and the benefits that were given him. We remember the magnificent example of the Apostles Peter and John who went to the Temple and to whom a beggar asked for alms; "Peter and John went up to the temple together at the time of prayer: it was the ninth hour. There was a man born lame, who was carried and placed every day at the door of the temple called the Beauty, to ask alms to those who entered the temple. This man, seeing Peter and John going in, asked them for alms. Peter, like John, looked at him, and said, Look at us. And he looked at them attentively, expecting to receive something from them. Then Peter said to him: I have neither silver nor gold; but what I have, I give you: in the name of Jesus Christ of Nazareth, rise up and walk. And taking him by the right hand, he made him rise. At the same time his feet and ankles became firm; With a jump he stood and began to walk. He entered the temple with them, walking, jumping, and praising God." (Acts 3:1-9). Peter and John take great care to specify: "I have neither silver nor gold". Like them, the Church has nothing, difficult for some to get used to this reality, which is also a primary truth highlighted in this other passage: "I am the vine, you are the branches. He who dwells in me and in whom I dwell bears much fruit, for without me you can do nothing" (Jn 15:5). Where is the wealth of the Church? How to convey the message of his kingdom made of; "justice, peace and joy" as the apostle Paul clearly defined it in his epistle to the Romans (Rom 14:17). The Church, having nothing of its own, must rely solely on God's intervention to transmit its message. No force other than that of God himself can convince a heart of "sin, justice and judgment" as the Gospel of John states in this passage; "And when he comes, he will convince the world of sin, righteousness, and judgment" (John 16:8). But quickly on the scale of universal history, by disbelief, by complacency, by inferiority complex, passing from one compromise to another in relation to the texts of the Bible, the Church becomes both in East and in West this institution that we know, of an indecipherable heaviness and opacity for the human heart. Very far from the simplicity of the Gospel, it now relies on the power of the emperor, then on that of the kings who followed him, in all Europe, after the fall of the empires of the West and East. It dominated by the sword, later with the inquisition, it even created a police force of dogma with powers of constraint very extended to the right of life and death on those who fall under its judgment. By levying the ecclesiastical tax, it became immensely rich and built sumptuous buildings for worship, as well as for its great servants, cardinals, bishops, and other dignitaries. It interfered everywhere and defended by iron and by the verb its own empire which extended in a few centuries, on an immense perimeter, even superior to that of the two former Roman empires combined.

6.2 The will to win more than to convince.

We see throughout the New Testament that the transmission of the Gospel can only be done by the action of the Holy Spirit in hearts. This means that it is based both on a personal experience of conversion to which knowledge is added that it is in conformity with the teachings of Jesus Christ. The witness tells the listener what the circumstances of his encounter with Jesus Christ were and how he will continue his earthly pilgrimage with him. His mission to bear witness is therefore not only punctual, it lasts during his lifetime, since he is also to give testimony by his actions and words, of the works of the Lord Jesus Christ into his life. With this necessary perspective on the transmission of the Gospel, it is easier to understand the infinite precautions taken by the Apostle Paul to convince his audience when he is in the gallery of the Aeropagus in Athens and said; "Knowing then the fear of the Lord, we seek to convince men" 2 Corinthians 5:11. This passage clearly indicates Paul's approach; He tries to convince men and the implication is that this is neither easy nor improvised. The beginning of his sentence is like a prerequisite to this research, because he specifies that knowledge of the fear of the Lord is indispensable to this search. We measure here the extreme precautions that the apostle takes to convince. Indeed, we see that he would be able to adapt to each of the different audiences, as well as to each person he would meet with, in his ministry, as an evangelist. In front of the Areopagus in Athens, for example in Acts 17, he witnessed his listeners and asked them about a metaphysical problem that they had not solved, namely that of creation. Some Epicurean and Stoic philosophers began to speak with him. And some said, what does this discourser mean? Others, hearing him proclaim Jesus and the resurrection, said: It seems that he announces foreign deities. Then they took him, and led him to the Areopagus, saying, could we know what this new doctrine you're teaching? Because you make us hear strange things. So, we would like to know what that could be. All the Athenians and foreigners living in Athens spent their time only to say or to listen to news. Paul, standing in the midst of the Areopagus, said: Athenian men, I find you in every respect extremely religious. For, while walking through your city and considering the objects of your devotion, I even discovered an altar with this inscription: To an unknown god! What you reverence without knowing is what I'm telling you. The God who made the world and all that is in it, being the Lord of heaven and earth, does not dwell in temples made of man's hand; he is not served by human hands, as if he needed anything, he who gives all life, breath, and all things. He caused all men, coming out of one blood, to dwell on the whole surface of the earth, having determined the length of time and the bounds of their abode; he willed that they seek the Lord, and that they strive to find him groping, though he is not far from each of us, for in him we have life, movement, and being. This is what some of your poets have also said: Of him we are the race... Thus, being the race of God, we must not believe that divinity is like gold, silver, or stone, carved by the art and industry of man. God, regardless of the times of ignorance, now announces to all men, in all places, that they should repent, because He has fixed a day when He will judge the world according to righteousness, by the man He has appointed, what he gave to all a certain proof by raising him from the dead... When they heard of the resurrection of the dead, some laughed, and others said, «We will hear you about this another time". So, Paul withdrew from among them. Some, however, became attached to him and believed, Dionysius the Areopagite, a woman named Damaris, and others with them" (Acts 17:18-34). This remarkable work of pedagogy to bring his hearers to faith and salvation in Jesus Christ begins with what their intelligence can comprehend: universalism of the human condition. Indeed, he says that we came out of the same blood and that our life at all is limited in time. In his short presentation, however, he emphasizes the need for repentance in order to approach God because "he judges the earth and its inhabitants" according to his justice. This speech is not easy and the text shows that its result is rather meager; many laughed, others politely walked away, verse 30 tells us that only a few became attached to him and believed." This passage also emphasizes that preaching is a risky exercise because not all are convinced, many turn away from the Word of Jesus Christ and that of his witnesses. In this passage the Apostle also emphasizes: "All Scripture is inspired by God, and useful to teach, to convince, to correct, to instruct in righteousness". 2 Timothy 3:16. It demonstrates how much is the transmission of the gospel to be done in strict doctrinal conformity with the whole Word of God. Thus, it was necessary to preserve the transmission of the Gospel, that is, by witnessing and conforming to the teachings of Jesus Christ, with the risk of not being understood by some. But the historical evolution of Christianity shows a completely different path; whether it is the difficulty of preaching, the persecution or the illusion of the exercise of power, Christianity from the Fourth Century on, seeks more to win than to convince. Its evolution is reminiscent of the one that Jesus Christ reproached the Judaism of his time. Indeed, it is structured around the Bishop of Rome in its western part into a powerful center of spiritual but also temporal power, as we described earlier in part 2.4. It is a huge, sprawling organization that, from Rome, holds kings and people under its spiritual control and governs them more than it seems, with an iron hand. By fighting the innumerable heresies that weaken its conception of Christianity, it departs from the simplicity of the Gospel and does not forget to fight Judaism either.

6.3 Forgetting the prophetic words of the Bible about the restoration of Israel.

There has not been for the church of spontaneous generation, we have seen in the first part, that it was born in and through the synagogue. So, whether it please or not, the Church is closely associated with the destiny of Israel. Jesus strengthens this bond when he tells the Samaritan woman: "You worship what you do not know; we worship what we know because salvation comes from the Jews" (Jn 4:22). This capital word is covered with the seal of eternity, it means, among other things, that the teachings and experiences of Judaism over the centuries have kept all their value for the Christianity as a whole and for individual born again Christian throughout the centuries. The proof of this is that in all the Evangelical Churches of the whole world, the texts of Judaism, of the Old as well as of the New Testament are abundantly read and commented by the servants of God for the people of the faithful. Moreover, there is in this word, the thought, which the pagans worshipped for a long time, what they did not know according to their imagination while, from the highest antiquity, the Jews sought the Eternal God, creator of all things and they found him. They did so first with their patriarchs and then, with Moses all the people were instructed and finally, the succession of their kings and prophets helped to perfect their search and knowledge of God. This, in spite of its errors at times, has been constant and constitutes the distinctive element of Judaism with other peoples. There is also in this thought, the vision of the future with the persecutions that the Jews will have to suffer from the so-called Christians. But above all, there is the restoration of Israel prophesied several times in the Old Testament as in the prophet Jeremiah when he declares; "Thus saith the Lord: Behold, I bring the captives of the tents of Jacob; I have compassion for his dwellings; The city will be rebuilt on its ruins, the palace will be restored as it was." (Jer 30:18). As in the days of Ezra and Nehemiah, the restoration of the city and its mansions is only a reflection of the restoration of hearts. This is what the prophecy speaks of constantly; more than the restoration of walls, it is the restoration of hearts that counts for the Lord the Lord. About 740 BC, during the reign of King Zechariah in Israel, Amos the one who was not even a recognized prophet, had made a remarkable description of what the restoration of Israel could be. We see men at work, sowing and plowing a prosperous country, buildings that were once demolished and now rebuilt and converted for residents from all over the world. This is a vision very close to what happened in 1948, about 2700 years later, with the declaration of independence of the country of Israel proclaimed by its then Prime Minister, Mr. David Ben Gurion. "At that time I will lift up the house of David from its fall, and I will repair its breaches, and I will restore its ruins, and I will rebuild it as it once was, so that they may possess the remnant of Edom, and all the nations upon which my name was invoked, who will do these things. Behold, the days are coming, saith the LORD, Wherein the ploughman shall follow the reaper closely, And he that treadeth the grape shall he that soweth the seed, Wherein the wort shall flow out of the mountains, and shall flow forth from all the hills. I will bring back the captives of my people from Israel; They will rebuild the devastated cities and inhabit them, plant vines and drink the wine, establish gardens and eat the fruits. I will plant them in their land, and they will no longer be taken from the land I have given them, says the Lord your God (Am 9:11-15). Never has this prophecy been erased from the Bible, however, some theologians believed they could say that Israel's recovery would never take place. We read this, under the pen of Origen[134], theologian of the 3rd century; "We can therefore confidently affirm that the Jews will not recover their former situation, for they have committed the most abominable of crimes, by plotting this plot against the savior of mankind... It was necessary, therefore, that the city in which Jesus suffered was destroyed from top to bottom, that the Jewish people were expelled from their homes, and that others called by God to the blessed election". The restoration of Israel for the most eminent theologians is therefore impossible despite the many promises contained in the Bible texts.

6.4 The Affirmation of Anti-Judaism as a Pledge of Better Christianity

Human nature often surrenders to excesses of all kinds and fanaticism is one of its most common forms. According to the Larousse dictionary, this word means; Absolute and exclusive dedication to a cause that incites religious or political intolerance and leads to acts of violence". This short definition makes an important reference to two factors that push fanaticism, namely, religion and politics. We can admit other factors that push fanaticism, such as passion, artistic sports, or love... In general, it is all that leads a person or a group towards the passion or passions beyond any reasoning, common sense, and what is the fruit of reflection. Nations as a group are capable of fanaticism, and Israel throughout its long history has been no exception, especially in fighting against the many attempts to dissolve the people, to destroy their worship and culture. This fanaticism, as the dictionary definition indicates, is aroused mainly by the religious world. We remember the prophets, like Elijah and many others, who in the Old Testament excited the people to revolt against foreigners: the Assyrians, the Babylonians, the Greeks, who tried in various ways to make him forget his religious and cultural roots. Jesus Christ prophesied this when he said to his disciples in this passage from the Gospel of John (16:2); "They will exclude you from the synagogues; and even the hour comes when whoever causes you to die will believe that he is worshipping God". This fanaticism found itself in-extenso

---

[134] Léon Poliakov, History of Anti-Semitism; the age of faith P 32 Citation.

in Christianity, as if it too had to defend a cultural and religious perimeter by iron and fire. The great Christian dignitaries mentioned above and so many others after them made anti-Judaism one of the centerpieces of their theology, and to assert their Christianity, they wanted to be all the more anti-Jewish. Thus, in its paraphrased Christian version, the verse found in the Gospel of John (16:2) could have become, "They will exclude you from the churches; and even the hour comes when whoever causes you to die will believe that he is worshipping God". As if fanaticism were not enough to annihilate every trace of Judaism in its midst, an authoritarian Christianity will acquire from the so-called Gregorian reform[135] more and more coercive means to control not only the institution of the church itself, but soon the whole society. The inquisition[136] that appeared in France in the 13th century will be that ecclesiastical police charged with examining hearts and consciences to eradicate the heresies of the Cathars and Waldensians, considered in many respects as precursors of the Protestant Reformation. In Spain, it will use all the resources of exorcism to erase even the trace of Judaism among former Jews, who have become by force, new converts to Catholicism but whose sincerity it strongly doubted. A significant number of them will be subjected to burning, torture and crime, at the mercy of these shameful excesses of zeal.

6.5 The amplification effect by the religious repetition of anti-Judaism from generation to generation.

Jews become the main cause of all the evils of society. Monotheistic religions have largely triumphed over pagan cults, from Greco-Roman antiquity, and later, with the emergence of Islam in the East and on the shores of the Mediterranean. Historians have extensively studied and determined the causes. One area of particular interest in our study is the practice of incantatory repetition, which involves repetitive recitation of fundamental truths from religious dogma. This repetition is often associated with singing and becomes a sung prayer. Christianity did not invent it, since it was present from the earliest times in Judaism and it formed the well-known verb Psalmody. The cantors had this function as one reads

---

[135] The Bible: 1R 18.1-40
[136] Sylvain Gouguenheim, The Gregorian Reform. From the struggle for the sacred to the secularization of the world, Temps Présent, Paris, 2010

it abundantly in the books of the Psalms, the Chronicles, Ezra and Nehemiah, and others. There is often in these prayers a part of incantation; that is, intense wishes, sometimes extreme vows made with an oath against oneself. Here lies the boundary between truth and error, legitimate praise to God and uncontrolled mysticism. In his time Jesus Christ had warned against such excesses when he declared in the Gospel of Matthew; "But I tell you not to swear at all, neither by heaven, because it is the throne of God, nor by the earth, because it is his footstool; nor by Jerusalem, because it is the city of the great king. Don't swear with your head either, because you can't make any of your hair white or black. Let your word be yes, yes, no, no; what is added to it comes from the evil one." (Ma 5:34-37). The Apostle James expressed the same thought in almost identical terms when he said: "First of all, brethren, swear not by heaven, or earth, or any other oath. But let your yes be yes, and your no be no, so that you will not fall under the judgment". The message is clear; no one can systematically ask for God's support for their thoughts as in his undertakings. These councils of prudence on the relationship of man to the sacred, recorded for eternity in the Word of God, have nevertheless been neglected by generations of Christianized peoples. They were enjoined to chant, following their spiritual leaders, from the 7th century until the Second Vatican Council in 1965, the prayer of Good Friday called "Oremus et pro perfidis Judaeis[137]", that is to say: Let us also pray for the unfaithful Jews". It can be understood without difficulty that this prayer and many others of this kind, constantly repeated over the centuries, had an effect of a "Tam-Tam" which has expanded to the most remote parts of Europe since the early Middle Ages, until very recently on a historical scale. We also think of this comparison made by the Lord Jesus Christ, with the little seed of mustard that grows with the seasons, a great tree in the garden; "He says again, What is the kingdom of God like, and what shall I compare it to? It is like a mustard seed that a man took and threw into his garden; it grows, becomes a tree, and the birds of heaven dwell in its branches" (Lk 13:19). In this passage it is a question of the kingdom of heaven that prospers and develops in the hearts of believers for their greatest happiness. On the other hand, however, it also shows that evil, initially insignificant, can become if it is not uprooted promptly, a great tree

---

[137] https://theologicalstudies.net/8.1.3.pdf

growing branches and deadly fruits everywhere for humans, as this passage from the Epistle to the Hebrews clearly indicates; "See that no one deprives himself of the grace of God; that no root of bitterness, growing offspring, produces trouble, and that many are infected with it" (Heb 12:15).

6.6 Hostility to Jews when they are blessed.

The condition of the Jews in the West as in the Christian East will never be stable or guaranteed by law. They are sometimes sought because of their ability to work and their intelligence of things, men and situations. Like the patriarch Joseph in his time, they became advisers to kings, experts in the trade of goods and services, wealthy landowners, and scrupulous jurists. The biblical prophecy below then applies perfectly to their condition. "If you obey the voice of the Lord your God, observing and putting into practice all his commandments that I prescribe to you today, the Lord your God will give you superiority over all the nations of the earth. These are all the blessings which will be poured out upon you and which will be your sharing, when you obey the voice of the Lord your God: You will be blessed in the city, and you will be blessed in the fields. The fruit of your bowels, the fruit of your soil, the fruit of your herds, the litters of your big and your small cattle, all these things will be blessed. Your basket and your crib will be blessed. You will be blessed when you arrive, and you will be blessed when you leave. The Lord will give you victory over your enemies who will rise against you; they will come out against you in one way, and they will flee before you in seven ways. The Lord will command the blessing to be with you in your granaries and in all your undertakings. He will bless you in the land that the Lord your God gives you. You will be holy to the Lord, as he has sworn to you, when you keep the commandments of the Lord your God and walk in his ways. All the people will see that you are called by the name of the Lord, and they will fear you. The Lord will fill you with goods, multiplying the fruit of your bowels, the fruit of your flocks and the fruit of your soil, in the land which the Lord has sworn to your fathers to give you. The Lord will open to you his good treasure, heaven, to send rain to your country in its time and to bless all the work of your hands; you will lend to many nations, and you will not borrow. The Lord will make you the head and not the tail, you will always be above and you will never be below, when you will obey the commandments of the Lord your God, which I prescribe to you today, when you will observe and put them into practice, and that you will not turn away from all the commandments I give you today, to go after other gods and serve them" (Dt 28:1-14). In medieval Europe a place of choice was soon assigned to them; This is the money business. The loan at interest being considered a sin by the church institution, this activity nevertheless, necessary is soon devolved to the Jews alone. Through this exclusive trading, they sometimes become immensely rich, but the risks of bankruptcy are also present everywhere. Indeed, the princes, the great of the various kingdoms, are careful not to help them in case of default of their creditors.

6.7 Hostility to the Jews when they are cursed.

The verses quoted below (De 28. 58) follow the blessings pronounced by the Lord. They show that the people of Israel can fall from the grace described above. There are no unconditional vested rights or income. His fortune and happiness are entirely conditioned by his disposition of heart to the Lord. "But if you do not obey the voice of the Lord your God, if you do not keep and put into practice all his commandments and laws which I prescribe to you today, these are the curses which will come upon you and which will be your share: You will be cursed in the city, and you will be cursed in the fields. Your basket and your crib will be cursed. The fruit of your bowels, the fruit of your soil, the litter of your big and your small cattle, all these things will be cursed. You will be cursed when you arrive, and you will be cursed when you leave. The Lord will send against you the curse, the trouble and the threat, in the midst of all the undertakings you will do, until you are destroyed, until you perish promptly, because of the wickedness of your actions, which will cause you to abandon me. The Lord will bind the plague to you, until it consumes you in the land which you are about to take possession of. The Lord will smite you with consumption, with fever, with inflammation, with burning heat, with dryness, with jaundice, and with gangrene, which will pursue you until you perish. The sky on your head shall be brass, and the earth beneath you shall be iron. The Lord will send dust and powder to your land for rain; It will come down from heaven upon you until you are destroyed. The Lord will make you beat by your enemies; you will go out against them in one way, and you will flee before them in seven ways; and you will be an object of fear to all the kingdoms of the earth. Your corpse will be the pasture of all the birds of the sky and the beasts of the earth, and there will be no one to trouble them. The Lord will smite thee with the ulcer of Egypt, with hemorrhoids, with scabies, and with ringworm, from which thou canst not heal. The Lord will strike you with delirium, blindness, and delusion of mind, and you will grope in the middle of the day like the blind man in the darkness, and you will have no success in your undertakings, and you will be oppressed every day, stripped, and there will be no one to come to your rescue... Just as the Lord took pleasure in doing you good and multiplying you, so the Lord will take pleasure in making you perish and destroy you; and you will be taken out of the land you are about to take possession of. The Lord will scatter you among all peoples, from one end of the earth to the other; And there you will serve other gods whom neither you nor your fathers knew, wood and stone. Among these nations, you will not be quiet, and you will not have a resting place for the soles of your feet. The Lord will make your heart restless, your eyes languid, your soul suffering. Your life will be suspended before you, you will tremble at night and day, you will doubt your existence. In fear that will fill your heart and in the presence of what your eyes will see, you will say in the morning: May evening be there! And say in the evening: May the morning be here! And the Lord will bring you back to the ships in Egypt, and you will make the way I told you: You will not see him again! There you will offer yourselves for sale to your enemies, like slaves and servants; and there will be no one to buy you." (Dt 28:15-68). These warnings that the Lord addresses to his people through Moses in the book of Deuteronomy, were written about 7 centuries before the arrival of the Messiah Jesus Christ. However, they are so representative of the destiny of the people of Israel that they would readily believe that they were recorded afterwards, rather as the account of a faithful historian. Now this prophetic text describes with a luxury of detail, what will be the destiny of Israel according to its obedience or disobedience to the Word of God. It is immediately noticeable that curses occupy more than three times the space of blessings, that the parallelism between what they affirm, and the historical reality lived by Israel is absolutely striking. For some, the blessing has been manifested in every respect throughout history, it has been such that verses 1 to 14 indicate it, namely: intelligence, fortune, fruitfulness, power, influence. For others, it is on the contrary: misfortune, dispersion, persecution, permanent failure, destitution... and many other calamities. The primary cause of this destiny, results from the conscious or unconscious choice to have obeyed or not the Word of God. From this point of view, the persecution against Judaism that begins in mass Christianity and never stops, could be understood and internalized in thought, as in Jewish piety for centuries. From this point of view also, it can be added that the Lord knew that the universal ministry of his Son Jesus Christ would precipitate the fall of Israel before its recovery. Thus, in prosperity as in persecution, the people of Israel remain throughout the centuries the witness of God. However, as the apostle Paul emphasizes in a passage from his epistle to the Romans; Woe to him and to those by whom these misfortunes would come: for if God has not spared the natural branches, he will not spare you" (Rom 11:21). Here the apostle merely recalls the 12fundamental principle established for eternity by the Lord himself; "... and I will curse those who curse you" (Gen 12:3). Indeed, one should not believe that the apparent power of the Christian institution could immunize him against these words because, anti-Judaism institutionalized from top to bottom of the hierarchy in the church of multitude was judged by the Lord through various historical circumstances. Thus, even as it continued its rise to power in the Roman Empire, it broke under its feet. The political and religious unity desired and celebrated by Eusebius of Caesarea as the joint triumph of the state and Christianity, is no more than an illusion after the collapse of the Western empire. This happened in 476, when the last emperor, Romulus Augustulus abdicated in favor of the king of barbarians from the far lands of the empire. Strange coincidence, despite the efforts of emperors and popes, despite their desire for power, the empire did not resist for more than 100 years to the forced Christianization of its peoples, and it will never again find the unity and power that had made its strength and glory. Latin, its unifying language, quickly fell into oblivion in favor of multiple regional dialects. Having become a dead language, it nevertheless forms the etymological root of many European languages, mainly in southern Europe. The Catholic religion continues to borrow many terms and formulas from it for its liturgy. This use of a dead language that will last a very long time, until the 2nd half of the XXth century, will only increase its hermetic and mysterious character. It will be one of the causes of his separation from the people ignorant of the subtlety of the texts in Latin. It will also be one of the causes of the rise of anticlericalism, still very present in southern Europe, where Catholicism has long reigned. From the end of the Fourth Century, it was therefore a shaky Christianity, sometimes weak, sometimes brutal, that reigned in Rome and Constantinople. Very far from the biblical texts, these two versions of the same religion have at least in common: their anti-Judaism, which is recorded in their respective theology. It is as if the curse written in Genesis 12:3 had fallen upon these churches of multitude and upon the peoples they had enlisted. Words are very insufficient to translate such a phenomenon, triple fold: spiritual, historical, and social and mine are no exception. Indeed, in this chiaroscuro, there has been, many men of faith and truth, an authentic Christianity, true; there have been genius, sparkling lights to which we should also pay tribute. Thus, the promise of God remained true in all generations, and all those who blessed Israel were blessed indeed.

6.8 The empire is defeated from within; Was the Judeo-Christian pill too big to swallow?

The image used for the title of this section is deliberately caricatural; it evokes this animal that dies by swallowing another smaller than itself without realizing that, seemingly weak, this animal possesses a deadly venom that kills the big one from inside. So, the question is: did the weak get the better of the strongest in Roman history?

7. State Christianity and the Fall of the Roman Empire

One is justified in asking the question of the preceding section, considering the brutal fall of the empire after the triumph within it of a state Christianity. The adjective is not exaggerated since the collapse is spectacular and follows quickly over less than a century. When one considers, indeed, that this immense empire built for more than a thousand years around Rome its capital, capable of resisting invasions from all sides and founder of an extraordinary civilization, one is surprised that its end is so rapid and so definitive. Historians have done extensive investigative work on the causes of its fall and their conclusions emphasize both its external and internal factors. However, we want to make here an additional contribution that has not often been mentioned in the existing amount of work on this issue. Did not the Eternal God himself precipitate the fall of this empire? The question is worth asking when we consider that Christianity is already very far from its biblical roots and its founding texts, when the emperor Constantine recognized it in 313 by the Edict of Milan and converted himself in the year 326. At this time it is estimated that[138] it already represents between 7 and 10% of the population of the empire, and it will pass almost without transition from the situation of the minority persecuted under the emperor Diocletian (303-311) to the official religion of the empire in 380. Only eleven years later, it was declared an exclusive religion in 391, with the promulgation of the edict of Emperor Theodosius I[139]. Was the Eternal God in agreement with this nationalization by forced march of a Christianity that had no more Christian than the name? He was certainly not consulted, nor his Word, which in none of its lines teaches that Christianity must become a state religion. Where then, is the individual and voluntary act of faith, which Jesus Christ indicates when he says: "... he who believes and is baptized will be saved" (Mk 16:16)? The pill having been swallowed despite everything, it was without the support of the Lord of armies that the empire went into battle against its enemies and was defeated, as in ancient times, Israel sometimes went to fight its enemies without first consulting the Lord and was defeated. Shattered into a multitude of rival nations and tribes, the empire was torn apart, splintered into numerous factions, and finally disappeared in the year 476. In rereading the passage from the Book of Daniel, which prophesies the fall of this great Colossus with feet of clay, one cannot help but think of the colossal Roman Empire destroyed by this detached stone without the help of any human hand and which struck it at its base, made of a mixture of clay and iron unable to support the building. In Daniel's book we read this description: "The head of this statue was pure gold; his chest and arms were silver; his belly and thighs were brass; his legs, of iron; his feet, partly iron and partly clay. You

---

[138] Constantine 1er: https://www.britannica.com/biography/Constantine-I-Roman-emperor
[139] Theodosius 1er https://www.britannica.com/biography/Roman-emperor-Theodosius-I

looked, when a stone came loose without the help of any hand, struck the iron and clay feet of the statue, and tore them to pieces. Then iron, clay, brass, silver, and gold were broken together and became like the bullet that escapes from an area in summer; the wind carried them away, and no trace was found. But the stone that struck the statue became a great mountain and filled the whole earth" (Dan 2:32-35). One thinks even more of the messiah of Israel because in the whole Bible, this Savior is also presented as a solid rock. Indeed, he is the "Rock of the ages", He is solid as the rock as this passage tells us; "Trust in the Lord in perpetuity, for the Lord, the Lord, is the rock of ages (Es 26:4)." For his part, the psalmist cries out; "Let us shout with joy to the rock of our salvation (Ps 95:1)". In the New Testament they read that he is, "... the cornerstone" on which rests the whole spiritual construction of Israel's hope; "For it is said in Scripture: Behold, I put in Zion a cornerstone, chosen, precious; And he who believes in it will not be confused." (1Pi 2:6), another example found in the epistle of the apostle Paul to the Ephesians shows Jesus Christ as the stone on which the whole spiritual edifice of Christianity rests; "You were built on the foundation of the apostles and prophets, Jesus Christ himself being the cornerstone." (Eph 2:20). If we continue the biblical analysis of the prophecy of Daniel to its end, we conclude that he was Jesus Christ himself who brought down the Roman Empire, this military-religious colossus, to establish in hearts an eternal kingdom of peace of justice and love that will have no boundaries and no end. Although the empire disappeared, it bequeathed to posterity a considerable civilization and culture, and yet it also bequeathed for their greatest misfortune, this link of union between its many peoples, namely, a deep anti-Judaism spread from east to west and north to south. [140]

7.1 Jews are ultimately the cause of all the evils of society.

Chapter 28 of the book of Deuteronomy quoted above is both a realistic description of the condition of the Jews in exile and deportation. It is also a no less realistic prophecy of its destiny until the middle of the twentieth century. Who could formulate it better than the Lord himself about 700 years before

---

[140] The Bible: Book of Daniel 2:37-45

it materialized? Indeed, such foreknowledge is not given to anyone under the heavens because everything is written in advance in its smallest details. For example, verse 29 states: you will be oppressed every day, robbed, and there will be no one to come to your rescue". Such is the fate of Israel, defenseless, scattered in small communities throughout medieval Europe. From the year 636, they were banned and expelled from Rome by Pope Honorius 1st, and they had to flee. This is the beginning of an endless series of exiles, deportations, expulsions, which will make Jews this, "wandering people", constantly uprooted from its precarious places of reception. Expelled but still present, they become a subject of fear among the nations, as this passage among others, of the prophet Amos describes so well; "They will then be wandering from sea to sea, from north to east, and will go here and there to seek the word of the Lord, and they will not find it (Am 8:12)."

7.2 Dispersal and expulsion

The dispersal of the Jews throughout the Mediterranean basin and even beyond is not a consequence of the destruction of Jerusalem in the year 70 by the armies of Titus. A large diaspora already existed, since remote times difficult to date if not for those who remained in Babylon and in the Persian empire after exile in the 6th century BC. On the other hand, we know that important communities existed in Egypt, in Cyrenaica, throughout the Maghreb, and even in Spain long before the advent of the messiah of Christians; it was a voluntary emigration and not forced. The texts of the New Testament, including this one: "[141] Now there were in Jerusalem Jews, pious men, of all the nations under heaven.(Acts 2:5)" , evoke these important Jewish communities scattered in the nations and in their great metropolises such as: Alexandria, Corinth, Rome, Antioch, Ephesus, Thessaloniki and many other places, where the apostles exercised their ministry. Defeat certainly renewed this dispersion later and even accentuated it, but it was not, it's the primary cause. However, some Christian theologians, including Tertullian and Chrysostomea, wanted to make it believed later, from the[142] Fifth Century,

---

[141] Jewish Diaspora: www.jewishvirtuallibrary.org/The Diaspora
[142] Anti-Judaism: Why the Jews: History of Antisemitism/www.ushmm.org

to emphasize the ruin and curse that fell on Israel. Consequently, from their teachings, this new exile was gradually interpreted, in the popular imagination, as a heavenly sanction, a proof of God's existence and his power. The Jews expelled from the land which the Lord had given them were proof of their guilt, and that they should be treated as guilty. In an extremely diverse Europe of the Middle Ages, which a facade of Christianity cannot manage to unite, the permanent trial enforced against Judaism, nevertheless becomes one of its common features. In France, history will retain 12 expulsions of Jews, not counting those ordered by the autonomous powers of the provinces. The first is that decreed in 533, by the son of Clovis, Childebert[143] Ist, because the Jews refused to convert to Christianity, the second is pronounced in 633 by King Dagobert Ist for the same reason. The third comes after the destruction of the Holy Sepulcher in Jerusalem in 1009, by order of the caliph Fatimid. Through circumstances that will never be fully understood, the Jews were accused of being responsible for this sacrilege. As a result, they were once again expelled. King Philip Augustus in 1182, again signed a decree of expulsion, accompanied by the spoliation of their property and ransoms on their person. The fifth was imposed by Louis IX in 1254. This king is also called "Saint Louis" after being canonized by the Catholic Church in 1297, in view of his great merits for it. It is with such a legacy that we must still live today in the 21st century, where there are countless streets "Saint Louis", squares "Saint Louis", neighborhoods "Saint Louis", religious buildings "Saint Louis", Catholic high schools and colleges, "Saint Louis". It is still to pay tribute to the king and to the anti-Jewish prejudice to honor in this way such a man who contributed much to the misfortunes of the Jews in France. At the beginning of the XIVth, under the reign of Philip IV said, "the Bel", there was about 100,000 Jews and from 1292, their condition deteriorated. From confiscations to dispossession and arbitrary arrests, Judaism must constantly pay to exist in the kingdom. This disqualification ended with a deportation order signed in June 1306, which left them only one month to leave the kingdom. This expulsion is done, "at their expense", since they must abandon to the king all their claims. However, these are often written in Hebrew, it was necessary to bring back from exile, translators so that they are effectively monetizable. However, this return is only

---

[143] Expulsion of Jews: Judaism - Marginalization, Expulsion, Diaspora | Britannica.com

temporary, and their final expulsion is pronounced in 1311. In 1322, the seventh expulsion is more regional, it is ordered by Charles IV called "le Bel", it is applied in Languedoc and Burgundy. The eighth expulsion in 1394, that of King Charles VI, was to be definitive and national, but there were still others in 1491 and 1501, after the attachment of Provence to France. Later in 1683 and 1724, Louis XIV and Louis XV respectively carried out the expulsion of Jews from the West Indies and Louisiana, then French possession. In England it was King Edward I[st] who decreed in 1290 the Edict of expulsion of the Jews from the kingdom but also from Aquitaine, then under English domination. This single decree was repealed only 366 years later in 1656, thanks to the will of the "Lord Protector", Oliver Cromwell. Rigorous Protestant and very inspired by his Bible readings, he had seen in this decree the sign of a curse for the country, and he wanted, rather than to bless Israel. Without being able to account for all the particular situations of Judaism in this tormented Europe between paganism and Christianity, one can nevertheless cite four examples with the help of the remarkable work of the historian Leon Poliakov. The most important development we will make summarizes the historical evolution of the situation of the Jews in Spain. They are indeed there, much more numerous than elsewhere in Europe, and it is the only country where, for about eight centuries, three religions coexisted: Muslim, Christian, and Jewish.

7.3 Spain at the time of the three religions[144]

Divided into rival factions, the Visigoth dynasties were not able to oppose the victorious Muslim invaders from the south from the year 711 onwards. Cities and countryside have been taken away one after the other with a disconcerting facility like Toledo, the capital, abandoned by its leaders and its population. On the religious level, it is a very weak, divided and inconsistent Catholicism that they found before them. The very numerous Jews in the country already at this time, were very often auxiliaries of this conquest; they inherited in many places the administration of the towns and villages abandoned by their former masters. Christianity managed to maintain itself only in a few mountainous,

---

[144] Léon Poliakov History of anti-Semitism P 95 to 199 Editions Calmann-Lévy

poor, and remote provinces in the north of the country: Leon, Galicia, and Navarre. Nevertheless, these will form the basis of what will later become, "The Reconquista". It is a slow mystic-political epic, which ended only in 1492 with the victory of Queen Isabella the Catholic and Ferdinand of Aragon, over the last caliphate of Granada still in the hands of Muslims in the peninsula. In the Arab part of Spain, the principles of government proven elsewhere were gradually put in place. Religious minorities were tolerated at first, then after a certain time, they would be enjoined to convert to Islam by persuasion or coercion if necessary. In this context, Judaism resists rather well, probably because of its great dogmatic stability, and probably also, because of its Abrahamic source recognized by the Muslims themselves. Nevertheless, they are considered "dhimmis", that is to say, strangers to Islam. They are subject to a specific tax, and the time will come when they have to wear on their clothing a distinctive sign visible. They are generally treated with a certain condescension, "a slightly disdainful benevolence", says Léon Poliakov[145]. Christianity remained a minority in the Spain of the caliphs. It is also "dhimmis", it must comply towards their Muslim masters to the duties related to its condition. It must be recognized that in the long run, this multi-stage society is working well. Historians continue to analyze with great interest the considerable legacy of the Hispano-Moresque Middle Ages. A climate of mutual tolerance is established between the communities, which promotes the intellectual, artistic, and moral influence of this period. We are witnessing the rise of philosophy, natural sciences, mathematics, medicine, the arts in general, and so many others benefited the society as a whole. It greatly benefited the Jews, whose population grew strongly with immigration from North Africa. Influential, and colorful figures close to Arab power emerged at that time. They inaugurated from the 9th century onwards, what the historians call: "The golden age" of Judaism in Spain. This is particularly true of the figure of the sage, Hasdai ibn Chaprout , whose correspondence with the Jewish king Joseph, from a distant country, the Khazar located on the shores of the Caspian Sea, tells us at the same time of the existence of this kingdom, and how much he enjoyed titles, powers and prerogatives with its Arab monarch. Another famous name among many, was illustrated at the beginning of the eleventh century; Samuel ibn Nagrela,

---

[145] Léon Poliakov History of Anti-Semitism P 98 Ed Points

minister to King Nablus of Granada. He remained famous for his intellectual qualities as a writer and court poet, but also for those he demonstrated as a warlord at the service of his king. Moreover, by his work, he added his name: "Mebo ha-Talmud[146]", to the list of commentators of the Babylonian Talmud that can still be consulted today. At that time, there were no restrictions on the activities of the Jews, who owned land, cultivated grains and vines, bought and sold all kinds of goods, and were able to access the various levels of territorial administration. In general, the Jewish communities of Zaragoza, Cordoba, and those of the coast from Tarragona to the province of Huelva in the extreme south, played an effective role of intermediaries between the Arab civilization in the south, in all the cities of the Maghreb to Egypt and those of Christian Europe to the north. With this tolerance between the three communities, their remarkable achievements, which can still be admired today, in Sevilla, Cordoba, Granada, and many other places, it was indeed for the Jews "The golden century". "Spain during the time of the three religions", reminds us more of the "Renaissance" as the whole of Europe will experience it five centuries later, than in the Middle Ages of obscurantism and the retreat of civilization, as people used to live further north, at that time beyond the Pyrenees.[147]

7.4 "The Reconquista"

The enterprise of the reconquest of Christianity is just beginning when that of the Muslims is completed. Poor and remote areas in the North refuse submission to the new masters of the peninsula. Despised and neglected by them, they are nevertheless the leaven of a challenge to their hegemony that will only spread. A mythology is gradually built to animate the faith of the fighters of a "reconquista" within Christianity. Thus, it was under the patronage of Saint James, the younger brother of the Lord Jesus Christ, that the battalions of Christians went into battle. Saint Jacques of Compostela became over time a high place of resistance against the invading Saracens. It also became a center of pilgrimage where all kinds of people converged from all of medieval Europe, humble and prominent. Some

---

[146] Léon Poliakov History of Antisemitism P 102 Ed Points
[147] Léon Poliakov History of Anti-Semitism P 104 Ed Points

were eager for glory, others for the forgiveness of their sins, and together they were ready for the ultimate sacrifice for the cause of Christ. From this period, one would also remember the emblematic figure of the "Cid Campeador", Knight of King Alfonso VI, then of the Muslim kings of Zaragoza Al-Muqtadir and Al-Mutamán, then again in the service of the first. He was victorious over the Saracens in Valencia in 1094. He established in this city a principality which was returned under Muslim domination only in 1102[148]. The legend would make this character one of the guardian heroes of the "Reconquista", with almost mystical attributes. From all the nations of Europe came also in the peninsula missionaries who helped in the reconstitution of a vigorous Christianity wherever possible. This period was also that of the crusades to liberate Jerusalem from the domination of Islam and maintain ancient Judea and Samaria under the banner of Christianity. The re-establishment of Christianity in Spain, from where it had been expelled in the 8th century, is therefore very comparable; it is again a question of driving Islam out of medieval Europe with the same means everywhere: war, crusade, murder, iron, fire, and blood. This reconquest is very long; eight centuries from beginning to end, it is indecisive, sometimes very violent, sometimes less. The ebb and flow of the belligerents is difficult to follow, and the Jews do not frankly take sides for one or the other cause, and they rarely participate in the fighting. The historian Léon Poliakov tells us that whenever the Muslims had recourse to the particularly fanatical and intolerant Almohad warriors from the Maghreb, the Jews migrated further north and put themselves under the protection of Christian kings. As the reconquest progressed, this movement continued to gain in importance and allowed the Jews to be objective artisans of it. In this bilateral conflict, they often obtained the spoils of victory, such as the administration of cities, the cultivation of fields, and the occupation of commercial and craft offices deserted by the vanquished. A few centuries apart, they once again took advantage of the change of power. Soon they formed the structure of the territorial collectivities in the regions won by the "Reconquista", leaving to them the indelible mark of their rules of rights and jurisprudence. Everyone was winning at this change, and the positive role of Judaism was recognized at all levels of the social and religious pyramid of the

---

[148] Rodrigo Díaz de Vivar: El Cid: The True Story of Spain's Greatest Hero

time. This country, which passed at random battles, from one dominant religion to another, had as mediator Judaism. It learned long before the other European nations what tolerance was, the plurality of cults, and their benefits. However, the pendulum of history has gradually shifted in the other direction because, from the end of the eleventh century, the papacy was concerned about the influence of the Jews and their rise in power within the Spanish courts and recommended that a remedy be found. Anti-Jewish revolts broke out here and there during the 11th and 12th centuries, but overall, the social consensus of "Spain of the three religions" remained solid for a long time. In Castilla, for example, the Mosaic cult was respected and protected, in defense of Christians, from attacking synagogues and objects of Jewish piety. It was recalled dispelling possible misunderstandings that the very name of "Judah" was that of the noble tribe that gave Israel its kings and great warlords. Conversions from one religion to another remained individual approaches, but relations between Christian and Jewish theologians were close and frequent, because the overlap of their reference texts is strong. The clouds on this harmonious cohabitation arrived gradually in the thirteenth century. In the IVth Concile of Lateran[149] in 1215, Pope Innocent III had prescribed for the Jews the wearing of the "rouelle". This marking was another sign of the humiliation of the Jews in the north of the Pyrenees, but it was not yet in the south because in fact, in certain regions of Spain, the Jews already distinguished themselves by particular dress signs. The long process of the "Reconquista" is also accompanied by a progressive Latinization of religious life and correlatively of its feudal institutions, also called the "Subreconquista" or, inner reconquest. The religious orders of the Franciscans and Dominicans were particularly active in this inner crusade. They tended to place Spain in the European context, that of a rival and triumphant Christianity over Judaism, with varying degrees of success. The Inquisition Court, established in the 13th century, was charged with criminalizing any form of opposition to the dogmas and powers of the Roman church. It was used to fight against the heresies declared as those of the Cathars, Albigensians and Vaudois. It will not appear until the end of the fifteenth century in Spain and Portugal. However, this is in these two countries that it will be the most virulent because of the innumerable lawsuits it will bring

---

[149] Fourth Lateran Council | Church History, Purpose, & Outcome | Britannica

against all those whom they suspected, the lack of sincerity of their conversion. The "Subreconquista" moved according to circumstances; it reached, particularly the capital of Castilla, the city of Valladolid, where a very important Jewish community lived. Fueled by these crusaders from within, increasingly frequent troubles erupted against the Jews. To the rich intellectual debates of the early times among specialists, succeeded the clashes in public places, which had everything of theological lynching against Judaism. Those of Barcelona in the middle of the 13th century, the meeting of Tortosa at the beginning of the 16th century remained famous. The latter, long and exhausting, since it lasted almost two years, in various forms, generalizes this kind of theological dispute, followed by mass conversions. The rabbis were slow to understand that they were trapped from the very beginning, with no other way out than their personal denial and the conversion of their entire community. The increasing number of anti-Jewish riots each time left a trail of blood in the cities and villages with one only remedy: the conversion. This one seemed very simple indeed, and the nobility of the city of Perpignan in today France, said to King John I[st] of Aragon[150], "Let the Jews become Christians and all the tumult will end". It was like a permanent contest to know which bishop, priest, or simple parish clerk had converted the most Jews. After the disputation of Tortosa, the omen of the disappearance of Judaism in Spain[151] became more probable and more palpable every day. This century would also retain the development of a very strange complex that the doctors of the soul would not be able to cure, it is the, "marranism". For the one who has been forced to convert, there remains in his heart and mind such a strong memory of his Judaism that he cannot get rid of it. Therefore, in his own eyes, he is no longer Jewish without becoming a Christian. What fate is reserved for him then; In the end, it is rather the despair he must bear each day in his condition of being neither one nor the other. The more Latin term "conversos" has the same meaning as "marrane", it designates like it, these Jews converted without really being catholic and who continue to Judaize more or less openly. Marranism will see the most extravagant forms of spiritual compromise between opposing obedience's, accompanied by the confused mysticism of the in-between religion.

---

[150] Léon Poliakov History of Antisemitism P 149 Ed Points
[151] Léon Poliakov History of Antisemitism P 153 Ed Points

Note that France would also know its "marrane" period, during nearly three centuries indeed, when the Catholic clergy would force conversion, the Protestants who fell in their power after the Reformation of 1517. Note also the attempts of Pope Martin V to bring the clergy back in Spain, to a conception of conversion to Christianity more faithful to the Scriptures. He did so, in two documents in 1421 and 1422, in which he recalls that forced baptism is not Christian baptism. Lost time: the ancient anti-Jewish texts of this same papacy, the injunctions to the conversion of his predecessors, the legitimacy of the contempt long taught, the just discrimination against Judaism decreed by the papal institution were the strongest. Thus, swimming from one contradiction to another, in turn defender and aggressor of Judaism, the papacy will never find the strength or the courage of a clear position to defend the innocent persecuted by its own power.

7.5 In two centuries, the most tolerant country in Europe becomes the most intolerant.

In parallel with the "Reconquista" in pursuit of the last bastions of the Arab presence in Spain the "Subreconquista" continues its work of religious unification for the exclusive benefit of Catholicism. The important Muslim minorities that remained here and there in the newly conquered regions had no other choice but conversion, exile or death. This warrior Christianity descended on the Jewish communities with the same violent determination and stripped them of all that had previously made the wise Judeo-Christian balance and transforming one after the other, synagogues into churches. Everywhere triumphed an arrogant and self-assured Catholicism. The country achieved political unity among its various provinces in 1491. A year later, it culminated in a triple consecration; It is first of all on January 2, the triumphant entry of Isabella the Catholic and Ferdinand of Aragon in Granada, the last bastion of the Arab presence in Spain. It is then on March 31st of that same year, the publication of the decree of the Alhambra by which all Jews are expelled from the kingdom. The Court of the Inquisition did appear in Spain only in 1478, that is to say late compared to other regions of Europe, however, it will remain there much more present and much more active than everywhere else, being suppressed in this country, only in the 19th century, in 1834[152]. On the advice of the great inquisitor Tomas de Torquemada, the Queen and the King of Spain are now convinced to have to expel the Jews after having done so for the Arabs. The conditions of this departure are calamitous; after having resided there for more than a millennium, they have barely 3 months to leave the country after liquidation of all their property and possessions. The decree records in writing the hypocrisy of its authors when it brings this useless precision; "… it is open to them (to the Jews) to take away all their movable property and to convert their immovable property in order to take away its equivalent value in any form… with the exception of gold, silver or currency". It was enough to simply write that, as far as they were concerned, "robberies, looting and dispossession" were allowed. This is what happened during this lamentable expulsion; huge estates, entire buildings, countless works of art, have gone for a tiny fraction of their value. The only way to escape the rigors of this decree was conversion, to which many resolved. Unfortunately for them, very often becoming "Marranes", the fussy suspicion of the inquisition, its long memory did not leave them, and many were victims of its trials, its pyres, its executions and its persecutions of all kinds, for centuries to come. The third major event occurred in October of 1492, which was the discovery of the Americas by the Genoese adventurer Christopher Columbus in the service of the Spanish royalty. The relation with the condition of the Jews in the kingdom of Spain is indirect because this discovery did not have any immediate consequence on their condition in the country. However, it would allow Spain to become the leading maritime and economic power in 16th century Europe, because of the influx of wealth and precious metals it found there, was a guarantee of its power and of a great monetary creation of the kingdom. The brilliance and power of the Spanish monarchy then, resounded in all European capitals. Thanks to her possessions in America, it would reign over an empire, "where the sun never sets". It was even larger than that of ancient Rome. This Habsburg dynasty of which Charles V was the emperor from 1519, was present in Madrid and Vienna in Austria, and up to the heart of Europe, in the Netherlands, in Burgundy, in much of Germany and Italy. Where would its power end? Everything succeeded in this kingdom, which seemed promised to unite all the opposite parts of Europe

---

[152] Alhambra Decree: Vidéos Bing (1:03:02)

and to revive the Ancient Roman Empire, Christianized by Catholicism. His king Philip II, son of Charles V, further increased this power with his marriage to Mary Tudor, the Catholic daughter of the King of England, Henry VIII. This was the omen of an expansion to the north, intended among other things to bring the British Isles back into the fold of Catholicism. He also succeeded in unifying the Iberian Peninsula by annexing Portugal in 1580, thereby taking control of its immense possessions in Brazil and the Far East. His art flourished, especially that of painting with a series of great names such as; El Greco, Diego Velázquez, Estéban Murillo, Francisco de Zurbaran, and their talented successors such as, Francisco de Goya, Miquel Utrillo, Pablo Picasso and Salvador Dáli, who until today have made this art a centerpiece of Spanish culture. [153]

7.6 Is Abraham's blessing given to those who curse Israel?

Would Spain and with it its ruling dynasty have managed to prosper and flourish while banishing, cursing, and expelling Israel? Could one who cursed Israel be blessed? Considering all this glory, this wealth, this power, and this influence, one can legitimately ask the question. The promise made by the Lord to Abraham, "... I will bless those who bless you, and I will curse those who curse you." (Gen 12:3), was it in vain? However, thinking that way would only make the history of nations a superficial reading, looking only at the appearance of things. The fleeting brilliance of their glory, and that of their men. In fact, even as it prospered and would enrich itself on the one hand, at numerous sources, it became impoverished on the other and ruined itself in vain and costly battles, some of which can be considered directly committed against God himself. Without being able to detail this double process of greatness and decadence of the Spanish power, we can nevertheless remember some key dates and events. The bankruptcy of Spain in 1557 is one of the first signs that the fortune of this kingdom was finally very precarious. The massive increase in money in circulation within the kingdom was not used for productive investment; it was often wasted in futility, hardly cashed in. At sea, 1588 is another historical date; it is the year in which "the Invincible Armada", this huge fleet of ships destined to invade England to re-establish a

---

[153] Spanish Inquisition: www.britannica.com/Search?query=Spanish+Inquisition

Catholic dynasty there, was defeated and annihilated, both by the skill of the English sailors and by the elements unleashed against it. Queen Elizabeth I[st] was saved and Protestantism in England and Scotland as well, and with them, new forms of Protestant piety would be born after this memorable date, namely, the Puritans, Baptists, Quakers, and many others. Another major event that caused the powerful Spain to falter was the 80-year war[154] (1568-1648) by which the United Protestant Provinces of the Netherlands, long Spanish possessions in the Holy Roman Empire, emancipated themselves from its heavy guardianship. Paradoxically, this deadly war for both sides, saw Spain become permanently impoverished while the Netherlands at the same time, enriched considerably. At the same time, engaged in the 30 years' war[155] (1618 ~1648) on the side of Austria of the Habsburgs, Spain will still lose some jewels of its crown to the treaty of Westphalia in 1648, whether in France, provinces in the south, in the north, in Flanders, in Germany from the Holy Empire to Italy. In its very borders, centrifugal forces appeared with the secession of Portugal in 1648, which regained its sovereignty and the war of independence of Catalonia, the main manufacturing province of the peninsula. At sea, his navy was defeated by that of the United Provinces, much more modern and better commanded than its own. It was not until the survival of the ruling dynasty, which was threatened by the succession of inbred marriages it had contracted for three generations[156]. Indeed, King Charles II, who was sterile and suffered from several diseases that were incurable at the time, died in 1700 at the age of 39, without any descendants. Therefore, two ruling families, the French Bourbons and the Austrian Habsburgs, competed for the throne, and this was finally the Duke of Anjou, son of Louis XIV[th,] who became king of Spain under the name of Philip V. The Habsburg dynasty in Spain died out and was replaced to this day by that of the Bourbons. The very long reign of his first king, 45 years old, is not that of the restoration of Spanish power. Now vassalized, politically weakened, it is a poor, underdeveloped country. Spain is now subject to the law of the great European powers, first that of France, then that of Great Britain in the 18th century. A church which sometimes resembled

---

[154] Eighty Years War: www.britannica.com/Search?query=Eightyyears+war
[155] Thirty Years' War: www.britannica.com/Search?query=Thirtyyears+war
[156] Consanguinity within the Habsburg Dynasty: The rampant consanguinity in the Spanish branch of the Habsburg family | UCL Researchers in Museums

more of a political police than of a pastoral ministry, vigorously fought three plagues which it deemed intolerable in Spain namely; the Saracens or what remained of them, Judaism often hidden under the, "Marranism" and Protestantism, which will never find sufficient political and social support. Thus, in less than two centuries, the country moved from the summit of power to a secondary role in the concert of European nations. To this rapid politico-economic picture of its greatness and decadence, we can add this window open to the Spanish man of that time, which the historian Leon Poliakov offers us in his long study on the fortune and misfortune of Judaism in Spain. He says to him that he is now the well-known type of dilettante, "Gentleman", friend of the arts and the greats of this world. He tells us that he hates to work and that science annoys him, but that he finds his pleasure in the narcissistic representation he has of himself. Thus, he sees himself in "Caballero", that is to say, as a victorious knight in battle and charmer with the ladies. He likes to be served and does not conceive his status without a large domesticity. He is shady on matters of honor and a poet in his time. He is light on the fundamental questions of philosophy, politics, religion, life, and death. For him, appearance is reality; So, he wears beautiful clothes in all circumstances, it is them that ensures his promotion to the great, not his talents nor his work. Others do this for him. He is or sees himself as a landowner with vast estates exploited by peasants, all at his exclusive service. To have the right filiation, to make a beautiful marriage, inherit from a great estate; these are his main concerns. He is particularly careful to purifying his genealogy of any trace of Judaism. Indeed, how many were unmasked by a fierce inquisition, who believed that their titles, rank, and birth would enable them to escape its fierce struggle against the Jews and their descendants. From this absolute quest for purity of blood, the absurd idea of a Jewish race, characterized by direct or indirect filiation with its representatives in previous generations, is born. If there is a Jewish race, then there is necessarily one, non-Jewish, endogenous or indigenous, whose molecular constitution is different, for the sole reason of being pure of any mixture with the first. A pseudo-science then develops, on the objective existence of particular Jewish genetics, on the pure and impure blood on one side and the other. We know that this racist idea will be taken up and amplified later in Germany and placed at the heart of the doctrine of the Germanic superiority of National Socialism, and that it will follow everywhere in Europe, the advance of the German troops. This attitude, as well as this behavior at the national level, will lead Spain to retain until the middle of the[157] 20th century a very archaic social structure. It is very hierarchical between masters and servants, it is characterized among other things by what sociologists have called: the power "Latifundiaire", a word derived from the Spanish "Latifundia" which designates these immense agricultural areas, often under-exploited and neglected. They are the possession of a minority of aristocrats concentrated in the major cities of the country. They were one of the main causes of the deadly Spanish Civil War that tore the country apart from 1936 to 1939. It is a backward Spain, bruised, poor and locked in its borders as in an intolerant Catholicism, which survives the aftermath of this fratricidal war. General Franco, winner and new absolute master of the country, will make this final declaration; "En España, o se católico o se nada", that is to say in English: In Spain one is Catholic, or one is nothing[158]. The whole country reminds us of this Word of the Bible already quoted: "... I will curse him who curses you" (Gen 12:3). Finally, we can conclude this brief historical and social picture, highlighting the strength and permanence of the Word of God; Despite its gold, its empire and its power, this kingdom was brought down, and cursed in some way. None of what it undertook after expelling the Jews from its soil really prospered, either its empire or its monarchical institutions or its industry and commerce or its Christian state. It only managed to transport to its colonies its own archaisms. Salvation finally returned to this country through the little gate, through some simple but genuine acts of repentance. First, the repeal of the Alhambra decree in 1967, during the dictatorship of General Franco, was followed a year later by the inauguration of the first synagogue in Spain in Madrid since 1492. Then there was the recognition of Israel as a nation in 1986, which was rather laborious and conditional in view of Spain's important ties with the Arab countries. It was also in 1992, the day of remembrance of the 500 years after the memorable date of the decree of the Alhambra, in which the King and Queen of Spain participated. It was also and above all, the "Law of return" promulgated in 2015[159] at the initiative of the 1st minister of the time, Mariano

---

[157] Léon Poliakov; History of anti-Semitism P 185 – 198. The cult of blood purity or Iberian racism Edition: Calmann - Lévy
[158] Léon Poliakov History of Antisemitism P 155 to 169 Ed Points
[159] Léon Poliakov History of Antisemitism P 193 Ed Points

Rajoy, and unanimously adopted by the Cortes, the Spanish parliament. This law allows, in order to "repair a historical error", the obtaining of Spanish citizenship and the return to the country of the Jewish descendants expelled in the 15th century by this infamous decree. Today, unrecognizable compared to the years after the civil war, this country with democratic institutions is well integrated into the European Community, and it has considerably enriched itself. It has regained the tolerance of "Spain of the three religions" and the openness to a pluralistic world, both from the point of view of opinions and religions. Has the blessing of the Lord promised to those who would bless Israel, returned? One can legitimately think that, yes, the blessing came back.[160]

8. Crusades and expulsions of Jews from France, England and the Holy Roman Empire

In the extremely fragmented Europe of the Middle Ages, these two kingdoms had in common being relatively large in comparison with others both by their surface and their population[161]. Despite the doctrine of the official church already marked by anti-Judaism, prosperous Jewish communities were established there since time immemorial, well before the Carolingian era. Great autonomy was left to them by kings and princes, since they had legal and administrative arsenal far more sophisticated for the time than theirs. They were therefore present and active in all the towns, fertile valleys and ports of France and England. Although living separately from the local populations because of their different religious practices, the Jews were nevertheless well integrated everywhere and contributed to the influence of their city. One example among many others is given to us in the person of Rabbi Chlomo ben Itzhak HaTzarfat (1040-1105)[162], originally from the city of Troyes in France, who is better known as "Rashi". At the end of the 11th century, he left behind a considerable amount of commentary on the Talmud. His thought, still widely disseminated today, would bring great renewal in the exegesis of the Old Testament. It has since been a fundamental reference, not

---

[160] Quoted in the documentary film on the Spanish Civil War " Dying in Madrid" – Frédéric Rossif 1963
[161] Google estimate: Population of France in 1300 & population of England in 1300, 7 and 5 million inhabitants respectively.
[162] Rashi: Who Was Rashi? | My Jewish Learning

only in Jewish circles throughout Europe, but also among Christian theologians, including later the reformer Martin Luther. A relative calm seemed to prevail in this period of the High Middle Ages when the official Christian religion had not yet completely conquered hearts and minds. However, everything changed radically or almost, in 1096 on November 27 exactly, when Pope Urban II preached to the council of Clermont-Ferrand the 1st crusade, which was followed by many others. The use of the verb, "to preach" taken up by most historians, to describe the profound meaning of this expedition, armed as well as spiritual, gave it its major characteristic; this crusade was more than a duty, it was a divine order delivered to believers by the one who was supposed to represent God Almighty on earth, namely, the pope. It was "preached", that is, proclaimed from the altar during this famous council, as a revelation from the Almighty God himself. Therefore, it imposed itself on all the faithful, without exception, without the shadow of a discussion or even less of a contestation. The theme of this crusade was to wrest from the Arabs by war the possession of the "Holy Land". Although there are very few evocations in the Bible of what a land is, "Holy", except in a few passages like these; "God says, stay away from here, take your shoes off your feet, for the place where you stand is holy land. (Ex 3:5) and also "The Lord will possess Judah as his part in the holy land, and he will choose Jerusalem again" (Za 2:12). These two terms associated with each other, still refer today in Catholic phraseology, to the country of Israel and mainly, Judea and Samaria, as well as its ancient cities, Jerusalem, Bethlehem, Nazareth and everywhere where Jesus Christ taught and exercised his ministry. At first glance, the papacy's injunction to go on a crusade should have left the Jews out of it. However, very quickly a simple, even simplistic, but logical reasoning tends to prevail among a large number of crusaders; "Why go a thousand leagues to the land of the Saracens to fight the infidels, while in our towns and countryside live, near us, declared enemies of the Christian faith; the Jews? ". The crusade being "preached", it moves from all Europe towards the countries of the Levant. It is a motley cohort that is shaking, it is made of people of all conditions, nobles, knights, peasants, religious, and adventurers of all kinds. Some are motivated only by plunder, ransom, and flight far from their creditors, while others feel invested with a divine order, to bring back the "Holy Land" under Christian jurisdiction. The journey acts as a liberation of morals and all the inhibitions that weigh on the individual in the conformism of medieval society.

As a result, the crusaders quickly engaged in all kinds of violence and massacres. Nowhere were they more terrible than in the Holy Empire. With these great mystic-religious adventures, looting and killing against the Jews would follow one after the other, especially along the Rhine valley and its tributaries, where many communities existed. The cities of Worms, Mainz, and Regensburg to name but a few, were particularly targeted, and it is a trail of blood that remains throughout these valleys, after the passage of the Crusaders, which will focus on Christianity and the Crusades, the indelible stain of crime and sacrilege. Attempts by the nobility and clergy to stem the flow of bloodshed were made here and there, but they remained powerless precisely because of the unfairness of the project and the objectives of the crusade. Indeed, why spare one and fight the other when they are all, according to official doctrine, enemies of Christianity? The estimates of historians vary greatly on the number of victims of the crusaders, Léon Poliakov, citing the sources he had in hand, indicates for his part, the figure of 100,000 dead. Accompanied by forced conversions, looting, and extreme violence, these massacres nevertheless forged in the Jewish soul a will to resist even beyond life. It is sometimes the memory of the citadel of Masada that was evoked, when thousands of Jews entrenched on this rocky peak of the desert of Judea, preferred death to capitulation before the Romans in the year 73, three years after the fall of Jerusalem. After the Crusades, a slow migration of the Jews occurred towards the east, towards Poland and to the north, towards the Baltic countries: Lithuania, Estonia and Latvia. The excesses committed during the First Crusade remained in the Jewish memory as in their writings of the time. The following ones were also deadly for them, the second less so than the first, but during the Third Crusade[163] (1188) large-scale massacres were carried out in England, in London, York, Norwich, Stamford, and many other places[164]. The crusade had become much more than the distant struggle to take back the holy places from the Saracens. It was a means of unifying Christianity through war and violence under the exclusive domination of Catholicism. We saw that "The Reconquista" in Spain was very similar to the crusade, with in parallel: war and conversions. In France "The Albigensian crusade" is one, directed against

---

[163] Léon Poliakov; History of anti-Semitism P 242, 247. Calmann Lévy Publishing
[164] Léon Poliakov; History of anti-Semitism P 243. Calmann Lévy Publishing

the heresy "Cathars". It was preached by Pope Innocent III in 1209. From a purely internal problem to Catholicism, the struggle against heresy extends to Judaism, also guilty of resistance to conversion. It followed massacres and looting in the South of France and by extension in the north of the country[165]. Whenever it is necessary to defend a great cause of Christianity, whenever religious exaltation is aroused from the altar by a fanatical clergy, the Jews are their direct or indirect victims. When the adventure of the crusades was closed, anti-Judaism found other springs to reflect here and there, in a medieval Europe in perpetual crisis. [166] [167] [168]

8.1 Jews in the Holy Roman Empire & Emergence of the Yiddishland

Time of grace and prosperity. This central part of Europe formed after the death of Charlemagne, extending at the beginning of the 16th century from the Vosges Mountains in the west, in present-day France, to Silesia and Poland in the east. To the north it was bounded by the sea and its border with Denmark, while to the south it reached the shores of the Adriatic Sea after having long encompassed Rome and much of northern Italy. Unlike France and England, this vast expanse of various territories had never known any real political unity nor clearly established borders. Until its fall with the abdication of Emperor Francis II[sd] of Austria and the decree of Napoleon the I[st], the French emperor, who abruptly ended its political existence in 1806, the Holy Roman Empire had remained a loose ensemble of very small states with limited sovereignty, vassals of the emperor who oversaw them from Vienna in Austria. Since the Legacy of Charlemagne and the Carolingian kings, several dynasties succeeded at the head of this Holy Roman Empire. That of the Habsburgs lasted the longest, from 1437 to 1806; it would disappear completely only at the end of the First World War with the defeat and the dissolution of the empire of Austria-Hungary in 1918. Although very dispersed in various or even opposite principalities, there is an interesting feature

---

[165] Léon Poliakov; History of anti-Semitism P 241 to 266. Editions Calmann-Lévy
[166] Masada: https://www.biblicalarchaeology.org/masada
[167] Léon Poliakov; History of anti-Semitism P 248. Editions Calmann-Lévy
[168] Léon Poliakov; History of anti-Semitism P 248 et seq. Editions Calmann-Lévy

in the founding myth of this aggregate of multiple sovereignties. It is the idea of perpetuating in Europe an empire, both Roman and Christian. It was an obsession propagated by an imperialist Church aspiring to universal domination, thanks to the power of the rediscovered ancient Rome. The term "Saint" was associated from the beginning of the 12th century with the other three terms: empire, Roman, and Germanic, because the popes wanted it to be entirely at the service of Catholic Christianity. The latter, with its bishoprics, dioceses and parishes, constituted already the local political and administrative backbone of these very diverse territories, without any other form of unity than the divine right that the papacy had granted to its successive emperors. In the context of unstable feudalism and a more theoretical than real central power, the Jews experienced relative peace and a great expansion of their community networks in the valleys of the great German rivers and their tributaries. Everywhere, they contributed by their unrestricted activities to the prosperity of these great German metropolises at the confluence of the many waterways of the country.

We have seen above, however, that the time of the crusades had been throughout Europe, that of doctrinal stiffening and religious fanaticism, with serious consequences for the Jewish people.

8.2 The multiplier effects of anti-Judaism in the Holy Roman Empire

The extreme decentralization of power in the Holy Empire has played a positive role in building an industrious, agile and prosperous society, especially along its major waterways. This is evidenced by the "Hanseatic League", this association of trading cities formed in the 13th century linking, from the Baltic Sea to the North Sea, its main economic centers. The "Hanse" began in 1241 as an association of two cities, Lübeck and Hamburg, one on the shores of the Baltic Sea and the other on the banks of the Elbe not far from the North Sea. Its objective was to promote and protect trade between these two cities. They were gradually joined in the "Hanse" by all the major port cities of northern Europe, from London in the extreme west to the Russian city of Novgorod in the extreme northeast. Enjoying important privileges and being able to impose its views even on the emperor, this alliance demonstrated before the time of the great international companies the strength of associations, of shared power, of consensual decisions, and even a primitive form of political democracy. The comparison with the network of Jewish communities scattered throughout the Holy Empire, is meaningful because it highlights the major role of a kind of cellular division of power in these two types of alliance, opposed to the pyramidal hierarchical power that the church institution tried to impose everywhere. They share similar ideological foundations and values; on both sides, there is the will to promote a pluralistic power quite different from that of the princes and the emperor and also, enrichment through trade. Among their common features is the establishment of a set of precise legal rules for the common good, a relative equality of their representatives in their respective governing bodies. The free entry and exit into the alliance they each formed is also part of it. The "Hanse" would have a major contribution in the promotion of the German language, it promoted the unification of northern dialects, first through texts, then in universities and schools, from the region of Bremen to the west, to Königsberg in the east on the shores of the Baltic Sea. The etymology itself of the adjective "Allemands" has the root: "Alle", "man", that is, "all men". Judaism, for its part, borrowed much of its linguistic structure and vocabulary from German, to which it added elements of Hebrew and Slavic languages. They thus gradually created the "Yiddish[169]" from the early Middle Ages, which became, over time, the common language of most Jewish communities in Germany, Central Europe and the South, and even in distant Russia. The extent of the use of this language was such that it formed this Jewish nation without king or border often called, the "Yiddishland". With Yiddish, the communication within intra-European Judaism was greatly promoted, allowing the formation of a political, intellectual, and financial elite, which in turn, played a major role in structuring the institutions and administrations of the backward countries of Eastern Europe. Yddishland did not survive World War II; Decimated by the Nazis and their accomplices, it lost all of its small and large urban centers. Before this terrible war, it was still spoken by 11 million people and[170] was the subject of abundant literature. Today it is only

---

[169] Hanse: Discover the Hanseatic cities
[170] Yiddish: Yiddish language | History, Culture & Alphabet | Britannica

a language of remembrance, understood and spoken by a few scholars in Israel, the United States and the major Jewish universities. A Polish writer naturalized American Isaac Bashevis Singer, remained faithful to this literary expression and he obtained the Nobel Prize in 1978, for his work written and published in Yiddish. We have seen how the crusades have upset the social context in Europe and how in a few years, the relations between Jews and Christians have stretched to the breaking point. Henceforth, the "People of the Book" became the enemy people within the popular imagination. The historian Léon Poliakov explained that in an extremely divided Holy Empire, the persecutions in one state were quickly known and sometimes amplified in another. They became a recurring phenomenon throughout those small countries and principalities; they turned the victims into guilty of their own condemnation because being Jewish was now a crime. Mildly condemned here and there by bishops and princes, anti-Semitism settled permanently in the Holy Roman Empire from the[171] 13th century, including in states where no Jewish community existed. It became a phantasm, the Jew was the invisible enemy and yet everywhere present, they act in the shadows, they became the ultimate cause of all the misfortunes of the people. It was the whole mythology of the deicide people, sacrilege, adversary of the Gospel, profaner of the hosts and profiteer of the misery of the poor people, which spread in all principalities and cities of the empire. Unlike the great centralized kingdoms of the time, such as France and England, which only expelled their respective Jews a limited number of times, twelve times for the first and only once for the latter, these expulsions were more frequent in the Holy Roman Empire. Moving from one region to another[172], they were often expelled, and, on the whole, a hostile population multiplied against them the most absurd prejudices. One can see in the generalization of his anti-Jewish feelings, without being able to make the formal demonstration, the historical cause of the will to annihilate once and for all, the Jewish people who resurfaced with Nazism in the troubled Germany of the 1930s.

---

[171] Anti-Semitism in the Holy Roman Empire: How anti-Semitism was used to gain political power in medieval Germany - UW Stroum Center for Jewish Studies

[172] History of the Jews in Germany: Jews and Gentiles in the Holy Roman Empire - A Comment (Chapter 4) - In and out of the Ghetto

8.3 Expulsion of Jews in Europe from the[173] 12th to the 16th century

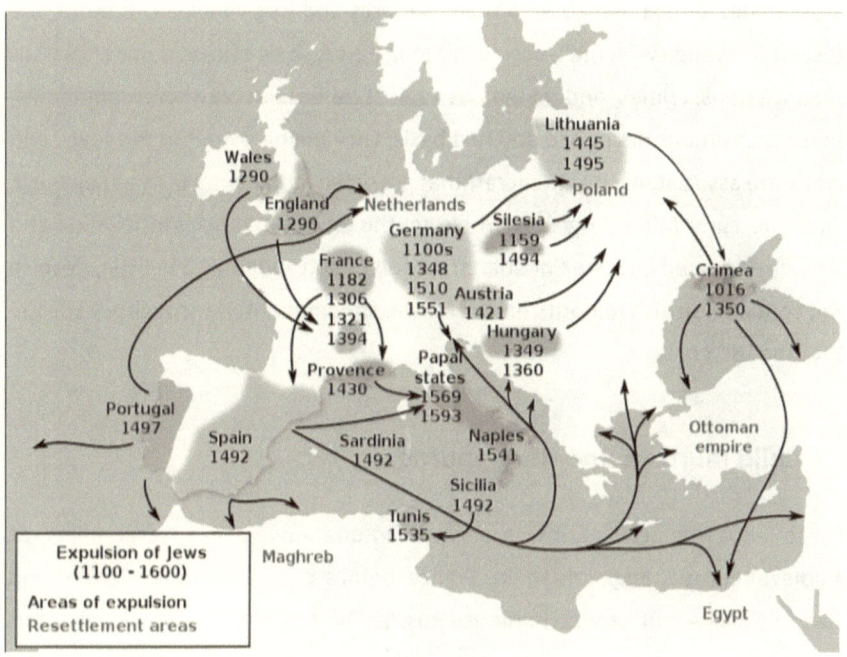

8.4 Main accusations against Israel and Jews

This section develops some of the best-known but also the most emblematic accusations of mass Christianity against Jews. Their main characteristics are to be systematic and outrageous, soliciting the absurd and fanaticism in ignorant populations.

8.5 The profanation of hosts,

The host is declared sacred in Catholicism since it is according to dogma, the very body of Jesus Christ. Accordingly, the suspicion or accusation of having profaned

---

[173] Expulsion of Jews: No Return: Jews, Christian Usurers, and the Spread of Mass Expulsion in Medieval Europe | Department of History

the host is instructed by a clergy who does not shrink from any excesses in order to pursue the Jews with a merciless zeal and to raise from during the Middle age, the indignation and anger of a people largely ignorant and more sensitive to condemnation and anathema than to mercy and forgiveness. Therefore, the desire for revenge will entail, during this long period, a significant number of trials of convictions, crimes, and massacres against defenseless Jewish communities. These accusations never had any real basis; they mainly targeted the Jews, and they were associated with witchcraft that persisted at the same time as paganism since the early Middle Ages. A whole mythology of extravagant legends and prejudices passed into the Christian tradition of anti-Judaism to belittle, despise and condemn Jewish minority and defenseless communities throughout Europe until the 18th century.

8.6 Child murders and ritual murders

These extreme accusations appeared simultaneously in several parts of medieval Europe, England, Spain, France before passing through Central and Eastern Europe and into the immense Russia. This not only criminal act was, but moreover, considered an abomination by the Lord in Judaism, underlined by this passage from the Book of Deuteronomy, "Let no one in you be found to carry his son or daughter by fire... For whoever does these things is an abomination to the Lord; and it is because of these abominations that the Lord your God will cast out these nations before you" (Deu 18:10, 12). This is a reminder that the God of Isaac, Jacob, Moses, and the whole nation of Israel is above all the God of life and that, beyond religious, national and cultural differences, he is the one who blesses life and especially that of children. Pope Innocent IV[174] himself had to intervene to try to bring back to reason the fanatical propagators of these fantasies. In a text addressed to the German episcopate in 1247, he recalled the flagrant contradiction between this stupid accusation and Jewish theology when he stated: "We have heard of the deplorable situation of the Jews against whom some spiritual and temporal princes and other powerful lords in your

---

[174] Innocent IV (1247) to the German episcopate quoted in Johannes Oesterreicher. Racism, anti-Semitism, anti-Christianism. DEER 1940 P 61-62

countries and bishoprics imagine all kinds of pretexts, in order to attack them, to plunder them and strip them of their property in an unjust manner. Though Sacred Scripture says to them, "Thou shalt not kill" and forbids them to touch during the Passover to something dead, they are charged with the crime of taking communion that day with the heart of a child killed, and they are done as if the law prescribed it to them, while this act would clearly be contrary to the Law...[175]
. Unfortunately, this plea for Jews supported by biblical references remained very isolated, and it did little or nothing to detach the Roman institution from its militant anti-Judaism theorized in its founding texts for centuries. Indeed, in the twelfth century, the accusation of ritual murder was launched, and pyres were lit against the Jews, especially in the city of Blois[176] in 1171.

8.7 The job of usurers; the starvers of the people

Very early the church institution condemned the loan with interest as a disguised theft, it wrote this about it[177]; "To receive an interest for the use of the loaned money is in itself unfair, because it is to make pay what does not exist; what is, of course, unevenness contrary to justice... what is usury. And since one is obliged to return property acquired unjustly, one is also obliged to return money received as interest". From trade to usury, the step was taken by Judaism, finally reduced to this end by the evolution of the economic and social circumstances where it found itself in medieval Europe. Indeed, the prohibition of the loan with interest made the currency extremely rare and its circulation between the economic agents of the time all the more difficult. Who could have had interest in lending without being able to get any remuneration[178] from his loan? Although it was never completely absent from the contracts signed between Christian economic agents, this singular activity returned almost naturally to the Jews. The first element of this professional evolution towards loan sharking was the ban on them exercising an increasing number of other professions. These prohibitions appeared between the 10th and 13th centuries, namely, the maritime trade with

---

[175] Anti-Judaism: Various accusations and expulsions
[176] Anti-Semitism in France: Anti-Judaism before the revolution.
[177] Usury (finance) History: The usury - Jewish Community of Venice
[178] Léon Poliakov History of Antisemitism P 267 – 269 – Editions Calmann-Lévy

the East, the possession of land and buildings, the teaching of Christians, and the exercise of justice at any level. The second element of this evolution was the extreme precariousness of their condition as a minority exposed to the abuse and persecution of a population hostile to their very existence. It was therefore necessary for them to possess at all times, this money in liquid form to be able to leave or even flee away from their attackers. The need to be "liquid", placed them at the same time in ideal conditions to lend to princes, kings, the church and its dignitaries, cardinals, bishops and all its representatives. Being "liquid" was also necessary to pay the countless specific taxes, duties, and fees to which they were subjected by civil, religious, royal, state, urban authorities, and much more... Now deprived of any other outlet on the social scene, they have gradually evolved towards this despised but necessary function of lending money with interest. The link between money and life only strengthened for the local community, often grouped around a banker able to provide resources and organize its life so that it never lacks this precious "liquid". Money, the real umbilical cord of Judaism during the Middle Ages, played a major role in the birth of the mythology of the "avaricious" Jew, usurper and starver of the people. He is the man without conscience, but no, without interest. He constantly recalls in popular imagery Judas Iscariot, the one who sold his master for 30 silver coins. This is at least a reason to believe, what the priests say about them, since it is a fact that can be seen in the everyday social life. Condemning with its voice and texts the loan with interest, the church and its dignitaries, were nevertheless among the first beneficiaries of the system, an English lawyer of the XIIIth century, named Bracton[179], summarizes the Jewish condition with these words; "The Jew can have nothing of his own: everything he acquires becomes the property of the king not his own, the Jews do not live for themselves but for others, so it is for others that they acquire and not for them". In his work, "Somme Angélique" the Franciscan Angel of Chivasso theologian of the XIIIth century has this abrupt definition of the Jew, taken as a legal entity; "Being Jewish is a crime not punishable by the Christian, however, as it is the case with the heretic[180]". This definition of the Jew, the perpetrator of a crime under the law because of his birth alone, is

---

[179] Quote: Léon Poliakov History of Anti-Semitism P 270
[180] Quote: Léon Poliakov History of Anti-Semitism P 270

not only scandalous, but rather reverses the condemnation on the one who pronounced it. However, it also reflects the monstrous idea that never ceased to germinate until the Nuremberg laws and the Nazi persecutions that followed them, according to which, the Jew is placed from his birth to his death in the box of the defendants of a court that holds hearings permanently because he is part of a race justiciable under religious and civil laws.

8.8 Isolation: Life in the Ghetto

Because of their religious practices and strong community ties, the Jews of the diaspora, wherever they were present, lived together in a well-defined perimeter. De facto, this grouping gave rise to the creation of Jewish neighborhoods in some cities, and it gave rise to a very particular urbanism since the exile that followed the fall of Jerusalem at the time of King Zedekiah in 587 AD, until today. The word used in France in the Middle Ages to designate such neighborhoods was, "the Jewry" and, even today, there are not less than 300 streets called by the name of, "the Jewry" or even, "street of the Jews" in various cities of the country. However, with the expansion of Christianity what was only a habit without restriction of right or obligation of residence became an increasingly strong constraint accompanied by vexatious and discriminatory measures. The reform of the so-called Gregorian Catholic institution in the 11th century marked a hardening of the papacy towards the Jewish communities present in the states of the pope and even beyond. Later, the Lateran Council in 1215 made it compulsory for Christians to sever all relations with the Jews. This exclusion reinforced the compartmentalization of Jewish communities in their neighborhoods throughout Europe. In 1515, the Jewish quarter of Venice took the name of "Ghetto", which means the "foundry", in Venetian dialect. It was there, on the site of an old foundry, that the Jews had settled for a long time, but now they were constrained to do so. In 1555, Pope Paul IV published the papal bull; "Cum nimis absurdum" by which, he recalls all previous jurisdictions made against the Jews and specifies new provisions even more binding as the wearing of different clothes for men and women, putting in place a fence around their neighborhood with a single entry and exit point. It was thus closed and more guarded night and day by a Christian agent paid by the community. The limitation of relations with Christians extended to many areas of work and service, as the following excerpt states: "How absurd and totally inappropriate it is to find oneself in a situation where Christian piety allows the Jews, who by their own fault have been condemned by God to perpetual slavery, to have access to our society and even to live among us; in truth, they are without gratitude to Christians because, instead of thanking us for the benevolent treatment, they return invective to us, and among them, instead of slavery, which they deserve, they arrange to claim their superiority: we, who have recently learned that these Jews have invaded Rome from several Papal States, territories and domains, to the extent that they mix with Christians, even those near their churches, and wear no dress to identify them, and also that they reside in houses, even in the noblest residences of the States, territories and estates, in which they linger, conducting their affairs from their homes and in the street and trading real estate; they even have Christian nurses and maids they employ...[181]

....

1) We order that for the rest of the time, in the City [of Rome], as well as in all the other States, territories and domains of the Church of Rome, all Jews will have to live in one district, which will have only one entrance, and only one exit, and that if there are not enough places [in this neighborhood, then], in two or three or the necessary number; in any case, they must reside entirely among themselves in designated streets and be fundamentally separated from the residences of Christians, [this must be applied] by our authority in the City and by that of our representatives in other States, lands and estates mentioned above.

2) Moreover, in all the states, territories, and areas in which they live, they will have only one synagogue, in the usual place, and they will not build new ones, nor will they own their own buildings. In addition, all their synagogues, other than the one authorized, will have to be destroyed and demolished. And the properties they currently own will have to be

---

[181] Cum nimis absurdum: July 14, 1555, Pope Paul IV publishes the "Cum nimis absurdum"

sold to Christians within a time to be determined by the magistrates themselves.

3) Moreover, concerning the question that the Jews should be recognizable everywhere: [to this end] men should wear a hat, women, some obvious sign, of yellow color, which should not be hidden or covered in any way, and should be firmly affixed [sewn] ; and in addition, they shall not be absolved or excused from their obligation to wear the hat or any other emblem of this kind on any occasion and under any pretext, regardless of their rank or importance or ability to tolerate [this] adversity, whether by a chamberlain of the Church, clerics of an Apostolic Chamber, or their superiors, or by legates of the Holy See, or their immediate subordinates.

4) Also, they will not be able to have nannies or servants or any other Christian servant, nor use Christian women to breastfeed or feed their children.

5) ....

15) And if in any way they should not submit to the foregoing, it must be treated as a crime: in Rome, by us or by our clergy, or by anyone authorized by us, and in the above-mentioned States, territories and fields, by their respective magistrates, exactly as if they were rebels or criminals according to the jurisdiction where the offence was committed; they will be accused by all the Christian people, by us and by our clergy, and may be punished at the discretion of the appropriate authorities and judges."

8.9 Marking of the Jews: the rouelle and the yellow star.

The[182] spinning wheel, or wheel, is a small piece of cloth whose ostensible wearing is imposed on the Jews as a distinctive dress sign by Pope Innocent III and widely respected by the civil authorities, from the thirteenth century. This period is

---

[182] Léon Poliakov: History of Anti-Semitism P 259 – Edition Calmann-Lévy

clearly one of rigor and increasing discrimination against Jews. Canon No. 3 of the Council of Lateran 1215 is unambiguous in its terms when it states: "We excommunicated and anathematized all heresy against the holy faith, orthodox and catholic". Jews naturally, but also Saracens are targeted. It is about ruling by exclusion, religious authority, political, and exceptional laws. This century comes after the so-called "Gregorian" reform (1049-1085), which had the first, followed the path of firmness, the will for power, the moral and institutional recovery of the papacy and the entire ecclesial hierarchy. Historians believe that its effect lasted for more than 3 centuries and that it preceded increasingly authoritarian measures against any form of dissent whether those of the, "Cathars", that of "Vaudois" or that of "Marranes", the latter being the converted Jews, whose religious organization suspected of conversion, lack of sincerity. The best known of the institutions of the repressive arsenal implemented by the imperialist church is the Inquisition, which from the 13th century would hear trials in heresy of all kinds, persecuted any dissent, and sent to the pyre or torture many of its victims. Marking as a sign of infamy will be part of these repressive measures decided against the Jews. It was imported from the East by the Crusaders, and it was imposed on the Jews by Pope Innocent III at the Council of Lateran[183] (1215) in its canon number 68. The historian Léon Poliakov[184] traces the evolution of this infamous obligation, marking, like cattle, individuals with a distinctive sign. This was the wheel or a small wheel, a piece of round fabric sewn upon the garment. Its shape was supposed to represent the thirty silver coins received by Judah for the payment of his betrayal of Jesus Christ. The wearing of this badge should allow everyone at once to distinguish Jews from Christians, to avoid dating between the two communities, and, above all, to prevent the possible risks of union between their members. In accordance with the provisions of the Council of Lateran[185], in France King Saint Louis and in England King Henry III, ordered the wearing of the rouelle to their respective Jews. At the same time in most states of the Holy Roman Empire, the distinctive sign for Jews would be the yellow or red cap. This sign remained in use until the sixteenth century and was replaced

---

[183] Léon Poliakov, History of Antisemitism The Age of Faith volume 1 P 259-260 Edition Calmann-Lévy
[184] Anti-Judaism: From the First Crusade to the Renaissance. Antisemitism in History: From the Early Church to 1400 | Holocaust Encyclopedia
[185] Fourth Lateran Council 1215: Strengthening the exclusion of "Jews and Saracens"

by the yellow star, the symbolic color of the betrayal that would continue for a long time. A popular expression has even remained in contemporary language in France, to denote in contempt the one who is a traitor or unworthy of trust, it is said of him; «He is a yellow one".

The yellow star: This star is a distinctive sign of Judaism in the form of two equilateral triangles superimposed in opposition to each other. It is called "Maguen David" in Hebrew, it also represents the "Shield of David". Present since antiquity as a sign of identification of Judaism, it symbolizes the reign of King David and that of his lineage after him. Today, the Star of David is at the center of the flag of Israel, it is placed on the pediment of its public and religious buildings. Originally, it was by no means a discriminatory sign, rather, it was the testimony of Jewish national pride and deep messianic hope. This sign has received many symbolic and poetic meanings, including: the six days of creation represented by the six branches of the hexagram within the center, on the seventh day, that of the Sabbath of the Lord. After the destruction of the second temple and the dispersal of the Jewish people to the four corners of Europe, this star takes on the meaning of discrimination and later, infamy. In the regions won by Islam, it was first imposed on the Jews in order to mark their submission as Dhimmis, that is, foreigners, non-Muslims, and subject to a special tax. This sign was reintroduced by the Nazi regime in 1942, during the occupation of Europe. The regimes of collaboration with the German occupier would apply, not without stormy debates sometimes, this discriminatory measure, in spite of the reprobation that it would generate in general among the populations.

9. Triumph and Decline of the Papal Institution, Prelude to the Reformation

9.1 1Timothy 6.10: "For the love of money is a root of all evils."

This process of apogee and perigee is spread over more than five centuries, it has all the characteristics of these human organizations that go through the hesitant or chaotic beginnings, then a complete triumph before experiencing a more or less long decline. Jules-Marcel Nicole in his, "Précis d'Histoire de l'Église" speaks in his

3rd part of, "The Church at the Apogee of the Papal Power", which he situates[186] from the 11th to the 13th century. It is characterized by the concentration of power within it, far superior to that of the kings and princes of a Europe that will never find its unity, neither institutional nor political. From this period remained several characteristic features of the institution, which neither time nor contradictions related to the Bible have removed. It is first of all, the election of the pope by a college of cardinals decreed under the pontificate of Nicholas II in 1059 at the Synod of Lateran and maintained to this day. It had the double advantage of removing it from the many palace intrigues and of supporting it on a representation much better distributed throughout Catholic Christianity. It is then, the so-called reform, "Gregorian" of the name of Gregory VII its initiator. It is characterized by a strengthening of the papal authority, by a great effort of discipline, by the fight against corruption in the institution. It imposed by decree in 1074 the celibacy for all clergymen. The biblical texts are thus diverted in order to impose in the society a vision of, "the man of the church" different from, "the lay man" or secular, that is to say, of the present age, when the former are timeless because they are spiritually married to the eternal Church of God. Before this date, celibacy was highly regarded in the ecclesial hierarchy, without being obligatory. With this decree, the clergy was supposed to live without any existential concern other than their ministry and incidentally, it helped the church avoid the fragmentation of its vast domains by successive inheritances because the venality of ecclesial offices was often the rule. There was also during this period the affirmation of the superiority of spiritual power over the temporal; "going to Canossa" remained one of the most famous expressions in the popular language. It means for a great dignitary of this world, to submit to the pope, and it has become, by extension, to submit to any holder of authority. In fact, King Henry IV of the Holy Empire believed he could depose this pope in question so intransigent, but his enterprise failed, and he had to go to Canossa in Tuscany, imploring his forgiveness, barefoot and dressed in the rags of the penitent. France also had to suffer from the immense power of the pope, when Innocent III in 1200, placed it under ban because his king Philip Augustus II, had repudiated his wife without any valid reason. This act of papal

---

[186] Jules-Marcel Nicole: Church History Précis, P 97 to 101. Editions of the Bible Institute of Nogent-sur-Marne

authority released the subjects from their oath of allegiance to their king, closed small and large parishes and no longer allowed the celebration of church services or the registration of births and deaths. In the end, it was a shameful monarch who was forced to yield and take back his legitimate wife, to obtain the lifting of the ban. A similar misadventure happened to the King of England John without Land, following a conflict with the Archbishop of Canterbury. After a stalemate of several years, the king made an act of submission in 1215, recognizing that his country was now a vassal of the papacy; he also agreed to pay him a significant annual tribute, not without raising the violent opposition of a large part of the nobility of the country. These examples, to which many more could be added, give a glimpse of this unequalled power of the pontiffs over kings, their kingdom, and their subjects. In the fourth part of his recently quoted opening, Jules Marcel Nicole speaks of the decline of the Catholic system at the height of its power. It is a slow erosion that runs through the fourteenth century, it is marked by a succession of failures that arouse so many counterpowers. First of all, the failure of the Crusades made missionary zeal for the conquest of the holy places fall into indifference. It was also the unfortunate episode of the reign of the popes in Avignon from 1309 to 1378, and of the inversion of power that thus passes brutally from the papacy to the king of France. After these 70 years, another no less chaotic period opens between 1378 and 1417 with what historians have called "the Great Western Schism". Indeed, for nearly 40 years, no less than three popes fought for spiritual power over Christianity in the West. One seat in Rome, he is recognized by the Holy Empire, England and Italy, the other remained in Avignon, it was supported by France and Spain. To remedy this disastrous testimony of quarrels at the top of the institution, a council meeting in Pisa in 1409 deposed the first two popes and elected a third, Alexander V (1409 ~1410). The worst was then to come because the two popes in question refused their relegation and excommunicated the cardinals who made this new election. Catholicism found itself for a time, with three leaders claiming succession to the papal throne. The remedy was much worse than evil because John XXIII, who succeeded in the ephemeral Alexander V, was only an intriguing, licentious, perverse, and greedy adventurer. He was even suspected of the murder of his predecessor. He was finally deposed and as well as the two other popes at the Council of Constance in 1415, which put an end to this extravagant schism, by electing Martin V, who finally brought the papacy back to Rome. The latter has not yet finished with scandals and infighting because the councils and the elected popes did not rely on the authority of the Bible. Indeed, at the end of the 15th century, they brought to power Alexander IV Borgia (1492 ~1503) and with him, his family and illegitimate descendants entered the papal affairs. It was through intrigue and poison that he plundered more than governed an institution that inspired only fear and contempt in the popular conscience. His successor, Julius II (1503~1513), more a soldier than prelate, was concerned only with the extension of the pope's states. He dreamed of an entire Italy submitted to the papacy and fought constantly to increase its possessions. His successor, Leo X (1513~1521), more peaceful but not much more inspired, loved the arts and luxury. Having great need of money for the construction of the Basilica of Rome, he was an ardent promoter throughout Europe of the sale of indulgences, those false promises by which the clergy made a promise to all those who gave their money for the immediate; the forgiveness of sins and for eternity, the reduction of the sojourn in purgatory with the entry into heaven in the presence of God. This financial manna, along with the many other ecclesiastical benefits, generated a huge flow of money into the Vatican coffers. Leo X did not see the rising of a new era before this manifest abuse of power over consciences, a humble monk by the name of Martin Luther, who denounced him forcefully to the point of bringing about the total collapse of Catholic Christianity over much of northern Europe with the advent of Protestantism. [187]

9.2 The Reformation or the restoration of the authority of the Bible

Among the main events preceding the Reformation, historians readily cited the invention of Johannes Gutenberg's movable type printing. Indeed, it was the Bible in the version of Saint Jerome, known as the "Vulgate" that was chosen to inaugurate the new page of human scholarship between 1452 and 1455. This invention brought with it first access to sacred texts and then, by extension, the diffusion of knowledge, culture, intellectual and metaphysical speculation to the greatest number. Thanks to it, the knowledge hitherto confiscated by the clergy in

---

[187] Jules-Marcel Nicole: Church History Diary, P 124 to 134. Editions of the Bible Institute of Nogent-sur-Marne

monasteries and abbeys multiplied and overflew their borders. This time was also characterized by great anguish about death, with this pending question: can one be saved, and can one be sure of his salvation? Epidemics, wars, disorders in religion, and the fragility of life lead many to seek in God and him alone, the foundations of human destiny. The arts, literature, and philosophy of the time bore witness to this anguish of nations and their spiritual needs. An Augustinian monk, Martin Luther, will embody this turning point in theological reflection by giving it this orientation closer to the texts of the Bible than to the Catholic scholastic. In his confrontation with the power of the papacy, he will be led to specify the 5 founding principles for a revival of Christianity described below. They had everything to radically change the Christian perspective as a whole and to bring it back to its original purity.

9.3 "Sola Scriptura" or Scripture Alone

This first principle expresses the idea that it is the Scripture of the texts of the Bible alone, which is authoritative for the life of the Christian as for that of the Church. Thus, the Reformation passed, the spiritual authority, from the changing reign of men, kings, popes, and their councils, to that of the Sacred Book, which contains God's eternal thought for his people, for each individual, and all humanity. This principle has undoubtedly and durably brought Christianity closer to its origin, namely Judaism. Indeed, when the apostle Paul declares to his disciple Timothy: "All Scripture is inspired by God, and useful for teaching, for convincing, for correcting, for teaching in righteousness" (2Tim 3:16), he does not speak of the New Testament, which is not yet completed nor compiled, he speaks of the Old or First Testament that already existed. It was therefore in Jewish wisdom and inspiration that the first disciples and the nascent Church were formed. It is in these that the reformer Martin Luther intended to restore the inspiration, order, and structure of a Reformed Church.

9.4 "Sola fide" or, By faith alone.

The second principle of the Reformation expresses the fundamental idea that man's salvation comes only through "faith alone". It is opposed to the Catholic idea of that time, according to which it was possible to buy one's salvation, by the papal indulgences, at the price of money. Deepening this principle makes it clear that it is more generally opposed to the notion of salvation through works, often expressed in Catholicism through penances, personal sacrifices, and various wishes intended to obtain from God a special favor. In other words, this principle expresses this fundamental truth: we do not buy God, and it is by faith in his Word that man can be saved. This second principle leads directly to the third.

9.5 "Sola gratia" by Grace alone.

What is "grace"? The Bible, from its first lines to its last, speaks of the guilty and lost man without God. In chapter 3 of the book of Genesis, because of the sin that entered their lives, the Eternal God drove Adam and Eve away from the Garden of Eden, he declared: "You are dust and you will return to dust" (Gen 3:19). Thus, the biblical conception of man is that of a sinful living being lost in the immensity of creation. Grace is therefore necessary since he is guilty and constantly on trial with God. In his situation, he can only plead guilty and accept the grace that God offers him in Jesus Christ, his only Son, who died for the forgiveness of his sins. In one person, only Jesus Christ, the Christian obtains grace and forgiveness, which is why the fourth principle of the Reformation bears the name of the Savior himself.

9.6 "Solus Christus" in Jesus Christ only.

This is a powerful reminder that all of Christianity since its origin brings the believer back to the example of Jesus Christ. He is the one who accepted to give his life for his people, but also for all people, "in as many as our God will call them" (Acts 2:39). He is the eternal Son of God, he is the incarnate God, living among men and sharing their burdens. He is also Eternal and risen from the dead after his crucifixion. This fourth principle, which bears the very name of the Messiah of Israel, shows that he alone is worthy of worship as God the Father and God the Spirit. This fourth principle also shows that the many mythologies built over the centuries on the life of the "saints" and on all the dignitaries of the church-institution are vain, false, illusory, and that we must not address them with our prayers and worship them.

9.7 "Soli Deo Gloria" for the glory of God alone

The fifth principle of the Reformation is that of "Soli Deo Gloria", which means: for the glory of God alone. It could serve as a starting point for a long meditation so rich in meaning and depth. It certainly inspired generations of men and women who, in response to God's love, wanted to put their lives at the service of his glory. For what is doing the "Glory of God" if it is not doing good by applying one's heart to put into practice, in one's daily life, the Word of God, one's Law and one's basic principles. From then on, the "Glory of God" becomes accessible to all people of goodwill. Far from the splendor of the clergy, the gigantic basilicas, and the snoring titles, the "Glory of God" is cultivated in humility, faith, and obedience to his Word. Protestantism, therefore brought Christianity back to its point of origin, namely the Bible. The great reformer Martin Luther, at the beginning of his work, linked with Judaism very naturally and multiplied the contacts and the relations with its representatives. Thus, he wrote several texts on this subject like this one in 1523: "That Jesus is Jewish by birth", to affirm this organic link between Judaism and Christianity. He rather naively hoped that the Jews would convert "en masse" to the new Reformed religion stripped of the errors and artifices of the old and based on authentically biblical roots. However, what he hoped for would never happen, and at the end of his life, he was a bitter man who wrote violent pamphlets against the Jews, the best known of which is this one: "The Jews and their lies", composed in 1543 three years before his death. As we know, Protestantism in several forms would spread like wildfire throughout Europe, mainly to the north. It would allow a great return to the founding texts of Christianity. Besides the innumerable advances that it would allow in Christian universalism, Protestantism would not foster the flourishing of the personal expression of the faith as Jesus-Christ himself wanted it for his disciples and for all those who followed him around the world when he declared to them in his last message; "... he who believes and is baptized will be saved, but he who does not believe will be condemned" (Ma 16:16).

9.8 From collective to the individual or the difficult emancipation of Protestant Christianity

Whether Lutheran, Reformed or Anglican, Protestantism will often remain locked into political and social issues from birth until today. Indeed, history has not spared them. Where they laid down the principles and words of biblical wisdom in universities and libraries, through their writings and speeches, they often received in return threats, blows, insults, persecutions, and finally war. The resumption in hand of a Christianity of state very far from its evangelical bases, could not be done serenely in dialogue and peace. Whether in France with the wars of religion, in Germany with the terrible "30 years' war" or in Great Britain with the civil war and the fall of the Stuarts dynasty at the end of the "Glorious Revolution" in 1688. Everywhere, it was war that decided what the humble citizen was allowed to believe and not to believe. Entire regions went from Catholic to Protestant or vice versa, without popular consent and with the application of this absurd rule, which followed the Augsburg Peace of 1555. It is called in Latin: "Cujus regio, ejus religio" and means that the faith of the prince decides that of the population. For a long period of time the prince considered himself invested with a divine right, with a special higher authority to decide in the place of his subjects which articles of faith they should believe. In the 16th century, the temporal and spiritual powers of the churches remained inseparable and in general, faith was not personal, but rather a vague collective custom. That is to say, it often boils down to conformism, passive obedience to the prince's injunctions, and it remained very far from what the texts of the Bible have said. The promise of individual freedom in relation to the Word of God contained in the Book of Deuteronomy of the Bible (Dt 30:15-16) remained a dead letter, most of the time. Fortunately, and despite these adverse conditions, it was in Protestantism that the power of the biblical message was finally able to express itself freely. It allowed, often despite the resistance of their hierarchy, the emergence of spiritual awakening movements, here and there in these Protestant countries. Together, they brought the true renewal of a Christianity centered on the revelation of the Word of God at the elementary level, that is, at the level of the individual. Since the Anabaptists of the time of Luther from 1523, Puritans, Baptists, then Methodists in the eighteenth century, and until today Pentecostals have succeeded one another. Together they formed what is called the "Evangelical Churches", whose world has difficulty understanding the phenomenal expansion in the 21st century, while official Christianity is everywhere in decline.

10. Consequences: the legitimacy of the right to hatred and contempt

As the ebb of the tide reveals on the beach, relief and underwater life, the retreat of the religious practice at the end of the 20th century puts in the light of day its legacy accumulated by history. The human church-institution did not delay in borrowing from man rather than from God, its most questionable character traits, namely; compromises, corruptions, nepotism, interest, ambitions, abuse of power, hypocrisy, and so many other faults that are not the fruits of the Holy Spirit. Its historical and theological journey is ultimately parallel to that of the synagogue-institution, which Jesus Christ denounced in his time when he told his disciples, "... How can you not understand that it is not about bread that I have spoken to you? Save yourselves from the leaven of the Pharisees and the Sadducees. Then they understood that it was not the leaven of bread that he had told them to keep, but the teaching of the Pharisees and the Sadducees." (Ma 16:11-12). These two verses could be paraphrased by replacing "Pharisees and Sadducees" with "priests, pastors, and theologians". This would certainly be a hasty generalization, for many, like the Pharisees, have exercised their ministry honestly, and it must be taken into account, however, this comparison is necessary given the evolution of what was at the beginning only a modest, "small flock" (Lu 12:32) and which became in a few centuries this colossal spiritual and temporal empire. It will not be stripped of all the greatness of its past, of its brave men and of their timeless works, whether in the cultural, artistic, religious, social, or moral fields. However, the cost of this colossal undertaking is exorbitant considering the benefits obtained; it is unbearable in many respects and still weighs on the shoulders of European society as a whole, even in its diversity as of today. How to get rid of anti-Semitic legislation still engraved in the texts of the so-called Christian theology? How to erase these centuries of contempt against the people of God? How to rehabilitate those whose very birth is a crime? How can we propose the message of love and grace of the

Gospel to those who, through dogma, have been excluded from it? How do we get back from the death camps all the innocent people who were sent there? These are impossible things for men, and all that remains is to listen to this word of Jesus Christ found in the Gospel of Mark; "What is impossible to men is possible to God" (Mk 18:27). This legacy is unbearable because instead of the Bible, it is contempt that has been taught for centuries. For his work on this poisoned legacy, the Jewish historian Jules Isaac has indeed chosen this title: "The teaching of contempt". He wrote it the day after the Second World War in which he lost his entire family in Auschwitz. After long being with his Catholic colleague Albert Malet, the preferred historian of French schoolchildren because of the quality of their schoolbooks. He was revoked from national education by the German puppet government of Marshal Pétain in 1940. According to the racist principles of the Vichy regime and his leader, who concluded; a Jew could not teach their own history to the little French schoolchildren. His book, whose reading is still topical, shows how the successive layers of theologies, of various theories, of popular uses, have grown, and how they produced this monstrous and devastating torrent of hatred and crimes that we are all still drenched in today. This inexorable path of the right to hatred and contempt was perfectly described by the apostle James in his epistle. Indeed, he speaks of this cumulative process that can be implemented in a heart, as this passage perfectly describes: "But everyone is tempted when he is attracted and initiated by his own lust. Then covetousness when it conceived begets sin; and sin, being consumed, produces death" (Jas 1:14). The apostle first evokes a desire that would be very personal. In religious anti-Judaism, what lust can it be? We have explained this partially above by showing that it may be related to the claim of having replaced Israel in the heart of God. This lust is an excessive ambition that cannot be fulfilled. It is even aberrant because, according to the whole Bible, no one can qualify himself in the eyes of God. It is easy to be convinced that there has not been a replacement when one is attentive to the whole Bible and particularly to this verse already quoted: "For God does not repent of his gifts and his call" (Rom 11:29). However, the mystic-religious desire to replace Israel in the heart of God did exist. From personal, it became collective as we have emphasized and it attracted to it, many religious men, the dignitaries of a church of the first centuries who sought a power very different from that of the Holy

Spirit. Fascinated by the military and political prestige of the Roman Empire, it was rather this power that they sought and not that of the Holy Spirit, which God gives to his children to do good. Thus, according to the sequence described by the apostle James, this lust became a sin. It is a new doctrine alien to the Gospels that appeared, was written, and formalized in a pseudo-Christian theology, as we have seen it above. As for childbirth, it took it time to conceive and give birth to anti-Judaism, from her first roots in a Marcion of Sinope until the modern era. In the next stage, sin is consumed, that is, it becomes food for the one who eats it. This food goes through the body; it spreads and diffuses to its smallest parts. Thus, from the top down of the religious pyramid, the teaching of contempt is dispensed, and with it, the right to hatred is legitimized. This is the last step in the process described by the apostle: the consumption of this sin produces death. It is the direct consequence of this sin; spiritual death for the institution that planted these seeds of death, spiritual death for the one who taught or teaches these doctrines of death. Spiritual death finally, for one who listens and believes in these doctrines of death rather than the message of life taught by the Bible. Dominating and self-confident, the politico-religious nomenclature installed in power among kings and powerful, inspires and produces a set of rules of law and social norms that are slowly spreading throughout society (See Annexes). Among these are the right to hatred and contempt of the Jews. This right falls within a particular legal category of civil law, as well as property law, constitutional law, commercial law, and many other categories of law. Thus, the right that normally protects and regulates social life becomes the right that accuses, punishes, and excludes a part of the population without real cause. In examining these distortions of meaning introduced into our law based on anti-Jewish religious prejudice, we think of these prophetic words, one found in the Gospel of John: "But this has happened so that the word written in their law may be fulfilled: They have hated me without cause" (Jn 15:25) , the second in Psalms 119:86; "All your commandments are fidelity; They persecute me without cause: help me!" and also this third also in Psalms 69:4, "They are more numerous than the hair of my head, those who hate me without cause; They are powerful, those who want to lose me…". The repetition of the two words, "… without cause", emphasizes the absence of rational or emotional, objective or subjective justification and the fundamental unfairness of the process; It is hatred by decree.

10.1 A major oversight: the co-responsibility of the Jewish religious world and the Roman pagan world in the condemnation of Jesus Christ.

The discourse of official Christianity, points exclusively to the guilt of the condemnation of Jesus Christ on the Jewish people and on its religious leaders, while it passes entirely under silence the guilt of the pagan authorities of Rome, who also participated in this condemnation in the person of Pontius Pilate, their local chief and soldiers performing his low works. It is necessary to recall here that in the 10 commandments, the one who executes the crime is no less guilty than the one who orders it. Indeed, we remember that at the Nuremberg trial and the others that followed it, at the liberation of Europe at the end of 1945; It was not only the people who were convicted of the Nazi crimes, but also the people who carried out the crimes at the lowest level. It is an important historical reminder that the Law of God is valid for those who exercise power as for those who apply it and that the individual can never free himself from his personal conscience in the acts he performs. In his writings, Augustine d'Hippone tried to exonerate the Roman procurator Pontius Pilate of all complicity and therefore of all guilt with regard to the murder of Jesus Christ. He will be careful to explain in detail that the ultimate responsibility lies with the Jews and with them alone when he writes in his Commentaries of[188] Psalm 63 :"That the Jews do not come to say: "It is not we who put Christ to death." For if they delivered him to the court of Pilate, it is to appear innocent of his death. […] But did they think they were deceiving the sovereign Judge who was God? What Pilate did, to the extent that he did, somehow made him their accomplice. But compared to them, he's much less guilty. […] If it was Pilate who pronounced the sentence and gave the order to crucify him, if it was, he who somehow killed him, you Jews also put him to death. [...] When you shouted, "Cross! In cross!". This essay of rhetoric to exonerate the Roman part, does not resist the examination of the politico-legal context of the time because indeed, in this part of the Roman Empire as in the others besides, only the Roman courts had the right to render justice and enforce the death sentence. Consequently, the decree, issued against Jesus by the Sanhedrin,

---

[188] Augustine of Hippo: Relations with Judaism, AUGUSTINE - JewishEncyclopedia.com

could only be executed by another decree, that of the Roman occupier. These are the facts; The latter is therefore well, "wet" in a way up to his neck, in this unjust condemnation. More than juridical-historical arguments on the real or supposed guilt of the Roman occupier in relation to the proven guilt of the Jewish Sanhedrin, one must take height and examine the eschatological meaning of this double death sentence. It refers an effect on another condemnation; that of the whole human race, represented on the one hand by the Jewish religious world and by the pagan world of the Romans on the other. Together, religious and pagans condemned Jesus Christ and so they placed themselves together, under the condemnation of the judgment of God as shown by the many passages of the Bible found in the book of the prophet Jeremiah when he said; "A voice is heard in high places; These are the cries and supplications of the children of Israel; For they have perverted their way, and have forgotten the Lord their God" (Jer: 3:21). In this passage, as in many others, the root cause of the perversion of the children of Israel is only that they have forgotten the Lord their God. What can be said then of this exceptional tribunal assembled in haste to make Jesus a mock trial condemning him to death? What about Pontius Pilate who will execute the sentence, as much for fear of this new "King of the Jews" as for need to please the Jewish religious leaders who ask him? According to Jeremiah's text; They have perverted each other, their way and, "They have forgotten the Lord, their God." But beyond these particular circumstances, they are representative of a humanity of which each of us is a part, which lives in injustice, and which has forgotten that there is over it a God of righteousness. They embody as much as ourselves, this humanity that does not know God and needs to come or return to him, repent and convert. The Psalms also speak of the human condition, marked by original sin, the figure of Adam to which we all resemble; "All are lost, all are perverted; No one does good, not even one." (Ps 14:3). The passages of the New Testament already quoted are no less explicit when they state: "For all have sinned and are deprived of the glory of God" (Rom 3:23) and also some verses before this one; "No one is intelligent, no one seeks God; all are lost, all are perverted" (Rom 3:11). For centuries, this major oversight that made the Jews the only culprits of this unjust condemnation, made Christians by contrast, the innocents of it. So, to be and appear more Christian, it was necessary in certain circles to be and appear all the more anti-Jewish. So much so that the Catholic daily[189] "La Croix" founded in Paris in 1883 did not hesitate to promote itself with this slogan: "The most anti-Jewish daily in France". Nothing, however, was or is false still today, than this dichotomy that would make some, the damned of the earth and others, the elect of heaven. The truth to which we must return is this one: Jesus Christ the Son of God, pure and innocent of all sin, gave his life for the whole of humanity, for the Jews as for the Romans and well beyond, for all of us, originating from all nations in all centuries. The texts of both the Old and New Testaments abound to emphasize the eschatological perspective of the Bible message, especially the one that is perhaps the best known of them found in the Gospel of John; "for God so loved the world that He gave His only begotten Son that whoever believes in Him may not perish, but may have eternal life" (I 3:16). The very general scope of this beautiful promise, addressed to the inhabitants of the whole world does not hide, however, the necessary and sufficient condition for it to be effective; you have to believe in Him. Offered to humanity without exclusion from anyone, this promise can only be received individually and has value only for the one who actually believes in him. But believing in him is not a simple one-day religious and family ceremony. It is much more, since this same chapter of verses 1 to 9, speaks of the need to be born again, that is, to be born of the Spirit. These words explain with remarkable brevity the individual process of conversion to God through Jesus Christ, which transforms the whole person through repentance and faith. At the same time, they give him new aspirations and the ardent desire to serve God throughout his life. In summary on this, "oblivion of size", one can see three trials in the condemnation and crucifixion of Jesus Christ; the first is naturally that of the collusion between the Sanhedrin and the Romans to condemn Jesus-Christ the righteous, the second is that of the righteousness of God against the authors of the first and the third is instructed to charge but also to discharge against all humanity. Indeed, in this last trial, the unjust and guilty man before God can be saved and redeemed if he believes in the sacrifice of Jesus Christ. This is indicated by numerous biblical references to the subject, including this one found in Paul's epistle to the Romans (Rom 10:9); " If you confess the Lord Jesus with your mouth, and believe in your heart that God raised him from the dead, you will be saved."

---

[189] "The Cross" Catholic newspaper: Dreyfus Affair and Newspaper Anti-Semitism

10.2 From the religious to the political: nationalism in Europe is a factor of amplification of secular religious antisemitism.

If, from the sixteenth century, we make the rapprochement of European political and religious history on the one hand and on the other, we can see the gradual disappearance of the power and role of Christianity in its evolution. We have seen how wars, intrigues, greed, and the will to power have diverted people everywhere from the Christian religion and its biblical roots. However, the void it left in hearts and consciences was filled by other forms of metaphysical and intellectual research and speculation. The arts and sciences are reborn together from this century to the detriment of religion, and from the seventeenth century, philosophy, law, and politics are undermining feudalism and the power of churches over consciences as well as over societies. It seems that a new era of progress is emerging for the greater good of humanity. It is an age during which man seems to have permanently freed himself from the dual guardianship of nature and religion. However, one never builds only on the legacy of the past, and although they defend themselves from it by the voice and the pen of their thurifers, these centuries that come up to us, have preserved within them, the references, the feelings and the images, that have transferred to them a Christianity that is fundamentally anti-Jewish. By taking several shortcuts to European history between the 16th and 20th centuries, as in the following paragraphs, we can see how anti-Judaism has passed from the religious to the social domain.

10.3 Influence of the Protestant Reformation

In the north of Europe, the Reformation generally triumphs, in the south it remains a minority, and it is constantly threatened with destruction, as it is the case in France until the Revolution of 1789. Everywhere it brings a new conception of Christianity by questioning the Holy Scriptures and also by the constitution of national Churches, England, Scandinavia, United Provinces of the Netherlands, Principalities of the Holy Roman Empire, Swiss Cantons, etc. In its work of returning to the teachings of the Bible, it allowed a deepening by any individual of the biblical texts and their interpretation in a systematic search for them, regardless of the religious conformity of traditions. As a result, religious currents soon appeared in their wake, independent of the national structure of each Church and sometimes even butted with it. This is the case in England, where Puritanism allowed the emergence of professing churches such as the Baptist Churches and later during the eighteenth century, the Methodist Churches. These have given pride of place to the Old Testament and allow a very progressive rapprochement with Jewish spirituality. However, official Protestantism will never complete its logic of a radical return to the inspiration of the Holy Scriptures and their Jewish roots. Caught in the turmoil of the wars of religions, as in France, it would rather seek to define and implement the perfect society, the holy city, as John Calvin tried to do in Geneva. Further north, during the 80-year war (1568 ~1648), the United Provinces made Protestantism an essential and discriminating feature of their identity against their Spanish enemies. It is much more the legitimacy and the organization of powers in society, which would be at the heart of the reflection and dynamics of Protestantism until the end of the eighteenth century, to bring out the idea of tolerance and plurality of cults. It is true that almost everywhere Catholicism took up arms against the new religion, which was forced to defend itself by ideology and of course, by arms. Quickly, it was more in military terms that the two sides clashed, rather than in terms of theological exchanges of views. The will to destroy the other took hold, and there was nothing left of the evangelical inspiration in both camps. The worst is probably reached during the Thirty Years' War[190] (1618 ~1648) which set the heart of Europe to fire and blood. Although mixed with court intrigues, this war wanted by Emperor Ferdinand II of Habsburg and supported by Pope Paul V as a new crusade, was nothing but an attempt to reconquer by arms the ground lost in ideas and theology by Catholicism. The strong confessional identity of both sides left no room for doubt on the stakes of the conflict; It was about destroying the other. Historians estimate that several million people have died during this conflict or that one in five inhabitants in certain regions of the Holy Roman Empire, both civilian and military, were the victims of this fratricidal war. This is particularly the case for Pomerania in present days Germany, which lost 65% of its population compared to the pre-war

---

[190] La Guerre de Trente Ans, Henri Sacchi - Paris, Éditions L'Harmattan, coll. "Chemins de la mémoire", 1991

period, and in Silesia further south, which lost 25% of its own. It was also called, "The European Civil War", so much it mixed kings, princes, nations and peoples on the continent. Today's Germany has been the main theatre of the military operations; it was ravaged from north to south and from east to west by the unceasing displacement of conflicts and armies. The peasants, plundered and ruined, often had no other resource than to enlist themselves in this or that army and to participate in their turn in new pillages. Only two major European countries would be absent from this conflict, namely England itself in the midst of their civil war and distant Russia without any stake for itself in this war. In 1648, the Treaty of Westphalia put an end to hostilities without providing peace on a continent where everywhere succeeded attempts to dominate one nation over others. The two official winners of the conflict are France, which is expanding to the east and Sweden, which soon dominates the two shores of the Baltic Sea. The power of the Habsburg house was reduced in both Spain and Austria. However, the great vanquished of this war is undoubtedly Christianity, whether Catholic or Protestant, in whose name the belligerents fought beyond their respective kingdom. The popular conscience would hold it directly responsible for these many massacres, these lives lost, these years lost in development and social progress. Everywhere in Europe, voices were raised, and pens were working hard to revise man's relationship to God, to the power of the prince, of the Church, to nature, and to life itself. This was the time when philosophy and science, with Baruch Spinoza, René Descartes, and many others, replaced theology in an attempt to respond to the ambiguity of time and eternity. On the other hand, the Catholic religion was thwarted against science in its lawsuit against Galileo[191] over the roundness of the Earth and the movement of the planets. It was also completely overwhelmed by the progress of the arts, sciences, and culture. In mathematics, the invention of logarithms allowed astronomy to make great progress, while in the field of political science, appeared the principle of the "Social Contract", elaborated by the English philosophers, Thomas Hobbes and John Locke, in which the role of Christianity was marginalized and confined to the private sphere, while the natural rights of the individual and the just government of peoples were exposed. Consequently, the divine right of the dynasties to

---

[191] Galileo (scholar): Galileo Vs the Church | All About History

power supported by the official church was also gradually challenged by the emergence of the opposite idea, namely, that of popular sovereignty. In all fields of intellectual, scientific, philosophical, and moral speculation, the traditional churches appeared as an enemy of the freedom of conscience and expression of human genius. It was without them and sometimes against them that cultural, technical progress and the emancipation of men from the forces of nature were made. Without them, the Jews also emerged from the ghetto, and their influence gradually increased in all areas of Western European life. From the seventeenth century on, the time of crimes and massacres against Jewish communities was fortunately over, and their integration into modern society would be made without major difficulty. However, if religion and its stereotypes passed into the background of social life, they remained present in the collective unconscious, and they would wake up much later during the 20th century, in an extremely violent way against the Jews.

10.4 Four centuries of European revolutions (1688, 1789, 1848, 1917)

During these four centuries, Europe experienced several successive revolutions, although very different in their purpose and in the circumstances of their appearance. The first that can be quoted quickly is called the "Glorious Revolution". This revolution, which took place in England in 1688, is called "Glorious" because it led peacefully to a transition; the power eventually returned to parliament, to the detriment of the monarchy and the aristocracy. It marked the end of the reign of the Stuart dynasty, which had been preceded by several tragedies, including the civil war in England, the death sentence, and the execution of King Charles 1st in January 1649 and the eviction of his son James II in 1688, by the Protestant dynasty of the Orange in the person of the own daughter of the deposed king. It was also the end of Catholicism's attempts to reconquer the British Isles, through its more or less explicit alliance with the Stuarts. Now, except for Ireland, they would remain firmly attached to the Protestant Reformation. By making history a certain approximation, one can say that this 'Glorious Revolution' puts an end to the civil war that ravaged England from 1641 to 1645, and which had brought in its wake Scotland, Ireland, and Wales. The final point was also that of the reign of the

Stuart dynasty and its more or less strong collusion with the Catholic party and France. With the "Bill of Rights", that is to say, the charter of rights, it is the final point, finally, to the will of the monarch to exercise absolute and personal power, in the manner of the king of France Louis XIV, on the 4 kingdoms which will soon constitute from 1705, Great Britain. This "Glorious Revolution" marks an entirely new era for what will become, just in a few decades, the first European power in the middle of the eighteenth century to replace the kingdom of France. The new dynasty came to power in a wise balance between monarchy and parliament. Over time, the Prime Minister will become stronger and will occupy the full place of the executive in the person of the Prime Minister. With this positive evolution England and the British islands with them, will know an unprecedented prosperity and a political pre-eminence over all Europe. It was also at this time that the Jews were liberated by the Lord Protector, Oliver Cromwell and they were gradually recognized as equal citizens in rights and duties throughout the empire. This key figure in British history led his entire political commitment, inspired by the Bible. It was to defend religious and political freedoms threatened by Charles 1st that he raised the Parliamentary army against him and defeated the king. It was also inspired by the Bible that he wanted to bring back the Jews who had been expelled from the kingdom in 1290 and had been banished ever since. Initially, he did not succeed against the opposition of parliament. However, after he died in 1650, the Jews were gradually allowed to return, and they contributed significantly to the prosperity and social progress of the United Kingdom.

10.5 The Enlightenment, the Emancipation of the Jews and the French Revolution in 1789

Historians generally consider that the end of the 30-year war in 1648 marks a new era in Europe, radically different from the previous one. It is first of all the erasure of the papacy in the influence it had previously on the courts and dynasties in Western Europe. It was also the reduction of the power of the Habsburg dynasty, which lost a number of their possessions in the Holy Empire, including Alsace and Lorraine, which was granted to France. It is finally the awakening of peoples with the advent of "nation-states", this somewhat hybrid regime in which the role of the church is replaced by "national consciousness" and soon by nationalism. The development of national sentiment is accompanied by a spectacular strengthening of the power of the state as an entity capable of producing a coherent and dynamic legislative framework at the service of the public good. This is the case in France, in England where the parliamentary way triumphs at the expense of the power of the king and that of the church. At the same time, science, philosophy and law assert themselves in opposition to the teachings of the churches and open up new moral and spiritual perspectives for individuals and societies. In a few decades, the Europe of darkness and clashes between Christian religions reached, "the age of enlightenment". For the Jews, it was soon the end of the rules dating from the Lateran Council in 1215. They were gradually emancipated throughout Western Europe, except in Spain and Portugal. The Netherlands is the first to recognize them, equality of status at the beginning of the 17th century de facto if not de jure. In the same way, England again opened its doors to the Jews, from the reign of William III and his wife Mary at the beginning of the eighteenth century. At a time when the "philosophy of enlightenment" triumphs, relations with Judaism can no longer be treated according to outdated religious prejudices. Everywhere, Rationality, knowledge and science, prevail over religion, over the curse in that has enclosed these people. While this was his vocation, it is not Christianity that liberates the Jews, it is rather this humanist philosophy, called enlightenment that highlights them as well as all men. The monumental work of the French authors Denis Diderot and Jean le Rond d'Alembert published between 1751 and 1765 is entitled: "L'encyclopédie raisonnée des sciences des arts et des métiers", Reason will have a great influence on the ideas of this time. It develops a complete chapter on the Jewish people, in which the two philosophers do not fail to pay tribute to their great tenacity, their great faith in the many persecutions inflicted on them by Christianity over the ages. At the same time, Judaism itself experienced an important movement of openness, mainly in the Holy Empire. This is the "Hashkalah", a Hebrew word meaning "Education". Rather than cultivating bitterness about its fate, this movement develops within communities the idea of cultural openness. It accompanies and promotes the development of a dynamic Jewish bourgeoisie in the field of economic and social affairs, and they were well-integrated into the ruling circles of the contemporary world. Moses Mendelssohn, the grandfather of the famous musician Felix, will be one of his brightest representatives, ardent defender of this "Hashkalah", he would spread it internally in Judaism as well as externally to the benches of the University of Berlin where he would be in contact with the great philosopher Emmanuel Kant. The years of the late 18th century were favorable to the emancipation of the Jews. It is indeed the era of "enlightened despotism", these monarchs enlightened by the philosophy of enlightenment, of which Frederick II says, "The Great", king of Prussia (1712 ~ 1786) is one of the most prominent representatives. From step to step, whether de jure or de facto, most European nations will recognize the equality of Jews with their other citizens, this is notably the case of Joseph II, emperor of Austria, who by his "Edict of tolerance" in 1781, granted Jews and Protestants the recognition of civil status and equality in rights and duties before the law. In France, the process is also irreversible. Under the influence of its many lawyers and defenders, the Enlightenment philosophy penetrated to the top of the state and throughout its territorial administration with the Revolution of 14 July 1789. It was a radical challenge to the power exercised jointly by the monarchy, the aristocracy, and the clergy over French society. This test of strength ended with the destruction of the feudal orders that had governed the entire French nation since the beginning of the Capetian dynasty in 987. It is interesting to note that this revolutionary epoch is also that of the emancipation of the Jews, and we note again that it is neither the official church nor the royal power that freed them, but rather a popular assembly inspired by feelings of justice and reparation. Indeed, it is by a decree[192] of September 27th of 1791, voted by the National Assembly, that the Jews are definitively recognized as citizens in the same way as any Frenchman, regardless of their origin and their religious practice. The period of Terror from September of 1792 until the end of 1794 prevented the expression of religious freedom and it was not until the end of the revolutionary troubles with the reign of Emperor Napoleon I[st][193] that Judaism was again recognized and confirmed in its rights and duties in 1807. Later, in October 1870, the Crémieux Decree[194] granted French citizenship to the Sephardic Jews of North Africa.

---

[192] "Admission of Jews to Rights of Citizenship," 27 September 1791 · LIBERTY, EQUALITY, FRATERNITY: EXPLORING THE FRENCH REVOUTION
[193] DELAGE Irène, PAPOT Emmanuelle: Napoleon I and the integration of the Jews in France: some points of interest - napoleon.org
[194] Adolphe Crémieux: The Crémieux decree, Decree of October 24, 1870, Algeria

10.6 The 19th century: The End of the Enlightenment, the beginning of darkness, and the revolutions of 1848

The Age of Enlightenment would not withstand the repeated assaults against it during the French Revolution, which ended in the blood of the "Terror" period. The dream of a democratic republic, just and governed by law, collapses due to a lack of faith, a lack of inspiration, and intellectual and spiritual resources. It was an ambitious young general, Napoleon Bonaparte, who picked it up after a coup d'état on 9 November 1799 and made it his thing before replacing it with a politico-military empire. It would put almost the whole of Europe in a state of permanent war until its fall after its defeat at Waterloo in 1815. It was the end of the Enlightenment because the sad epilogue of what had been the great hope of the peoples; a government by reason, by a positive human philosophy and by the progress of knowledge, demonstrated that it was not enough to drive God away from the heart and the nation to rebuild a humanistic philosophy by which man alone could ensure his happiness and destiny. It must be concluded that human philosophy was not able to replace the Word of God, and that religion had not fulfilled its pedagogical role toward peoples, and that politics had neither responded to their deepest aspirations. The nineteenth century thus remains ambiguous with, on the one hand, the pursuit of great progress on the scientific, economic and institutional level, but on the other, the pronounced return to the darkness of the past in the form of nationalism and anti-Judaism. In the years of what has been called, "Restoration" after Napoleon, the legacy of imperial France is not yet seen very well, however it is real and in many ways it is positive. It is first of all the civil code, monumental legal work also called "Code Napoleon", which draws largely from the revolutionary legislation and tends to gather in a single legal body the rules, formerly disparate and regional, on the status of persons, property and relationships between people. This underground work is accompanied by the transmission of the ideals of the Revolution, in particular on public and religious freedoms guaranteed and protected by law for the citizen. The recognition of individual freedoms implies that both Judaism and Protestantism are irreversible; the table below shows in what year Jews were recognized as full citizens throughout Europe, or almost during the[195] 19th century.

---

[195] Emancipation of Jews: Jewish Emancipation in Western Europe | My Jewish Learning

Year in which Jews obtained equal rights in Europe			
Year	Country	Year	Country
1791	France	1848	Kingdom of Sardinia
1796	Batavian Republic	1849	Hamburg, Denmark
1808	Grand Duchy of Hesse	1851	Norway
	Kingdom of Westphalia	1858	United Kingdom
1811	Grand Duchy of Frankfurt	1861	Italy
1812	Mecklemburg-Schwerin, Kingdom of Prussia	1862	Grand Duchy of Baden
		1863	Duchy of Holstein
1828	Kingdom of Wurtemberg	1864	Free City of Frankfurt
1830	Belgium, Greece	1866 -74	Switzerland
1832	Canada	1867	Autria-Hungaria
1833	Electorate of Hesse	1867	Germany
1834	Low-Country	1878	Bulgaria, Serbia
1835	Sweden	1890	Brazil
1830	Ottoman Empire	1917	Russia
1832	Canada	1923	Romania
1842	Kingdom of Hanover		

The Congress of Vienna (1814 ~1815) was gathered under the tutelage of the 4 victorious nations of the wars against imperial France: Great Britain, Austria, Prussia, and Russia, all that Europe had of kingdoms, of principalities, and more or less sovereign states, and belligerents of the Napoleonic wars. It did considerable work for European reconstruction after the great disorder left by the Napoleonic adventure. The most important modification of its geopolitical map was undoubtedly that of the Germanic Confederation, a new name given in 1815 to the ephemeral Confederation of the Rhine, which had itself succeeded in 1806, to the very old, Holy Roman Empire. Thus, the new complex, dominated by a brand-new power, Prussia, was simplified and had only 39 states instead of 350 in 1792. On the other hand, the poisoned legacy of imperial France was also the will for national power and pride, and its translation into strong nationalist feelings, sometimes positive when it genuinely seeks the public good and the recognition of the values of the nation and sometimes awfully negative when it manifests, national pride, a will of power, and a spirit of revenge and superiority compared to other people. From this point of view, the march to German unity heralded conflicts to come in the nineteenth to the twentieth century. It begun in 1807, with the famous "Speech to the German Nation" of the philosopher Johannes Gottlieb Fichte, pronounced in Berlin after the defeat of Prussia against Napoleon at the battle of Jena in 1806. The discourses tended to exalt patriotic sentiment and the need for national recovery after this terrible defeat. They highlighted the common heritage of the Germanic peoples, namely the German language, that of the Protestant Reformation soon put at the service of the cause of German nationalism, especially in the unfortunate episode of the "Kulturkampf" or "Fight for civilization", translation of its real meaning into English. Indeed, for a short but brutal period (1873 ~ 1878), the Prussian Chancellor Bismarck, tried to obtain from certain regions of southern Germany, the abandonment of their Catholic faith, considered archaic and too close to its Latin roots, by their forced Germanization in a nationalized Protestantism at the service of the greatness of the Hohenzollern dynasty. This policy was met with no success and was definitively abandoned in 1887. The desire for recovery after the defeat of Jena in question is accompanied by the dream of a united and powerful Germany; powerful because united and able to resist France in particular. The Jewish philosopher and theologian Franz Rosenzweig (1886, 1929) saw in these discourses a very clear desire for power when he emphasized this passage: "this (German) people of humanity would then have been destined, with the Reformation and idealism, to constitute the truly dominant experiences of the human race". Orchestrated by Prussia, which, after 1815, extended considerably westward to the borders of France, the march towards German unity under the impulse of its Prime Minister Otto von Bismarck was characterized by an ardent nationalism, which encompassed the entire Germanic space. What was for centuries a confederation before the time, very decentralized where parliamentary life could flourish, becomes in a few decades a military dictatorship that extended at the end of the nineteenth century "by iron and blood" according to the expression of Chancellor Bismarck, from the hills of the Vosges in eastern France to the banks of the Niemen more than 1600 km to the east. This expansion began with the war against the Danes in 1864, then against the Austrians in 1866, and finally against the French in 1870. In three giant steps, Germany had become the leading European economic and military power. It was now a great empire of more than 80 million inhabitants that reigned over central Europe. It was the golden age of, "Pan Germanism" this political movement where the defenders and promoters of Greater Germany, "Großdeutschland" in German, found any reason to hail "Deutschland Über alles" (Germany above all). We can cite three of its main founders in addition to the philosopher Johannes Gottlieb Fichte, presented earlier in this paragraph. There is, indeed, Johann Gottfried von Herder[196] (1744-1803), who developed the Idea of the "Volk", that is, the people in the sense of an organic unity by the unity of blood. It was very far from the social contract of the "Enlightenment" philosophy because this unity is fleshly, powerful and organic by all the social elements that compose the "Volk". Are naturally excluded from this "Volk": the Jews, although they have been present and active in the country since antiquity, they are excluded because they have another conception of man, society, and the universe. There is also the well-known and highly respected philosopher in universities throughout Europe today, Georg Wilhelm Friedrich Hegel[197] (1770-1831), for whom: "The most fatal mistake for a people is to abandon its biological character. Germany itself remained pure of any mixture, except on its southern and western border where the strip of territory bordering the Danube and the Rhine was submitted to the Romans. The region between the Elbe and the Rhine has remained absolutely indigenous". Since ancient times, history has shown the opposite, with incessant migratory flows through Germany, favored by its wide rivers, the Rhine, Weser, and Elbe, all oriented from south to north. But, in this period when the will to power seeks good scientific arguments, including biological and racial ones to express itself, the formula pleased a lot in universities and chancelleries. For Friedrich Wilhelm Joseph von Schelling[198] (1775-1854) there was a sort of initiatory journey in the people's accession to political consciousness when he declared: "The organic creation of states is what allows a mass of human beings to reach the union of

---

[196] Biography of JOHANN GOTTFRIED HERDER (1744-1803) - Encyclopédie Universalis
[197] Franz Rosenzweig, Hegel and the State, PUF, 1991, p. 217.Henri Lasvignes: Antisemitism in Germany – La Revue blanche Volume XV p 282 - 287
[198] Friedrich Wilhelm Joseph von Schelling: Sundheim.pdf

heart and mind, that is to say to become one, "Volk". For German Jews, the nineteenth century was a time of emancipation and development in cultural, social, and economic domains. They kept many of their ancient institutions while being at the forefront of intellectual, artistic and social progress. They helped the communities of Poland's Russia and much of Yiddisland, some of which remained backward and oppressed in their ghetto. However, with German nationalism, anti-Semitism was also reborn, and very few were moved by its first manifestations, yet it heralded the most violent that came later. The word itself was formed in Germany under the pen of journalist Wilhelm Marr, who used it in 1879 to talk about a new "anti-Semitic" league. The "discourses on the German nation", soon served as the basis for various doctrines of German nationalism in which the idea of a German ethnic unity, a community of destiny to dominate and lead the other European peoples, emerged. German nationalism soon doubled with a complex of purity and racial superiority, specifically Nordic was opposed to the inferiority and impurity of the Latin, Semitic peoples of the East and the South, and specifically to the Jewish in Europe. After several hundred years, we find again the idea of an inferior Jewish degenerate race, which had been developed in Spain at the time of the ethnic and religious cleansing of the XVth and XVIth centuries (see § 7.3, 7.4, 7.5). Henceforth, it was given irrefutable scientific value with the work of the Prussian historian Heinrich von Treitschke[199]. This nationalism was also revanchist, it emphasized this dubious factor of "the homogeneous evolution of the peoples", which concretely meant that, "Generations are in solidarity with each other". This new de facto solidarity made it possible to declare the French of 1870 guilty of the defeat of Jena in 1806 and to avenge it, 64 years later, with the capitulation of the French 3^{td} empire in 1870. For some thinkers like Nietzsche and Dühring, the Jewish conception of man was incompatible with that of the new man, "German and Aryan". Some of the most prominent Christians awakened the old antagonism between Christianity and Judaism, rather than preaching the gospel of love and peace. This is the case of Pastor Stoecker[200], a preacher at the Hohenzollern court and supporter of German imperialism. He fought against Judaism in its social form, especially because of

---

[199] Heinrich von Treitschke in: The State, the Nation, and the Jews: Liberalism and the Antisemitism Dispute in Bismarck's Germany on JSTOR

[200] Court Chaplain Adolf Stoecker (1880) | German History in Documents and Images

its growing assimilation into modern German society. In fact, they succeeded more socially than Protestants and Catholics, as the German sociologist Max Weber would emphasize this fact later. His rigorous study, published in 1904 and 1905 on social classes in Germany, entitled "The Protestant Ethics and the Spirit of Capitalism," indeed showed this pyramid, where Jews were at the top of income and business successes, Protestants were second, and Catholics third. Pastor Stoecker puts all his energy into arousing the anger of the people against the Jews. With a population of around 500,000, he thought that Jews were really too many in Germany and that they had to disappear at all costs, including through physical violence. He said: "Anti-Semitism will triumph through revolution; the people must be raised against the Jews; A revolution is needed, and it will come, be sure, it is mathematical". If he and his colleagues did not see it, Germany, for its greatest shame and misfortune, would see this anti-Semitic revolution during the III^{td} Reich. On the religious level, he recycled all the old prejudices of the deicide people, of the fall of Israel after the destruction of the Great Temple of Jerusalem in the year 70 with all the old anti-Jewish resentments. He multiplied the attacks against the Talmud and Jewish thought, which, according to him, penetrated too much into Christian circles. Although a pastor, he did not see that the entire Bible, that is, the Old and New Testaments alike, are and remain for eternity an entirely Jewish work. He did not see that it is being preached and taught every Sunday in all Christian assemblies around the world. Knowing this, why would one be scandalized that Jewish thought had penetrated Christian circles? Was it not destined to do so by God's will from eternity?

Further south, the nineteenth century is that of the great social upheavals, and many ideas of the French Revolution remained with the people after the departure of Napoleon's troops. This is particularly the case for those ideas which promoted individual freedom, freedom of political opinion, and press, universal suffrage, and the expression of a national culture. From this point of view, the kingdom most exposed to internal dissent was undoubtedly that of the Habsburgs in Austria. In competition with the Kingdom of Prussia, it found itself increasingly confined to the south and the east of Europe, where many people had much difficulty accepting its tutelage. In 1848, there was suddenly an explosion all over Europe. This year is also called by historians "The spring of the peoples[201]" because most of the revolts that run through it took place during this spring. It was first in France, in Paris, that the people brought down the monarchy in February of that year. King Louis-Philippe left Paris for exile. He was the last king of France; his regime was worn out, and the political, social, and fiscal measures taken by his government were rejected by a large part of the political spectrum, with the support of the liberals and the republicans. The Second Republic was proclaimed on 24 February. This revival of an experience of political democracy was highly acclaimed among the European peoples, and it opened great prospects of emancipation for them. In Berlin, riots broke out in March of this year, which are called, "Märzrevolution[202]" in German and reflected both, the need for public freedom and for national unity. Here again, the awareness is great; with industrial development, the formation of a proletariat in the big cities, social questions arose which the ruling dynasties were unable to answer. In most German states, there were demonstrations to obtain deep reforms and at the same time to express national unity. The liberal deputies sent to the Assembly in Frankfurt, from May 1848 and for a year, drew up a constitution to meet these aspirations. Austria also has large Jewish communities in permanent contact with their German counterparts, whose language they share with Yiddish. They contributed greatly to the difficult emancipation of Judaism from central and eastern Europe. Their contribution was also important in the diffusion of a particular Jewish socialism, which would give birth in the 1880s to the "Bund[203]", a Jewish socialist and secular party sometimes very close to the future revolutionary Marxist parties. The Habsburg dynasty was reigning over a large number of people, the system of the "Holy Alliance[204]" set up by Chancellor Wenzel von Metternich in 1819 was undermined by the political and social revolution that shook the old empire on March 13, 1848. Only a month after the revolutionary demonstrations in Paris, the man who had led European diplomacy and had ruled the country de facto since 1809, had to flee Vienna. Emperor Ferdinand granted quickly, the nation under his rule a constitution of bourgeois and liberal inspiration that abolished feudal rights. However, the

---

[201] The European People's Spring, 1848 | EHNE
[202] Deutscher Bundestag - Die Revolution von 1848/49
[203] https://www.jewishvirtuallibrairy.org/bund
[204] Holy Alliance | Austria, Prussia, Russia | Britannica.com

fire moved from the political to the national level. The Czechs demanded their autonomy, while Lombardy rose on 18 March announcing the beginning of the wars of independence of Italy. Hungarians established their "Parliamentary Ministry" from which the government derived its legitimacy. They thus departed from the heavy guardianship of Vienna. However, despite their energy and sometimes their radicalism, the movements of liberal and national inspiration fail to achieve unity of project and action. They were finally defeated one after the other by the central power of Vienna, by the aristocracy, the clergy, and the ruling classes who feared the contagion of the French ideas with the proclamation of a republic. Everywhere, the repression led by the imperial army spread, and it took more than a year to reintegrate Hungary by force into the empire that would become from 1867, "The Empire of Austria-Hungary". Ferdinand Ist was forced to abdicate, he had to give his place to his nephew, Francis Joseph Ist, infamous for having jointly with his rival, Nicholas II^{sd} Tsar of All Russia, triggered in July 1914, the First World War. Political and social upheavals, new popular ambitions, new rights, new dynasties, so many changes in 1848. However, everywhere, it is the reaction to political and national liberation movements that triumphs. In France, Napoleon III, nephew of Napoleon Bonaparte, confiscated the Republic for his own benefits and decreed, on December 2, 1852, by a coup d'état, the "Second Empire", authoritarian and dynastic. In Germany, the march towards unity also took an authoritarian and nationalist turn, particularly under the leadership of Chancellor Otto von Bismarck. Austria-Hungary, for a time, defeated these centrifugal forces that, however, prepared underground, its final disintegration. Everywhere, nationalism and anti-Semitism won against the hope of the people. With these two plagues came together: the exaltation of the superiority of the nation with that of race and xenophobia is interpreted rather as a cardinal virtue than as a defect in the relationship between men. The hatred of the stranger is justified; the rejection of the one who is different, not reducible to the injunctions of social conformity, is legitimized when it is not encouraged. In this context, the Jew appeared increasingly as the disruptive element. He was the international element by definition, therefore the one who could challenge this newly established order. The Bible that he held in his hand could judge kings, emperors, princes, church leaders, and prominent people at their service. This was a distant descendant of what was "the nation-state" at the end of the

Thirty-Year War in the seventeenth century, but this new order turned out to be monstrous. It was a new nationalist religion that took place throughout the European area, where competition between nations was exacerbated. God is quickly put at the service of the national cause; Catholicism in southern Europe, Protestantism in the north, and Orthodoxy in the east are cleverly mixed with the specific virtues of race and nation to allow each to assert its superiority over the other. Theorists in large numbers do important historical, sociological, and biological work for this double cause[205]. The mixture between the virtues of Christianity and those of nationalism reaches heights, and who wants to be a good Christian must also be an ardent nationalist and a good soldier of its cause. [206]

10.7 Anti-Semitism and Nationalism

In France, examples of this anti-Jewish relentlessness are present everywhere in the news of the late nineteenth century. Poorly recovered from its defeat in 1870 against Germany, France became a republic by default in 1876, following a long process during which the royalists, divided between Legitimists and Orleanists, fought against each other. Although it was proclaimed on September 4, 1870, only 2 days after the capitulation of Napoleon III in the city of Sedan, it was recognized in practice and in the texts only in 1875 and still it was, by a majority of only one vote. It is a republic that does not dare to say its name because indeed, we only discover the form of this new political regime through the Wallon amendment, which is the only one in the end of the entire constitutional text to mention the word "Republic", with the expression, "President of the Republic". This brief reminder of the context of France at that time shows that the defeat in no way prevented the royalist and Bonapartist conservative forces from wanting to redo history for their benefit. This important part of the country was above all; rural, Catholic, still largely illiterate, anti-protestant, and anti-Jewish. It was influenced by a far-right press that attacks Judaism, whether nationally or internationally. The case that would raise passions in these late nineteenth-century years was

---

[205] Hugh McLeod: Christianity and nationalism in nineteenth-century Europe p 7-22
[206] (PDF) Nationalism, Militarism, and Imperialism and its Impact on the Outbreak of The Great War

that of Captain Alfred Dreyfus[207], wrongly accused of espionage for the benefit of Germany. Of Jewish faith, one was very surprised on the political right that he was accepted into the ranks of the army. Convicted without evidence after a quick trial in 1894, he was degraded and then exiled to French Guiana in one of its worst prisons. The Catholic right was in the majority against Dreyfus, while the Protestants were in the majority for the innocence of the captain. The anti-Jewish press of that time spoke of the "Judeo-Protestant Conspiracy" against the army, the Catholic Church, and the nation in general. Passions were unleashed throughout the country to such an extent that the young republic was threatened. If the truth finally triumphed, the guilty ones unmasked and the innocence of Alfred Dreyfus established, the traces left by this state affair were very important. On the one hand, it was the victory of law and justice that strengthened the Republic. It allowed it to emancipate itself from the heavy guardianship that the Catholic Church still made it wear. It also opened up the possibility of better defining its nature as a "secular republic" and finally affirming the separation of churches and the state by the laws of 1901 and 1905. This had long been demanded by the nascent Evangelical Churches throughout the country, notably at the Congress of the Evangelical Alliance held in England in 1846, which had seen the birth of the Free Evangelical Protestant Churches, as opposed to the Concordat Churches, whose pastors remained state-paid officials. For its part, the right-wing was defeated in this showdown; of the law against passion, however, it did not stand defeated. For years, it maintained a large press animated by theorists of anti-Judaism and public agitators. This national affair gave this political wing the audience it was actively seeking, trying to restore royalty with strong power. The best known of his propagandists is the journalist and novelist Édouard Drumont[208], who multiplied in the articles of his newspaper, "La Libre Parole" his anti-Jewish positions. They gradually permeated almost the entire French right. He was not alone, far from it, as evidenced by the large number and virulence of anti-Semitic publications in France. Paul Déroulède, a poet, playwright and political activist from Pamphlet, denounces the Jewish danger in these terms: "Demilitarizing, decatholicizing, denationalizing France, that is their triple goal". The new Catholic

---

[207] Captain Alfred Dreyfus trial: Dreyfus affair | Definition, Summary, History, Significance, & Facts | Britannica

[208] https://pantheon.world/profile/person/%C3%89douard_Drumont

daily newspaper, "La Croix", founded in 1883, proclaimed this editorial motto: "the most anti-Jewish newspaper in France[209]". In France, the most famous anti-Semitic intellectuals in the[210] 20th century are, in addition to those already mentioned, Charles Maurras, Maurice Barrès and Louis Ferdinand Céline. This anti-Jewish militancy would accompany the entire political life of the French Third Republic until the tragic defeat of 1940. It was mainly of the right-wing, but it was not absent from the left either, where the real or supposed power of the Jews was denounced, with international capitalism. Indeed, on the left, it was often accused of controlling finance and large international companies and thus, it became the very embodiment of capitalism. Karl Marx[211] (1818-1883), a German historian, sociologist and economist, was born into a Jewish family, which in their time had given several Ashkenazi rabbis to their communities. Theorist of socialism, he formalized its founding concepts, the first and the main one being this: "historical materialism". It is the application to the historical and social realm of the laws of physics and their force, as they exist in nature. In this universe, God is absent; the same is true of the Bible, as well as others spiritual references. Based on this fundamental axiom, Karl Marx developed his corollary, namely that of the "Class struggle." According to him, society has always been, since the dawn of time, a place where the social classes that compose it clash against each other. The challenge of this endless struggle is not so much political power, which is only the ephemeral translation of a power that is far superior to it, namely, economic power. In the historical period in which Karl Marx lived, it was the merchant and the enterprising bourgeoisie that held the reality of power. It conquered it by the expropriation of workers and wage workers of their tools and means of production. Indeed, the wage-earner, which developed from the nineteenth century, testified to this growing separation between labor and capital and the emergence of a social class dispossessed of the means of production. According to Karl Marx, work and salaried workers are therefore "alienated" from their own existence since the salary is only the counterpart of the time spent on the service of the company and its owner. On the contrary, the annuity and fees guaranteed to

---

[209] Anti-Semitic Publications in France: Ideology and Experience: Anti-Semitism in France at the Time of the Dreyfus Affair on JSTOR

[210] Paul Déroulède: Anti-Semitic propaganda notes. Paris, late 19th century - DYNASTY AUCTIONS

[211] Karl Marx: philosophy and politics pdf - Recherche Vidéos

those who received them, the implicit recognition of a right and its use in the first case, and the talent that one was ready to pay for in the second case. In these two examples man was not separated from the source of his wealth for which he was paid, and he kept it as much as he lived. With the wage-earner, the link between talent and work done in the company has been detached, and the wage-earner is substitutable indefinitely. The sharing of the value of the output of a company, is also fundamentally unequal, since the capital is permanently remunerated and serves future investments as well as the payment of dividends to bourgeois shareholders, while work is only one factor of production among others and it last only during the actual time spent at the service of the company. Based on these observations, to which Karl Marx gave scientific value, he founded a materialist, historical and revolutionary socialism in his book co-authored in 1848 with Friedrich Engels entitled: "The Communist Manifesto". The consequence of the class struggle is the inexorable rise in power of the wage-earner and the imminent overthrow of the domination of social relations for the benefit of the workers and wage-earners of the world of work. The bourgeoisie, in fact, has against itself, to be only a minority of capitalists who command the whole of society. Its power can therefore be challenged by those it exploits. This is the third floor of Karl Marx's vision, for whom the purpose of the class struggle is the establishment of the dictatorship of the proletariat. This stage, which can be violent, is necessary for the ultimate foundation of a fraternal society without class, with, among other things, the motto; "From each according to his means, to each according to his needs". In France, socialism was more a philosophical legacy of the Revolution of 1789, revised and adapted to the modern world. It fed on various currents, one of the most radical being that of Pierre-Joseph Proudhon[212] (1809-1865), author of the famous formula, "Property is theft". He was revolutionary and anarchist, but also violently anti-Jewish and anti-clerical, he wrote this appeal for the murder of the Jews in his "Carnets" on December 26, 1847; «The Jew is the enemy of mankind. This race must be sent back to Asia or exterminated... by iron, fire or expulsion, the Jew must disappear". Before being totally marginalized, his thought exerted a great influence on the workers'

---

[212] Pierre Joseph Proudhon: Hubert Bouccara. Proudhon, antisémite obsessionnel - Tribune Juive

movements of the nineteenth century and especially during the insurrectionary days of the "Paris Commune" in 1871. Apart from Marxism, socialism, until today attempted the difficult synthesis between two ideals often opposed, that is, the guarantee of individual freedom and the distribution of the fruits of economic progress equally. It was not fundamentally anti-Jewish, even if this current existed within it. In the Judaism of Central Europe of the second half of the 19th century, socialism nevertheless found a broad echo, since it provided at the same time the concepts, the words, and the ideals of a new human hope, built on the ruins of the ancient religious and monarchical order. However, the Jewish conspiracy theory[213] gained popularity throughout Europe in the years following the great economic and financial crisis of 1929. At the time, it was supported mainly by the right and the extreme right: strongly nationalist, these movements vowed an unlimited hatred, both to the stateless capitalist Jew and to the communist Jew because of their atheistic inspiration and spiritual affiliation with the Jew Karl Marx. The Bible had prophetically announced the birth of these violent ideological currents which are only the manifestation of the pride of nations, particularly in Psalm 2, where it is said; "Why is this tumult among the nations, these vain thoughts among the peoples? Why do the kings of the earth rise up and the princes join with them against the Lord and his anointed? Let us free ourselves from their chains! .... And now, kings, behave wisely! Judges of the earth, receive instruction! Serve the Lord with fear and rejoice with trembling."

10.8 The Jewish International

This is the expression that the Jewish diaspora itself constitutes a network of business and influence, tending to dominate international relations and local governments. This theory is based on an objective reality, that of the dispersion of Jewish communities in the world. However, it draws some hazardous conclusions about a so-called Jewish conspiracy on a world scale, tending to the enslavement of peoples and nations for the sole benefit of international Judaism. This phantasm fed a sometimes-violent anti-Semitism, which inspired a whole part of the right and left in Europe for years.

---

[213] Conspiracy Theories and the Jews | My Jewish Learning

10.9 Colonialism and the triumph of nationalism

Colonial expansion is another expression of the pride of European nations; strong in their advance in agricultural and industrial techniques, they subdue one after other nations and vast areas on all continents. This adventure started in the 16th century by the Spanish, the Portuguese and the Dutch, is prodigiously developed especially by Great Britain and France until the end of the 19th century. At that time, there was virtually no more virgin territory or nation left to conquer. Like the countries that colonized them, the record of colonialism is highly contrasted; if it has undoubtedly brought great progress to distant backward countries, whether in the fields of health, agriculture, education, transport, civil engineering, and many other fields... It was, nevertheless, an enterprise of domination of the European peoples over the others and the expression of the power of the colonizers. For this reason, in less than a century, it has been rejected everywhere, sometimes, and by excessive reaction, it was synonymous with enslavement and oppression. Mass Christianity spread widely in the wake of the colonizers, and the confusion of one with the other was often detrimental to its positive work for the peoples. One aspect of this rejection is frequently found in anti-Zionism, which brings together the various tendencies of opposition to modern and democratic Israel. We have seen previously that a significant fraction of Judaism was, from its origin, opposed to the Zionist project and that this opposition was very present among the religious circles of Judaism in the countries of Central Europe and Russia. Today we see that, anti-Zionism has nothing to do with what it was originally. It is often traditional anti-Semitism disguised as anti-Zionism that resurfaces. He took up the cause of the Arab-Muslim party and frequently repeated the accents of traditional anti-Semitism.

10.10 Being Jewish in the land of pogroms.

The empire of the Tsars of Russia, the Romanov dynasty, seemed to be quite the opposite of Western Europe, with its small vindictive nations. As much as this one was fragmented, divided from every point of view, as much as that one was united, by language, the orthodox religion, by serfdom, which was still the social norm until 1861 in this immense country where nothing seemed to have to move.

In the 19th century, it expanded to the west by absorbing Poland and Ukraine. After a war with Sweden in 1808, it obtained Finland and the three small Baltic states, Latvia, Lithuania, and Estonia. In the south, the "Great Catherine II of Russia", had already taken advantage of the decline of the Ottoman Empire to enlarge its possessions by absorbing Crimea in 1783, then later Russification would reach Azerbaijan, Armenia and all of Kazakhstan. A true geographical border with the mountainous reliefs from the Caucasus going east, as a cultural rift with Islam, prevented it from going further south. However, it was towards the Levant that its true territorial expansion took place. No people, no natural border stood in the way of Russia's eastern expansion to the shores of the Pacific Ocean. Ultimately, it founded at the extreme east of the land, the city of Petropavlovsk in 1740, south of the long peninsula of Kamchatka. A year later, the Russian Empire entered North America through the Bering Strait and Alaska became, for a time, "Russian America" until March 30, 1867, date of its purchase for 7.2 million dollars by the USA. There was, however, one thing in common with Western Europe which must be stressed; it was the presence of many Jewish communities in Russia. In total, the empire had more than 5 million Jews in 1897, more than in the entire European West combined. Another common point was an institutional anti-Judaism, both that of the empire's aristocracy and that of the Orthodox Church. Important difference, however, was that the emancipation of the Jews did not take place during the time of the Romanovs, who ruled the country until their ouster from power in 1917. It would be one of the very first decisions of the new revolutionary Duma. Before this date, Jews still lived largely in ghettos, in communities closely united by religion and traditions. They were generally poor, lived on restricted and regulated activities, remained in a Middle Ages status, and did not have access to the administrative functions of the state or the ranks in the army. The same causes producing the same effects; it was Pan-Slavism, this grandiloquent nationalism of "Greater Russia" which was expressed during the[214] nineteenth century. Then, rivalry emerged between the nations, and Pan-Slavism was opposed to Pan-Germanism, Catholicism against Orthodoxy met in Sarajevo, where in June 1914 the attack against the heir to the throne of Austria-Hungary, Archduke Franz Ferdinand, is known, to have started

---

[214] Petropavlovsk-Kamchatsky | Location, Population, & Earthquake | Britannica

the terrible war of 1914-1918. The same causes produce the same consequences: the persecutions against the Jewish communities accompanied the progression of the pride of the nation. They started very early, but nothing stopped them. They gave birth to a word that has since been used for many forms of anti-Jewish persecution, it is the Russian word "pogrom". It means all at once: destruction, looting, massacre, rape and other misdeeds of the people unleashed specifically against the Jews. Nothing original in these acts, nor in this word which, however avoids, to the one who uses it, to pronounce in his mother tongue the horrors which it evokes. Pogroms came in a context of political and social tension in the greater Russia after the assassination of Tsar Alexander II in 1881. His successor Alexander III put an end to a relative period of freedom for the Jews. Anti-Judaism was then, endorsed by the Holy Synod, this collegial institution of the Orthodox Church, placed at the top of its hierarchy. Suspected of having participated in the attack against the Tsar, the pogroms against the Jews were linked one after the other with the tacit approval of the political and religious authorities. From 1881 in Kiev, Odessa, Warsaw, cities then part of the Russian empire, as well as everywhere in urban centers and villages, where Jews could be found, pogroms multiplied. The French historian Gérard Nahon in his "History of the Jewish people[215]", evokes the deliberate program of the Russian political and religious authorities of the time concerning the Jews, which holds in a few words: "A third of the Jews will be converted, a third will emigrate, a third will perish". Another historian, Salomon Reinach[216], in his "History of the Russian Revolution – 1905 ~1917", indicates that, "This way of seeing had the approval of Nicholas II, convinced that the 1905 revolution attempt had been the work of the Jews". To serve his anti-Jewish propaganda, the Jewish conspiracy theory was widespread throughout the empire and beyond, including through a document attributed to them. Its title, "The Protocols of the Elders of Zion", was published in 1903 and contained the Jewish program for world domination, just that. It quickly became a very successful work; however, it was only the product of the imagination of a Russian anti-Semitic forger named, Matveï Golovinski, working for the Tsar's police. A significant part of the Jews nevertheless managed to get out of this

---

[215] Publications de Gérard Nahon: Histoire du peuple Juif, Encyclopædia Universalis, DVD 2007.
[216] An intellectual of his time, Salomon Reinach (1858-1932) - Jews, Europe, the XXIst century

confinement both material and psychological. Together with the communities of Central Europe, which often shared the same condition, they campaigned for their rights as a minority among many others. The prospects remained narrow, however, with many siding with systematic resistance to oppression, others choosing emigration, which grew significantly during these years. Two main paths soon opened up to the hopes of emancipation for the Jews of Central Europe, deaf to any assimilation effort. This was Zionism on the one hand and socialism on the other. The first way was nationalist, in a way, it goes without saying because in a distant past, still alive by the reminder of rabbis and religion, Israel was a great nation blessed by the Eternal God. Indeed, the verses of Psalm 137 are frequently recalled in synagogues; "If I forget you, Jerusalem, let my right hand forget me! If I do not remember you, if I do not make Jerusalem the main subject of my joy!" (Ps 137:6). Moreover, in this execrable context of pogrom and racism, where nationalism everywhere becomes the cardinal value of European nations, Zionism puts the return of the children of Israel to the land of promise, at the center of its national and political program. The formation of Italian unity in 1861, then that of Germany in 1871 both served as an inspiration for the future gathering of the exiles of the Jewish people. Consequently, the eternal prayer of the return to Zion pronounced at each Passover; "...next year in Jerusalem..." now seemed credible in one form or another, in the last years of the 19th century. Thinkers, philosophers and essayists promoted this idea in the scattered communities of Europe. It should be noted that the rabbis were mostly hostile to the Zionist project; for them the salvation of Israel would come only in a supernatural way in an eschatological time impossible to define. Hence the conflict that would arise within the communities made this project a rather secular than religious undertaking. One of the ideologues of Zionism, Moses Hess, a German philosopher and historian, was close to Karl Marx and was the author of a book written in 1862, under the eminently prophetic title "Rome and Jerusalem: The Last National Question[217]". A unifying current of Zionism appeared after the pogroms of 1881, it was animated by Leon Pinsker doctor from Odessa in Ukraine, it was called, "The Lovers of Zion"[218], name evocative of the indissoluble

---

[217] Gérard Nahon: History of the Jewish People, Encyclopædia Universalis, DVD 2007.
[218] Moses Hess: Rome and Jerusalem: The Last National Question - Moses Hess – Google.com

link of Judaism with the land of Israel. In 1897 in Basel, Switzerland, Zionist activists gathered under the leadership of Theodore Herzl to organize the 1st Zionist Congress[219] and give the project its first contours. Journalist and writer, he is the author of an essay dealing with the future of the Jewish people whose title clearly announces the whole program, "The Jewish State: a modern solution to the Jewish question". At that time, we were in the midst of the Dreyfus affair in France, and more than ever, the Zionists were convinced that assimilation by the "Haskalah" could not meet the deepest aspirations of the Jewish people. Zionism also took concrete form when the Universal Israelite Alliance, founded near Jaffa, in what was still a neglected region of the Ottoman Empire, the first specifically Jewish agricultural settlement. It was soon followed by many Jewish settlement initiatives, which gave rise to the Kibbutz movement, these collective farms a model of unique in the world. Zionism benefited from an exceptional window of opportunity because the territories of ancient Judea and Samaria were not autonomous at the end of the 19th and beginning of the 20th century. They were part of the Ottoman Empire itself, in decline in the face of Russian expansion and the emancipation of the nations it had dominated for centuries in the Balkans. It was therefore possible to buy farmland there and to set up vast modern social organizations benefiting both Jewish and Arab inhabitants from these territories. Therefore, Bankers like the Rothschilds in France and Great Britain, Jewish investment funds in the United States, bought vast tracts of land from Arab landowners, who did nothing or so little with it. The socialist inspiration of the Zionist movement proved particularly effective in endowing the country with the attributes of a modern nation. Trade unions, mutual organizations for pensions, medical dispensaries, banks, cooperatives, and all kinds of businesses emerged at the same time as successive waves of emigrants arrived from Europe and Russia. The inhabitants of the kibbutz, and the mochavim were also early socialist idealists, who often understood the messianic dimension of the Zionist project. They cleared and exploited these formerly neglected territories and sometimes without their knowledge, they fulfilled the biblical prophecy of Psalm 107; «He turns the desert into a pond and the arid land into a source of water" (Ps 107:35). The second path of liberation announced above was that of socialism.

---

[219] First Zionist Congress & Basel Program (1897): https://www.jewishvirtuallibrary.org

In it, there were references to numerous Judeo-Christian sources but also humanists, academics and scientists or such to be more rooted in scientific truths. The French Revolution of 1789 occupied a great place there, but not only because its limits have highlighted the need for methodical and theoretical pillars much stronger than those it had at its time. Now, it was science that would serve as the basis for understanding the world, not only physically but also, and by extension, politically and socially. Already, the great Protestant universities put forward their philosophical and historical research more than the revelation of God contained in the Holy Scriptures. From the great philosopher Emmanuel Kant (1724~1804), the major Universities would retain more of the philosopher than of the theologian. With Karl Marx socialism became radicalized; it went far beyond its idealist period of "social Christianity" and took the form of an indisputable scientific truth. Thus conceived, it had something to seduce people in the ghettos, in the circles of progressive Jewish students of Eastern Europe, who often rejected a religion that had locked them in the unbearable ostracism of the outside world and deprived them of the intellectual and scientific openness to which many aspired. Circles of study and reflection on political and social issues were formed everywhere in the Yiddishland, from which more or less radical socialist currents were born. It is in Lithuania that took shape, what has been called in Yiddish and in short, "The Bund", but which was called in extenso: The General Union of Jewish Workers of Lithuania, Poland and Russia. It is interesting to note the Germanic root of the word "Bund", itself derived from the expression, "Covenant between God and men". This word, whose meaning has been attenuated and secularized over time, is found in a large number of German expressions and words in which it emphasizes the idea of forming a whole, a coherence, or a collectivity. The following examples, taken among many others: Bundestag (Parliament), Bundeswehr (Army), Deutscher Bund (German Confederation), amply demonstrate this. By a singular irony of history, "The Bund", of the Jews who wanted to be atheists after rejecting references to their own religious history, found themselves in 1897, under the umbrella of a collective organization whose name had a distant origin with "the Alliance with God". The "Bund" was a socialist and secular Jewish political party advocating for the recognition of the rights of the Jewish minority in the Russian Empire and in Central Europe. It was created by the Vilnius Circle in Lithuania in September 1897 by Aaron Liberman[220] (1844-1908), himself from a religious background but he became a socialist activist and by Arkadi Kremer[221], nicknamed "the Father". He too had left his very religious milieu, and he would be arrested several times because of his political commitment close to the Marxist revolutionaries. The Bund militants were in constant struggle with the Tsarist police, which did not tolerate any freedom of expression for the different ideological currents that were born in the country. The Bund fought for the social transformation of Tsarist Russia so that the Jews would be recognized as one of the nationalities of this vast empire. The will to separate the political from the religious was very strong, until wanting to make it disappear off the Bund and off the Jewish identity. Professor Rachel Ertl[222], a specialist in Yiddish literature at the University of Paris La Sorbonne, talks about those activists for whom, "Socialist literature is our Torah" and who were willing to die for atheism as the elders were willing to do for "The Name...". The Bund found itself in disagreement with the Zionists on the one hand, which perpetuated the messianic hope of the return to Zion and on the other hand with the Marxist socialists, who did not see the need to preserve a Jewish specificity in the general struggle against tsarism and the representatives of the bourgeois order. Although having joined the movement of the Second[223] Socialist International, the Bund remained marked by its Jewish origins, its cultural and social struggle, and despite its rejection of any religious content, it wanted to keep in Judaism, its culture, theater, literature, and especially the language. For them, it was the Yiddish, and not the Hebrew, which was the subject of a resurrection orchestrated by the Zionists. The fate of the Bund is tragic in many ways, and the rejection of the Torah would not bring luck to the movement. After having counted up to 30,000 members in the 1900s, having multiplied social institutions for the benefit of communities, the Bund was confronted with its internal contradictions. The most difficult to overcome was that of a Judaism without Torah or religion, and as a result, the nagging question of its integration into the Social Democratic Workers' Party of Russia (ODSP)

---

[220] Liberman, Arn-Shmuel (Aaron Samuel Liebermann) (1845–November 18, 1880): A member of the Vilnius Revolutionary Circle | Congress for Jewish Culture

[221] Arkadi Kremer: leader of a Jewish social-democratic circle | Kremer, Arkadii - YIVO Encyclopedia

[222] Rachel Ertel | Maison de la culture yiddish | Rachel Ertel | Jewish Women's Archive

[223] History of the Second International: https://www.marxists.org/

remained. Finally, the Bund withdrew from the party at the Congress of London in 1903, and later in the 1917 revolution, it supported the "Menshevik" faction (minority) opposed to that of the Bolsheviks (majority) and led by Wladimir Ilyich Lenin. In an atheist socialist republic, the relation to any religion no longer made sense and the Bund disappeared from the USSR in 1922 by merging its instances with those of the communist party of the USSR. This atheistic revolution nevertheless carried the hopes of a large number of Jews who fought in its ranks. However, it often gave them a tragic end because it did not forgive them for having been rather "Menshevik" and they would be many of its leaders and militants to be hunted down and executed during the Stalinist purges of the 1930s. In the west, the Bund did not survive another tragedy, that of the occupation of Poland in 1939 by the Nazis and the implementation of the "final solution". Crushed on both sides of the Vistula, European Judaism disappeared in the roar of the weapons and persecution of the Second World War. What remained of the Bund, of the Yiddish, of the Jewish specificity in Central Europe elaborated over more than a thousand years? Nothing, had the nations and their religions won against Judaism? No, they lost, they collapsed on themselves; especially the Christian religions today are called into question and deserted in relation to a past still close. Their buildings, sometimes of great beauty, belong to their people; they have, above all, a cultural value. They testify more to the greatness of their past than of their future. The Jews have left, we Europeans can weep bitterly at this departure, and we still need to repent today of having to endure the ambient idolatry of the nations, which has distanced us from the Word of God. We indeed live in an environment where the "Fathers of the Church" continue to be glorified by ignoring the extremely violent remarks of some of them against Jews and Judaism in general. In France, how many avenues, public squares and prestigious buildings are named after Voltaire, the philosopher of the Enlightenment or Jacques Bossuet, the bishop of the town of Meaux at the end of the 17th century, both of whom were notoriously anti-Semitic. The glorious memory of figures of the past, such as John Chrysostom, Jerome of Stridon, and Augustine of Hippône, continues to be celebrated in prestigious academies, while their insulting remarks about Israel, the people of God, are ignored. We could multiply these examples and this tendency to pay tribute to those who have taught contempt or even hatred of the Jews, reminding us of the thought of the prophet Isaiah when he declared: "Woe to those who call evil good, and good evil, who change darkness into light, and light into darkness, who change bitterness gently, and gentleness into bitterness!" (Is 5:20). The Jews are gone, and they left a great void behind them, which would never be closed and now their destiny is written elsewhere. Although they have often wished the Jewish would leave, the official Christian religions had no reason to congratulate themselves on this final departure. It proves to them de facto that they were by no means universal since they did not know how to integrate Judaism through dialogue and harmony into the eternal questioning of God's revelation. They did not know how to live the promises made to those who would bless the Jewish people, nor were they able to see in them a gift from the Almighty God for the understanding of the Word of God among the peoples. Another consequence of these dramatic events was the relegation of European nations as an institutional, political and social model for the world. Since 1948, the two main poles of Judaism, are Israel on the one hand, but also the USA where they are more than 6 million to live without ever having to permanently justify their right to exist and their religious identity. It also flourishes in those small and great nations that have blessed Israel, according to the Word of the Lord repeated many times; "I will bless those who bless you" (Gen 12:2).

10.11 The 2 World Wars 1914 ~1918 and 1939 ~1945

The dangers of competition between nations were exacerbated until the 20th century with the two deadliest world wars in the history of humanity. For many historians, these two world wars make only one in reality. Indeed, in the aftermath of the First World War, Europe remained an unstable powder keg of nations in perpetual rivalry, waiting to explode. As these exacerbated nationalisms clashed, the Jews found themselves in the center of the common hostility. France but also Germany, Spain, Italy and all Central Europe, as well as Soviet Russia, fed together the hatred of the Jews, symbol of all the rejections, they concentrated on them at the same time, the causes as well as the consequences of all the hatred and failures of nations. The Second World War appears in many respects as a double enterprise of Nazi Germany; the conquest on the one hand, to regain the "Großdeutschland" by erasing Europe from the treaty of Versailles of 1919 and the civil war against the Jews, on the other hand, with a view to their total extermination in the conquered countries.

10.12 Responsibility of religions in the spread of anti-Semitism in Europe

If anti-Semitism is not a uniquely European phenomenon, it will never reach such a high level of violence as in Europe, going so far as to attempt systematic destruction, as implemented by Nazi ideology and their accomplices. One can therefore wonder about the ultimate responsibilities that led to such a progression to the crime of genocide. As the main vector of morality in society, representatives of its highest collective and individual values, religions, and especially the Christianity of the multitude, bear a major responsibility in this anti-Jewish relentlessness. We have seen that this is, first of all a rhetorical issue that is rapidly emerging in Christianity itself from its origin. The erasure of the religious domain from the seventeenth century on did not prevent this mortal message from remaining since then, as an indelible legacy in all European societies. The transmission to the philosophical, intellectual, and political sphere of this poison, in no way exonerates the responsibility of the religions of the multitude, since they did not carry out any work of rehabilitation of Judaism as a source of Christianity between the 17th and the 20th century. On the contrary, during this long period, this message of condemnation was found, as we have seen, in all the pages of its doctrine concerning the Jewish people. Certainly, repentance always comes after the crime, and it is in the order of things, but for these organizations that have had no other care than themselves for centuries, can they reinvent or reform themselves as the Reformers of the sixteenth century wanted? Nothing is less certain, since their audience and attractiveness collapsed after the Second World War.

10.13 The Shoah, the ultimate outcome of anti-Semitism among the nations

No word is enough to speak with reason of what exceeds it so much. Neither ours nor those of men of letters and history have the capacity to describe the immensity of this crime. Our development will therefore be short and sober if not to recall what is "The **Shoah**[224]" in <u>Hebrew</u>: שואה, "the catastrophe". Moreover, we refer to the voluminous studies that have been made on this major question, which still tirelessly questions human consciousness today. Indeed, it is the systematic extermination enterprise, led by Nazi Germany and its allies, against the Jewish people during the Second World War, It led to the disappearance of more than six million Jews, or the two third of the Jews then present in Europe and about 40% of the Jewish population in the world. We also use the terms "Holocaust" or, "Jewish genocide", "Judecide" or "destruction of the Jews of Europe" (Raul Hilberg). Historians and linguists are still debating the right term to use to qualify the unqualified, and they cannot find one. What is important to remember is that Europe in this attempt to destroy its Jewish population, has destroyed itself. It no longer exerts the predominant influence it had until this brutal fall in the ruins of Berlin. The power passed elsewhere, exercised by other nations, on other continents, the religious practice in the official churches collapsed, while it progressed in the evangelical churches of professing type. In total during the 3rd Reich[225] , it took more than 9 million German civilian and military deaths combined to murder more than 6 million European Jews all civilians. Israel has left Europe, as he had left Egypt, thus listening to the call of the Lord, launched in chapter 37 of the book of Ezekiel (1-28), in order to settle in the land that was given to him forever by the Lord himself. In this moral and spiritual disaster, the official religions have demonstrated their inability to accept Christian universalism, for which they were in charge of, since they have not been able to maintain a respectful and fraternal dialogue with Israel and their religious representatives. [226]

---

[224] Holocaust & Shoah: The Slaughter of Six Million Jews: A Holocaust or a Shoah? - TheTorah.com

[225] Raul Hilberg: The Destruction of the European Jews: Third Edition on JSTOR

[226] REPERES: module 1-2-0, notice - Balance sheet of the Second World War - EN - final. pdf centre-robert-schuman.org

CHAPTER III

Reconciliation between the Synagogue and the Church

1. Introduction to this Kingdom, which is not of this world.

The apostle Paul explains in depth the relationship of humility, love and balance between the Synagogue and the Church, between the Jew and the pagan converted to God by Jesus Christ. Indeed, the Epistle to the Romans contains all the explanations and instructions necessary for harmony between the Synagogue and the Church. What dominates in his magisterial presentation is the fulfilment of God's plan both for the Jew and for the newly converted Christian. No opposition or distance because all the revelation of God is contained in the message of love of the Gospel, consubstantial extension to the First Testament. This is why the apostle Paul, in his entire letter to the Romans, wisely advises the pagans who have just converted to Christianity to have respect and consideration for the Synagogue and, more broadly, for the people of Israel who gather there. He unequivocally declares that God did not reject his people: "So I say, Did God reject his people? Far from it! For I, too am an Israelite, of the seed of Abraham, of the tribe of Benjamin. God did not reject his people, whom he knew in advance. Do you not know what the Scripture tells of Elijah, how he addresses to God this complaint against Israel: Lord, they have killed your prophets, they have overthrown your altars; I was left alone, and they're trying to take my life? But what answer does God give him? I have reserved for myself seven thousand men who have not bowed their knees before Baal" (Rom 11:1-4). Then he exhorts them in verses 17 and 18 to humility towards Judaism with this comparison between the two olive trees; Israel is holy and the pagan world is wild. This means, that the latter a priori, does not know God, nor the election, nor the Law, nor the prophets, nor the long memory of the Jewish people, but, that it can access it through Jesus Christ. Paul renews this exhortation in verse 21, with this premonitory warning: "... do not abandon yourself to pride but fear". In addition, let us add what he says in chapter 3 of verses 27 to 31. "Where then is the subject of glorifying? It is excluded. By what law? By the law of works? No, but by the law of faith. For we think that man is justified by faith, without the works of the law. Or is God only the God of the Jews? Is He not so with the pagans? Yes, so are the pagans, since there is only one God, who will justify by faith the circumcised, and by faith the uncircumcised. Do we destroy the law by faith? Far from it! On the contrary, we confirm the law". This statement of the apostle announces the inclusion of the First Testament in Christian universalism. This is all the more understandable since at the time when Paul wrote these words, the New Testament did not exist. It can also be noted that it echoes the promise made by the Eternal God to Abraham; "all the families of the earth will be blessed in you" (Gen 12:3). Consequently, and in his own words, the Ministry of the Law is thus confirmed at the same time as that of Grace, several centuries apart. The extent of this reign coming from God is poorly measured, for it is not the nations which will claim to be Christians which will effectively establish, on earth, this reign of, "... peace, justice and joy" (Rom 14:17). Fortunately, it will come instead, in open hearts ready to receive this Realm in all his fullness, in accordance with the biblical thought expressed in the first chapter of the Gospel of John; "But to all who have received him, to those who believe in his name, he has given the power to become children of God, born not of the blood, nor of the will of the flesh, nor of the will of man, but of God" (Jn 1:12-13). It is a question here of receiving the "light" and of being born no longer of the union of a man and a woman, but rather of the only will of God. When the individual receives his Word in his heart, he welcomes with it the Lord and the Savior of his soul. Indeed, verse 14 specifies that this Word in question was made flesh, that is, his Word was incarnated. After centuries of messianic prayers and hope, the connection between the Word of God and the life of man was finally manifested in Jesus Christ the Messiah of

Israel. Thousands, if not millions, of men and women became; "children of God", starting from Judea and Samaria, that is, from the historical heart of this revelation, would travel the known and unknown world to bring it to the "ends of the earth". It is not easy to grasp the importance of their legacy to the generations that followed them; however, they were the true pioneers of Judeo-Christian civilization that we know. Working for justice, peace, and love, they often received in this world nothing but mockery and contempt for any reward, but they have been welcomed into the Kingdom of Heaven. Others have reached the steps of fame, but they have not yielded to its mirages, as this comparison with Moses in the Epistle to the Hebrews indicates; "It was by faith that Moses, having grown great, refused to be called the son of the daughter of Pharaoh, who loved to be mistreated better with the people of God than to have for a time the enjoyment of sin, seeing the reproach of Christ as a greater treasure than the treasures of Egypt, for he had his eyes fixed on remuneration" (Heb 11:24-26). Humble fathers, housewives, in all the simplicity of their daily tasks, they are the heroes of the New Testament, they have built a kingdom that will never be destroyed. This is the one that Daniel's prophecy (Dn 2:33-46) speaks of, which is based on justice, peace, and love (Rom 14:17), as Jesus Christ taught. Through the witness and fidelity of these humble servants, life has been built over the centuries, on the solid foundations of the Bible, despite the gesticulation of the great of this world. For them, the connection with Judaism was self-evident because; from where did the Word of God come except from the spiritual and intellectual heritage of Judaism, compiled by generations of wise men and scholars dedicated to its service? The law of God is addressed to the intelligence of man, but even more, to his conscience and his heart; it is a doctrine of good that goes as far as the intimacy of the person. This is what makes it special, compared to all other laws written by men. It is placed above them and as a source of water follows its slope, it irrigates the entire legal and regulatory arsenal of our social and personal life in the Occident. In his commentary on the Sermon on the Mount (Mat 5), the theologian and sociologist Frédérique De Coninck[227] speaks with accuracy of this kingdom both invisible and yet very real

---

[227] Frédéric de Coninck: Regards Protestant «Happy the gentle, because they will inherit the earth" 4,23/6,35 - YouTube

when he says: "of these people who live and exchange in network of friendship", stressing the necessary prerequisites for its existence, namely, the esteem of the other, mutual respect, mutual trust. He shows that a large part of the exchanges between these people are in fact free because at its base, there existed these values, both social and moral. He looks in particular at Matthew 5 verse 5, where Jesus declares that the "meek shall inherit the earth". In ancient times, this adjective was used to describe a man of good "origin", i.e. of good extraction, noble or middle-class, who could be associated with a genealogy of good reputation. Over the centuries, the evolution of meaning has shifted towards psychological value; In popular language, the meaning of the word has even evolved into a pejorative qualifier, close to, "simple, silly, naive...". However, in the Bible, it is indeed a value of the spirit by which one who possesses it can inherit the earth. At the same time, we note that for Jesus Christ, the earth is a good inheritance, which brings us back to the time before the fall of Adam and Eve, when God had given man the mission of cultivating and guarding the garden of Eden (Gen 2:15). Our modern age confirms this idea of the meek man who by his intelligence of men, situations and by his work, legitimately reaches the top of institutions and companies. It also shows us that real progress is no different. It is customary to say or think that "Happy people have no history", implying; they have nothing to tell. This formula also said: "Trains arriving on time do not interest anyone". In fact, the media, the cinema, and opinions are generally most often focused on what is exceptional, provocative, scandalous, and shocking... It is as if we had to be constantly on the verge of a nervous crisis to have the feeling of existence. An important sector of the modern economy lives on this permanent tension between the law and its transgression, between social norms and scandal. In this third part, we want to honor these happy people who, on the contrary, have a beautiful story to tell; we want to try to understand why the trains that arrive on time are very interesting. The sermon on the mount indicates the opposite of the common thought, that there is great richness in listening to the testimony of happy people, blessed by the Lord, according to this chapter 5 of the Gospel of Matthew. It also indicates that we should be interested in trains that always arrive on time rather than those that derail because the good quality of services does not come without the deployment of great intelligence, sustained work, and intense mutual service within the teams that set the trains in motion.

Chapter 5 of the Gospel of Matthew brings everyone back to his or her elementary condition of mortal being, transient on this earth and also depositary of a seed of eternity placed in him or her by the Eternal God. As a "Kingdom", it was to be defined in terms of places, government, principles and rules, yet Jesus Christ presents it exclusively in experimental form; some experiences are desirable, others are bad or harmful, and we must flee from them. He exposes the true characteristics of the Kingdom of Heaven, starting with the best, namely a philosophy of happiness to which even the sages of ancient Greece had not thought. Rather than indicating what the conditions for happiness are, the first 10 verses show who these happy people are, without having reached the fullness of personal fulfillment or being spared from the trials of life. They are happy because.... They nurture in their hearts the values and thoughts of the Kingdom of Heaven. This is the explanation; we do not know more about their conditions and the circumstances of their lives, but we know that they are happy. At the same time as they are declared happy, these people give a glimpse of the Kingdom of Heaven; it is a question of consolation, inheritance, the earth, justice, obtaining mercy, seeing God, bringing peace and being called a son of God, possessing the Kingdom, being happy even in persecution. This kingdom, built on virtues, good feelings, expectations, and sufferings sometimes, is inherited from the messianic hope amply developed in the First Testament. Indeed, since the patriarchs, and even before them, we see these men in pursuit of an ideal of peace, justice and love constantly pushed back into a hypothetical future. The present devours the future, with its struggles, intrigues, prohibitions, wars and mourning, to such an extent that Jesus Christ does not even speak of it and demonstrates that the Kingdom can only be an interior disposition of the heart and mind. My kingdom is not of this world" (I 18:36), he told his accusers at his trial shortly before the crucifixion. In each verse in Matthew 5, he also points out that it is an intentional and personal search. The emphasis is on the individual character of the quest for these cardinal virtues. Following this general introduction, verses 13-16 address the audience directly with a comparison of salt and light. First are the qualities that protect the flavors from surrounding corruption. The reader does not have the impression that he speaks to an elite particularly gifted in terms of their qualities of mind, intelligence, and culture. However, it is as a representative of the Jewish people that he compares his audience to the salt that gives taste to food and, by extension, to life itself. He emphasizes only in a word, "the salt", the exceptional destiny of the Jewish people, made by the will of the Eternal Almighty, the people both witness and conservative of his divine Law. Light allows intelligence to penetrate the darkness of certain texts and explain them so that they become permanent landmarks for the individual. The light not only highlights previously hidden details but also carries far, as a city located at the top of a hill, its radiation is visible to a great distance. This is the vocation of these people, recalls Jesus Christ, to shine forth with good works so that men may glorify God. There is a mystery in this link of cause and effect because it goes through no explanation nor demonstration. However, he indicates that the men of every other nation in this world would know immediately when a good work has been done, and ipso facto, they would understand the testimony given on the existence of God and on the glory that it would bring to his name. Thus, according to this word, this or that act becomes like a ray of light, penetrating in a flash, the hearts to reveal God and his nature. These good works are not necessarily accompanied by words or religion, but they touch with sufficient strength for all men to glorify God. It is a direct appeal to the human conscience and perhaps even more, a revelation of the Holy Spirit. The Roman centurion is an example; he knew that the God of the Jews was the true God, unlike the idols of Rome. The Gospel text of Luke (7:5) tells us, "He loves our nation, and it is he who built our synagogue". There were many pagans, far more than we suppose, who were sensitive to the testimonies that the Jews brought about a God of eternity, truth, and beneficence for humanity. Despite the heaviness and inadequacies of religion to meet the aspirations of the human heart, Jesus Christ confirms in the Gospel of John, the central position of the Jewish people in the revelation of God, creator of the universe and Savior of men, when he declares to the Samaritan woman but also to all of us; "You love what you don't know; we worship what we know, for salvation comes from the Jews" (I 4:22). Following his remarks on salt and light, Jesus honors the Law and the prophets in verses 17 to 20. We could move distractedly from the salt to the light without making any link, while they are obvious. Indeed, the Jewish people are both salt and light because they are the people of the Law of God and his prophets. It is the people of the Book and also of its memory, Jesus Christ recalls this truth with these capital words; "Do not believe that I have come to abolish the law or the prophets; I came not to abolish, but to accomplish" (Ma 5:17). Faced with the difficulty, even the impossibility of perfectly fulfilling the Law of God, the temptation was great at that time, as it is today, to completely free oneself from it. We have seen in the second part how theologians, philosophers, and historians gave in to this seduction, to deny the Jewish origins of Christianity. Here however, the text recalls that, for time and eternity, one can never do without the Law of God or the jurisprudence that it left in the writings and preaching of their envoys and prophets in Israel. He even announces judgments on those who would alter their letter and spirit. The conclusion of verse 17 brings us back to the idea of salt and light because it is a question of doing more and better than the religious world, more and better than what is visible to men and strikes the eye; it is about being happy, according to the beginning of chapter 5. Verses 21 to 26 draw a parallel between murder and anger. It may come as a surprise, but both must be punished by the judges according to Jesus Christ, that is to say, it requires the intervention of a third party, namely that of a magistrate, to treat fairly, according to the law, the problem posed, both by anger and by murder. That means it's as bad to get angry with your brother as it is to kill him. Anger is seen as the beginning of murder because in the Kingdom of Heaven, the act as well as the thought of the act has equal value, as seen in the following concerning adultery in verses 27 to 29. This principle of the Kingdom of Heaven can be generalized to other examples of faults such as the thought of fraud is equal to fraud itself, the thought of theft is equal to theft itself, the thought of false testimony is equal to false testimony itself etc. The teaching on divorce follows this principle and shows that nothing, except marital infidelity, does not dispense man from loving his wife unconditionally in the same way as; "Christ loved his Church and gave himself up for her", as the apostle Paul states in his epistle to the Ephesians ch 5 v 25. The habit of swearing higher than oneself was a common practice in the time of Jesus Christ, it still is today, although it is, in general, out of the vocabulary intended to deal with business and conflict. At the time, it was to involve all kinds of abuse and false oaths taken with heaven or Jerusalem as a witness. To these excesses of all kinds, in which the sacred and the profane are easily mixed, he opposes the simple force of yes or no for any form of answer (v 33 to 37). The question of love for one's enemies is very difficult to assimilate; it goes against the instinct of conservation that every individual possesses, pushing anyone to defend themselves against any aggression. It even opposes the teachings of the Law in Exodus chapter 21. It begins in verse 38, with this quote: "You have learned that it has been said: eye for eye, and tooth for tooth." (Ex 21:24). The problem raised by this verse and the following is that of the equivalence of the penalty between that of the victim and that to be inflicted on the offender. In a search for fairness, the legislator found no better than to make both equal and that of the offender proportional to that which he caused to the victim. Is it restorative justice? At first sight not, because in the various cases cited, the harm caused is irreparable and the penalty imposed on the offender does not relieve the injured person. Nevertheless, it is noted that it seeks a form of balance; the harm done to one is balanced by the punishment imposed on the other. Since the writing of the Law, the wisdom of generations of jurists in Israel has tried to find a nuanced answer to this first formalization of what was later called the "Law of Talion". Numerous case studies and abundant jurisprudence appeared in the Mishnah and the Talmud, to expose the exceptions, the particular points, and the infinite declensions of what seems so abrupt in the general law. However, they will never manage to cover all the complexity of the real experiences in social life. To this difficulty of human understanding, Jesus Christ opposes the non-violence of one who does not resist oppression, who even goes in the direction of the aggressor when he declares; "But I tell you not to resist the wicked. If someone hits you on the right cheek, introduce the other as well. If anyone wants to plead against you, and take your tunic, give him your coat again. If someone forces you to make a mile, make two with him" (Ma 5:39-41). The meaning of this teaching is difficult to grasp. However, it can be said that it demonstrates that there is a pedagogy in non-violence, likely to modify the behavior of the aggressor. The one who stretches the other cheek, believes that his absence of violent reaction, and his contempt of the offense, will disarm the opponent, that he will be led to think rather than obey his anger or his will of power. Not to resist the wicked, to go in his direction rather than to oppose force against force is however a fundamental law of the Kingdom of Heaven, honored many times during the ministry of the apostle Paul, especially in the passage of his second epistle to the Corinthians; "Five times I have received forty blows less one from the Jews" (2Co 11:24). In the course of his career, the apostle suffered all kinds of opposition to his ministry and yet his non-violent attitude, his resilience, his will to pass the righteousness of God rather than that of men, finally triumphed in the history of the Church as in that of men. We realize here that this Kingdom, with laws and rules that are sometimes non-transferable in human societies, remains first made for the individual and not for the national community. Indeed, Jesus Christ never speaks of disarming the nation, he does not oppose the condition of the soldier whose very existence serves to defend the nation, its territorial integrity, its institutions, its culture, and its traditions. His Kingdom does not need these human and very derisory defenses in view of their effectiveness in universal history. The conclusion of this passage, so difficult to understand and put into practice, is said in verse 44; "Love your enemies, bless those who curse you, do good to those who hate you, and pray for those who mistreat you and persecute you, that you may be children of your Father who is in heaven." The purpose is therefore to be "sons of the Father", with this idea; "such a father, such a son" and this reminder of the human condition, whether good or evil; "... it rains on the just and on the unjust"(Ma 5:45). The last verse of chapter 5 sounds like a challenge to human understanding, since it is a matter of getting out of our earthly condition and being "Perfect", as our heavenly Father is perfect. The sermon on the Mount continues in chapters 6 and 7 of the Gospel of Matthew and Jesus once again emphasizes the inner life of those whom he calls into his special Kingdom. In verses 1 and 2 it is a question of reward and Jesus shows that it is advantageous to receive the one that the Father gives rather than that obtained from men. Indeed, the two are not equal, although the first is not detailed, we understand that it is very different from the second, ephemeral and immediate glory granted by men. On the one hand we are told; "the memory of the just lasts forever" (Ps 112:6), of the other; "For they loved the glory of men more than the glory of God" (Jn 12:43). Thus, in an act of justice, the reward may be chosen; that of God or that of men. Jesus encourages his disciples to seek justice from above, that of the Father who is often invisible to men, that which produces fruit for a long time, that which instructs and edifies them. With regard to prayer, teaching follows the same principle; it is better to practice discretion and sincerity than to display one's oratory skills before others. In the latter case, the expression "... they receive their reward", means that it is immediate, it does not last and only helps to flatter their ego. In verse 7, Jesus teaches not to multiply vain words as the pagans do. There is indeed a danger in letting one's heart speak faster than one's mind because, in this verbal outburst, one risks pronouncing the name of the Lord in vain and thus transgressing the 1st Commandment of the Torah; "Thou shalt not take the name of the Lord thy God in vain; for the Lord will not let him who takes his name go unpunished" (Ex 20:7). Today, in some evangelical assemblies, this abuse of language and personal expression harms their spiritual life and the sincerity of the people's praise. Pastors have the difficult task of encouraging, while controlling, the freedom of the expression of individual prayers, so that it does not overflow into the multiplication of vain, often egocentric, words that do not glorify God. After indicating what prayer should not be, Jesus Christ shows what it should be in verses 9 to 15. Entirely turned towards the Eternal God, it consists of a dialogue with him in which no selfish request enters, but rather the sincere expression of humility in the face of Almighty God. After the: Amen! of verse 13, comes this equivalence between the Kingdom of Heaven and that of men concerning forgiveness; to be forgiven by God, we must learn to forgive men their offenses. Logically, the pedagogy on fasting follows that on prayer, again, it is not a question of impressing others, but rather of devoting oneself sincerely to God who will bless one who does so. The riches in heaven are preferable to the riches of this earth because indeed, some are imperishable while others are corruptible and disappear with time. The conclusion of these three verses sounds like a warning to the conscience of each because it abruptly raises the question: "... where is your treasure?" The answer given is unambiguous: "it is where your heart is" (v 21). This is followed in verse 22, a demonstration which is psychoanalytical because, in fact, the eye is the organ of the representation of the external world, and it reveals only a part of it that is chosen by the individual. This is precisely where his personal disposition comes in: what does he see when he opens his eyes? This world is vast, it reveals what is good and what is bad. The eye and what it sees influences the whole body and places it whole, in the Light or in the darkness. Verse 24 sets out a new radical principle of the kingdom of heaven; the money presented as a master occupies the whole life of the one it possesses, there is no longer any place for God, these two kingdoms are exclusive of each other. Social life shows the truth of this opposition when one considers the numerous examples of those who have strayed from spiritual life to attach themselves to the riches of this world. However, these are derisory according to Jesus Christ, they are summed up in two essential needs; food and clothing, housing and transport are not even mentioned in what constitutes earthly life. He says in the Gospel of Matthew 8:20, not to have for himself a place of habitation or rest; "Foxes have dens, and birds in the sky have nests; but the Son of man has no place to rest his head". The link he makes between the accumulation of the riches of this world and the belief that one can add a cubit to the length of his life, is a new page of psychoanalysis that he opens on human behavior in verse 27. He thus shows, that this frequent tendency in humans to amass wealth is only an expression of, "the instinct of death", described and studied by the founder of psychoanalysis, Professor Sigmund Freund (1856 – 1939) and that it is only an illusory protection against death. The conclusion of chapter 6 is a call to trust in God for all matters of earthly life. Rather than concentrating on the often-made present, of uncertainties and frustrations, the Lord invites us in verse 32, to seek first the Kingdom of Heaven and the righteousness of God, knowing that everything necessary for life, we will be granted because Heavenly Father knows what we need (v 33). In the Kingdom of Heaven, we do not judge because it is the Law that judges, with the judges established for this and the sovereign Judge, that is, God himself the supreme legislator. However, by habit and temperament, our fellow men are willingly and frequently judged, for all sorts of very superficial reasons. Some others are much more serious; they have much more serious issues. Both are in any case dangerous for interpersonal relationships, without realizing it, they create barriers between individuals, groups, diverse communities. Judgments often lead to hasty generalizations between groups, religions, nations. One will say willingly, the Germans are this or that, the French are like that etc, without realizing that one has passed from the observation, results, sometimes erroneous to the moral judgment which brings a verdict: guilty or innocent, good or bad, good or bad, etc. The process of the upbringing of the child involves an infinity of judgments which define for him what is good and evil. It is mostly the result of experiences made by parents, which are transmitted to him for his good, for his education and for the construction of his personality. The rules of practical life are indistinctly mixed with the moral and spiritual rules that parents communicate and when adulthood comes, it is the time of choice to know how to consider the environment in which the grown-up child is placed. Will the discovery of this world, of the society of men, with its imperfections, its wars, its compromises, its scandals, push him to judgment or to compassion, Will he be able to distinguish between the observation necessary to understand the facts and the judgment on them, which brings a sanction? The first verse of chapter 7 is unambiguous; "Judge not, that ye may not be judged". It is difficult to renounce what appears to be a natural and legitimate tendency in man. However, Jesus Christ gives an excellent reason for this renunciation because he clearly shows that the one who judges draws attention to himself and on his own faults. The one who judges necessarily rises above the others, and he interprets the Law and yet he is no longer subject to it. But spontaneously others will question his role as judge, they will say, like this Hebrew, who quarreled with another, said to Moses who wanted to separate them; "Who made you chief and judge over us? Are you thinking of killing me like you killed the Egyptian? Moses was afraid and said, "certainly the thing is known..." (Ex 2.13-14). Standing as the judge over his brothers, Moses is brutally brought back to his own faults. He collapses morally and finds his salvation only in flight. As in this case, the defense of the accused is often stronger than that of the accuser and here we find the comparison between the one who wants to remove the straw that is in the eye of his brother, while he has a beam in his own (Ma 7:2-5). The position of the judge is therefore eminently critical, this first verse of chapter 7 shows that this role cannot be attributed to just anyone. In the old covenant, the Levites had this particular ministry at the same time as that of the celebration of worship of the Lord (No 18). They were detached from material contingencies since each tribe had a duty to maintain them (Num 18:20-24). This transversal position should ensure, in principle, neutrality and impartiality of their judgments. Judges are therefore servants of the Law of God and as such, they cannot take sides for any cause presented before them. They simply have to say what the law states on a particular matter and highlight what is right in a case in relation to the articles of the Law. This mediation role is absent when one person judges another, and quickly, he wants to do justice himself at the expense of the other. Man's natural inclination to judge his neighbor is proscribed in the Kingdom of Heaven, yet he who is born again, and who has received the Holy Spirit, receives the ability to judge. In some cases, it is even a duty. For example, 1 Corinthians 2:15 states: ".... The spiritual man judges of everything, he himself is not judged by anyone". The important thing in this passage is the, "of everything", it does not say that he judges "everything" or, "everyone". The preposition "of" used here shows that he judges with the necessary hindsight that the Holy Spirit gives him. Appreciates context, origin, location, cause, quality, circumstances... and he judges events, situations, doctrines, and in some cases men, according to the truth and justice of God, revealed in his Word. He becomes, for a time, a "Levite" when circumstances require it. His judgment is inspired by the truth of the Word as well as by the spirit of grace, everywhere present in his teachings. He remains in complete control of his own feelings and interests in relation to the case he is examining or the one he is talking about. Does spiritual man have universal jurisdiction? No, since all man's abilities are limited and rather than pronouncing on what he knows not or does not control, he would declare himself incompetent and would rely on the advice of experts on the case. This admission of ignorance is nevertheless positive because it allows truth and justice to progress by appealing to the qualifications of specialists. In this sense, the spiritual man judges well "of everything", even if, in many cases, it is not his opinion that will retain the conclusion of the debates. Verse 6 invites caution on the sharing of the treasures of the Kingdom and conversion, even more, it invites sanctification that is to say, the radical separation of the two domains, the spiritual and the material. This verse reminds us that these are holy things that cannot be mixed with the secular world. Here we find, even indirectly, the idea of the separation of domains and powers, developed in § 2 on pages 14 and 55. Like these two liquids that do not mix with each other, but can exist one in addition to the other, those who convert to God through Jesus Christ must take care to separate themselves from the polemics, quarrels of words, which according to the apostle Paul, give rise to; "envy, quarrels, slander, evil suspicion" (1Tim 6:4). For those who want to enter it, the Kingdom of Heaven remains a very personal path of life, the verses in Mat (5:7-12), explains this very well since it is necessary to show will to constantly: ask, seek and knock at the door, to get answers and solutions. These action verbs are used to stress at once the intentional nature of entry into the Kingdom and the perseverance required to truly remain in it. The comparison made with the father who gives good things to his children (v 9 to 11) shows the nature of the heavenly Father who gives, not like the world to take back afterwards (Jn 14:27), but definitively. Another principle of the Kingdom that is not necessarily intuitive is reciprocity. Verse 12 point out, "Whatever you want men to do for you, do for them, for it is the law and the prophets". This is a teaching on the logical equivalence of behavior between people; "Do to the other what you would like him to do to you". However, there is more because it is also a summary of the whole law and the prophets, that is, the ultimate synthesis of all that the prophets and sages of biblical thought have said and written to this day. This expression of common sense is given the sanctity of an eternal law. The logical rule is mixed with the spiritual rule in this sentence; the two kingdoms, one celestial and the other terrestrial, touch each other on this particular point. This is not the only example where Jesus Christ will call upon the most elementary common sense to explain, elucidate and liberate the captive thought of men concerning these two kingdoms, distinct but sometimes so close. The narrow door follows the previous idea; "ask, search and knock on the door". It is a very selective route to reach a door that is also narrow. One cannot enter it cluttered with his titles and possessions, his qualities and experiences good or bad. The door is narrow, and you have to strip yourself of the artifices that you tend to add during your life to compensate for its imminent disappearance. The door is narrow but opens to an immense kingdom where abundant graces, virtues, happiness, values of the spirit, consolations and true joys etc. Conversely, the path of perdition is wide because it passes through all the seductions that can be offered to human lust. It is wide at first, but it gradually tightens until the end of life and all hope for eternity. The idea of the narrow door is developed in the warning against the false prophets (v 15-20), against those who know how to hide the substance behind the form, those whose fruit is pleasant to look at but bitter to taste, those whose promises engage only those who listen to them.... The Old Testament warned against false prophets with these words; "Thus says the Lord of hosts: Do not listen to the words of the prophets who prophesy to you! They lead you to things of nothingness; They speak the visions of their hearts, not what comes from the mouth of the Lord (Jer 23:16). Even today, this warning has retained its full value because the reckless abuse of prophecy undermines the authority of the preaching of the biblical message. The criterion of the authenticity of the prophecy according to the teaching of Jesus Christ in this passage, is not only that it is realized in a more or less near future, but even more, it is the credibility of the prophet himself that counts more than anything, as verses 16 indicates; "You will recognize them by their fruits (the prophets). Are grapes picked from thorns, or figs from thistles?" and verse 20; "So you will recognize them by their fruits".

This thought is confirmed in the letters of the apostle Paul, especially in this passage from the first epistle to the Corinthians; "The spirits of the prophets are subject to the prophets" (1 Cor 14:32). This means that the prophets control each other and are indebted to each other in what they advance. There follows a direct link between saying it and doing it, between speech and action (v 21-23). This reminder of the need to align our actions with our thoughts and words, is not the simplest requirement to satisfy in the Kingdom of Heaven. This is a stumbling block because the feelings, thoughts and words jostle in the mind of man, and they are not proportional to our actions, as the apostle James emphasizes in his epistle when he speaks of the language and the ravages it can cause. On four occasions, he warns of its excesses and abuses, he says in the first chapter; "If one believes to be religious, without holding his tongue in check, but by deceiving his heart, the religion of this man is vain" (Jam 1:26). In chapter 3, the apostle makes a detailed analysis of the problems related to the untimely use of the word, he says from verse 5; "Similarly, the language is a small member, and it boasts great things. This is how a small fire can burn a large forest". Small in size and sound, words can ignite hearts, cause murder and war, seal conflicts between families for generations. However, it can also bless, heal, teach, and build. In the next verse he likens the tongue to a devouring fire; "Language is also a fire; it is the world of iniquity. The tongue is placed among our limbs, defiling the whole body, and inflaming the course of life, being itself inflamed by Gehenna". In verse 8, he notes that evil has no solution; "but no man can tame his tongue; it is an evil that cannot be repressed; it is full of deadly venom" (Ja 3:8). The tongue is an absolute evil in the mouth of the fallen man and there will always be this mixture of purity with impurity, of life with death until he turns to the God of his salvation. For this reason, Jesus Christ does not make access to the Kingdom of Heaven dependent on the words spoken by those who have confessed his name before men, but rather on their acts; "Many will tell me on that day: Lord, Lord, have we not prophesied by your name? Have we not cast out demons by your name? And have we not done many miracles by your name? Then I will tell them openly: I have never known you, withdraw from me, you who commit iniquity" (Ma 7:22-23). The conclusion of the sermon on the Mount is given by this comparison between the two houses; one is built on the rock, that is, on the eternal words of Jesus Christ, the other is built on the sand because it ignores them, the first resists bad weather but not the second. The testimony of the apostle Matthew in verses 28 and 29 of chapter 7 is that the words of Jesus Christ are striking. They strike individuals but also collectively, the crowd is "… struck by his doctrine". It spontaneously assimilates his words to a doctrine unique in its kind. Then, it is "his doctrine", it is like no other and very different from what their scribes and Pharisees teach them, for he teaches with authority. This last word indicates that he adds experience to knowledge, incarnation to theory, which is why his doctrine is, "… striking". We remember again, this enigmatic kingdom described by the prophet Daniel in the vision he is explaining to King Nebuchadnezzar; "You looked, when a stone came loose without the help of any hand, struck the iron and clay feet of the statue, and tore them to pieces" (Da 2:34). Further on (v 35) it is said that; «…. The stone that struck the statue became a great mountain and filled the whole earth". The doctrine of Jesus Christ has indeed struck hearts, but even more, it has struck kingdoms, empires, kings and princes who have collapsed (v 43) because they had made only human alliances between them, forgetting to do so first with the Eternal God. The analogy between this stone which struck the feet of iron and clay and the rock on which the prudent man built his house is also striking; it refers to the many comparisons made in the Bible with the God of Israel who is also called "The Rock of Ages" (Is 26:4). The pedagogy of the Kingdom of Heaven is the subject of most of the concrete and detailed teachings of the New Testament, and we cannot do more than what they themselves say. Jesus Christ develops them in the context of the Judaism of his time, and they follow the work of the Law of God and the prophets of the First Testament. It is a moral of the individual who is called to reform his heart and his ways unceasingly, knowing that it is corrupted because of sin present everywhere in his life and works. There is no scriptural basis for the Christian anti-Semitism described in the second part of this book, except by making the texts say what they do not say. It is also a doctrine of the universal love of God revealed in Jesus Christ by his atoning sacrifice on the Cross. In his three epistles, the apostle John is even more direct when he defines the very nature of God by these four words; "… for God is love" (1Jo 4.8 & 16). This doctrine is therefore unique: it is the point of departure and arrival of all metaphysical speculation. It is a perfect summary of the general thought outlined in the Law and the Prophets of the Bible. For this reason, there is no trace of the will to exclude anyone from accessing the Kingdom of Heaven in the texts of the New Testament and it is also for this reason that we must hasten to rebuild what has been destroyed. The reconciliation plan we propose begins with an awareness of what we owe to Israel, then we will make a quick comparison between the evolution of the nations that bless Israel and the one that curses it. In this part we also want to pay a sustained tribute to those who, despite anti-Jewish prejudices of all kinds have understood the message of the Jewish people addressed to this world and have been advocates of the defense of a Jewish harmony-Christian against religious and social prejudice. Without being able to cite them all, we will talk about some whose profile stands out particularly well for this cause. Finally, we will talk about the remarkable work of Evangelical associations that work for a complete rehabilitation of Judaism in memory as in the practice of Christianity. With these developments in multiple chains, we will have contributed together to this work of justice and truth to bring peace and serenity between these two pillars of solidarity of the faith of Abraham.

1.1 Humility of King David, humility of the Christian

Behind the two terms of this paragraph, one can discover all the ambiguity of the Church's relations with the Synagogue. Indeed, as a born-again Christian, when one considers the destiny of Israel, one cannot do better than to imitate David's attitude towards King Saul, fallen from his title of king, but not of "the anointing of the Lord". In this story, despite the advice of those close to him, despite the murderous intentions of King Saul towards him, David retains respect and deference to the one whom he will always consider "the Anointed One" (1Sa 24:2 et s). He answers to his companions (v 6); "And he said unto his people, The Lord forbid me to do against my lord, the anointed of the Lord, such an action as to lay my hand upon him! for he is the anointed of the Lord." David three times invokes the name "The Lord" to justify before his people, his refusal to lay hands on the king. This refusal and the others that follow, will remain in the jurisprudence of Judaism as a marker of the distance that must be taken with regard to those who are custodians of, "the Anointing of the Eternal". This is not an exorbitant privilege, but rather a sign that in the last resort, the one who judges "the Anointed" is ultimately God himself and no one else, even if he was

King of Israel. What we must remember from this seemingly unequal struggle between strength and law is finally the triumph of the second over the first. It is also expectation and faith in the manifestation of divine justice that will come, no matter what happens in the present. This attitude of heart and mind will be one of the main characteristics of Jewish piety. Expectation, resilience, prayers, and reflections will help us understand God's plans, even through trials that can be very challenging at times. In the New Testament this principle is confirmed by the Apostle Paul who will say, "Do not avenge yourselves, beloved, but let anger act; For it is written, To me is vengeance, to me is retribution, says the Lord" (Rom 12:19). In the history of Christianity very often, the manifestation of the righteousness of God was not expected and many were the men of a church that became imperialist who wanted, by sword and fire, forced the hand of God and obtain without any resistance the conversion of Jews to Christianity. Yet the Lord did not grant them what they sought with their own strength, and conversion to the Christianity of the nation of Israel as a whole remains a mystery to this day. On the other hand, individual conversions by the "New Birth", according to the plan of God explained by Jesus to Nicodemus in the Gospel of John (3:4) and following, are not and confirm that Jesus Christ is well; the "Messiah who came to save the lost sheep of the House of Israel" (Mat 15:24). Far from religious passions and invective, a New Testament man in the book of Acts (5:34-42) shows the continuity of this thought; "But a Pharisee, named Gamaliel, doctor of the law, esteemed by all the people, rose in the Sanhedrin, and ordered the apostles to leave for a moment. Then he said to them, Men of Israel, beware of what you will do with these people. For it was not long ago that Theudas appeared, who gave himself for something, and to whom about four hundred men rallied: he was killed, and all who had followed him were routed and reduced to nothing. Judas the Galilean appeared after him at the time of the census, and he attracted people to his party. He also perished, and all who had followed him were scattered. And now, I tell you, take care of these men no more, and let them go. If this enterprise or this work comes from men, it will be destroyed; but if it comes from God, you cannot destroy it. Do not run the risk of having fought against God. They sided with him. "This man placed the answer to the Sanhedrin's questions in the hands of God himself. In either case, this attitude protects against error, prejudice, and ultimately sin. This is valuable advice that we do not want to forget for the future in this book, and especially for this part on "Reconciliation".

1.2 What We Owe Israel: The Plan of Biblical Revelation

The genius of God's revelation for man lies in the construction of the Bible itself; from a man, Abraham, it extends gradually by the transmission of the message to his family, then from it to the nation of Israel, and finally to all humanity through Jesus Christ the Messiah. The link between the generations found in the lines of the Bible is fundamental; it demonstrates that the message of God for man is not only, individual revelation, it is also testimony and transmission from age to age into eternity, a declaration of love, forgiveness, and reconciliation between man and his creator. In the paragraphs that follow, we evoke this family bond, then tribal, then national, and finally universal that unites from the origin the families of the earth to the faith of Abraham.

1.3 A man, Abraham

He listens to the Eternal God and submits to his will; better still, he knows how to transmit to the generation that follows him this disposition both that of the heart and that of the spirit, which became the foundation of Judaism and subsequently of Christianity. He is not free of weaknesses and occasionally lacks faith. He leaves the security of his country, without knowing where he is going, simply guided by the voice of the Eternal God, "Leave your country, your homeland and your family and go to the country that I will show you" (Gen 12:1). This absolute trust in the Word of his God is an example for all the generations who have followed him until today. Thus, he inherited the title of; "Father of the believers". However, he doubts God's protection when he arrives in Egypt, and he lies to Pharaoh about his wife (Gen 12:11-20) for fear of being put to death because of her beauty. In this he is close to each one of us who often alternate methodical doubt and the purest faith with God. Abraham leaves us the testimony of a powerful relationship with God. Above all religious formalism, he is the one who listens to him and questions him, as each of us can do, and he gets answers, which are not always in accordance with his desires. He is, therefore for us, the founder of a metaphysics unique in its kind, as much made of certainties about the existence of God as of questions about his interventions in the human experience.

1.4 One who walks with God and goes where he tells him to go.

Abram of his first name is the man on the move, since his departure from Babylonia he has been searching for the concrete answer to this word which has served as his guide (Gen 12:1). He arrives in Canaan, where he stops only at Shechem (v 6) there, he builds an altar in honor of the Lord (v 7). He continued by step towards the Negev desert (v 9). Then he was forced to leave for Egypt because of the famine in the land of Canaan. It is during this trip that he invents this subterfuge, making his wife Saraï, who is very beautiful, for his sister in order to have his life saved. But misfortune struck Pharaoh, who had believed this lie and had had Sarai kidnapped, whose beauty had been praised to him. He dismissed her immediately, not without reproaching Abram for his deception (v 18-20). Abraham repeats this ploy to King Abimelech to avoid being put to death or mistreated because of the beauty of his wife. Yet God threatens the king who also renounces touching her out of fear of death and the great calamities of which the Lord has threatened all his subjects. This episode teaches us that God always puts a limit to the wanderings of our heart when he is overwhelmed by fear or the strongest emotions. Without having sought God's counsel in prayer, the one who has become Abraham in the meantime nevertheless twice receives confirmation that he and his wife are under God's protection. Returning to Canaan, he settled where he had erected an altar to the Lord and first established himself between Bethel and Ai (Gen 13:3). This place will later become the city of Beer-sheva, meaning "Well of the Oath," when Abraham makes a covenant with Abimelech (Gen 21:22-34). The promise of a country is still far away for Abram, who must separate himself from his nephew Lot because there is not enough living space for both families and their immense possessions in servants in herds and goods of all kinds. Abram poses as a man of peace (Gen 12:8), when he avoids the conflicts that might have arisen on the occasion of this difficult sharing. He leaves it to his nephew to decide which region he prefers to settle in. At first glance, Lot chose the best share; the plain of the green and fertile Jordan, like a garden of the

Lord, says the text (v 10). According to their agreement, Abram goes to the west in an area both more deserted and more rugged. He settled in a wooded place, "among the oaks of Mamré, which are near Hebron" (v 18). More difficult to cultivate, more difficult to irrigate, this region nevertheless allows him to prosper, all his servants and his herds. Lot soon finds himself a prisoner of his seemingly best choice because it is also that of the cities of Sodom and Gomorrah, which the Lord will destroy because there, evil and debauchery reign. He who in the meantime has become Abraham stands in his way to save these cities from a cataclysm, with this fundamental idea that the influence of the just extends even to the benefit of the unjust. His justice is communicative; it is transmitted in the manner of the concentric waves around his person and thus allows him to bless, to a certain degree, his entourage. Will the recurrence calculation proposed to the Eternal God by Abraham in favor of the two sinful cities work? Starting from the modest number of 50, he asks if these cities will be destroyed if there were 50 righteous. The bar being still too high, he first lowers his request from five to five to forty righteous and each time the Lord shows his nature by showing mercy to all the inhabitants (v 29). Not even finding forty righteous, Abraham again lowers the thresholds of his request, this time from ten to ten, until he asks only ten righteous for these two cities. Unfortunately, they are not even found, and as a result, they have been destroyed. This pathetic intervention by Abraham shows, before the sermon on the Mount of Jesus Christ in chapter 5 of the Gospel of Matthew, a fundamental value of the Kingdom of Heaven, namely; mercy, both that of the Eternal God and that of Abraham; "Blessed are the merciful, for they will have mercy" (Ma 5:7). We owe to Abraham this introduction to mercy, that is to say; if there is one righteous among the unrighteous then the judgment of God stops and allows the wicked to repent and convert. How many were saved by this countdown, because of the righteousness of one! This shows how useful it is to bear witness to the blessings of God, even if there are no apparent signs of hope that one is listened to or even heard. In the secret place of prayer, God works, answers, sanctifies, forgives, purifies, and heals every person, city, region, and nation. In chapter 17 Abram changed his name to Abraham (v 5-6); "... for I make you the father of many nations. I will make you fertile to infinite, I will make you nations; and kings will come out of you". What we owe to Abraham is the demonstration of the faith that carries the mountains and especially that of the biological clock, when he becomes a father at an advanced age (Gen 21:1-5). The very unlikely birth of Isaac, his son, announces other miraculous events that often exceed human understanding. One thinks of the sacrifice of Isaac, the son of the promise, this act of absolute obedience by Abraham to his God, which he had no doubt had provided a divine provision with this ram held by the horns in a bush (Gen 22:1-14). The examples left by Abraham have helped generations of believers to enter this dimension of faith in a God of miracles and revelations. Improbable acts, miracles, the restoration of some who had fallen, healings, and many other benefits were received and accepted by those who, like Abraham, had the faith to believe that; "… what is impossible to men is possible to God" (Lu 18:27).

1.5 A Family, Isaac, Jacob, and the Patriarchs (Map of the Tribes of Israel – Appendix P 313)

According to the will of God, this man Abraham creates a family from Isaac, their son. The children that he will have are the first milestones of immense posterity still present and clearly visible today. What is remarkable, despite appearances to the contrary, is the strength of the covenant that God maintains in this family, and whose circumcision is the emblematic sign. Without being fully aware of it, Isaac's sons fulfill God's plans and forge exemplary filial and spiritual bonds with their unloved grandson Joseph. Thus, the Lord shows how the children of faith and of common hope are created among the members of the same family. This example will become universal in nations where the faith of parents will be transmitted by cultural as well as religious heritage to the children of the same family. Throughout the centuries, God will bless this model of family development, until it is challenged by the Bible itself, because of the abuses of power and injustices it will give rise to. The individual conversion preached by Jesus Christ (Ma 16:16) and the apostles will balance this type of family relationship so that it is not too abusive, as unfortunately it was often the case. Indeed, it allows the choice of one's own destiny with God and personal emancipation from any link that would upset him. The fierce struggle between Jacob and the angel of the Lord at the ford of Jabbok (Gen 32:24-32) readily compares itself with that which some men know in order to emancipate themselves from all ties and access the truth of God. Like him, they sometimes come out: wounded, transformed, edified, but also bearers of a powerful message of authenticity about the living and true God, invisible and yet so present among men. It is also close to this teaching of the sermon on the mount, in which Jesus emphasizes that the truth that sets free must be sought with insistence and perseverance; "Ask, and you will be given; search, and you will find; Knock, and you will be opened. For whoever asks receives, the seeker finds, and the one who strikes is opened" (Ma 7:7-8). What can be observed, however, is the strength of the generational bond that has allowed the transmission of the faith of Abraham to the posterity of Isaac, Jacob, the patriarchs, and so on from the exit of Egypt to the present day. Thus, faith in a creator God, good, just, and merciful, of a man, was passed on to his family. This example demonstrates that God wants to be at the very heart of the family. That he blesses the natural and spiritual bonds that are woven in his womb; that he gives a broad and general blessing to man and woman in marriage as described in the first chapter of Genesis (Gen 1:26-29), and that it is accompanied by a spiritual dimension that is also strong if not stronger than the natural one. For the hearers and readers of the Word of God to cling to it, it was necessary to this family, these sometimes incredible experiences like those of Jacob, the deceived, then those of his child, Joseph, who from the preferred son, is soon sold by his brothers, he then passes through the prison cell and nevertheless reaches the peak of power with Pharaoh. The theologian Didier Van Heck[228] speaks of a "prodigious literary success" because not only are we captivated by these texts, which possess all the elements of an epic story, but we also see in them an inexhaustible source of inspiration. Finally, we believe in these stories because they are embodied, fleshly, and passionate; their characters resemble us, rational, emotional, calculating, and sentimental. Thus, the fate of the patriarchs recounted in these chapters of Genesis becomes more important than the simple historical sequence of a chronicle. On the contrary, it is an exceptional destiny that founds a spiritual dynasty represented by these patriarchs, who take up for themselves the faith in a single God, creator of the entire universe, and towards whom each must pledge allegiance by the sign of circumcision. It is therefore much more than the story of a family; it is also ours

---

[228] fr. Didier van HECKE, GB GSA: The Pentateuch, 2014/2015

because at each of its lines, any reader can get involved both as judge and actor. He can identify himself at leisure with these epic characters, Jacob and Esau, with their story thwarted both. He may wonder about this God whose designs are obscure in appearance and favoritism for some, seems to be a mode of governance for others, such as Jacob and later Moses saved from the waters, and David, the smallest of the sons of Isaiah the shepherd. The essential function of this family is to form the matrix of several tribes that will live and grow in Egypt (Ex 1:1-7) for a very long period until Moses. During this time, the transmission of the spiritual heritage in question will be carried out through an oral tradition, and each character of this fabulous story will become, by the voice of the elders, a legendary and tutelary figure for successive generations of the children of Israel while in Egypt. The portrait that can be made of this family is quite in contrast since the twelve sons come from the same father Jacob, but from four different mothers; there are his two legitimate wives, Leah and Rachel, whose turbulent relations with him are described in the book of Genesis from chapter 29, then the two concubines, Bilha and Zilpa, one servant of Rachel and the other of Leah. His twelve sons are each: founder of a tribe that bears their name respectively. The first is called Ruben[229], after the name given to the son of Leah, although the eldest of his brothers, he is removed from his birthright passed to Joseph the firstborn of Rachel, for having committed an irreparable contempt against his father (1Chr 5:1). An important tribe during the conquest of the land of Canaan, it is only a small group in the time of the Judges. It occupies with Gad and Manasseh, a semi-arid part of the southern region east of the Jordan. Its implantation is difficult because, in addition to the unforgiving terrain, there are numerous conflicts against the Moabites, the descendants of Esau, still hostile to Israel. Jacob's last words to his sons, seen in verse 28 as a blessing, are in fact full of reproaches for Reuben (Gen 49:3-4). Moses' words to him are more positive; "Let Ruben live, let him not die, yet his men are reduced to a small number!" (Deut 33:6). However, they already reflect the little consideration given to this tribe that will have a hard time surviving. Later, between 845 and 800 BC, it will be absorbed by that of Gad during the reign of King Hazael[230] of Syria. In his

---

[229] King James Bible Dictionary - Reference List - Reuben
[230] King James Bible Dictionary - Reference List - Hazael

address to his sons, Simeon[231] and Levi[232] receive rather a curse from their father than a blessing; "Their swords are instruments of violence. Let not my soul enter into their conciliation, nor my spirit unite with their assembly! For in their anger, they have killed men, and in their wickedness, they have cut off the hocks of the bulls. Curse their anger, for it is violent, and their fury, for it is cruel! I will separate them in Jacob and scatter them in Israel" (Gen 49:5-7). In fact, Simeon will have to settle in the south of the country, in its driest part where only livestock is practicable. He must constantly fight against the Philistines on his left, the Edomites on his right, and the Canaanites in the south. For his survival, he relied on Judah, who settled further north and had significant human and agricultural resources. This tribe is no longer mentioned in the battles of the period of the Judges against the invaders, and the song of Deborah (Gen 5:1-31) does not mention it. The book of Chronicles (1Chr 4:41-43) evokes a major feat accomplished by the people of Simeon against King Amalek, but the tribe does not seem to have survived long after the conquest of the land of Canaan. The one of Levi is not mentioned because it has not received territory in Israel, having inherited religious and legal functions, it has a transversal destiny throughout the country (P 18, 1st part), it benefits from the assistance and protection of all Israel, it perceives the size of the communities and has many cities in the country. Judah[233], the fourth son of Jacob and Leah, had a destiny and power far superior to that of his other brothers. However, his morality is not exemplary; he sells his brother Joseph for thirty shekels of money and embezzles some of that money (), then he is involved in a morality affair with his daughter-in-law Thamar () (Gen 38:1-23). Prestigious names like Caleb, King David and his descendants up to Jesus Christ come from this tribe. Settled in the heart of the country after absorbing that of Benjamin, it will keep Jerusalem the capital of Israel and its spiritual center. It also has important cities such as Hebron and Beth-Shemesh, still present and active today. Claimed by Caleb, chief of the tribe of Judah during the conquest of Canaan, this territory will remain in history as the crucible of the entire Jewish nation. It will become a kingdom under this name until it is destroyed by the empire of Babylon in 587 BC. Later, after the War of Independence led by the

---

[231] King James Bible Dictionary - Reference List - Simeon
[232] King James Bible Dictionary - Reference List - Levi
[233] The Story of Judah in the Bible - 1565-1446 BCE - Chabad.org

Maccabean brothers (174 to 150 BC), this region was extended to Galilee to the north and took the name of Judea, derived from its patronymic root, Judah. This name has remained to this day. It is in Judea that Jesus will come and preach his message of salvation, peace, justice, and love. It is again this name that will give birth to the word, "Jewish", which has taken a considerable extension since it designates both; the descendants of the twelve tribes of Israel, practitioners of the Jewish religion and multiple groups, such as the Ashkenazi and Sephardic, who claim religious, ethnic and cultural closeness to the Jewish people. Rachel, no longer bearing her sterility, obtains from Jacob a first son through her servant Bilha. He is for him the fifth son, his name is Dan[234], which means; "God has done justice", overcoming her sterility through a servant is a known stratagem in the family, it is quite similar to the one used by his grandmother Sarah, in the fourth generation before her. Sarah was also impatient to have a child but barren, she gave her servant Hagar to her husband Abraham. The continuation, as the text of Genesis 16:1-14 tells us, is not particularly happy and even leads Abraham to expel this woman with her child Ishmael. Similarly, the relations between the two sisters, Leah and Rachel, were greatly degraded until later, when she healed of her sterility and gave birth to her two sons, Joseph and Benjamin. The area of Dan was bounded to the east by that of Benjamin and it was bordered by the sea to the west, to the north was Ephraim and to the south Judah. It is a small territory, barely larger than that of Benjamin[235]. Its existence was difficult because of the many incursions from the country of the Philistines to the south. It is famous for its great soldier, Samson (Ju 13-16), who won many victories over their enemies. Despite this, the precariousness of its position pushed part of the tribe to migrate completely to the north of the country, to the hills of Mount Hermon, where it gave the city of Laïs the name of Dan, after their victory against this city. (Ju 18:1-13,27-29). This enterprise saved the tribe for a time, which in the south was assimilated by both, Judah and the philistines. However, it also disappeared after the exile, carried away by the conquerors who came later, from all sides in the centuries that followed the conquest of Canaan. Rachel once again renews her ruse with her husband Jacob and through Bilha, she gets for her and him a

---

[234] King James Bible Dictionary - Reference List - Dan
[235] See Appendix Map P 307

sixth son whom she calls Nephtali[236] (Gen 35.25 46.24). Located between Aser to the west, Manasseh to the east, Zabulon and Issacar to the south, it is a rich and fertile country bordering Lake Kinneret later called the Sea of Galilee and the Jordan Valley in its upper northern part of the lake. It is also a land of trade to the sea as well as to Damascus and the East. In his song of blessings, Moses said of him; «Nephthali, satisfied with the blessings of the Lord, takes possession of the west and the south" (Dt 33:23). Deborah also pays tribute to his courage in the battles of the conquest of Canaan saying; "Zabulon is a people that faces death, as well as Naphthalic" (Ju 5:18) and the famous Psalm 68 also called, Psalm of Battles, in verse 28 recalls the heroic memory of it; "There are Benjamin, the youngest, who dominates over them, the leaders of Judah and their troops, the leaders of Zabulon, the leaders of Naphthalic". Isaiah's prophecy speaks of a glorious future for this country (Isaiah 9:1-2) after the ravages of war and deportation; "If the past times have covered with reproach the land of Zabulon and the land of Naphthalic, the future times will cover with glory the neighboring land of the sea, beyond the Jordan, the territory of the Gentiles the people who walked in darkness see a great light; on those who lived in the land of the shadow of death a light shines". The Evangelist Matthew used this passage to describe the blessing received in the land when Jesus came to dwell in Capernaum (Ma 4:13-16). To increase her offspring, Leah imitates her sister and places Zilpa her servant in the bed of Jacob so that she is indirectly the mother of a seventh son whom she names Gad[237], which means in Hebrew: "Happiness has come" (Gen 30:13). The tribe that bears this name is known for its impetuous warriors (Gen 49:19) and the blessing pronounced by Moses on Gad testifies to this; "On Gad he says, Blessed is he who sets Gad off! Gad rests like a lioness, tearing his arm and head" (Deu 33:20). The Gadites supported David's cause in his struggles against Saul, and the book of Chronicles recalls their qualities as mountain warriors (1Chr 12:8). However, their territory east of the Jordan is not conducive to agriculture, it was also difficult to defend on its eastern part. The ammonites were constant opponents of Gad, and they suffered under their yoke until the great deliverance brought to them by the liberator Jephthah (Ju 11:32) around

---

236 King James Bible Dictionary - Reference List - Nephtali
237 King James Bible Dictionary - Reference List - Gad

1100 BC. In the eighth century, the land of Gad disappeared under the blows of invasions from Assyria between 745 and 727 BC, and it is no longer mentioned in the postexilic narratives. Leah, desiring to prolong her descendants, again uses the same stratagem to obtain from Jacob an eighth son by her servant Zilpa. She calls him Asser[238], which means, "happy," Moses' blessing for Asser is also full of optimism for him (De 33:24). It is said of this tribe, that it contributed to the struggle against the Midianites, but that its abstention during the war against King Jabin of Hathor who long oppressed Israel, is severely judged in the hymn of Deborah (Ju 5:17). Asser is located along the coast from the city of Dor in the south, to beyond Sidon, that of the Canaanites in the north. Its situation by the sea gives it prosperity, and it accommodates very well the Canaanite inhabitants who remain numerous on its territory, which corresponds approximately to the Lebanon of today. This social mix will not be without consequences because it will, unfortunately lead to any kind of compromise with pagan cults. The ruins of the monumental Phocaea city of Baalbek[239], located north of the Bekaa plain in Lebanon, still bear witness to the splendor of the Canaanite period. Erected in the 3rd millennium BC, at the time of the Phoenician colonization, it was a place of celebration and sacrifice to the God Baal and to Astarte, his companion, from where it takes its name. Today, one visits these strange places with the feeling of their immorality in relation to the rules of Judaism. In the blessing that Jacob gives to his ninth son Issachar[240], born by Leah, he is described as a simple, hardworking, robust character who is content with what he has received from God. He does not have to complain because his country, located between Mount Tabor in the west and the Jordan in the south-east, is fertile and has many sources of water. The tenth son of Jacob and Leah is called Zabulon[241], and Deborah's hymn gives strong praise (Gen 5:18) to this tribe for the courage it showed in the conquest of Canaan. It is a small tribe whose territory lies in a fertile valley west of Lake Tiberias, including the cities of Nazareth, Sarid to the south, Gath-Epher to the east and further north, the Levitical city of Rimmon. Its boundaries are imprecise (see map P 313), Joshua (Josh 19:10) does not give him access to the sea, while

---

[238] King James Bible Dictionary - Reference List - Asser
[239] Baalbek - World History Encyclopedia
[240] King James Bible Dictionary - Reference List - Issachar
[241] King James Bible Dictionary - Reference List - Zabulon

Jacob in his words of blessings says; "Zabulon shall dwell on the coast of ships, and his limit shall extend to the side of Sidon" (Gen 49:13). Moses also gives it access to the sea in his last words (De 33:18); "Be happy, Zabulon, in your travels... They will exploit the riches of the seas and the treasures hidden in the sand". Small in size and territory, Zabulon will stand out for his unwavering support alongside David in his wars to conquer the power in Israel (1Ch 12:33,40). Rachel's first son, Joseph, is the eleventh of Jacob. He is best known for his exceptional destiny, although he himself does not constitute a tribe like his other brothers. His legacy, however, is extremely important; it is more spiritual and ideological than tribal, because it is under the name of his son Manasseh[242] and not under his own that he will establish a tribe. In the first stage of his life, he is the privileged heir, the one whom Father Jacob loves more than his other sons (Gen 37). Sold by his brothers, he goes through suffering and humiliation. However, it is in this stage of his life that he learns the most to believe in this God who saves those who trust in him. In a third stage, he is raised in dignity with Pharaoh and becomes himself a savior for his family. His journey with a few differences is reminiscent of that of the prodigal son of the Gospel of Luke in chapter 15, when he leaves for a distant country and finds himself in great distress. It is there, in fact, that he addresses God and finds the way of life because his father, who represents God in the parable, was waiting for him and saved him. Thus, Joseph is an emblematic figure of the faith and salvation that God grants to those who seek him with sincerity, even when they are going through great difficulties. Symbol of resilience and perseverance in the trial, he shows the descendants of Israel the path to follow, even when it is long and dangerous. Rachel's second son and her father's twelfth, Jacob, is called Benjamin[243]. By his birth, he caused the death of his mother, so she gave him this name before leaving: Ben-Oni, which means "Son of my pain" (Gen 35:18.18). His father changed it, and he became "Benjamin", which means "Son of my right". This much more honorific name reflected the importance he attached to the offspring he had had with Rachel, the one he loved most. When Joseph disappeared, Jacob reported all his affection to Benjamin, and he would not let him go to Egypt, at the request of this

---

[242] King James Bible Dictionary - Reference List - Manasseh
[243] King James Bible Dictionary - Reference List - Benjamin

mysterious great ruler of the country, who was none other than Joseph, his firstborn son of Rachel (Gen 42 & 43). Benjamin will form a small tribe throughout Israel, as Saul says (1Sa 9:21), surrounded by Judah to the south, Ephraim to the north, Gad to the east, and Dan to the west. On this small territory, however, there are cities of great renown, starting with Jerusalem, the capital before it passed into Judah, but also Jericho, MIT spa, Ramah, Bethel, and Anathoth. It disappeared almost completely during the Civil War in the days of the Judges (Jg 19:21) before being restored and giving the country great names such as Ehud (Jg 3:12), who was the Judge in Israel, and Saul, its first king. Small in size, however, this tribe contributed greatly to the greatness of the kingdom by the glorious names of its sons and by its ardor in battle (1Ch 8:40). Later will come Jeremiah, the prophet as well as, in the role of Savior of the nation at the time of exile, Esther and Mordecai. With the remains of Levi and Judah, Benjamin will form the nucleus of the revival of postexilic Israel. Saul of Tarsus, a great Benjaminite, will even be at the center of the New Testament. Manasseh is not the son of Jacob but his grandson by Joseph, the beloved, this ninth descendant of Jacob, gives his name to a tribe and receives a vast and fertile territory. It is located north of Benjamin and Dan (see map P 313) and has important cities such as Samaria, which will become the capital of Israel after the division of the kingdom in 931 BC. There is also the city of Dothan (Ju 3.9 & 4.8), a transit city ideally placed on the road to Damascus, between the Mediterranean and further north the plain of Jezreel. Manasseh has another even larger territory (see map P 313) on the eastern bank of the Jordan, including the heights of the current Golan Heights, formerly called Gueshur. He also received Basan, the plain that descends gently to Damascus and east Hauran, region crossed by a tributary of the Jordan, the Yarmouk (cf: map P 313). Like many tribes of Israel, Manasseh would not manage to drive out the important Canaanite minorities which would often make war on him. Add to this that the difficult administration of a large territory separated into two almost autonomous entities will not facilitate the political stability of the region. The prophet Isaiah condemns the fratricidal struggles between Manasseh and Ephraim (Isaiah 9:20). Later, there was a king of Judah by the name of Manasseh, he was the son of King Hezekiah and ascended the throne in the year 698 BC from where he reigned 55 years. His long and tumultuous reign was marked by a return to idols, astrology and foreign cults that had been driven out while his father's time... What this family picture brings to us is as contrasted as the tunic of Joseph (), which provoked the jealousy of his brothers. One can see the diversity of the people of God, its struggles, its victories, its defeats, the major transgressions that prevented the conquest of the country from being complete, but also the great blessings received from the Eternal God who led them from the exit of Egypt to the reign of King David and beyond, until our days. We can also see the strength of the Word of God because it is the Word of the Lord and the Word alone, which would maintain the national unity of Israel despite its great diversity in space and time. It is enough to consider the map of the geography of the time of the conquest of Canaan (P 313), to note that all the kingdoms, empires, and nations of that time disappeared, except Israel. The generational link that allowed this miracle is a spiritual, scriptural, moral and theological link. The tumult of internal troubles, wars from elsewhere and other calamities did not prevent the tireless and patient work of the prophets of the Lord, the elders of the people, the Levite scribes of all generations and a multitude of faithful in all ages, to bear witness to the truth of God the Creator and Savior of Israel and of all humanity.

1.6 The successful transition from family to nation

The map of the land of Israel (P 313) at the time of the conquest of the land of Canaan that we have in all our Bibles is very approximate. It corresponds to the indications of the book of Joshua, from chapters 13 to 21. The general impression it gives is the imbalance of wealth between the south, arid and desert, and the north, fertile and rich, it is also the inequality in the allocation of territories, some very small, others much larger and diversified, Finally, it is the vulnerability to enemies inside and outside this country. We ask ourselves questions like this: why had Israel not already made its political unity before the conquest? Were not the forty years spent in the Sinai desert sufficient to make it? Why this inequitable sharing of resources and opportunities? Was it not likely to create dissension and political instability within the tribes? And again, why does the Lord give to his people a space inhabited by enemies and which is only a region of passage between Egypt in the south and Syria in the north? Other questions come to mind, which the Bible often answers only with the words of faith and hope; yes, it is the land of promise, the land that God gave to the children of Israel through the descendants of Abraham, a land of justice and peace where milk and honey flow (No 13:27). There is not always an answer to our questions about the plan of sharing the country of Canaan. However, reality, as we know, will sometimes clash violently with this hope of personal and collective fulfillment for the Hebrews, in this land of blessings where God has placed them. Indeed, there is at the beginning neither milk nor honey and the history of each tribe shows very diverse fortunes. Some will prosper while others will collapse until being absorbed by their powerful neighbor. From more or less respected alliances to not always successful integration and assimilation of foreign cultures, the country remains politically rather unstable. It is threatened, both inside and outside, by numerous enemies. The tendency is, nevertheless, to the gradual integration of the various tribes into a single entity called by the Old Testament: Israel. Despite the tireless work of the tribe of Levi throughout the country, it struggles to find its political stability and maintain its territorial integrity. The Word of God could have served as a guide and legislator for the twelve tribes, unfortunately this was not the case and Samuel the prophet, servant of the Most High God, is the last of the Judges in Israel (1Sa 7:15). The Book of Judges does not particularly focus on the chronology of events that will take the country from tribal rule to empirical unity, then to royalty when the prophet Samuel anoints Saul king over Israel. But isn't the important thing elsewhere? Is it not in the scripting of these events with his key characters from the great Judges: Othniel, Ehud, Shamgar, Débora, Gédéon, to Samson and finally Samuel? From these four and a half centuries[244], we retain the links, both fleshly and spiritual, which nevertheless unite the descendants of the twelve sons of Jacob. Indeed, the texts of the Bible teach us more about life, morality, theology, and philosophy than about history. They tell us that in the face of the inability of the sons of Samuel, Abiah, and Joel to assume their office as Judge in Israel with dignity, the elders of the people demanded a king (1Sa 8:4-22) in imitation of the use of the surrounding nations. Despite the warnings of the old sages, the people refused to listen to them and the Eternal God himself made this premonitory declaration

---

[244] Estimate: According to 1Ro 6:1, the period of exit from Egypt was estimated at four hundred and eighty years

of great difficulties ahead; "_The Lord said to Samuel, Listen to the voice of the people in everything they say to you; For it is not you that they reject, but I that they reject, that I may no longer reign over them. They act upon you as they have always acted since I brought them up from Egypt to this day; they have forsaken me to serve other gods" (1Sa 8:7-8). Those words are far from a blessing on royalty and even further from on the "Divine Right", which will become much later, the justification of royal dynasties in medieval European Christian nations. Starting from these family and spiritual roots, having served much as a political message, the tribes gradually merged into a single entity during the period of the Judges. From the prophet Samuel, the distinction between the tribes fades clearly without ever completely erasing itself, and the work of the kings who succeed them consists in federating them into a nation so that they better serve the Lord. Their mission, therefore, is to bear witness to him before other nations; "to the ends of the earth" (Ps 48:10). Chapter 12 of Samuel's 1st work is in fact a trial against the people and their unjustified desire to have a king. The prophet anointed Saul king over Israel, but it was more at the people's request than to do God's will. This passage shows again clearly the separation of the powers that the Eternal God wanted to establish in his people, to the Levites the priestly and juridical functions, and to the kings the political and military offices. However, originally it was the Levites who anointed the kings and gave them a form of spiritual accreditation so that they would not forget that power was ultimately granted to them by the Eternal God himself. The principle was excellent, but its application in the history of the kings of Israel will often be perverted by violence and intrigue and of the 42 kings of the kingdoms of Israel and Judah, only 9 kings will make: "... what is right before the Lord". However, this chaotic national life is also spiritual, and from this point of view, it is much more stable, and it will succeed where great empires have failed. This nation will survive the greatest attempts at destruction that human history has ever conceived against it. From tribe to nation, it is good to be interested in what the link was and the strength of it. Originally, the word "nation" is borrowed from the Latin "Nascio, -onis", itself derived from "Nasci" which means "To be born". In French the word knows several spellings, including that which is attested in the[245] twelfth century,

---

[245] Dictionnaire historique de la langue française – Mot Nation P 2345

namely, "nascion" and finally, "nation" at the end of the fifteenth century. Its meaning has evolved to characterize, "Those born together in the same place". To this idea is added later that of the community of origin, lineage, language, culture, and religion. So, when we consider the "nation of Israel", we are in the presence of those who were born together in Egypt and who will remain there for more than 400 years. They already have the embryo of a culture and a religion with the covenant of circumcision contracted with the Lord, the God of Israel, and thus they can claim the seed of Abraham. During this long period, the tribes of Israel developed by natural increase and probably also by the assimilation of other ethnic groups, passing from the 12 sons of Jacob, its original founders, to several hundred thousand families as they left Egypt under the guidance of Moses. With the divine Law given to Israel at the foot of Mount Sinai (Ex 20), these people who had only a tribal existence like many others, became a nation with a very precise legal and institutional framework of great modernity. The Law of God serves as both a moral law for the individual and a civil constitution for the nation. Its application to individual and collective life is accompanied by many promises of blessings and success. On the other hand, its transgression entails ipso facto curse and misfortune. Thus, even before possessing a territory, Israel already possesses all the characteristics of a nation, a people, and a state. Moreover, by its Law, it differs radically from the surrounding countries, which could not resist it during the conquest of the country of Canaan. However, despite its perfection and intangibility, the application of the divine law is a permanent challenge for the people of God. The fundamental problem is: how could imperfect men enforce a perfect law? This is the difficulty that the people of Israel will find themselves in for generations. The period of the kings and prophets of the Old Testament provides an abundant jurisprudence very useful until today to deal with difficult situations born of this major contradiction. For its part the Talmudic wisdom will, over the centuries, make a sum of case studies later called in Christianity, the casuistic in order to elucidate by its reflections and speculations, how to apply the Law of God to all the concrete circumstances and situations of life. These rules, these traditions and their developments added to the Law of God, will make it unclear to the people and very far from their daily life. They will be denounced by Jesus in the Gospel of Matthew, when he declares to the Pharisees: "Thus you cancel the word of God for the benefit of your tradition"

(Ma 15:6). Despite the difficulty of living according to the perfections of the Law of God, the Bible offers a unique and permanent model for the formation of a nation as for life at the individual level in a society. Every man can indeed recognize himself in this model, It is the perfect divine plan which is also chronological and genetic, it is declined thus: a man Abraham, a family the twelve tribes of Israel, a nation Israel and subsequently, the whole universe through Jesus Christ who is the "word incarnate, preached to the ends of the earth" (Acts 13:47). In this sense, Judaism is a founding religion of the history of all humanity.

1.7 Jesus Christ the Messiah of Israel who brings God's message to the whole world.

For centuries, kings and prophets had announced the coming of a messiah in Israel. He was to reign by righteousness and in peace, perfectly fulfilling the Law of God over the whole land and thus saving it from its enemies. We note again that salvation is a consequence of obedience to God's Law. This is how the disciples of Jesus Christ and the crowd with them understood the coming of the Messiah, relying on several passages of the Old Testament, including this one, Isaiah 11:2-5: "The Spirit of the Lord shall rest upon him: Spirit of wisdom and intelligence, Spirit of counsel and strength, Spirit of knowledge and fear of the Lord. He will breathe the fear of the Lord; He will not judge on appearance, nor pronounce on hearsay. But he will judge the poor with equity, and he will pronounce righteously upon the poor of the earth; He will strike the earth with his word like a rod, and with the breath of his lips he will make the wicked die. Justice will be the belt of his flanks, and faithfulness the belt of his loins". This messianic hope had two aspects that were difficult to reconcile; one was to guarantee the political and military integrity of the country, while the other was to reign in justice, righteousness, and fear of the Lord. In appearance, Jesus Christ does not correspond to either of these two criteria and his task to convince the people that he is indeed the envoy of the Father whom they all expected is monumental. Indeed, for many, he has nothing of a king, neither political program nor party to impose himself and his law, from this point of view, he will even have this disappointing word; "We must give credit to Caesar for what is Caesar's and to God for what is God's" (Ma 22:21). With these words he prophesies even the dichotomy of the two kingdoms; one earthly and the other heavenly according to him, the first can wait, the second is the most important when he says; "Seek first the kingdom and righteousness of God; and all these things will be given to you above" (Ma 6:33). He thus puts the political sustainability of the country of Israel in the background, he even suggests with these words; "and all these things will be given to you", that one day they will come, as a consequence of having first sought the, "Kingdom of heaven and its justice". The priority given to the search for the Spirit rather than an earthly kingdom is confirmed by his dilatory response to his disciples on the question of the restoration of Israel's sovereignty; ".... He replied to them: It is not for you to know the times or moments that the Father has fixed with his own authority. But you will receive power, the Holy Spirit coming upon you, and you will be my witnesses in Jerusalem, in all of Judea, in Samaria, and to the ends of the earth" (Acts 1:7-8). In other words, without completely dismissing the answer to the question that he refers to be the sole sovereignty of the Father, he traces a new path for them, which can never be taken except with the help of the Holy Spirit. From now on, their destiny has nothing political, it is spiritual, and they must serve as witnesses of the things they have seen and heard. This is the monumental challenge facing the Israelites of that time, and it is understandable that "some of his disciples withdrew" (Jn 6:66). This monumental work will therefore be undertaken by the least qualified party leader that could have been found. Indeed, among the twelve quoted in the 3 synoptic[246] Gospels, most are fishermen or sons of fishermen; there is also the tax collector, Matthew, and there are the sons of Zebedee, himself a fisherman, James and John. The only one who has received significant theological training is not one of the twelve; he is Saul of Tarsus, who will become the apostle Paul after his encounter with Jesus Christ on the road to Damascus (Acts 9:3-12). Despite the lack of initial qualifications to accomplish this monumental task, this small group of twelve will succeed in spreading the message of Jesus Christ throughout the Mediterranean basin and even far beyond in the East, Persia, Armenia, and later, "... to the ends of the earth". Historians and theologians generally attribute this feat to two key factors: Firstly, the quality of the network of Roman roads traced by the occupier, which greatly facilitated long-distance communications. Second

---

[246] Twelve Apostles: John and the Synoptic Gospels | N.T. Wright Online

factor; the existence of a written reference in Greek, the Bible of the Seventy speaking of the messiah of Israel, this language was indeed, the most practiced in the entire eastern part of the Mediterranean. In addition to these undeniable assets, Christians put forward the main role of the Holy Spirit who came upon the Apostles in the upper chamber (Acts 2:1-42), "a... spirit of strength and wisdom" (1Ti 1:7). This wonderful spirit qualified them and made them capable of realizing what was impossible in human sight. We recall in the second part what was the perverted destiny of the "Christian State"; what must be emphasized in this one is the wonderful work of the Holy Spirit. Despite these adverse circumstances described, it has been able to touch and save millions of honest and pure believers across generations until today. The Holy Spirit, more powerful than doctrines and human philosophy, has penetrated the hearts of many faithful downs through the ages. Christianity has indeed reached all continents. Translated into more than 8,000 languages and dialects, the Bible and its promises to Abraham have become universal; "For the earth will be filled with the knowledge of the Lord, as the bottom of the sea by the waters that cover it. On that day, the Branch of Isai will stand as a banner for the peoples; nations will look to him, and his dwelling place will be glorious. (Isaiah 11:9-10)

1.8 The same conception of man lost without God.

The Bible already explains in chapter 3 of Genesis what is the condition of man in this world: he is lost because of death, he has fallen from his place in the kingdom of heaven, because of the sin that marks him forever throughout his life. Thus, the man who was to reign eternally with God must pass through death, and all that he undertakes is marked by time, ephemerality, failure, and imperfection; nothing lasts, neither his victories nor his failures nor his great achievements. His life oscillates between submission to the forces of nature and rebellion against God the Creator. Contrary to what the philosophy of the eighteenth century says, "of the age of enlightenment", man is not master of his destiny, just and rational, dominating the world and the forces of nature. According to the prophets and Jesus Christ himself, he must convert and go through the New Birth. These Old Testament passages bear witness to this (Ps 14:1-3); "To the chief of singers. Of David. The fool said in his heart: There is no God! They have become corrupt; they have committed abominable acts; There is none that does good. The Lord, from heaven, looks to the sons of man, to see if there is anyone who is intelligent, who seeks God. All are lost, all are perverted; There are none who do good, not even one... They do not know the way to peace; The fear of God is not before their eyes (v 17-18)". These verses are repeated in the New Testament by the apostle Paul in his epistle to the Romans (Rom 3:9-26) "Now we know that all that the law says, it says to those who are under the law, so that every mouth is closed, and everyone is found guilty before God". This fundamental guilt accompanies the whole history of the reign of man on earth. However, it is not recognized by humanity for what it is or for the consequences it entails, including in mass Christianity. We have seen how this one had tried to restore the greatness of a "spiritual Caesar" in Rome, rather than celebrating that of the Lord, King of Israel and of the nations. With the replacement of biblical baptism, we have seen how the process of individual conversion has been transformed into a gigantic factory of "little Christians", conditioned to the service of a religious organization. However, we must also see that a significant part of the very essence of the message of the Bible remained in the foundations of this mass Christianity because it was indelible and stronger than all the attacks that were made against it. It is first and foremost the one God and creator. The whole universe is his work, and the earth is his "footstool" (Ma 5:35). It is also the condition of man before God; he is marked by original sin, as was recalled in the first lines of this paragraph. Even if pedo-baptism removes much of its meaning from the act of conversion, it nevertheless remains in its etymology as in its biblical definition (1Pi 3.21), the witness of the need for a transformed life, passing from the natural state of sinner to that of redeemed before God. Even if the official churches wanted to standardize man and his condition in society, the individual remained at the center of Christian doctrine. We have also seen that Jesus Christ does not build a nation, but rather a people of cross-border believers. Therefore, is the whole reflection of philosophy largely derived from this imposing reality? What is a man? What is the individual? What are its rights and duties? What is his relationship to the real world? If these themes were present in Greco-Latin philosophy, they rarely went beyond the walls of religious universities until the Renaissance of the 16th Century. With it, and the invention of printing, literature, philosophy, and their authors came out of churches and reached a wider audience. Science, art, and astrology often compensate for what religion was not able to explain. We have seen the influence of Baruch Spinoza in the emancipation of culture from the religious world. We must also mention Desiderius Erasmus[247], who is considered by most philosophers and historians as the precursor of modern humanism. He is the founder of an evangelical humanism because of his more literal reading of the Bible, despite his membership in the order of the regular canons of Saint Augustine. He is famous for his positions very close to those of Luther concerning the theological wanderings of the papacy and the Roman curia. His books and treatises were burned at the same time as those of Luther in Milan in 1543. His major work, "The praise of madness" is put at the index in 1559 after the Council of Trent. Although he did not commit himself to the Reformation, his thoughts and work were very close to it. In these, getting as close as possible to the texts of the Bible he develops an individualistic conception of salvation. On the other hand, he radiates everywhere in Europe, which he feels at the same time; the underlying unity despite the precariousness of the small kingdoms that compose it and the strength it inherited from Judeo-Christianity. He is a humanist who sees Christianity as an opportunity for European unity. In this sense, he is one of the very first convinced Europeans. The writer Stephan Zweig[248] in his remarkable work on Erasmus writes about this; "Instead of listening to the vain claims of the kinglets, the sectarians and the national egoisms, the mission of the European is on the contrary to always insist on what binds and what unites the peoples, to affirm the preponderance of the European over the national, of humanity on the homeland and to transform the conception of Christianity, considered as a purely religious community, into that of a universal Christendom in a love of humanity humble, helpful, devoted". We know that Erasmus was not listened to, and that it was rather; the kinglets, the cultists and the national egoisms that prevailed in Europe, in the obsessive quest for power and the will to power of its potentates, after the Renaissance and the Protestant Reformation. In any case, his work greatly enabled the emergence of the central question of man, his salvation, and his destiny. In France, Michel Eyquem de Montaigne is another

---

[247] Desiderius Erasmus: Biography, Beliefs, Works, Books, & Facts | Britannica

[248] Stefan Zweig, Erasmus: Grandeur et décadence d'une idée "Triumph und Tragique des Erasmus von Rotterdam", Paris, Grasset, 2003, 187 pp., 19 cm (ISBN 978-2-246-16853-9, lire en ligne [archive]), pp. 87-88.

humanist who knew a great influence from the 16th century until today. He too, placed the question of the individual at the center of his thought. He admits that religion is part of his genetic heritage; He was born with it, and he would die with it without any support or rejection. On this question, he says indeed, "We are Christians in the same way as we are or Perigordians (Region of central France) or Germans[249]", and also, "It is not through reflection or intelligence that we have received our religion; it is through authority and an outward order[250]". This thought sounds like an admission of indifference to his own religion; it is a determinism like any other, as if he had blue or brown eyes, he cannot change anything. It also shows the little consideration he has for what is not the fruit of his adhesion or his decision and allows, for himself and for several generations of European philosophers and scholars of great talent, the emancipation of the mind and the search for meaning outside religion. Shared by a large number of scholars, this thought became a general attitude of men of letters and sciences of this time; it prefigured the coming of "the age of enlightenment". This "age" is the opposite of the teachings of the New Testament, but it is nevertheless highlighted by all that Europe has, writers, philosophers, scientists, academics, and artists, who seek a way other than that of the church-institution to discover and understand the world and the human being in their complexity. Despite all their discoveries and the progress they bring, many return to the starting point and show, each with their words, the difficulty or even the impossibility of explaining creation without the "Creator", the persistence of evil in the life of man without the necessity of the "Savior".

1.9 Salvation by faith

Faith and its manifestations in human life are attested among the founders of the nation of Israel; "Abram trusted in the Lord, who put him to justice" (Gen 15:6). Thus, faith in the Word of God has become the distinctive mark for a man of a life lived in righteousness. From ancient times the servants of the Eternal God emphasize this formula: "...the righteous will live by faith..." (Ha 2:4). It shows

---

[249] Michel Eyquem de Montaigne: Essays, II, 12, p. 540.
[250] Michel Eyquem de Montaigne: Essays, II, 12, p. 608.

the need to live the commandments of the Law by faith, for they all implicitly recognize the impossibility for man to live it perfectly without ever transgressing it. The Apostle Paul recalls this human incapacity from the first chapter of his epistle to the Romans; "For I am not ashamed of the Gospel; it is a power of God for the salvation of all who believe, first of all the Jew, then the Greek, because in him is revealed the righteousness of God by faith and for faith, as it is written: The righteous will live by faith" (Rom 1:16-17). Similarly, the new birth promised by Jesus Christ is only possible by exercising faith, according to what is written in the Gospel of Mark: "He who believes and is baptized will be saved". This faith is therefore common to us with Israel, it is also manifested in the hope that is ours: on the one hand, the coming of the messiah for the Jewish world, and on the other hand, the return of the Lord Jesus in glory for the Christian world.

1.10 The foundations of Judeo-Christianity

The Synagogue and the Church is a story intertwined; we showed in the first part the filiation between the Synagogue and the Church, and in the second, the unfortunate divorce that occurred. However, from the beginning of Christianity until today, our destinies are linked; no effort of all anti-Semitism combined, including those of religions, could separate the Jewish and Christian world from each other. The work of the Protestant Reformation, from its origins to the present day, and despite its shortcomings, has largely contributed to the awareness of an authentic "Judeo-Christianity" which spread at the same time as the proclamation of the message of the Bible. Since then, wherever it has been proclaimed, even in difficult contexts of war and major conflict, institutions, courts, universities, the economy, social customs, education, and even the private lives of individuals have evolved toward a Judeo-Christian model. Examples abound in this direction, whether in England and Scotland from the 17th century, these two nations take their first steps towards unification and especially towards political democracy. Another example: France, with its revolution of 1789, freed itself at the same time from the yoke of royal power, that of the clergy, and that of the aristocracy, in favor of the "Universal Declaration of the Rights of Man and of the Citizen", largely inspired by the Bible. Although its political and social evolution was very chaotic during the 19th century, this famous Declaration supplanted forever the royal power of "divine right" and all the feudal jurisdictions that went hand in hand with this regime. It proclaims the emancipation of the nation and its inhabitants under the motto "Freedom, Equality, Fraternity", which is reminiscent of the promise of Jesus Christ: "He that the freed Son is truly free" (John 8:36), even if it is only civil liberty. Let us quote again the most important and emblematic example of this historical dynamic of Judeo-Christianity, namely, that of the United States of America, which was founded on the biblical bases brought by the Puritan refugees of Mayflower[251] in 1626. It was the new country of promise, the country of refuge for Protestants and Evangelical Christians persecuted in Europe and France in particular. The formation of this country, which has become the most powerful in the world in just two and a half centuries of existence, acquired from its beginning a biblical dimension that still characterizes it today. It is clearly found in its constitutional, legal, regulatory texts and in its most symbolic political acts as the oath of its successive Presidents on the Bible. The American Pastor, John Hagee, founder of a great evangelical movement called "Christian United for Israel[252]", considering the history of the USA since their creation, made this statement: "We have been blessed in an extraordinary way". This blessing has several aspects, which show the fundamental differences that exist between the formation of the USA and that of Europe. The first point to emphasize is the absence of official anti-Semitism at the top of the state and the states of the union. Formed based on the principles of the Bible, a country of refuge for persecuted minorities in Europe, the US has never taken over official anti-Judaism from authoritarian European regimes. Based on an enlightened and thorough reading of the Bible, they immediately decreed the separation of churches and the state. The clear distinction between spiritual power and the temporal, they avoided the submission of one to the other, as happened in Europe. The American Constitution, remarkable for its sobriety and precision, still in force today, states in its first words; "We the people...[253]". It is written for the people and by the people, its writers were pastors and jurists[254], inspired by the texts of the Bible. They had a clear vision of what this new nation should be,

---

251 Mayflower: Mayflower | History, Voyage, Landing, & Facts | Britannica
252 Christians united for Israel: The Fight Against Antisemitism | Christians United for Israel
253 In French: Nous le peuple
254 Who Wrote the Constitution? Will the True Author Please Stand Up?!

conceived more by the bonds of spirit than by those of flesh and blood. Contrary to the European evolution where Christianity has much declined between the sixteenth and twenty-first centuries, this provision has allowed, on the contrary, the Evangelical Churches professing, but also the other Christian confessions, to know a great development and to send missionaries of the, "Good News, to the ends of the earth". The major difference in historical and social paradigm is underlined by the French sociologist and historian, Alexis De Tocqueville in the 1830s, when he finally demonstrates in his major work; "Democracy in America" as in Europe, religion is synonymous with repression, while in the US it is synonymous with liberation"[255]. From the 1850s, the USA received Jewish emigrants fleeing persecution in Central Europe. Then after 1883, the year of the assassination of Tsar Alexander II, a considerable flow of Jews fleeing the pogroms of Tsarist Russia, came to settle in this country formed by the Bible, where they could prosper according to the talent of each one. All these Jewish communities arrived at the end of the nineteenth century, have greatly contributed to the economic and cultural development of the nation. Another major difference between the US and Europe is the value of the individual as a basic element of society and national wealth. This characteristic, derived from biblical thought, accompanies all the development of personality from youth in most Americans. It fosters the taking of responsibilities in the community, the desire to undertake and innovate, the major decisions of existence, such as individual conversion to Christianity, marriage, professional orientation, education given to children. It is strongly oriented in project mode, towards understanding the real world and personal fulfillment. While Europe remains partitioned into nations hostile to each other, and within them, into rigid social classes equally hostile to each other, the United States develops without an aristocracy other than that of merit and social utility. The unity and solidarity between the small and large States is a success unparalleled in the world. That is why during the 20th century they became the first economic power in the world, and their industry exceeds in wealth and innovations all the others combined. Even today, the USA, despite the criticism and all the evil that some media say, remains powerfully attractive to the

---

[255] Alexis de Tocqueville: Democracy in America Chapter V: How in the United States religion knows how to use democratic instincts.

people and continues to attract talent from all over the world. However, it should not be inferred that the nation is a cardinal model of political and social balance and harmony. Unfortunately, there are too many denials to list; wars, scandals, racism, and bankruptcies have marked the development of the country. This is what tends to prove that even with the best intentions, the best institutional and social framework inspired by the Bible, the reign of men is always chaotic, marked by injustice, violence, and bankruptcy.

1.11 The Law of God: source of our laws and political democracy, the emergence of the "Biblical Law"

From now on, the Decalogue, that is, the Law of God, takes place today in all our national and international jurisdictions. It is present everywhere in our constitutional law and all our jurisdictions, whatever they are: civil, criminal, commercial, matrimonial, and in all other areas of law and regulation. It protects social life while limiting individual power against others. Certainly, the first commandment, which is to say, the worship that must be rendered to the eternal and creator God, is absent, but from the fifth commandment it concerns the whole social life. This consideration allows us to ask the following question: have we returned to the time of the Judges in Israel? It is legitimate to ask this question when we see that today, political democracies are all governed by texts, as in the days of the Judges in Israel, the country was to be governed by the Law of God. In these texts are provided the provisions that allow the continuity of the state, national representation, successive governments, national defense, the rights of people, etc. Men and ideas of their time pass, the nation and all its institutions remain. This is the meaning of "the rule of law" which gradually spread from east to west and from north to south Europe, especially after the Second World War. It can be noted that this form of government of the people by law, although it has had great difficulty in imposing itself in Europe, this is the one that best guarantees the development of men and their multiple talents. The analogy with the time of the Judges is undoubtedly excessive; however, this biblical period is the one where the people of Israel also had to experience a political and social life directed solely according to the principles, the terms, the texts, and all the commandments of the Word of God. It is known that it was not so, but the mercy of the Eternal God, his great patience with men allowed this time to return. Rather than the "time of the Judges", it is the "time of Grace" which is proposed from the foundation of Christianity to the contemporary generations. What characterizes it is that Law and Grace are present and act at the same time, and not, one excluding the other as it has long been taught. It is the fulfillment of the words of Jesus Christ found in the Gospel of Matthew 5. 17-19; "Do not believe that I have come to abolish the law or the prophets; I came not to abolish, but to accomplish". Thus, we must live with these two dimensions of divine revelation, the Law which was not abolished and the Grace, which was already present before the coming of Jesus Christ, but which is in him; revealed, incarnate and granted to anyone who asks it in humility and faith, as this passage from the Epistle to the Hebrews (Heb 4:16) advises: "Let us therefore confidently approach the throne of grace in order to obtain mercy and find grace, to be rescued in our needs". This duality, "Law and Grace", allows the emergence of what can be called; the "Biblical law". Is this a new legal field or, on the contrary, a very old body of work put back in the spotlight? The ease would tip for the second alternative, but on closer inspection, it is not about either. Today, this expression is placed in quotation marks because it is used neither in the circle of jurists nor in that of theologians. Will it be more widely recognized and used by these same circles tomorrow? Will "Biblical law" be anything other than an awareness that will help the individual to better morally qualify each of his acts? It is to be hoped that it is much more than that and that it will take root in his heart and conscience, to the point of helping him to recognize the author and founder of this right, that is, God himself. This evolution would be one more step towards conversion, towards the new birth of which Jesus speaks in the Gospel of John in chapter 3 and verses 3 to 8. One of the major characteristics of the "biblical law" is its emergence in many societies like these giant bubbles that sometimes pierce the surface of a lake. From a small town in central Europe in 1517, the message of the Bible has continued, despite constant and sometimes violent opposition, to spread all over the world. Indeed, for historians it is from Wittenberg, where Luther plastered on the doors of the church of which he was canon, his 95 theses that Protestantism was characterized by a return to the Bible in the life of the Church as a divine institution as in the individual life of the believer as a guide for his conscience. It will be objected not without reason that the biblical message was, before Luther, propagated by the Catholic churches in the West and the Orthodox in the East of Europe. Yet, their very superficial teachings and their many theological errors, both doctrinal and ecclesial, left little room for their true expression. By opening the Bible to people, by affirming that the ministry of the Word of God is universal, Luther places religious reflection in the biblical text itself rather than in the words of men and their changing traditions. He invites every believer to do the same for his own account. Thus, he is the one who restored all his strength and authority to Sacred Scripture, after the apostolic era and that of the first five centuries of Christianity. With their motto "Scriptura sola", the first reformers opened a real Pandora's box because they placed the Word of God above men and their institutions. From then on, the texts of the Bible are addressed directly to the believers, and they have inspired and still inspire them under all the heavens until today. Therefore, they influence them wherever they are in, family, company, society, and its institutions. From this point of view, we can clearly see the emerging and growing influence of "Biblical law" in Latin America, where the rapid transition to the rule of law and relative institutional and political stability, in many South-American countries, owes much to the rise of the Protestant and Evangelical churches.

1.12 Jurisprudence: from the time of the judges to the prophet Zechariah

After the Pentateuch, the conquest of the land of Canaan remains unfinished, despite the initial successes of Joshua. A long period of uncertainty, called the time of the Judges, follows these promising beginnings. We are told in this book (Jg 2:10) that after Joshua, Caleb and those who had conquered the land of promise, "... a generation rose up who did not know the Lord...". Then the time of the kings of Israel and until the conquest of the country by the Romans is hardly better, apart from the glorious reigns of King David and Solomon, his son. However, it is known that the latter, at the end of his life, abandoned the Lord, returned to idolatry, and a dissolute life. In the end, his kingdom did not survive him and was soon divided between Judah and Israel. After them, few kings would succeed them and did "...what is right in the sight of the Lord...". Only 9 of them would succeed out of the 42 kings who reigned during the period of the kings before the deportation. However, what contrast does this chaotic national journey offer compared to the spiritual, cultural, and intellectual riches that this long period left us? The biblical texts of this time are still today the common inheritance of Judaism and Christianity. Every Sabbath day in the synagogues and every Sunday in the churches, rabbis, pastors, and priests comment on the biblical texts and encourage generations of believers to observe their precepts, the commandments and even the abundant jurisprudence they teach us. This contribution is such that it has produced, since the Protestant Reformation, a set of norms for life in society, unanimously respected and put into practice, which migrated from Israel and the Church to all continents and in most countries. The Bible now serves as the basis for the ethical, moral, and institutional construction of many developing countries. Today, we could demonstrate, texts and historical references in support, although this is not the subject of this book, that political democracy is entirely contained in the Bible.

2 The rebirth of Israel according to the Prophet Ezekiel and his vision of withered bones

Exit from the death camps is prophesied in the book of Ezekiel, Chapter 37. 1-14. No text written by man's hand could prophesy with such precision what the Lord revealed to his servant Ezekiel nearly 2,500 years before these events occurred. There is at the same time, the destruction of Israel, then its rebirth, and finally its blossoming among the nations. In addition to this magnificent revelation, there are several confirmations in the New Testament, including the passage in the book of the Acts of the Apostles chapter 1 v, 6 to 8, where Jesus Christ explains to them that the rebirth of Israel as a nation will not be revealed to them; "… it is not for you to know the times or moments that God has fixed with his own authority". Thus, Jesus Christ unambiguously confirms Ezekiel's prophecy of the restoration of the nation of Israel. It is also found, under the pen of the apostle Paul, especially when he declares that; their reintegration into the grace of God and the concert of nations will be like: "the life from the dead" (Romans 11:15). He continues (Romans 11:16-24), demonstrating that Christianity was grafted onto Israel, which he calls "a good olive tree", and as such has no superiority or specific glory.

2.1 Israel's creation in 1948 changed hearts and minds.

The gestation and rebirth of Israel as a nation are associated with a vast plan for reconfiguring world geopolitics. It was designed by the Eternal God in the late nineteenth century. It was at this time, in fact, which proliferate in Europe, the most exacerbated nationalisms, the most anti-Semitic and it was also the time of pogroms in the Russia of the tsars. Both would reach the Jewish community and, within them, was born the desire to affirm a fervent Jewish nationalism and the need for security provided by a state based on law and justice. To achieve this double objective, long expressed in this famous prayer: "Next year in Jerusalem...", the first World Zionist Congress will be held in Basel in August 1897. Chaired by Theodore Herzl, founder of the Zionist movement and author of a book entitled in German "Judenstaat" (The Jewish State). This congress was intended to structure the project of implantation of a Jewish settlement in what was at the time only a neglected province of the Ottoman Empire. Therefore, even before the dark hours of Nazism, the project was taken shape with the arrival of a large number of Jews fleeing persecution in Europe or driven simply by the Zionist ideal. The concomitance of the destruction of European Judaism in 1945 and the rebirth of a Jewish national home in the Middle East in 1948 is striking; it has something miraculous. Death is immediately followed by rebirth in just 3 years apart. These three years are not without reminding us, the three days spent at the tomb by Jesus Christ after his crucifixion before his resurrection. It is like a refuge that would have been prepared in advance for the remains of European Judaism. It also reminds us that the Eternal God holds the destiny of the nations in his hands, as this passage from the Bible found in Psalm 22 underlines: "For to the Lord is the kingdom: he rules over the nations" and this other in: Ezekiel: 39:21, "I will manifest my glory among the nations; And all the nations will see the judgments which I will exercise, and the punishments which my hand will strike them". Germany, which had taken the leadership of this frightening anti-Jewish crusade, is constrained and forced to consider with shame and sorrow the disasters it caused almost everywhere in Europe. After its capitulation, it was necessary to rebuild itself on entirely new bases. Denazification was vigorously carried out throughout the country, in all its administrations, particularly its justice, heavily compromised in the service of the Hitler regime. Repairs were also needed, and Germany finally contributed to the development of Israel after a historic agreement was signed on September 10th, 1952. This is the Luxembourg agreement, whereby Israel received financial compensation for its economic and social development. In addition, Israeli citizens who were robbed, uprooted, and persecuted in various forms received pensions and financial compensation from the state of Federal Germany. It should be noted that the eastern part, led de facto by the Soviet Union at the time, would not contribute to this effort of reparation. The religious world would not emerge unscathed from this moral and spiritual chaos. Although apparently nothing seemed to change, after sowing the seeds of anti-Judaism for centuries, the victory having changed sides, suddenly, the religious world is positively interested in Israel. These sudden changes in doctrine and dogmatic truths have had the effect of convincing the masses of the people of the vanity of the religious word, and in fact, between 1950 and 2010, religious practice fell sharply[256], and the number of vocations to the Catholic priesthood dropped in considerable proportions. There were more than 1,000 priests ordained every year in France in the early fifties; in 1970, there were only 285, and fewer than 100 per year since 2010. Many other factors contributed to this decline, however; one cannot help but think that the many curses that were pronounced and written by the institution against Israel finally drew upon it the curse of the Lord, in accordance with this famous verse quoted so many times (Gen 12:3): "I will curse the one who will curse you". It will take no less than 45 years for the Vatican to recognize Israel, but it will finally come on December 30, 1993, when the recognition agreement between the two states will be mutually signed. The institution will do even more to get rid of its secular anti-Judaism since Pope John Paul II, on March 26, 2000, visiting the Yad-Vachem Museum, then the Western Wall of Jerusalem, will file a written request for forgiveness in the name of the Church with these words; "God of our fathers, you chose Abraham and his descendants to bring your Name to the nations. We are deeply saddened by the behavior of those who in the course of history, have made your children suffer, and in asking for your forgiveness, we wish to engage in true brotherhood with the people of the Covenant. Jerusalem, 26 March 2000 Joannes Paulus II[257]".

---

[256] The slow death of the Catholic Church | Slate.fr
[257] Text communicated by Dr Jean-Igor Wolga.

Can the institution reform itself? It is allowed to doubt as much as to hope this. However, nothing unfortunately can erase the centuries of injustice, pride, and militant anti-Semitism, even in its theology and its founding texts. Moreover, if the institution can hardly change its history, we can hope that the men who compose it today and tomorrow are more animated by the texts of grace and love expressed throughout the Bible.

2.2 Men and women of reconciliation: those of the past

Those who worked for reconciliation between the Synagogue and the Church, had in fact no conflict with one or the other; they had their conscience for themselves. They have never believed in speeches of hatred and contempt, including those spoken from the highest ecclesiastical altars. What they have in common is that, in their time and under circumstances which were sometimes very difficult, they did their duties, which is to say, simple acts of humanity, respect, and love. They also share the modesty that makes their actions perfect; neither claim nor self-interest motivated them. Their memory is honored at the Yad Vashem Museum in Jerusalem, the memorial of the Shoah, under the name, "Righteous among the Nations[258]". It is also a great courage that characterizes them because they exposed their lives to save that of the Jews that the circumstances had entrusted to them. Today, 27712 of them share this honor of having together contributed to the salvation of several hundred thousand people. The notion of "Righteous among the nations" comes from the Talmudic tradition, which recognizes to some non-Jews, dispositions of heart and mind close to a Jewish conception of the universe and life. Thus, "Melchizedek" (Gen 14:18-20), king of Salem and priest of the Most High God, was an example of "Righteous among the nations", because he recognized in Abram a worshiper like him, of the Most High God. The Talmud[259] (Baba Batra Treatise, 15b) made long developments on this subject about these non-Jews, who nevertheless, by heart and spirit, love and understand Judaism. The historian of the first century, Flavius Joseph (Ant, I.10.27) makes them the very type of king of justice and peace. The epistle to the

---

[258] Just Among Nations: The Righteous Among the Nations | Yad Vashem
[259] Dominique Natanson, "Les Justes, le Bien et le Mal: critique d'une problématique, Imaginaire & Inconsciente", no 21, 2008 read online

Hebrews speaks of him as the forerunner of Jesus Christ, he is the founder of an order of a priest, "in the manner of Melchizedek" (Ps 110:3-4), to whom Abram gave the dime of everything. Among them are also, "those Fearing God", several times quoted in the New Testament (Acts 17:4), they love the Eternal God without knowing him too much, he is for them, the God of life. "... life was the light of men" according to chapter 1 of the Gospel of John (v 4), it was indeed, this light that guided their thoughts, their steps and their actions during the dark hours of the occupation of Europe by the Nazis because life had terribly retreated in the face of death. The list of these, "Just", is not closed yet, even if the years remove the last witnesses that could be added to it. It is scrupulously updated by the Yad Vashem memorial, and all the representatives of civil society, any profession, any confession are gathered in this great book. The three main nations represented out of a total of 48 are: Poland, the Netherlands, and France. The courage to save Jews was mostly individual; however, it was also sometimes collective despite the risks involved. This was the case for the Dutch village of Nieuwlanden, which, at the initiative of its municipal council, decided to hide Jews in its various farms. Another village, "Le Chambon-sur-Lignon", located in France received the title of "Juste parmi les nations" (Righteous Among the Nations), it is located in a Protestant region that has long suffered persecution. That is why, as soon as there were exceptional laws against the Jews in 1940, the inhabitants of this agricultural plateau organized themselves to thwart its application. With their Pastors, André Trocmé and Édouard Theis, the village became a city of refuge for Jews hunted by the Germans and their collaborators. They were particularly active in the defense of several thousand children who were thus removed from deportation. These two villages are accompanied by collective citations to several Polish networks of support for persecuted Jews, including those of the network, "Zégota", code name of the Commission for Assistance to Jews. In this country with the largest number of Jewish victims of Nazism, 7,232 people were distinguished, "Just among the nations". The Danish resistance was also honored by this title because it allowed the escape to neutral Sweden of its whole community. Eminent personalities have been declared "Just among the nations", this is the case of the French pastor Marc Boegner who very early in the occupation multiplied interventions in favor of displaced people, interned in insalubrious and overcrowded camps. Like the majority of the French, he did not see at first the extent of the betrayal of the republican ideals committed by the collaborative regime under the leadership of Maréchal Pétain. However, as President of the Protestant Federation of France, he wrote a pastoral letter in December 1940 to remind the state of its duty of impartiality towards all citizens and to emphasize that; "for the Church, there is no Jewish problem". A few months later, in his letter to the Chief Rabbi of France, Isaïe Schwarz, he was indignant against the racist laws decreed by the Vichy regime and assured him that the ERF (Reformed Church of France) would not stop fighting them. This was the first manifestation of Christian solidarity towards persecuted Jews. It was met with a very wide audience because it was reproduced by the entire collaborationist press, naturally to denounce the collusion of Protestants and Jews. Ignored by the representatives of the public authorities of the Vichy regime, his positions were widely read and commented on in the Protestant Churches. His high office as a representative of French Protestantism protected him from the severity of the laws of the Petainist dictatorship but they did not prevent the multiplication of the dramas of anti-Semitic persecution in France. In August 1942, one month after the Veld'hiv (Winter Velodrome) raid in Paris and following the strengthening of anti-Jewish measures throughout the country, Pastor Marc Boegner[260] wrote a letter to Marshal Pétain expressing his indignation at the same time as that of the multitude of Christians he represented. This message of revolt would also have a large audience because it was read and commented on in parishes, in the media of the time, as well as on the radio and in the international press. In 1943, he again protested against the introduction of the sinister STO for: "Service du Travail Obligatoire", (Compulsory Labor Service), intended to provide workers in large numbers to the German war machine. Although threatened himself by the occupier and his accomplices, he protected from his influence Protestant personalities and places of resistance located in the Cévennes and in the Drôme. (Southeast of France). At the end of the war, he testified on July 30, 1945, at the trial of Marshal Pétain, then he continued his activities within the Protestant Federation of France. He advocated ecumenism and increased interfaith contacts. He was elected in 1946, a member of the Academy of Moral and Political Sciences,

---

[260] François Boulet, "Pasteur Marc Boegner (1939-1945)", Le Lien. Resistance Friendship Newsletter, Vol. 26, May 2011, pp. 34-46

and later in 1962, he entered the prestigious Académie Française. The pastor André Trocmé[261] (1901 - 1971) carried out his ministry at the same time in the small town of Chambon-Sur-Lignon in Haute-Loire in the Southeast of France, already mentioned. Since the 16th century, the region and its surrounding villages have been mostly Protestant, and it has experienced the terrible hours of persecution, especially after the edict of Fontainebleau of 1685, which ended religious freedoms in Louis XIV's France by the revocation of the Edict of Nantes of 1598. In this historical and social context, the pastor André Trocmé quickly understood that the defeat of the French army in 1940 had paved the way for new forms of persecution with the collaborative regime installed in Vichy, under the presidency of Marshal Pétain. The day after the signing of the armistice of June 22sd, 1940, he gave a sermon on "The weapons of the Spirit", in which he warned the whole population against submission to a pagan ideology made of violence, idolatry, and racism. In particular, he stated: "To love, to forgive, to do good to our adversaries is our duty. But this must be done without abdication, without servility, without cowardice. We have to, resist when our adversaries demand of us submissions contrary to the orders of the Gospel. We have to do so without fear, as if without pride and hatred". He and his friend Pastor Édouard Theis (1899 - 1984) would lead a passive but effective resistance against official anti-Semitism, which would bring salvation to a large number of Jews. It is estimated that between 3,500 and 5,000 of these fugitives would have been collected, fed, helped, and saved from deportation. The two pastors will be later honored by the memorial of Yad Vaschem with the title of, "Just among the nations", as well as the modest city of Chambon-Sur-Lignon, which will receive this honor as a collective one. Unexpected personalities are included on this list of "Just", this is the case of Mr Aristide De Sousa Mendès[262] (1885 – 1954), that nothing predisposed to be included. However, he was the consul of his country, Portugal in June 1940 in Bordeaux, where tens of thousands of refugees were fleeing the advance of the German troops. Many were Jews, political refugees and sought to leave Nazi Europe through Portugal. Listening only to his courage and conscience, against the instructions of his government, chaired by the

---

[261] André Trocmé: André and Magda Trocmé, Daniel Trocmé | Righteous Among the Nations

[262] Aristides de Sousa Mendes: His Life and Legacy - Sousa Mendes Foundation

dictator, Antonio de Oliveira Salazar, he issued thousands of visas to these unfortunate people. It is estimated that about 30,000 people have benefited from visas issued by the Consul and among them, 10,000 were of Jewish faith. For his acts of disobedience, he was removed from office and demoted in the Portuguese diplomatic corps. He would know the misery he and his family of 15 people. In 1966 in recognition of his heroism, the Yad Vashem awarded him the title of, "Just Among the Nations" and in 1986, the President of the Portuguese Republic Mario Soarès posthumously awarded him the title, "Officer in the Order of Liberty" and he made public apologies on behalf of the Portuguese state to his entire family. Another unlikely personality to whom we must pay tribute in these lines is Miss Corrie Ten-Boom[263] who practiced with her father and sister Betsie, the clock-making trade in the city of Haarlem during the occupation of the Netherlands by the German. Of Protestant Reformed faith, they had for the Bible and for the people of God, a deep love, and they had arranged in their little house a space of refuge for the fugitives. Most peacefully they became resistant against anti-Jewish persecutions in their country and their house, would hide Jews proscribed and hunted by the occupier and their accomplices. In February 1944, they were reported to the gestapo and imprisoned before being deported to Ravensbrück concentration camp in Germany. The father did not survive the abuse and died at 85, one month after their detention. In December of that same year, Betsie also died in this sinister death camp. Then, a miracle happened: Corrie was released sometime later, following an error of the German administration of the camp, despite being known for its extreme rigor. Her life was broken, her little world had entirely collapsed because of the wickedness of men; however, she would take an extraordinary flight at the end of these years of darkness. Corrie would put on the clothes of an informal evangelist ministry, travelling the world to preach the Bible message of forgiveness and reconciliation, preaching that the life of the Spirit was stronger than the forces of evil. From conferences to international meetings, she carried this message to the ears of her former jailers of Ravensbrück, during a famous evening in 1947, where she found herself face to face with one of the worst guards of the camp. Invited many times for special occasions, she would tirelessly testify to her love for Israel. At the same time, she

---

[263] Corrie ten Boom | Encyclopédie multimédia de la Shoah

authored several books of testimonies, edification, and encouragement for present and future generations. His ordeal and that of his family was brought to the screen after being written in the form of a book of testimonies, both of which have the title in hell in French; "God in hell" and "The hiding place" in English. Its wide international spread continues to upset hearts and bring back to God souls in search of truth and meaning. Corrie Ten-Boom was honored with the title of "Just Among the Nations" by the Yad-Vashem Museum, and after this tireless work, she died in 1983, in Placentia, California. In Catholicism, there are also men and women of great compassion whose spirituality has directed them towards a deep love for Israel. Joseph André[264] (1908 – 1973) is one of them; he was a priest in Namur, Belgium, when the German occupation and the anti-Jewish persecution occurred. Despite his fragile health, he worked tirelessly to shelter, feed and save from deportation, a large number of Jewish families with their children and ancestors. Despite what is known of Catholic theology hostile to Judaism, he had kept intact a genuine fascination and love for Israel as the people of God and the "… light for the nations" (Is 50:3). He was a tireless friend and ally for the creation of Israel and in 1967 he received the title "Righteous Among the Nations". A year later, the "United Jewish Appeal" paid him a vibrant tribute in New York for his work on behalf of persecuted Jews. Another important name among Catholic religious is Pierre Chaillet[265] (1900 – 1972) he was a French priest, a member of the Jesuit order, a theologian and resistance fighter during the occupation. Unlike the majority of the Catholic clergy who saw in Philippe Pétain; «… the savior of France", he was well aware of the dangers of Nazism, having witnessed in 1940, the first anti-Jewish persecutions in Austria annexed by Nazi Germany. During this period, he refused any relationship with the regime of collaboration and became a liaison officer, then a resistance fighter in the ranks of France-Libre. Founder of a journal on spiritual warfare, Christian morality and political ethics; "Les Cahiers du Témoignage Chrétien", (The Christian witness Notebooks) it was declared, "Just among the nations" in 1981 for his actions in favor of the Jews persecuted during the war. Two Catholic bishops in the city of Toulouse helped to awaken consciences in the period before the Second World War, there is Jules

---

[264] Joseph André: (20+) Facebook
[265] Pierre Chaillet: Appendix: Biographies of Jesuit Righteous among the Nations in: Journal of Jesuit Studies Volume 5 Issue 2 (2018)

Saliège[266] (1870 – 1956), who had taken a position very early against the racist and anti-Jewish doctrines of Nazism. In one of his messages delivered on 12 April 1933 at the Théâtre du Capitole in Toulouse, he recalled the spiritual and memorial link that Christianity has maintained forever with Judaism with this sentence: "How can I not feel connected to Israel, like the branch of the trunk that carried it!". In the confusion that followed the capitulation of the French armies in June 1940, he supported the arrival to power of Marshal Pétain, the so-called "savior of France". However, the city of Toulouse was an essential crossing point on the road to Spain, and the diocese quickly became a center of assistance to the many refugees from all backgrounds who flocked there. The resistance begun there, in great destitution, before the need to help those who were persecuted because of their ideas or of their Jewish origins. In March 1941, Archbishop Jules Saliège concretely organized support to the prisoners of the concentration camps installed in the region and maintained in appalling conditions of survival. On Sunday, August 23, 1942, he had a pastoral letter read in all the parishes of his diocese in which he expressed his indignation: "In our diocese, scenes of terror took place in the camps of Noah and Récébédou. Jews are men, Jews are women. Strangers are men, strangers are women. Everything is not allowed against them, against these men, against these women, against these fathers and mothers. They are our brothers, like so many others. A Christian cannot forget it". At liberation, General De Gaulle appointed him: "Companion of liberation" and later, he was declared "Just among the nations" in recognition of his courageous positions, the personal risks he took to save and deliver those who were drawn to certain death. To this tribute, one can associate that which was rendered to the auxiliary bishop of Toulouse, Louis de Courrèges[267], who shared the same sentiments as Jules Saliège on the racist, anti-Jewish, and repressive measures of the government of Vichy. He participated in the same support and relief activities for the persecuted of the Vichy's regime. He was one of the main animators of the network, "Œuvres de secours aux enfants" (OSE - Relief works for children), which helped to rescue thousands of Jewish children in the south of France. Summoned by the French police in August 22[sd] 1942, he refused to cancel the

---

[266] They Are Our Brothers, Like So Many Others
[267] Louis de Courrèges: righteous among the nations

broadcast of the famous pastoral letter of protest that Jules Saliège wrote. Because of his actions, he was recognized, "Righteous among the nations" by the Yad Vashem. We add to this evocation a much less well-known personality who nevertheless showed that faith in the return to the promised land of the exiles of Zion was not exclusively reserved for Jews. He was a French soldier named Thadée Diffre[268] (1912 – 1971), from a bourgeois Catholic origin in the city of Arras in northern France. After his studies, he joined the colonial administration and as a result, he was in Africa, far from the fighting and defeat of the French army against the German forces in June 1940. However, because of his high sense of patriotic duty, he refused the armistice of 22 June 1940. He used his many relations in the colonial administration to keep French Africa on the side of General De Gaulle's Free France. He joined the army and took part in the fighting for liberation until the end of the war. Convinced of the rightness of Israel's struggle for independence, he enlisted in the service of the Haganah in 1948, under the pseudonym of Teddy Eitan and rose to the rank of commander and then to that of Lieutenant-Colonel. He created the "French Commando - ודנמוקה יתפרצה in Hebrew", which distinguished itself in the very hard battles, for the capture of the Negev and the access roads of the southern city, of Beer-Shev'a. He did not receive the title of "Just Among the Nations" however, a commemorative plaque recalls his achievements of arms and courage for the victory of Israel over its enemies. He died tragically in a traffic accident on December 30th, 1971. He is one of those many anonymous Christians, who have understood the exceptional destiny of the Jewish people to the point of risking their lives for their country by a commitment themselves in its fights and sometimes in its army. These few quick paintings of distinguished characters deserve much more than the modest lines above. It would also be necessary to pay a vibrant tribute to all those who in this tragedy have lost their lives either in deportation in the death camps, in the prisons of the gestapo and its collaborators, or on the battlefield, for helping in one way or another the Jews whom the fortunes of history had placed in their way. To obtain a more complete vision of the work of these, "Righteous among the nations", it is better to refer to the documentary collection on the Shoah

---

[268] IN MEMORIAM – Thadée DIFFRE, compagnon de la Libération (décédé le 30 décembre 1971) | Theatrum Belli

maintained by the Yad Vashem Museum of Jerusalem[269], which keeps the exhaustive list of these, 27712 "Righteous". For the French part, the historian Lucien Lazare[270] published in 2003 a dictionary of "Just of France". They all have a place at the heart of the double Jewish and universal memory for their major contribution to the work of reconciliation between Judaism on the one hand, Christianity and the whole of society on the other.

2.3 Official anti-Semitism defeated: The victory of a nation that was not a nation.

The defeat is not only German, but also that of Europe because in almost all the countries that compose it, the complicities in the murderous project of the Nazis had been very numerous. The defeat of totalitarian and racist states, the Nuremberg Trial, and the creation of Israel wiped out official and religious anti-Semitism. Although it still existed abundantly in different circles of thought generally placed at the extremes of the political chessboard, no state, except Iran of the ayatollahs, and no religion can any longer make it an essential vector of its preaching. Historian Léon Poliakov is one of the first to show that religious and official anti-Semitism quickly faded after the Second World War. Global sovereignty over nations changed places; universal dominion is taken away from Europe, much like royalty was taken away from King Saul by the Lord himself after his many transgressions (1Sa 15). It moves first to another continent: North America, and second, to a new ideology, that of the Soviet bloc led with an iron fist by the USSR. However, the victory of the US is more complete, more lasting, and it has a biblical significance that cannot be underestimated. It is the victory of the nation that was not a nation because indeed, the USA came out of the 2nd World War as an absolute winner; they fought successfully on all fronts, they supported all their allies, including the USSR, with the power of their industry. They put an end to the myths of European nationalism, since they do not form a homogeneous nation, but rather the sum and synthesis of all the exiles of the old continent, gathered under the banner of freedom promised by their constitution.

---

[269] The Righteous Among the Nations | Yad Vashem
[270] Lucien Lazare, Dictionnaire des Justes de France, Paris, Fayard, 2003

It is useful to recall in a few lines the originality of the formation of the United States, which is ultimately an integral part of the history of Europe. As soon as they arrived on American soil from 1626, the English, Dutch, French Huguenots, and other non-conformist Protestants, who came from the 4 corners of Europe to flee persecution, put the Bible at the center of their personal, social, and later national lives. In successive waves, they arrived and in just over 3 centuries, they gave full rise to the Evangelical Churches, pietists, Baptists, Methodists, Pentecostals, also called Professing Churches. These are characterized by the individual conversion of believers and the commitment to serve God in newness of life, according to the teachings of the Bible. The other Protestant, Anglican, Presbyterian, Lutheran, Reformed denominations were certainly not outdone, they thus reinforced the Protestant character of this young country, which would have a national constitution strongly influenced by the Bible at the end of its war of independence with Great Britain in 1776. The 13 colonies then that would soon become the first 13 states of the union had neither king, aristocracy, nor clergy to govern them, which was totally innovative in the context of the time. Rather, they had a constitution[271] placed at the top of the hierarchy of legal norms to which any citizen could refer. Moreover, in the whole country, thousands of churches were there to constantly recall their biblical inspiration. This reference text, still in force today, is remarkable for its clarity and simplicity; it is a hymn to freedom, individual right, and happiness, which has constantly attracted to it most of the national liberation movements all over the world. It spread beyond American borders and returned to Europe to give the foundations of political democracy to many nations of the old continent. Beyond the victory of weapons, the victory of the US over European nations is also ideological and economic. The first, however, is military; it brutally silenced the hate speech and anti-Semitism of Adolf Hitler and his accomplices, who had seized power almost everywhere in Europe in contempt of the law. The second is ideological and political indeed, even if the European nations, their leaders, and the cohort of their post-war intellectuals did not realize the extent of the victory of the US that followed that of their troops. Even if the wildest utopias of the pre-war era that had led to disaster, were reborn and abounded as soon as the liberation happened. This

---

[271] U.S. Constitution: U.S. Senate: Constitution of the United States

tumultuous period was, fortunately, over, and all the chimeras combined of ultra-nationalism, genius of race, fascism, and racism were rejected by the facts, by history, and by the millions of anonymous people who, coming out of the nightmare of war, aspired not to return to it. Europe, unaccustomed to political stability, peace at the borders, individual freedom, that of believing and undertaking, as well as other benefits provided by political democracy, will, however, make these experiences very beneficial for the development of its cultures and peoples, all of great wealth. However, the peace found again in Europe is in fact one, "Pax America", and it lasted for more than 80 years. The US brought to European nations a model of political democracy, "turnkey", ready for use. Having put the texts of the Bible to the test themselves, they can advise their application to European nations that were always hesitating between regimes of authority and the appeal of communism. This was the case of Italy where the fascist, monarchist and clerical regime was swept away by the popular revolt in April 1945. It was succeeded by a democratic system of parliamentary representation that was very fragile, but that would last much longer than the forecasts that had been made about it predicted. It was very fragile because it hesitated for a long time between a communism inspired by Moscow and the revanchism of the extreme right. Christian democracy, between crises and scandals, would do its best to keep the country in the camp of political and democratic freedom until today. This was also the case in Spain, where the violent civil war from 1936 to 1939 set up a severe dictatorship. However, the strong politico-military influence of the USA, the vital forces of the whole nation, turned towards institutional and political progress, advanced the idea of a democratic synthesis with the restoration of a constitutional monarchy. In this particular case, it should also be emphasized that the significant influence of mass tourism, which brought millions of silent "ambassadors" of the democratic life of northern Europe to Spain. The victory of the USA is also economic, since it is after the war, the Marshall Plan named after the American general who conceived it, which would help powerfully in the reconstruction of a large part of Europe. This plan is an entirely new way of conceiving peace and relations between victors and vanquished. Rather than overwhelm the perpetrators, Germany, Austria, Italy, and others, as was done by the Treaty of Versailles of 1919, the US would help the two opposing sides to recover and restart a social and political life in peace.

Thus, Germany would never pay for the extent of the ruins it had caused; it would not have been able to do so. The Marshall Plan would help the country to get its powerful industry back on its feet in the service of peace so that it becomes with France and Italy, one of the pillars of European construction, although it was very shaky at the beginning. The engine of victory was also the Dollar, which everywhere replaced gold and the British Pound Sterling as a means of payment in international exchanges. It was to become the financial instrument par excellence, accepted by all nations, including the fiercest enemies of the US, such as North Korea or Iran. It has been ever since easy to use for a large number of goods and services all over the world, and especially for the most important ones such as energy, grain, sea and air transport, banking, insurance, and so many other products essential to economic life. This victory even reached Vietnam, although militarily victorious in its war of reunification in 1975 against the Republic of the South, supported by the US, when it joined the WTO (World Trade Organization) in 2007, where the influence of the dollar predominated. Communist China with its immense human and technological resources, had preceded this movement since 2001, thus consecrating the hegemony of the dollar king. The global character of the US victory is only confirmed when the rival Marxist-Leninist model of the Soviet Union shows obvious signs of weakness before its final collapse in December 1989. Soon NATO, an organization of politico-military cooperation led de facto by the USA, welcomes the former members of the defunct Warsaw Pact of the former USSR. Historians, economists, politicians often talk about the post-war period until the collapse of the USSR as a bilateral period with the Atlantic bloc on the west side, led by the United States and the Soviet bloc on the other side of the Iron Curtain led by the Soviet Union. With the disappearance of the latter in 1991, the world became rather unilateral, and the political-military influence of the USA became almost universal. There is unquestionably a biblical significance to this pre-eminence of the nation which was not a nation. What we must remember from this total and multilateral victory is that it is also historical and philosophical, that everywhere it brings a biblical conception of man and his condition. This is reflected in the[272] preamble to the Charter of the United Nations, which was endorsed by most nations but

---

[272] Preamble of the United Nations: Preamble | United Nations

conceived mostly by the US. It recalls unequivocally several passages of the Bible, the following examples: "For to the Lord belongs the kingdom: He rules over the nations" (Ps 22:28). This word clearly shows that the Lord is not only King of Israel and Christians, but also of all peoples and nations. We can become aware of this when we see their progressive alignment with biblical values of peace, justice and respect for the human person. One will object to this idealism, the many conflicts existing nowadays between countries, ethnicities, groups and ideologies of all kinds. We will object to the recent wars between Russia and Ukraine, the much less publicized one in Sudan and the open war between Hamas and Israel after the terrible terrorist attacks of October 7th, 2023. However, it is undeniable that there is a charter of the United Nations, which establishes principles of equity between nations. Whether these are respected or not comes down to the same ethical and philosophical problem as collective and individual obedience or disobedience to the principles of the Bible. Psalm 67:4 says: "Nations rejoice and they shout with joy; For you judge the people with righteousness and lead the nations on earth". What is interesting to emphasize in this passage with regard to nations is the non-juridical notion of "rejoicing", although it is a question of the judgments of the Lord. Indeed, they cause joy and rejoicing; they act for the people as proof of God's existence, of sovereignty, and of goodness when he intervenes in human affairs. The beautiful example of these miraculous judgments and interventions of the Lord on behalf of the people is the story of Queen Esther, her uncle Mordecai and the entire Jewish people, was saved from a certain condemnation. In the epilogue, chapters 9 and 10 of these dramatic events and happy endings they experienced, there is great rejoicing among the people that testify to their gratitude towards the Lord's judgments. Even today the feast of Purim celebrated in all Jewish communities bears witness to the rejoicing of the people in the final victory of Queen Esther over the forces of evil. The last part of verse 4 of Psalm 67 quoted above, is an implicit recognition that the Lord alone, can lead the nations of the earth and that the reign of men is limited to one nation, or even an empire made of several of them but never to the whole universe. Psalm 82:8 states: "For all nations belong to you". We find here the notion of belonging, which is close to that of universalism. It is a reminder that the God of Israel is also creator of all things, founder of all tribes and nations. Far beyond the borders of the land of promise, he reigns over the kingdoms of the earth. The vision of the prophet Isaiah is a confirmation that the reign of the Eternal God is a reign of justice and peace for all the inhabitants of the earth when he declares; "He will judge between the nations, and will decide concerning many peoples; and they shall beat their swords into plowshares, and their spears into pruning hooks. Nations shall not lift up swords against nation, neither shall they learn war anymore" (Is 2.4). Certainly, these are allegories because the Bible does not speak precisely with characters, dates and key places. However, it clearly indicates in many similar passages, the advent of a time of relative peace for peoples, brought by a nation that was not a nation and by a God who does not dwell in temples made by the hand of man. It is indeed necessary to speak of a relative peace only, because the period from the post-war until today remains marked by many local conflicts, some like the Korean War, that of Vietnam, that between India and Pakistan and many others like the current conflict between Russia and Ukraine have been and are particularly violent and deadly.

2.4 The Conjunction of Powers for the Restoration of Israel

It was in this context of rebuilding European nations that the state of Israel was born in 1948; survivors of the death camps, idealists of the new world on the land of the ancestors, militants of a Jewish socialism in the kibbutz, religious of all tendencies... they meet in the territories of ancient Judah-Samaria, then under the administration of the Ottoman Empire, to rebuild against all odds, the nation of Israel with its own language that had not been spoken for more than 2500 years. This difficult reconstruction began with a war between May 1948 and January 1949 against neighboring Arab countries that did not accept Jewish sovereignty over a Muslim population. It was nevertheless endorsed by a positive vote of the United Nations on November 29th, 1947, despite the opposition of the surrounding Arab countries. The proclamation of the independence of Israel was made by the prime minister of the time, David Ben-Gurion, on May 14, 1948, and the very next day, it was the war that opposed the new state to all its neighbors. The conjunction of the votes of the 5 members of the Security Council in favor of the creation of the Jewish state, was miraculous enough for many and must be emphasized anyway, at the beginning of the cold war between the rival blocs of the West against communism, which were opposed on almost all the great diplomatic questions of the time. In civil society after the creation of Israel, the Jewish question is de facto raised in consciences with this question: "Why did you want to destroy the Jewish people?". Intellectuals in France like Jean-Paul Sartre, would bring to this question their answers, made of academic, philosophical reasoning, where the intelligence is sorry for the disaster of the Shoa. Their analyses and conclusions on this question were often reduced to a fundamental critique of the bourgeois capitalist society. Their relevant answers on many points, however, will never touch the heart of the mystical-theological problem because the distance that had been created between the two worlds, one academic and the other religious, was far too important in post-war Europe. The genocide against the Jewish nation became a subject of study led by great historians, sociologists, psychologists and even psychoanalysts because antisemitism soon passed from the status of politico-religious opinion widely spread in the society of the 30s, to a form of shameful illness that needed to be hidden at all costs, and which roots themselves reflected a profound imbalance of personality in the 1950s and 1960s. Without the problem being definitively resolved, it is necessary to recognize a positive evolution and the progress of consciousness in post-war civil society. The catastrophic outcome of the Second World War for Judaism emerged gradually in European opinions, opinions were untied, books were published, films, interviews with survivors, TV programs, a wide documentation of all kinds was being available to the public. It supported the case against criminal totalitarianism that prevailed in Europe before and during this period. This is how a culture of the memory of the Shoah was born, constantly recalled by witnesses, survivors, historians and all those who, believers or not, took to their heart these events. Moreover, the achievements of the small state of Israel, the exemplary character of its economic development, its military victories with biblical accents, all its men and women of heart and talent who made the desert bloom, attracted more and more both curiosities, the sympathy and finally the attachment of those who understood its historical significance and prophetic dimension. At the same time, the social evolution in Europe was characterized by the reverse movement of the decline of official religions and the expansion of professing Christian churches, Baptist and Pentecostal. Indeed, the USA arrived not only with weapons and luggage in Europe but also with many Evangelical missionaries who accompanied this landing. In the years following the war, they were to make a powerful contribution to the establishment of an important network of evangelical churches in Europe, which would allow the gradual spread of biblical thought, which would significantly influence classical Christianity and more broadly, public opinion. Finally, this positive evolution of Christianity greatly favored the support of Israel among the European peoples. Five wars in search for peace is the title that could be given to a film retracing the creation and struggles of Israel since 1948. The major conflicts between the Jewish state and its Arab opponents since that date have brought nothing conclusive except for one: to assert its rights to existence, and for the others to gradually recognize this nation. Nevertheless, since the Camp David agreements and the peace of Abraham signed in 1978 and 2020, respectively, we know that there is still a long way to go towards peace in this region.

2.5 Why is reconciliation necessary and urgent? The works of reconciliation.

To convince and convert to the teachings of Jesus Christ, Christians have received no power other than that of the Holy Spirit, as we have had the opportunity to write above by quoting this passage; "... but you shall receive power upon you, and you shall be my witnesses in Jerusalem, in all Judea, in Samaria, and to the ends of the earth" (Acts 1:8). When reading this text, it must be clearly understood that the ability to convince and convert belongs only to the Holy Spirit regardless of the witness, whatever his or her merits. He is simply there to honestly account for his experience with Jesus Christ the Lord and the savior of his soul. Thus, having no personal capacity to transmit the torch of faith, he is modestly brought back to this role of witness with every person, the Jew, the pagan, the Arab and finally whatever his or her condition and religion. The true power belongs to the Holy Spirit who alone, in fact, convinces one and the other to, "... sin, of justice and judgment", according to this passage from the Gospel of John (Jn 16:8). Moreover, the witness is exhorted to: gentleness, compassion, humility, he is an ambassador of a new world made of spiritual values and these good sentiments expressed in the whole Bible and clearly taught in many passages, including these two examples; "This is my commandment: Love one another as I have loved you" (Jn 15:12), and also; "Be good to one another, compassionate, forgiving one another, as God has forgiven you in Christ" (Eph 4:32). Consequently, the ultimate responsibility of the Christian is to be animated by feelings, love, forgiveness and compassion without which his message is devoid of all force and value. In the particular case of his relationship to Judaism, this love is coupled with the sense of filiation that we developed in the first part of the book. In this disposition of heart, he receives ipso-facto, the promise of peace and blessing according to this prophetic word already quoted, "I will bless those who bless you and I will curse those who curse you" (Gen 12:3). Christians cannot ignore or free themselves from this promise that God makes to his servant at the foundation of the first family of what would become later Israel, the people of God. There is therefore an individual part in this commitment to bless Israel, the Holy Spirit invites every born-again Christian to probe the scriptures, bless Israel and pray for the peace of Jerusalem. In his epistle to the Romans, the apostle Paul clearly explains what relations Christians should have with Israel. They are characterized by love, hope and humility with this blessed perspective expressed in Romans: 11.15 "For if their rejection was the reconciliation of the world, what will be their reintegration, if not a life from the dead?". He recalls that all the inspiration and wisdom of the Bible, including that of the New Testament, come from Judaism. He points out that the pagan world, of which most Christians are a part of, through the New Covenant in Jesus Christ, was grafted onto the Jewish world and not the other way around, as it was unfortunately taught for centuries. The attitude of the Christian is therefore made of gratitude towards Judaism, but also of circumspection and sometimes mistrust of the media of this world, always quick to show hostility towards Israel in the slightest politico-social affair which agitates the Middle East. More generally, the attitude of the evangelical Churches also reflects these same sentiments. This is evidenced by the important work done by these churches for the knowledge of Israel, its history, language, spirituality, and places of memory. Indeed, a biblical tourism animated by these churches, reaches impressive proportions when one relates it to the number of evangelical believers of each country. New and growing flows of tourists arrive, especially to visit the places of original Christianity and its biblical roots. They come from everywhere, "... from the ends of the earth" according to the prophecy and more concretely: from Brazil and all of Latin America, from South Korea, the Philippines, Africa, but also closer to us, from Spain, Portugal, France and Italy, where evangelical Christianity is experiencing a remarkable expansion. As it can be seen, these churches take their fair share in the blessing of Israel and in return; their vitality, their growth, their spiritual wealth, testify to the blessings promised by the Lord. On some occasions, evangelical Christianity does more than tourism; they take a firm stand in society. Thus, faced with the resurgence of anti-Semitic demonstrations in France, the CNEF (National Council of Evangelicals in France), which brings together almost all the unions of Evangelical Churches, takes a courageous and radical stand worthy of homage in defense of Judaism and Israel. In fact, at the end of 2018, the Council published a collective book of conviction written by several eminent personalities of the evangelical world in France entitled "Anti-Semitism; it is time to react". This collective commitment of the Evangelical Churches is positive; it also testifies that the Evangelical Churches continue to draw their inspiration and their messages largely from the very sources of Judaism. They have learned to bless Israel according to Genesis 12:1, rather than to curse, which is the opposite of their doctrine because it is written: "... Bless, do not curse" said the apostle Paul in his letter to the Romans (Rom 12:14). The question of conversion remains a hope similar to that which can be expressed with regard to all the nations of the world. However, as we have already seen, this is essentially the case of a person's choice who meets the God of Israel in his son Jesus Christ and decides to obey him by conversion and commitment to live according to his word. Conversion is above all not a prerequisite for the love that evangelical Christian's manifest for Israel. They have at their heart this thought always present in the texts and said by the Lord Jesus Christ himself: "... salvation comes from the Jews" (Jn 4:22). Given these historical and theological elements, it is clear that God did not want the disappearance of the nation of Israel, on the contrary he wants to bless and save it and all the others.

Numerous and diverse Evangelical associations have emphasized the expression of sincere love for Israel, in order to do more than simply recognize it. Indeed, this passage in Genesis 12:3; "I will bless those who bless you" clearly shows that it is about doing much more than knowing and recognizing Israel; it is about blessing, that is to say, loving, do good, listening to and give thanks to God for the role it has played as a witness people since its election. And indeed, when we look fairly at its history, it involves many more duties and responsibilities than privileges. The Word of God in this short passage insists on the voluntary and intentional character of the widespread blessing for Israel. He who acts in this way quickly realizes that the blessing he bears in his heart for Israel does not deprive other nations of his love and consideration. This thought actually has the effect of increasing the depth of his feelings of love for God and for all the nations he has created throughout the world. Many evangelical associations have made their support for Israel the essential mark of their ministry. To draw up an exhaustive list of these associations that advocate for the rapprochement of the evangelical churches with Judaism is an impossible task, as they are numerous and varied. They have all their merits, and the few presented quickly below, in no way diminish those of other associations, to which it would be good to pay special tribute. The best known of these is also the first of its kind in France, it is addressed to the whole of Christianity. It was created on February 26th, 1948, by the great historian Jules Isaac who, as a victim of Nazi persecution did much to develop interreligious dialogue and to stop the anti-Semitic message in the Catholic Church. This association is called "Jewish-Christian Friendships[273]" (JCF), the first team includes a small group of Protestants, Catholics, Orthodox, and Jews. Jules Isaac, as a founding member, had participated the previous year, with the Great Rabbi of France Jacob Kaplan, in the reflections and works of the Judeo-Christian conference of Seelisberg in Switzerland. In 1948, he explored in one of his works, "Jesus and Israel" the origin and fundamental paradox of Christianity, directly born from Judaism and nevertheless its most relentless enemy. In 1949, during his audience with the Pope, he asked for a revision of the teachings of the Catholic doctrine on Judaism and in particular, on the universal prayer of the Good Friday, with this passage; "Oremus et pro perfidis judaeis", which means; "pray also for the treacherous Jews". This prayer was rightly regarded as a grave offense against an entire nation. His request made to the timid and undecided Pope Pius XII, would only be accepted and followed by effects by Pope John XXIII, his successor in 1959, ten years later. Finally, it was in 1962 that the Second Vatican Council completely revised its doctrine of the "deicide" people and rejected the so-called responsibility of the Jewish people in the crucifixion of Jesus Christ by professing, rather as the Gospels put

---

[273] Natural Friends: Christians and Jews | Faithful Christian Friends | IFCJ

it, the universal and individual responsibility for it (). From his early years, one can also find in the ranks of the Christian Judeo Friendships (JCF), the pastor Jacques Martin, who received the title of "Just among the nations", the Protestant historian Fadiey Lovsky, Maurice Vanikoff, president of the Jewish veterans, Jean Daniélou, priest and later cardinal, Léon Zander, philosopher and orthodox religious. The list of its members will continue to grow as the enormity of the Nazi crimes and the parallel that could be drawn between incitement to hatred of Judaism in the Christian religions and the passage to the criminal act in Nazism were discovered. Even today, through seminars, conferences, and all kinds of activities, the JCF promotes Judeo-Christian dialogue in the French world by cultivating the ties that unite the two branches of the Abrahamic faith rather than what divides them. A JCF award is presented each year to Jewish and Christian personalities who have distinguished themselves by their contribution to Judeo-Christian dialogue. In 2022, the JCF prize was awarded to the Chief Rabbi of France, Mr Haïm Korsia. Articles 1 and 2 of the of JCF set out the goals of mutual rapprochement, collaboration on different subjects of society, and the fight against anti-Semitism and anti-Judaism in all its forms. Article 3[274] notably insists on the renunciation of proselytism, any attempt to dominate one group over another, and on the respect due to each confession represented within its ranks.

2.6 The Development of Messianic Christianity

The origin of this religious trend of Jews converted to Christianity can be found in England, especially at the beginning of the 19th century. This is where Protestantism would welcome scholars capable of making the connection between the New and the Old Testament. This is the case of the, "Church's Ministry Among the Jewish People", a branch of Anglicanism led by Pastor Joseph Frey[275], whose real name was Joseph Samuel Lévi and whose ministry was the development of Christianity among the Jewish population. He was the author of the first Hebrew translation of the New Testament in 1821. The "Church's Ministry among Jewish People" (CMJ) began to settle in Palestine in 1820 and pioneered modernization,

---

[274] AJCF Statutes, AJCF Website, 2007.
[275] Messianic Judaism: Pastor Joseph Frey (20+) Facebook

introducing the first modern building in Jerusalem that was the church "Christ Church", the chapel of the British Consulate in Jerusalem, which joined the CMJ in 1838, while the country was still under the Ottoman Empire governance. British consul James Finn was one of the pioneers of agricultural initiatives outside the walls of the old city. The first Western physician Irish George Dalton, the first modern hospital and the first modern education centers, were all part of the CMJ. One of the main activities of this institution was the "House of Industry", where Jews learned manual trades. Some non-Jews also joined them. In 1842, the first Protestant bishop, a converted former rabbi, Michael Solomon Alexander, arrived in Jerusalem. The CMJ also housed Jewish refugees who had survived the pogroms in Eastern Europe. This "missionary" activity of the Christian Zionists aroused the jealousy of philanthropists like Moses Montefiore and Baron Rothschild, who became deeply involved in the affairs of Jerusalem. Then came "The Hebrew and Christian Alliance", (Hebrew-Christian Alliance), created in the United Kingdom in 1866, then in 1915 it was the turn of the American branch, which would grow considerably with the expansion of Jewish communities throughout this new country. [276] On September 22, 1866, 157 American Christians "in love with Zion", members of the "Church of the Messiah", arrived in Palestine while sailing from Jonesport in the state of Maine, on the "Nellie Chapin" and landed in Jaffa bringing with them prefabricated wooden houses, because of the lack of trees on site, to found, long before, Tel Aviv in 1909, the neighborhood called American Colony north of Jaffa. Some of these houses are still there today. The municipality of Tel Aviv – Jaffa, gratefully installed a memorial stele on the seaside promenade near this neighborhood. These Christians had come in the hope of witnessing the return of the Jewish people to their land and the imminent return of the Messiah. Because of the difficult living conditions, most of these Americans left after a year or two, and they were replaced by a German group called «the Templars» (or the Temple Community) whose headquarters were set in a stone building in the center of the American Colony, which became the American-German Colony. Some of the wooden houses left by the Americans were bought by the CMJ, which was already present in the old city of Jaffa since 1844. The Templars created a school in the stone building. This building was then bought in 1878 by

---

[276] Messianic Judaism: Who Are Messianic "Jews"? | My Jewish Learning

a Russian Christian, Baron Plato Von Ustinov who made it a luxury hotel, then bought in 1926 by the CMJ which made it a high school for girls (Jewish, Muslim and Christian). Today, this building has become «Beit Immanuel» (the house of Emmanuel), which is both the second center of the CMJ in Israel after that of the Christ Church in Jerusalem, a Christian hotel, and a congregation of Messianic Jews and Arab Christians. At the end of the 19th century, many spiritual and cultural associations honored the filiation between Judaism and Christianity and willingly practiced a certain mix between the two confessions. This is the case of the large community founded in Chisinau in Moldova by a Jewish idealist named Joseph Rabinovitch, himself a baptized Protestant. This long-disputed region between Russia and Romania was the scene of many pogroms, massacres, and dispossession of all kinds against the Jewish populations during the 1880s and 1890s. The Judeo-Christian synthesis seemed to him to be the solution to the tensions between the two Bible communities. He introduced into his liturgy a preparation for the Sabbath by associating Christian and Jewish elements for the celebration of worship to the Lord. However, it is in the USA that this form of double piety would find its greatest expression through many messianic associations. The striking victory of the IDF (Israel Defense Forces) army of Israel in 1967 and the reunification of Jerusalem would be shocking for many among the Jews who would see it as a key step for the return of the Lord in glory. One of these messianic associations still active today is called "Jews for Jesus[277]"; it was founded in 1973 in the United States by Moishe Rosen, a pastor of Jewish origin converted to[278] Christianity in 1953. The organization is part of the growing evangelical movement all over the world, and now the majority in Protestantism. It claims that Jesus (Yeshua in Hebrew) is the Messiah announced by the prophets in the Old Testament. It proposes parallel studies between the Old and New Testaments to demonstrate that Jesus is also the Messiah of Israel and the savior of this world. It actively evangelizes in the streets by distributing leaflets and invitations to its lectures led by theologians, historians, and sociologists on the theme of the rapprochement between Judaism and Christianity. Present in churches, its members, who can, are sometimes asked to bring the light

---

[277] Home - Jews for Jesus
[278] Moishe Rosen: Jews for Jesus

of Judaism on certain aspects of Christianity. It has twenty offices in several countries: South Africa, Germany, England, Australia, Brazil, Canada, United States, France, Israel, Russia, Ukraine, etc. In this messianic current, there exists since 1980 an original work, it is the International Christian Embassy in Jerusalem (in English: International Christian Embassy in Jerusalem, ICEJ). It was born as a sign of support and solidarity of evangelical Christians towards Israel and the Jewish people following the departure of the embassies of several nations from the capital of Israel. Indeed that year, were approved by the Knesset, the laws, known under their English name, "Jerusalem Law[279]", extending the perimeter of Jerusalem on its eastern part. It had been annexed by Jordan after the fighting of 1948, like the rest of Judea and Samaria. Its location in the neighborhood, "Katamon" also called "Gonen", is at the center of the city, to affirm that for millions of Christians, Jerusalem is the eternal capital of Israel. This position was finally followed in 2018 by the United States, the most important country on the planet both from the Christian and Jewish point of view, which restored their embassy in Jerusalem. This name, "Embassy[280]" is also interesting because this time, Christianity did not want to occupy as a conqueror the country of Israel, as it had done during the Crusades but rather, to come as a benevolent guest, becoming, like any ambassador, accredited by local authorities. Today in a remarkable reversal of hearts and circumstances; it is headed by a certain Jürgen Bühler, the son of a German soldier of the Wehrmacht, taken prisoner in the USSR and cared for, fed and finally saved by a Jewish family. This Ambassy plays an important role today in the reconciliation movement that gathers more and more Christians, in love with Zion and convinced of the biblical meaning of the return of the Jews to the land of their ancestors. Whether from its center in Jerusalem or through its offices in more than 60 nations, ICEJ strives to motivate churches to take their biblical responsibilities towards the Jewish people. The Embassy has given itself the mandate in six points below:

— Be a source of comfort to the Jewish people according to the word of the prophet Isaiah 40:1;"Console, console my people, Say your God".

---

[279] Israel's Basic Laws | CIEA
[280] Our Work | International Christian Embassy Jerusalem - ICEJ UK

- Encourage Christians to pray for the peace of Jerusalem in the land of Israel.
- To teach and train churches concerning God's purposes for Israel and for the Middle East today.
- Defend and plead the cause of Israel worldwide and fight anti-Semitism in all its forms.
- Engage in humanitarian projects for the well-being of all peoples in the Land of Israel.
- Bring reconciliation between Jews, Christians, and Arabs, and support the churches and congregations of the Holy Land.

Moreover, in fulfillment of the prophecy of Zechariah, the Embassy invites Christians from all over the world to participate in the feast of Tabernacles according to what is written; "All that remain of all the nations that have come against Jerusalem will come up every year to prostrate before the king, the Lord of hosts, and to celebrate the feast of tabernacles" (Za 14:16). It is a major event to which the country's leaders, president, prime minister and key dignitaries pay a sustained tribute. It is followed by an annual conference in which pastors, Christian leaders, and supporters participate and meet. It addresses various themes useful to the understanding of the vocation of Israel among the nations according to the texts of the Bible and, the share that the churches can take in the fulfillment of the prophetic plan designed by the Eternal God. The Embassy provides concrete assistance to the needs of the large emigration of[281] Jews returning to Israel in accordance with the prophecy of Isaiah; "I will say to the north, Give up, and to the south, Do not withhold! Bring my sons from afar and my daughters from the end of the earth" (Is 43:6). We notice the imperative character of this order punctuated with an exclamation mark. There is anger against the nations in this double injunction, and indeed the persecuted people of Israel, helpless for centuries, were snatched from them by the Lord, who gave them this land, which today knows how to defend itself being feared and respected even by its worst enemies. The Embassy also offers young people aged 18 to 30, as part of the ICEJ Arise program, visits to emblematic places of

---

[281] (3) The Regathering of Exiles (Aliyah) | TBN Israel (Special) - YouTube

biblical history. This tourism greatly promotes the awareness that the Christian spiritual life is also part of the same unforgettable places of memory as Judaism. In all its activities, the Embassy expresses the love that Christians of all faiths, but especially evangelicals, have for Israel. Working against the current of bad feelings and the heavy past of relations between Jews and Christians, this embassy is aptly named in the heart of Israel for the reconciliation of the two branches of the Abrahamic faith. To conclude in beauty and thanksgiving the pages of this book on the indissoluble link that must exist between Christians and the Jewish people, and finally, according to the will of God himself, to "Reconciliation". It is important to mention the most important organization in the world that has made support for Israel the heart of its preaching. This is: Christians United for Israel[282] (CUFI); what is interesting about this evangelical revival movement is that it has found the theology that associates the love of Israel with the truth of the Gospel by a constant reminder of its key verses. It is an American organization founded in 1992 by Pastor John Hagee. His message indeed reminds everyone, what we also expressed in the first part of this essay, namely: filiation, continuity, brotherhood, and spirituality between the Synagogue and the Church. This offer of blessing to Israel is given for biblical reasons, as we have already mentioned. Today, the organization has more than 10 million members and is a strong expression of the indissoluble bond between Christians and Israel. It is still led by Pastor John Hagee responsible at the same time for a large evangelical church in San Antonio, Texas called "Cornerstone Church". He was invited by the Prime Minister of Israel Benyamin Netannyahou on May 14, 2018, to celebrate both the 70th anniversary of the creation of Israel and the inauguration of the US embassy in Jerusalem. His prayer at the conclusion of the dedication ceremony was to recall, drawing on numerous biblical references, the will of the Lord, to establish Israel in this land with Jerusalem as its capital. Its organization CUFI, is associated with various unions of Protestants churches, some Catholics also participate in its large gatherings and its many activities. These include the creation of student campuses in connection with American universities (CUFI on Campus), in order to develop the reflection and commitment of young people to support and bless Israel. Since their creation, several hundred chapters have joined CUFI on

---

[282] Christians united for Israel: The Fight Against Antisemitism | Christians United for Israel

Campus and they multiply the sensitivity to this effort of reconciliation between Jews and Christians. They are also known to help combat anti-Semitism in all its forms. A ministry of prayer organized by women called, "Daughters of Zion" was launched in 2007. They form a network throughout the country, wherever they can gather churches, public spaces, shops, houses, to pray for Israel and for the peace of Jerusalem. On the other hand, various events involve Christian members of CUFI with local Jewish communities to raise funds and support projects of general interest in Israel. Also noteworthy is the annual meeting in Washington of CUFI officials and delegates from all over the country who review the various aspects of their relations with Judaism and the country of Israel in connection with members of the American Congress.

2.7 A great name among many worth mentioning.

Among the artisans still very present in the memory of reconciliation between the Synagogue and the Church, we want to pay a heartfelt tribute to Pastor Jean Marc Thobois, who was its indefatigable advocate, mainly in France. Although he passed away in March 2020, at the age of 76, his ministry continues to inspire us, and he is still in the hearts of those who work, on the foundations of the Bible, for reconciliation between Judaism and Christianity.

Jean-Marc Thobois willingly spoke of his Huguenot ancestors, these Protestants scattered in a France that was hostile to them since the 16th century because of its kings then in power, their aristocracy, and Catholicism, until the year 1789, which took them away in a great political and social revolution. The Reformed Christians were the first authentic resistance fighters against the dictatorship; they were those who inspired the founding texts of our Republic and who gave to our country, great captains of industry. Jean-Marc Thobois also, in his way, was a great resistance against conformism, indifference, and apathy of consciences on the difficult question of relations between the Synagogue and the Church. By choosing this path in his ministry, he not only helped Christians rediscover the Jewish origins of their religion, but he also provided solutions to this problem by finding again the path of peace, of communion, and mutual understanding between these two branches of Abraham's faith. He often repeated during his lectures the words of his New Testament teacher, David Flusser, namely: "... Christianity is a Jewish religion". This simple and truthful statement has long remained shocking for many, and it is still sometimes even today. Very invested in Bible meditation and reading the testimonies of great evangelists such as Donal Gee and Billy Graham, Jean-Marc converted during his adolescence and went through the waters of baptism as a professed Christian, based on his personal statement of faith. He was able to seize the opportunities presented to him to make his first trip to Israel in 1962 and meet Professor Zeev Kofsmann, pastor of the Messianic Church of Jerusalem. He was excited by the truth of the prophecy about the restoration of the nation of Israel as much as by the wonderful connections he found with the Jewish roots of his Christianity. The professor encouraged him to study at the University of Jerusalem, where he rediscovered the teachings of Professor David Flusser. Despite the difficulty of following the courses taught in Hebrew, he greatly benefited from both their historical and theological contributions. These two years spent in contact with him were of great wealth for young Jean-Marc, both on the spiritual level at the Evangelical Messianic Church of Jerusalem and on the academic level to deepen his Jewish culture. In June 1967, he was surprised, like the whole world, by the 6-day war, which opened an entirely new page in the difficult history of relations between Israel and the Arab countries. The capture of the eastern part of Jerusalem, with Solomon's temple wall, triggered an extraordinary wave of enthusiasm and religious fervor throughout the country and far beyond. The words of Psalm 126 then resonated throughout the nation: "... We were like those who have a dream. Then our mouth was filled with shouts of joy, and our tongue with singing; then they said among the nations: 'The LORD has done great things for them!' (Ps 126 1-2). Returning to France in August of that year, he was successively pastor of an evangelical church, in Denain in the north of France then in Vannes in Brittany. There, he contributed to the spiritual and material edification of the church by working as a simple laborer and as a mason, building it with the young and not-so-young Christians that God sent him to this task. In 1976, after the death of the pastor Zeev Kofsmann, he resumed with the pastor Clément Le Cossec the publication of the magazine "Shalom," intended to offer a messianic point of view to evangelical Christians who were fond of culture and biblical teachings. Since it became "Keren Israel" in 1989, the journal has been enriched by the teachings of systematic theology that Jean-Marc gave at the Evangelical Missionary Center of Carhaix in Brittany. His teachings, in total 182, are of great human and theological richness; they were dispensed until 1992 and are still available (in French) today on the site: www.enseignements-bibliques-jmthobois.com. The continuation of his ministry was made up of trials and difficulties, but also of great victories and his faithfulness towards the churches and his relatives. Having reached the age of retirement, he nevertheless continued his ministry, receiving many invitations to share the message of the Bible and to strengthen everywhere the attachment of Christians to Israel and its history. He became an organizer of discovery and study trips to Israel that he traveled in all its dimensions a good number of times. At the same time, he established a close collaboration with the messianic publisher "Emeth Éditions" by publishing 9 reference works on the crossed destiny of Christians and Israel. He died on March 14, 2020, from the consequences of COVID 19, a disease he contracted during a stay in Alsace shortly before that date.

2.8 Fifty years later...

On 7 October 1973, Israel had left only a thin band of troops on its front line of the Suez Canal as a separation from Egypt. At its northern border with Syria, on the Golan Heights, a small tank unit and light military personnel had to watch over this very sensitive border. This fatal error of the high command was paid for by a very harsh war, also called the "Yom Kippur" war, because it was launched on this very day of this most sacred day in the Hebrew calendar. It resulted in the death of 2,700 soldiers on the Israeli side, 10,000 on the Egyptian side and 3,300 on the Syrian side. On October 7, 2023, fifty years to the day, Hamas, in power in the Gaza Strip, launched a war operation against some kibbutz located near its border with Israel. This one also very dangerous, with this cramped territory practically not guarded, the terrorists were able to cross it without encountering opposition and engage in all kinds of atrocities against civilians. The parallelism with the negligence committed on the eve of the Yom Kippur War is striking. Historians will debate the causes and consequences of this tragedy. Whether it was the overconfidence or the slackening of surveillance of this powder keg, fed by Hamas' war propaganda, the price paid by the inhabitants of the region has been exorbitant. For these unfortunate people who lived there peacefully, their end was terrible, and today it is estimated that between 1200 and 1350 victims of all ages, including infants, were massacred most brutally. It is hard to believe that this explosion of violence could not have been foreseen, given the accumulation of weapons stored in tunnels crisscrossing, at several levels of depth, the underground of Gaza. How has the earth and sand extracted for digging been hidden from the eyes of drones, airplanes, and satellites, which have been constantly monitoring for years, in this cramped territory where it is very difficult to hide? It was no mystery either that Hamas had vowed, since its installation in power in 2007, to wage war against Israel with a view to its destruction. This state of belligerence has turned it into an open-air prison surrounded by the stubborn mistrust of its Egyptian and Israeli neighbors. The living conditions of its inhabitants have deteriorated over time, and Iran and Qatar remained among the few donors to this island of hatred against Israel. Over the years, Gaza has become an issue in the struggles within the Muslim world, with Iran taking up the dream of Islamist nationalism, abandoned by many Arab countries, signatories of the 'Peace of Abraham' in 2020. Overall, the withdrawal of Israel in 2005 and the forced evacuation of the Jewish minority who lived in Gaza at "Gush Katif" was probably a historical error, as many commentators of the time pointed out, since Israel is forced to occupy it again today to ensure the safety of its citizens. This departure from Israel obtained for the Fatah party of Yasser Arafat, without any political, economic, or social counterpart, has not calmed the region, and everything must start again after countless deaths, tears, and destruction. Collateral damage is also social because the extent of destruction in Gaza has sparked an unexpected wave of sympathy for the cause of Hamas. Soon, the emotion caused by his odious massacres was forgotten; it gave way to a renewal of anti-Judaism that spread throughout Europe, as in the past, yet so close. We soon considered in many media the asymmetrical character of this war and reversed the roles by denouncing Israel as the aggressor and Hamas as the victim. Anti-Zionism has become the modest veil of resurgent anti-Semitism; the most prestigious universities, public institutions such as the French Parliament, have seen banners on their walls bearing the colors of a Palestine founded on the destruction of Israel. The future is dark because nothing indicates that violence will fade when all those who want the destruction of Israel consider the political benefit they derive from it, in the Middle East, in Europe, in the USA, in Canada, in Africa etc. However, on the other hand, millions of individuals, from evangelical Jewish and Christian communities, stood up in defense of Israel. From the first days of the attacks on 7 October, significant material and financial donations were sent to the various bodies responsible for victim assistance. Following the words of the book of Genesis (12.2), an immense international chain of prayers to bless Israel has been formed all over the world. If the borders of Israel are still not recognized by a large part of the Arab countries, the nation and the state, on the other hand, were recognized by the General Assembly of the United Nations on May 11, 1949. From then on, the ambition of Iran and its allies to make Palestine, "from the sea to the river," clashes with the international legitimacy of the existence of the Hebrew state. Therefore, there is a question of international law that cannot be resolved either by violence nor murder. The long-debated solution in the chancelleries and the media, of a land for two states, generates by itself great ambiguity because: can there be on this land two states, one of which seeks to destroy the other? This situation, contrary to the provisions provided for the recognition of a state by the international community at the United Nations is also a local obstacle to any progress in this direction, and the events of October 7, 2023, are a demonstration of the impossibility of such a solution. Since these dramatic events and in this period of war, it must nevertheless be emphasized that peace has also progressed. It bears the prestigious name of Abraham, the patriarch of the three monotheistic religions: Judaism, Christianity, and Islam. One wonders moreover, among specialists whether the war of October 7 would not be an initiative of its opponents, to mitigate its scope, without being able to permanently break it. Indeed, during the months that preceded this terrorist act, the dialogue between Israel and the Kingdom of Saudi Arabia progressed at a great pace, thus showing that the desire for peace was constantly spreading in the region. The well-named Peace of Abraham came towards the end of US President Donald Trump's term in late 2020. He contributed a lot with his son-in-law, Jared Kushner, to this great achievement. This is a peace treaty signed between Israel on the one hand, and the United Arab Emirates and Bahrain on the other hand, initially on September 15, 2020. This first agreement was quickly followed by many others, as the act of diplomatic normalization between Sudan, Morocco, and Israel was signed in October 2020. It is well known that diplomatic agreements do not even have the value of the paper on which they are signed if they are not accompanied by concrete and lasting acts of collaboration between the signatory states. From this point of view, the Peace of Abraham is promising because very quickly it allowed, among them, the opening of a vast field of exchange and cooperation. From the beginning of 2021, agreements in the fields of technology, air transport, media, financial services, tourism, energy, cyber security, of the fight against terrorism, and many others have been signed between Israel and its new partners. In 2022 alone, there were already nearly 250,000 Israeli visitors to the Emirates, and regular flights between the capitals have been scheduled. The head of the state of Israel, Mr. Isaac Herzog, was received in the United Arab Emirates with full honors at the end of January 2022. In just 2 years, total trade between the two countries has exceeded $2.5 billion since the signing of the agreements and sixty-five agreements and memoranda of understanding have been signed between the two countries, said the Minister of Foreign Trade of the Emirates, Mr. Thani bin Ahmed al-Zeyoudi, at the World Economic Forum in Davos. Even more significant, the agreements in the field of military technological cooperation were concluded and by the year 2021, Israel's military exports to Arab countries represented 9% of their total, climbing to 25% in 2022. The reason why this type of technological and industrial cooperation is particularly important is that it is necessarily a mutual long-term commitment. The states can only equip themselves with a country for very long periods because the time for study with their staff, interfacing with each army corpse, production and training of personnel, extends over several decades. There is therefore an extremely high level of trust between partners to obtain, maintain, and develop so that the country's client's army remains well equipped and fully operational. All these considerations mean that the peace of Abraham contains with these multiple agreements, and especially with its military security part, a real guarantee of survival in the long term. It has a beautiful prospect, despite the local situation now execrable at first glance, and a destiny, that many states of the region could soon join in this initial effort for peace.

2.9 Epilogue

We have received no other message to bring to Israel, or to the world, than that of the love of God, manifested in Jesus Christ. For the Christian, this translates into gratitude, recognition, blessing, and love towards Israel. It is the only proclamation in the entire Bible to be known; the universal love manifested in Jesus Christ, which is authorized for us. We witness what we have received from God, we invent nothing, and we sweep away all the theological wanderings that led to this calamitous divorce between the Synagogue and the Church. Nor is there a revolution in the functioning of Christian institutions or in the order of Sunday evangelical worship. It is certainly necessary to increase biblical and more broadly Hebrew culture in Christian assemblies, through the periodic intervention of scholars specialized in these questions. It is desirable to have periodically in the churches conferences and various events related to Israel, its history, and actuality. The great revolution to expect, however, is that of hearts, more sensitive to the Bible, the eternal Word of God, deeper in understanding the succession of generations of believers from Abraham to Jesus Christ, and then to us. A need for hearts more aware that Christian anti-Judaism is a heavy heritage, weighing like a curse on those peoples of Europe who have carried it for so long, and from which it is necessary to be purified individually and collectively. We want to buy back time, if possible; we must ask ourselves the question: how have we treated the people of Israel, in our hearts, in our homes, in our churches, and in our nation, until today? What have we done indeed to bless Israel as the Lord enjoins us to do so? To these questions we respond by expressing our solidarity with Israel in the face of its enemies who seek to annihilate it according to what the prophet says; "Isaiah 62:1 For the sake of Zion I will not shut up, for the sake of Jerusalem I will not rest, until his salvation appears, like the dawn, and his deliverance, like a blaze that lights." This passage, about 2700 years old, remains of burning relevance; it is not only a question of loving and supporting Israel with the slightest words, it is here to take sides and commit concretely so that the nation of Israel lives and that the nations live in peace with it.

Appendix

Quotations from the Bible: King James Bible, New Revised Standard Version

Some abbreviations and definitions:

AD: After Jesus Christ
BC: Before Jesus Christ
OT: Old Testament
NT: New Testament

Books of the Bibles abbreviated according to the translation in English of the Editions of the House of the Bible in Geneva

cf: compare	Galates: Ga	Nehemiah: Ne
ch: chapter	Genesis: Ge	1Pierre: 1P
Acts: Ac	Hebrews: Heb	2Pierre: 2P
Apocalypse: Ap	Job: Jb	Proverbs: Pr
1 Chronicles: 1Ch	James: Ja	Psalms: Ps
2 Chronicles: 2Ch	Judges: Jg	1Rois: 1R
1 Corinthians: 1Co	Joel: Jl	2Rois: 2R
2 Corinthians: 2Co	John: Jn	Romans: Rom
Colossians: Col	1 Jean: 1Jn	Ruth: Rt
Daniel: Dn	2 Jean: 2Jn	1 Samuel: 1S
Deuteronomy: Dt	3 Jean: 3Jn	2 Samuel: 2S
Ecclesiastes: Ec	Josué: Jos	1 Thessalonians: 1Th
Ephesians: Ep	Jeremy: Jr.	2 Thessalonians: 2Th

Isaiah: Is	Luke: Lk	1 Timothy: 1Tm
Esdras: Esd	Leviticus: Lv	2 Timothy: 2Tm
Esther: Es	Marck: Ma	Zechariah: Ze
Exodus: Ex	Matthew: Mt	Verse(s): v
Ezekiel: Ez	Numbers: Nb	

P 89. Minister: definition and origin of the name: servant

Origine

LATIN	LATIN	OLD FRENCH
minus →	minister →	ministre ────── → minister
less	servant	ministrer *Middle English*

Middle English (in <u>minister</u> (sense 2 of the noun)); also in the sense 'a person acting under the authority of another'): from Old French *ministre* (noun), *ministrer* (verb), from Latin *minister* 'servant', from *minus* 'less'.

P 129. Hermeneutics: Sciences of the interpretation of philosophical and theological texts. Historical dictionary of the French language P

P 133. Civilization of the Mines or Minoans: ancient civilization discovered in Crete (3100 – 1100 BC) from 1900. https://www.lemonde.fr/sciences/article

Synagogue and synagogue, Church and church: the capital letter serves to emphasize the unity of the community of believers in space and time. That is why in the title as in some passages of the book it is used. On the other hand, when the synagogue as the church designates a local community or both are related to a local event, it is not necessary to use the capital letter.

Expulsions of the Jews from France p. 163 (sources in French)

Expulsion of 533: Edict of Childebert I, breviary Richard Rossin.pdf

Expulsion 633: Edict of Dagobert I, breviary Richard Rossin.pdf

Expulsion of 1009: Bernhard Blumenkranz, Latin Christian authors of the Middle Ages on Jews and Judaism. (V), Revue des études juives, vol. 117, no. 17, 1958, p. 5–58 (Available online)

Expulsion of 1182: April 17, 1182 - Expulsion of the Jews by Philip Augustus - Herodote.net

Expulsion of 1254: Juliette Sibon - Chasing the Jews to reign: Expulsions by the kings of France in the Middle Ages - Louis IX, known as Saint Louis, expels the Jews - YouTube 2018 at 12:55

Expulsion of 1306: Juliette Sibon, 1306, the expulsion of the Jews from the Kingdom of France, Cahiers de recherches médiévales et humanistes, no. 16, 2008.

Expulsion of 1322: Juliette Sibon - Chasing the Jews to reign: Expulsions by the kings of France in the Middle Ages - YouTube 2018 – 13:40 to 15:49

Expulsion of 1394: Seventh edict expelling the Jews. Juliette Sibon - Chasing Jews to rule: Expulsions by the kings of France in the Middle Ages - YouTube 2018 – 14:21 to 15:49

Expulsions of 1491 and 1501 Following the annexation of Provence to the Kingdom of France. Juliette Sibon - Chasing Jews to rule: Expulsions by the kings of France in the Middle Ages - YouTube 2018 – 16:38 to 16:49

Expulsion of 1615: Decree of the tenth expulsion is purely formal and without effect.

Expulsions of 1683 and 1724: Eleventh and twelfth expulsions signed respectively by Louis XIV and Louis XV. Jews are expelled from the colonies.

Other interesting sources (In French)

JOURS DE COLÈRE | L'origine du christianisme (Episode 7) | ARTE - YouTube :

Rompre avec le judaïsme | L'origine du christianisme (Episode 9) | ARTE - YouTube

Marcion l'hérétique. - YouTube

Rompre avec le judaïsme | L'origine du christianisme (Episode 9) | ARTE - YouTube
A partir de 38 :32 Développement sur l'Hérésie de Marcion

Ces chrétiens qui défendent Israël - interview de Jean-Marc Thobois - YouTube

Jean-Marc Thobois: Israel dans le temps présent et l'attitude de l'Église vis à vis d'Israel - YouTube

Enseignement de Jean-Marc Thobois - Le procès des Nations contre Israël - YouTube

Rejet de l'évangile par les chefs de la diaspora juive - Jean-Marc Thobois - YouTube

Jésus avait ouvert l'évangile aux nations - Jean-Marc Thobois - YouTube

D'où vient le mythe du complot juif ? - YouTube

Histoire des juifs - Résumé depuis 750 av. J-C jusqu'aux conflit israélo-palestinien - YouTube

Jésus réformateur du judaïsme (JM Thobois 3'20 : (15) La voie de Jésus - Comment est arrivé le divorce entre juifs et chrétiens ? (Jean-Marc Thobois) - YouTube)

Naissance d christianisme dans le judaïsme (JM Thobois 5'30 : (15) La voie de Jésus - Comment est arrivé le divorce entre juifs et chrétiens ? (Jean-Marc Thobois) - YouTube) 1

(19) Rejet de l'évangile par les chefs de la diaspora juive - Jean-Marc Thobois - YouTube (3 44'20) la question du prosélytisme (prosélytes)

(19) Rejet de l'évangile par les chefs de la diaspora juive - Jean-Marc Thobois - YouTube (1'01''40) Proches d'Israël

(1) Why Support Israel - Christians United for Israel - YouTube

Christians United for Israel - Our Mission & Vision 2020 – YouTube

The sharing of Canaan

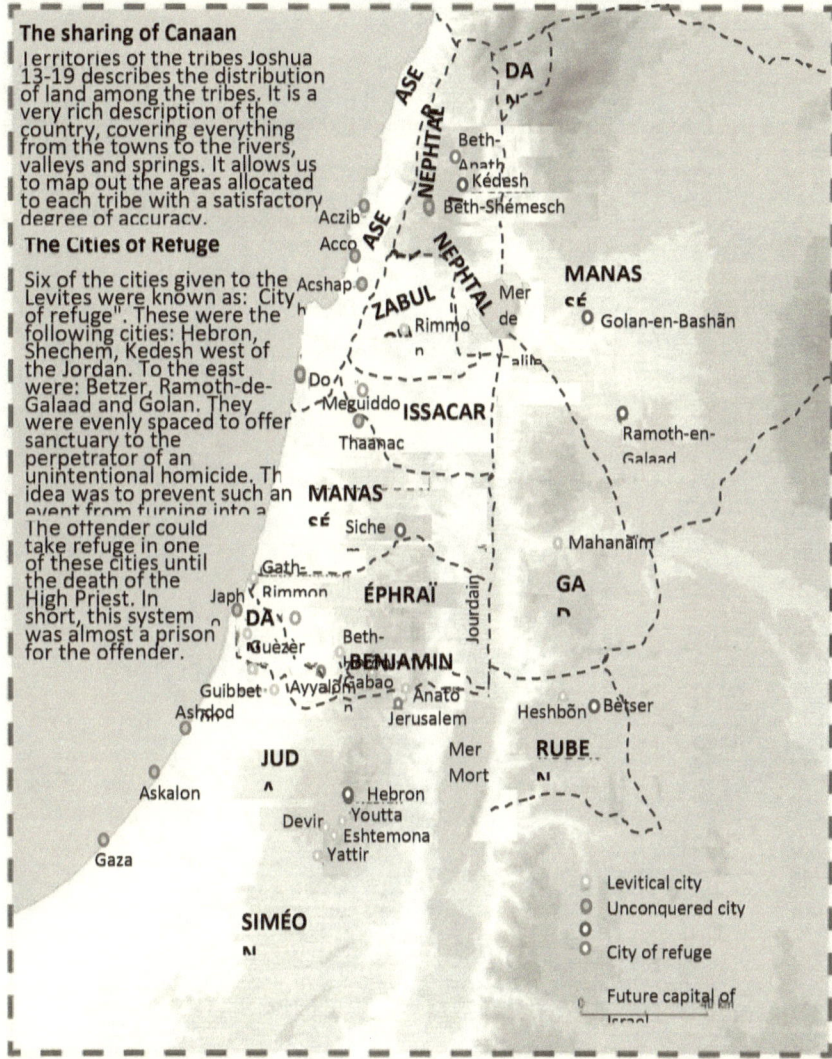

The sharing of Canaan

Territories of the tribes Joshua 13-19 describes the distribution of land among the tribes. It is a very rich description of the country, covering everything from the towns to the rivers, valleys and springs. It allows us to map out the areas allocated to each tribe with a satisfactory degree of accuracy.

The Cities of Refuge

Six of the cities given to the Levites were known as: City of refuge". These were the following cities: Hebron, Shechem, Kedesh west of the Jordan. To the east were: Betzer, Ramoth-de-Galaad and Golan. They were evenly spaced to offer sanctuary to the perpetrator of an unintentional homicide. Th idea was to prevent such an event from turning into a The offender could take refuge in one of these cities until the death of the High Priest. In short, this system was almost a prison for the offender.

Map labels: ASE, DA, NEPHTALI, Beth-Anath, Kédesh, Beth-Shémesch, Aczib, Acco, ASE, NEPHTALI, Acshap, MANAS cÉ, ZABULON, Mer de, Golan-en-Bashān, Rimmon, Don, Meguiddo, ISSACAR, Thaanac, Ramoth-en-Galaad, MANAS cÉ, Siche, Mahanaïm, Gath, Rimmon, Japh, ÉPHRAÏ, GA, DA, Jourdain, Guèzèr, Beth-, BENJAMIN, Guibbet, Ayyalo, Gabao, Anato, Ashdod, Jerusalem, Heshbōn, Betser, JUD, Mer Mort, RUBE, Askalon, Hebron, Devir, Youtta, Eshtemona, Gaza, Yattir, SIMÉO N

Legend:
○ Levitical city
◎ Unconquered city
○ City of refuge
○ Future capital of Israel

The boundaries between the tribes are approximate, drawn according to the indications found in the book of Joshua, chapters 13 to 21. The map is a simplified representation of the land of Canaan at the time of the division between the tribes of Israel. It appears on page 29 of the Nouvel Atlas de la Bible written by historian Nick Page. Éditions Empreinte temps Présent 2012.

Know the author.

Monique and Xavier Mainguy are part of the Evangelical Church of Versailles (France). They had a charming daughter, Mathilde, who herself gave them two little girls, Louise and Émilie. In their community, Monique put herself at the service of people and Xavier at the service of words. With these come ideas, poems, and messages of hope and love according to the Christian Faith. There are also history, theology, and sociology, and it is in these three areas that he works, through lectures on various social themes related to the message of the Bible, as indicated below:

- Under what Right do we live: the Napoleon Code, Roman Law, or Biblical Law?
- The legacy of the 20th century: the ruin of ideologies and the victory of the Bible
- Reform, Revocation, Revolution, Renaissance: or how does the Lord grant his grace again to France, our country.
- The Synagogue and the Church: filiation, divorce, and reconciliation
- The Gospel in the Land of Voltaire: The Evangelical Revival in France
- The Gospel succession: painful birth and affirmation of the Evangelical Churches
- Preaching the Bible Message: A Powerful Social Act
- The Bible and the Economy: convergences and divergences
- The biblical message and democracy why were it born, where was the Bible preached. Historical and contemporary examples

- Biblical message and entrepreneurship: a biblical explanation
- Freedom of worship: the one that conditions all other types of freedom.

There is currently no written book on each of these themes. On the other hand, there is ample documentation on them, which should be used for future literary projects.

Wishing that this study on the Synagogue and the Church interests you and finds its place among your works on the subject, I thank you for the time you will devote to it.

Xavier Mainguy

www.ingramcontent.com/pod-product-compliance
Lightning Source LLC
Chambersburg PA
CBHW030908120626
46554CB00001B/60